Chekhov

ANTON CHEKHOV, great Russian dramatist and short story writer, was born on January 29, 1860, in Taganrog, Russia. In 1876 his father went bankrupt and, with the rest of his family, fled to Moscow, leaving Chekhov behind to live by his wits. Supporting himself by tutoring, Chekhov was able to graduate from school at nineteen and win a scholarship to study medicine in Moscow. In Moscow he became the family breadwinner by writing short comic sketches under a pseudonym. His first story appeared in March, 1880, in a St. Petersburg magazine, *Strekoza* (Dragonfly).

In 1884, he received his medical degree and by this time had already contracted tuberculosis, the disease that would finally cause his death. Chekhov's prolific writing between 1884 and 1888 included the poignant stories "The Schoolmaster" (1886), "The Kiss" and "Volodya" (both 1887), and in 1888 "Steppe," one of his most famous stories, and the one which marked the beginning of the body of his mature work, including over fifty great short stories. In 1890 Chekhov journeyed alone to Sakhalin, a penal colony on an island off Siberia, and wrote his only nonfiction work, *The Island of Sakhalin* (1893–94), which remains a classic in penology. Chekhov also began experimenting with drama and wrote several successful one-act farces.

His first produced play was *Ivanov* (1887). On October 17, 1896, *The Seagull* was performed in St. Petersburg. It was practically hissed off the stage, and Chekhov vowed to give up dramatic writing forever. In March, 1897, he had a violent lung hemorrhage, and his health worsened, but with the formation of the Moscow Art Theatre, he again began to write for the stage. In 1898 at a rehearsal for a new production of *The Seagull* he met Olga Knipper, the actress whom he married in 1901. The Moscow Art Theatre also produced *Uncle Vanya* (1899) and *The Three Sisters* (1901). But Chekhov's health deteriorated, and his work on *The Cherry Orchard* during the Moscow winter of 1903–04 led to his complete collapse. He died on July 15, 1904, at Badenweiler, a health resort in southern Germany.

Bantam Classics
Ask your bookseller for these other World Classics.

THE BHAGAVAD-GITA (translated by Barbara Stoler Miller)

CHEKHOV: FIVE MAJOR PLAYS, Anton Chekhov
A DOCTOR'S VISIT: SHORT STORIES BY ANTON CHEKHOV

THE INFERNO, Dante (translated by Allen Mandelbaum)
PURGATORIO, Dante (translated by Allen Mandelbaum)
PARADISO, Dante (translated by Allen Mandelbaum)

THE BROTHERS KARAMAZOV, Fyodor Dostoevsky
CRIME AND PUNISHMENT, Fyodor Dostoevsky
THE IDIOT, Fyodor Dostoevsky
NOTES FROM UNDERGROUND, Fyodor Dostoevsky

THE COUNT OF MONTE CRISTO, Alexandre Dumas
THE THREE MUSKETEERS, Alexandre Dumas

MADAME BOVARY, Gustave Flaubert

FAUST, Johann Wolfgang von Goethe

THE COMPLETE FAIRYTALES OF THE BROTHERS GRIMM
   (translated by Jack Zipes)

THE HUNCHBACK OF NOTRE DAME, Victor Hugo

FOUR GREAT PLAYS, Henrik Ibsen

THE METAMORPHOSIS, Franz Kafka

THE PRINCE, Niccolo Machiavelli

GODS, DEMONS, AND OTHERS, R. K. Narayan

CYRANO DE BERGERAC, Edmond Rostand

ANNA KARENINA, Leo Tolstoy
THE DEATH OF IVAN ILYICH, Leo Tolstoy

FATHERS AND SONS, Ivan Turgenev

AROUND THE WORLD IN EIGHTY DAYS, Jules Verne
20,000 LEAGUES UNDER THE SEA, Jules Verne

CANDIDE, Voltaire

Five Major Plays
by Anton Chekhov

Translated
and with an Introduction
by Ronald Hingley

BANTAM BOOKS

NEW YORK · TORONTO · LONDON · SYDNEY · AUCKLAND

*This edition contains the complete text
of the original hardcover edition.*
NOT ONE WORD HAS BEEN OMITTED.

CHEKHOV: FIVE MAJOR PLAYS

*A Bantam Book / published by arrangement with
Oxford University Press*

PRINTING HISTORY
*Bantam Classic edition / May 1982
5 printings through July 1988*

The five plays first published by Oxford University Press, London: *Uncle
Vanya, Three Sisters, The Cherry Orchard* (1964); *Ivanov, The Seagull*
(1967). © Ronald Hingley, 1964, 1967.
Ivanov, The Seagull, Three Sisters first issued as an Oxford University Press
Paperback 1968. © Ronald Hingley 1968.
Uncle Vanya and *The Cherry Orchard* first issued as an Oxford University
Press Paperback 1965. © Ronald Hingley 1965.
First collected in this paperback edition, Oxford University, Press, New
York, 1977.

PUBLISHER'S NOTE

THE text of this edition of *Ivanov* and *The Seagull* is taken from Volume II of
The Oxford Chekhov, an edition of the plays and short stories newly
translated and edited by Ronald Hingley. *Three Sisters, Uncle Vanya*, and
The Cherry Orchard are taken from Volume III. Each of these volumes also
contains an introduction, bibliography, and appendixes, giving the early
history of the plays and their composition, with notes on allusions in the
texts and on Russian pronunciation.

ISBN 0-553-21211-7

Published simultaneously in the United States and Canada

Bantam Books are published by Bantam Books, a division of Bantam
Doubleday Dell Publishing Group, Inc. Its trademark, consisting of the
words "Bantam Books" and the portrayal of a rooster, is Registered
in U.S. Patent and Trademark Office and in other countries. Marca
Registrada. Bantam Books, 666 Fifth Avenue, New York, New York 10103.

PRINTED IN THE UNITED STATES OF AMERICA

O   14 13 12 11 10 9 8 7

PREFACE

The translations in this volume are taken from *The Oxford Chekhov*, as published from 1964 onwards by the Oxford University Press, London and New York. Volumes 1–3 of that edition contain Chekhov's entire dramatic writings, including all major variant versions, together with accounts of the composition of the plays and of the history of their texts as well as other explanatory material and bibliographies. The ten one-act plays, as published in Volume 1 of *The Oxford Chekhov*, are also available in paperback as *Chekhov: Short Plays* (1969). All Chekhov's short stories of 1888–1904 will be found in Volumes 4–9 of *The Oxford Chekhov* (though Volume 4 has yet to be completed). Two paperback anthologies, *Seven Stories* (1974) and *Eleven Stories* (1975), are based on these volumes.

More extensive information on Chekhov's dramatic evolution will be found in my recent *New Life of Anton Chekhov* (London and New York, 1976). I am most grateful to Alfred A. Knopf, Inc., of New York (and also to the Oxford University Press, London) for kind permission to make use of material from this biography in the Introduction to the present volume.

RONALD HINGLEY

Frilford,
Abingdon, England
1977

CONTENTS

INTRODUCTION

Few playwrights of the last two or three hundred years have had a greater impact than Anton Chekhov, and this despite his relatively small output. He left behind only five truly outstanding plays, all of four acts, and it is these which form the present collection.

Omitted from this volume are the ten one-acters, mainly farces, though several are masterpieces in their own limited genre. Omitted also are the two early four-acters, *Platonov* and *The Wood Demon*. Neither is a major work, but they will receive more prominence in this introduction than the one-acters, since both have a considerable bearing on the author's evolution.

Important though the theater was to Chekhov, he worked for it only sporadically and neglected it for years on end; to a large extent his playwriting was overshadowed until the end of his life by the claims of narrative fiction. Chekhov the short story writer was constantly developing and perfecting his craft; his stories take up six or seven times as much of his collected works as does his drama; he frequently referred to narrative as the "wife" to whom he considered himself respectably united for life, and to the theater as his fickle and temporary mistress. Yet to many of his admirers Chekhov still remains the great dramatist whose stories are less significant than his plays.

Chekhov's preoccupation with the theater ebbed and flowed throughout his life from adolescence onwards. It may be traced back to his school days in the early 1870s, and it ended only with his death in 1904. He loved the theater and he hated the theater. Now he would plan to write a hundred one-act plays a year; then, claiming to be disgusted with the stage, he would assert his intention of never penning another word of drama.

Chekhov was born in 1860 in Taganrog, a small and declining port on the Sea of Azov, six hundred miles south of Moscow. He was the third of the six children of a struggling and eventually bankrupt grocer. This pious martinet beat and bullied his offspring, but also ensured that they obtained a good education. At the Taganrog classical *gimnaziya*, or grammar school, Anton developed his early flair for the dramatic, displaying a love of practical jokes, mimicry, play acting. A skilled comic actor with a strong instinct for entertaining, he could imitate his elders' speech, walk, and gestures. His targets ranged from eccentric grammar school teachers, aged professors, and fatuous minor clerics to the Town Captain, in effect Taganrog's Governor. From such antics it was a short step to improvised charades and amateur theatricals at which Anton would impersonate a dentist or an aged village sacristan. More orthodox theatrical performances also took place, often at the homes of school friends. Himself the main organizer and producer, the boy is said to have written many plays of his own, only to destroy them. He also acted in established plays, including Gogol's famous comedy *The Inspector General*.

Comic acting figures little in Anton's mature years, for he gradually lost the knack or the interest. But an allied childhood pursuit, theatergoing, was to remain with him for life. Taganrog's theater gave him the opportunity to see the classics of the Russian stage, including Ostrovsky's plays; light opera such as Offenbach's *La Belle Hélène;* and a stage adaptation of *Uncle Tom's Cabin*.

Though Chekhov's efforts as a schoolboy playwright have not survived, he did not leave this interest behind when—in 1879, as a nineteen-year-old youth—he packed his bags and left Taganrog for Moscow. Here he joined his impoverished family, precariously established in the city for several years, and enrolled as a medical student. The five-year course, which he completed in 1884, was exacting. Meanwhile he had also managed to establish himself as a writer of sorts: he had become the increasingly prolific author of comic short stories and sketches published in a wide variety of periodicals. These trifles earned him enough to relieve his family's extreme poverty.

The same cannot be said of his dramatic writings of the period. Chekhov's earliest extant play was neither published nor performed during his lifetime, but was found—lacking any title—among his papers after his death and brought out posthumously in 1923. It is now known as *Platonov*, from the name of the principal character. Though the manuscript bears no date, the play may be assigned to 1880–81, partly on the evidence of Chekhov's youngest brother, Michael. His memoirs have the second-year student Anton offering *Platonov* to a well-known actress, Mariya Yermolov, and hoping to have it staged at the Moscow Maly Theater. That the play was turned down is not surprising, on grounds of length alone; at 160 pages it would take about as long to perform as *Uncle Vanya*, *Three Sisters*, and *The Cherry Orchard* put together.

Platonov eschews Chekhov's usual hints, half-statements, and eloquent silences, being as exuberant and outspoken as the later plays are evocative and reticent. Another contrast lies in the degree of emphasis placed on action. For a writer in whose later works "nothing happens," the Chekhov of *Platonov* makes far too many things happen. One of his heroines tries to throw herself under a passing train, on stage, and is saved by a horse thief who is later lynched by enraged peasants; the same young woman also saves her husband from being knifed and later tries to poison herself by eating sulfur matches. The play ends with a murder, its hero being shot in a fit of passion by one of three discarded or would-be mistresses. This concludes a sequence of intermeshed amatory and financial intrigues vaguely reminiscent of Dostoyevsky and revolving round a sexually irresistible village schoolmaster.

Absurd though *Platonov* must sound in this brief digest, and even more absurd though it may appear to those who read it through, the play has been successfully staged and contains many pointers to the mature Chekhov whose later techniques were very different. Nor can there be much doubt that the young man himself took his first extant play seriously at a time when most of his stories were still in a lighter vein. It would seem that his first interest as a would-be creative writer was the stage, not narrative fiction. And it was probably disappointment over the rejection of *Platonov* that temporarily diverted him from attempting any more serious plays for about six years. Periods of neglect were also to follow the unsuccessful production of his *Wood Demon* in 1889, and the disastrous flop of his *Seagull* in 1896.

Meanwhile the drama's loss was becoming more and more the short story's gain. After graduating as a doctor in 1884, Chekhov began practicing his new profession at once. This was never to become his full-time occupation, however, and although he hesitated between letters and medicine for a while, it soon became obvious that authorship was his chief vocation. Throughout the 1880s he was gradually abandoning his early facetious narrative vein, and producing stories more and more imbued with his own characteristic blend of poignancy, astringency, detachment, and carefully controlled humor. Meanwhile he continued to reside in Moscow, helping to provide for his parents, and also for his youngest brother and sister until they were old enough to fend for themselves.

When, in 1887, Chekhov reverted to serious dramatic writing he did so by invitation. A well-known impresario—F. A. Korsh, proprietor of a Moscow theater specializing in farces—suddenly commissioned him to write a four-act play, probably expecting the dramatic equivalent of the early comic stories on which alone the young man's reputation rested. The result was more than Korsh had bargained for: *Ivanov*, the work with which the present volume begins. This indeed does provide light entertainment in quantity, but it is also a disturbing and profound problem-drama.

The first draft of *Ivanov* was dashed off at high speed between September 20 and October 5, 1887, each act being rushed to Korsh so that he could submit it to the dramatic censor and put it into rehearsal. On November 19, exactly two months after Chekhov had first set pen to paper, *Ivanov* received its Moscow premiere at Korsh's theater. This first night developed into one of the scandals "without precedent in theatrical history" that figure so prominently in Russian stage annals. One theater critic spoke of a "storm of applause, curtain-calls and hissing," claiming that no author of recent times had made his bow to such a medley of praise and protest. The hissings and protests were partly due to the defects of the performance, for the play had been grossly under-rehearsed by actors who barely knew their parts.

It was not so much the quirks of the performance as Chekhov's controversial script that stimulated a response varying from extreme enthusiasm to extreme disapproval. Yet the general bewilderment did not derive from any obscurity in what is basically a simple plot. The play's main character, a landowner in his thirties called Nicholas Ivanov, has a Jewish wife, Sarah, who is dying of tuberculosis. Ivanov should have taken the sick woman to a warmer climate, thus giving her some hope of recovery, but instead he is busy seducing the daughter of a rich neighbor. For this caddish behavior he is repeatedly castigated by his wife's plain-speaking young doctor, Eugene Lvov. Sarah dies, and Ivanov marries again, but is subjected by Dr. Lvov to an especially severe final denunciation. This occurs on the very wedding day, when the young doctor turns on Ivanov with a denunciation so violent that, in the version of 1887, it causes the bridegroom to expire from shock on stage. In the final version of this much-revised ending, as translated in the present volume, he shoots himself.

Running an estate, coping with peasants, farming scientifically, falling into debt, marrying a doomed wife of alien faith—it had all been too much for Ivanov, whom we observe collapsing under the strain throughout the play's four acts. That his conduct is reprehensible must be admitted. But what on earth was there about it to tax an audience's comprehension? Or to provoke such violent reactions in the theater? Only this: that the author, insofar as his attitude seemed to emerge from the dialogue of his characters, came nowhere near outright condemnation of Ivanov. Indeed, far from pillorying that spineless individual as an arrant scoundrel, Chekhov seemed rather to sympathize with him, while displaying marked hostility towards the well-meaning young doctor who so persistently attempts to persuade Ivanov to do his duty by the dying Sarah.

Could the wicked Ivanov conceivably be Chekhov's hero? And could the priggish, self-righteous Dr. Lvov be his villain? Indeed they could, as is clear beyond a doubt from lengthy explanations in the author's correspondence. From these we also learn that the riddle of *Ivanov* did not lie in any obscurity of the script, but simply in Chekhov's failure to adopt a conventional moralizing attitude. Yet the play does have its own unconventional, paradoxical, characteristically Chekhovian moral: Do not moralize. Do not be too ready, that is, to imitate the stuffy Dr. Lvov by condemning a man, that all too complicated mechanism, on the basis of his behavior. An immoral scoundrel may be a better human being than a self-righteous prig.

By comparison with Chekhov's later pioneering drama, *Ivanov* now seems old-fashioned. One reason is the presence of a message, however paradoxical; another is the concentration on a single hero around whom all the action revolves; yet another lies in the emphasis placed on carefully orchestrated dramatic crises. Chekhov gave the audience "a punch on the nose" at the end of each act. So he himself pointed out at the time, not realizing that in his later dramatic career the cun-

ningly sprung dramatic climax would give way to something
far more impressive: the yet more cunningly sprung anti-
dramatic anticlimax. From crises to letdowns: such, in brief,
is Chekhov's evolution as a playwright.

While remaining comparatively conventional in structure
and technique, the thematically startling *Ivanov* is yet a
triumph of craftsmanship. The scenes are well put together;
the dialogue is subtle and lively; the background is suitably
light, introducing several comic minor characters who might
have stepped straight from the better passages of Chekhov's
early comic stories.

Ivanov, Chekhov's first dramatic work to appear on a public stage, immediately established its author as a figure to be
reckoned with in the Russian theater. This impact was reinforced when the play went into production in St. Petersburg
in January 1889 after extensive revision. By contrast with the
mixed reception given to *Ivanov* in Moscow in late 1887, the
St. Petersburg production was a resounding success. And
Chekhov was by now very much a man of the theater who
was often seen with actors and actresses, a familiar figure in
stage circles in both Moscow and St. Petersburg. He advised
on the production and casting of his own and others' plays;
and he wrote, between 1888 and 1891, his five famous one-act
farces: *The Bear*, *The Proposal*, *A Tragic Role*, *The Wedding*,
and *The Anniversary*. Yet he was anything but stagestruck.
The modern theater was to him "a skin rash, a sort of urban
venereal disease." Narrative was his legal wife, he was once
again insisting, whereas the drama was merely his "flamboyant, rowdy, impudent, exhausting mistress."

At the end of the decade this disillusionment was increased
by the failure of the new four-act play with which Chekhov
followed *Ivanov*: *The Wood Demon*, written in 1889. Here is
a comparatively lightweight effort, but one of crucial importance since it was to become the raw material for the mature
drama *Uncle Vanya*. That masterpiece contains large chunks
of dialogue quarried directly from *The Wood Demon*, and
several characters with the same or similar names; yet it
differs so markedly in tone and content that one hesitates to
call the earlier play a draft of the later. For the moment,
though, we are concerned with *The Wood Demon* alone. It
underwent many tribulations of its own long before Chekhov
was thinking of it in terms of *Uncle Vanya*.

Chekhov called *The Wood Demon* "a long romantic comedy"; it presented "good, healthy people who are half likeable; there is a happy ending; the general mood is one of sheer lyricism." A happy ending! That seemed a sinister augury. Could the play be shaping as one of those exceptional life-affirming moral tales, written under the influence of Tolstoy, which figure disastrously in Chekhov's fiction of a few years earlier? Fortunately, no. The play was indeed to turn out the romantic comedy that Chekhov had called it, yet with no little infusion of implied moralizing. After contemplating the negative, feckless, world-weary, demoralized Ivanov, we now meet more positive types: a very nest of Lvovs or potential Lvovs. In the character of the "Wood Demon" himself (Michael Khrushchov), Chekhov seems to commend the virtues of charity, contrition, and commitment to a good cause: nature conservation. Then again, a beautiful young wife seems to be applauded for "sacrificing herself" to her elderly, gout-ridden husband, while another character describes himself as having made ostentatious public confession of his sins.

That one should repent of one's sins, behave tolerantly, eschew malicious gossip: these are no bad guides to conduct. Yet to preach a worthy cause is not necessarily to compose a great work of art. With Chekhov, such implied exhortations were often aesthetically counter-productive. That he himself later found those of *The Wood Demon* unsatisfactory we know because he threw out all this moralizing when he converted the play into *Uncle Vanya*, which lacks such affirmations or certainties. Its characters move among shadows; the ground is nowhere firm beneath their feet; virtue goes wholly unrewarded.

By October 1889 the completed *Wood Demon* had been passed by the censor and was promised to two actor friends of Chekhov's for benefit performances at the Moscow Maly Theater and the St. Petersburg Alexandrine Theater. But both these prestigious projects fell through, and Chekhov resignedly sold the play to a Moscow house, Abramov's, which was on the verge of bankruptcy. Here *The Wood Demon* received an inadequate first performance on December 27, 1889, and it was taken out of production shortly afterwards. Thereafter Chekhov rejected all requests to stage or publish the play. Ten years later he remarked that he hated it and was trying to forget it.

Uncle Vanya—so different from, yet so extensively based on, the earlier play—is a pioneering dramatic masterpiece;

from which it by no means follows that the relatively conventional *Wood Demon* is a resounding failure. Chekhov, in his disillusioned later phase, was too hard on the earlier play—still eminently stageable, as shown by the fine production with which the British Actors' Company toured Britain and the United States in 1973–74. At the time, though, the disappointment aroused by *The Wood Demon* was so acute that Chekhov abandoned serious dramatic writing during the period between the completion of that play in late 1889 and the writing of *The Seagull* in 1895. He abandoned it, that is, with the exception of any work on the conversion of *The Wood Demon* into *Uncle Vanya:* an operation, conducted in total secrecy, which may have fallen within this period.

Though we do not know precisely when the transformation took place, we can be fairly certain that it was either in 1890 or at least five years later, not at any intermediate point. This seems clear from Chekhov's statement, made in April 1895, that he had "written nothing for the theater during the last five or six years." That the new drama had taken shape by November 1896 we learn from a reference of that date to the intended publication of Chekhov's collected plays. In this book my own feeling that the undatable *Uncle Vanya* is Chekhov's first fully mature play is expressed by the order in which the works are printed. This is in principle chronological. Since the chronology of *The Seagull* and *Uncle Vanya* simply cannot be established, I have not only been free to indulge my editorial taste in the matter, but have actually been compelled to do so.

So much for when the metamorphosis of *The Wood Demon* into *Uncle Vanya* took place. But what about the far more tantalizing problem of how it was brought about? To compare the earlier play with the later is to study the transformation of a gifted but uncertain, hesitant, and immature artist into a creative genius. In creating a new play out of an old one, Chekhov reduced the length by about a third and scrapped four major characters entirely. Yet he somehow retained substantial sections of the original dialogue while converting a play of action into a play of mood, and turning a piece of light entertainment into a work of genius. I know of no parallel for such a process; there is certainly none in Chekhov's other works. Everything that had been too clear-cut and brightly lit in the earlier play has become enchantingly indefinite, blurred, and atmospheric. For instance, the unfortunate Uncle *George*

Voynitsky, who had straightforwardly shot himself in Act Three of *The Wood Demon*, is replaced in the later play by the more puzzling Uncle *Vanya* Voynitsky whose main achievement or non-achievement is to fire a revolver at the hated Professor Serebryakov—and, of course, to miss. Then again, each play has its "Sonya." But how different the two girls are. *The Wood Demon*'s had been an elegant, rather silly, rich young woman who was cloyingly paired off in the finale with Michael Khrushchov, the play's doctor-forester. *Uncle Vanya*'s Sonya is a less handsome, more sensitive girl. She too loves the play's doctor-forester, Astrov—the counterpart to *The Wood Demon*'s Khrushchov, but a more subtly drawn character. And this later Sonya's love remains unrequited, since Astrov barely notices her, having eyes only for the beautiful Helen Serebryakov.

The conclusion of *Uncle Vanya* leaves the frustrated Sonya and her frustrated uncle facing a boring future together. This non-solution contrasts vividly with the fates of their counterparts in the earlier play: Sonya evidently destined to live her life happily ever after, her uncle dead by his own hand. Thus had *The Wood Demon* offered a tragic Act Three followed by a happy ending in Act Four, and no nonsense about either of them. With *Uncle Vanya*, though, we shall do better to look neither for tragedy nor comedy, but to realize that we have entered a strange anti-climactic, anti-romantic, anti-dramatic world such as had never existed on the stage before Chekhov, a world with its own laws, its own dimensions, its own brand of humor.

The period between the conception of *The Wood Demon*, in 1888, and the publication of *Uncle Vanya*, in 1897, had seen major changes in Chekhov's life. Weary of Moscow after residing there during the whole of the 1880s, he spent most of 1890 on a long and adventurous journey to the Russian penal settlement on Sakhalin Island, which lies to the north of Japan. In 1892 he embarked on another adventure by buying a farm at Melikhovo, a village about fifty miles south of Moscow. Here he spent seven years as a country squire, rural doctor, and author. It was his most prolific period as a short-story writer. But these were fallow years for dramatic writing until, in October 1895, he settled down to create *The Seagull* in a small cottage on the grounds of his estate. The first reference in his correspondence to the new drama occurs on October 21, 1895, when he speaks of enjoying the work; of playing fast and loose with stage conventions; of providing a landscape with a view of a lake, a lot of talk about literature, little action, and a hundredweight and a half of love. One month later Chekhov reports the play finished and is still harping on his rejection of theatrical conventions. "I began it *forte* and finished it *pianissimo*, contrary to all the laws of the theater." As these comments indicate, *The Seagull* abandoned the traditional concentration on a single star part and on the strong, carefully prepared dramatic crises that had characterized *Ivanov*. *The Seagull* stands, as it were, halfway between that earlier four-acter and Chekhov's mature drama.

From all Chekhov's major plays, earlier or later, *The Seagull* differs in the somber tone of its last act. It differs, too, in concentrating so heavily on the experiences of creative and performing artists—two actresses and two writers. And it differs yet again by a somewhat self-conscious flaunting of "modernistic" devices. There is the heavily obtruded symbol of the shot seagull, which represents the wanton ruining of Nina's life by Trigorin. No other such ponderous symbol, Ibsenite rather than Chekhovian, occurs anywhere else in the Russian master's work. Another "modernistic" feature of *The Seagull* is the interrupted play-within-the-play of Act One. This rhetorical monologue by a World Spirit is itself a fragment of non-realistic drama, such as his Russian contemporaries called "decadent." "We need new forms," proclaims Chekhov's Treplev, the author of that encapsulated playlet; this same sentiment was constantly on Chekhov's mind when he was writing *The Seagull*.

Though many dramatic novelties were to come from Chekhov's pen in the future, such items as dead fowl and tirades—however ironically intended—by a World Spirit were not to be among them. His new, unfamiliar, and as it was later to prove, still transitional dramatic technique contributed to the initial spectacular failure of *The Seagull*. Indeed, its first performance at the Alexandrine Theater in St. Petersburg was perhaps the most traumatic episode of Chekhov's life. It occurred on October 17, 1896, almost a year after the play had been completed, the interval having been largely devoted to tiresome negotiations with the dramatic censor.

The real cause of the play's failure lay less with Chekhov's unorthodox text than with the circumstances of the performance. For some reason a popular comic actress, Elizabeth Levkeyev, had chosen it for her benefit night, the twenty-fifth anniversary of her debut on the stage. She was one of those "fine old character actresses" who has only to emerge from the wings to provoke eruptions of mirth. Her large following consisted of unintellectual fans who liked their bit of fun, and who, if they knew Chekhov's work at all, would have been familiar only with the comic writer of the 1880s.

Miss Levkeyev's fans were bound to be disappointed at not seeing her—as they naturally expected on her own benefit night—in the actual play. That was quite out of the question, though, for the mere appearance on stage of so robust, so earthy, so grand a comic old trouper would have torn the delicate fabric of Chekhov's eccentric drama to ribbons. Thus was the failure of *The Seagull* doubly assured in advance. The audience was in a mutinous mood even before the curtain had gone up on the fateful night. Enraged by the absence of their favorite actress from the cast, these lovers of broad farce were not going to put up with any decadent highbrow rubbish. Knowing little or nothing of Chekhov, they cared still less about "new forms," whether in the theater or anywhere else.

The Seagull would thus have been foredoomed even if it had not been grossly under-rehearsed by a cast that barely knew its lines and had little confidence in the text. The actors and producer took the play seriously, but the decision to stage it at only nine days' notice was absurd. Chekhov himself had arrived in St. Petersburg in time to attend rehearsals. Visiting the theater every day, he discussed interpretation with the actors, stressing the need to avoid theatricality. According to the producer, "everything that could be done in this incredibly short space of time, with only eight rehearsals, for so subtly shaded a play as *The Seagull* . . . was done." But it was not enough, and the author himself was left with no illusions about the prospects for October 17.

The events of the unhappy first night exceeded his most gloomy forebodings, and have inevitably been described as "a spectacle truly unprecedented in the history of the theater." As the play proceeded, spectators in the front rows demonstratively turned their backs on the stage, hissed, whistled, laughed, and started rowdy private conversations. The uproar increased until the play was inaudible. Chekhov left the auditorium in Act Three and sat in a dressing room. After the performance he left the theater and wandered the streets on his own; not until 2 a.m. did he return to his lodgings, where he told his host that he would never offer another play to be staged even if he lived another seven hundred years. How profoundly distressed he was by *The Seagull*'s failure, inevitably shattering to so sensitive an artist, is evident from the way in which he later harped on this "fiasco beyond my wildest imaginings." It wasn't so much *The Seagull*'s failure that grated on him, he said, as the failure of his own personality.

In March 1897 Chekhov was found to be gravely ill with tuberculosis. Ordered by his doctors to winter in the south, he most unwillingly moved his home from Melikhovo to the Crimean resort of Yalta. But although he was henceforward a semi-invalid and had again abandoned all thought of writing for the stage, he was once more to be restored to the theater by the theater itself. In 1898 a newly formed company, the Moscow Art Theater, persuaded him to permit the staging of his disgraced *Seagull*. On September 9, on his way through Moscow to the Crimea, he attended an early rehearsal of this play; the date is also memorable as that of his first meeting with Olga Knipper—one of the new company's leading actresses, who was to become his wife three years later. Thus did the ailing Chekhov acquire intimate links with the theater during his last seven years of life; this despite being "exiled," as he called it, in uncongenial Yalta during most of the theatrical seasons.

The association between author and theater first attracted attention with the Art Theater's first performance of *The Seagull* on December 17, 1898. This took place in the author's absence and in an atmosphere of impending doom. What if his ill-starred play should flop again? Might another such fiasco conceivably prove fatal to the ailing author? Among those most closely concerned were Olga Knipper and the Art Theater's co-founders—Constantine Stanislavsky, Russia's most famous actor-manager, and Vladimir Nemirovich-Danchenko. Himself a playwright, Nemirovich-Danchenko was particularly concerned that *The Seagull* should succeed, since it was he who had taken the initiative in overcoming Chekhov's objections to the resuscitation of a work associated with so many painful memories.

When the curtain rose on *The Seagull*'s first act, members of the cast were very agitated. Everyone had taken valerian drops—the tranquilizer of the period—while Stanislavsky, as Trigorin, found it hard to control a twitching of the leg. As Act One proceeded audience reactions were hard to gauge, and when the curtain came down the house seemed frozen into immobility. Standing on the stage, Olga Knipper fought to control hysterical sobs amid the silence until, at last, when it seemed that not a single clap would reward so carefully nurtured a production, "like the bursting of a dam, like an exploding bomb a sudden deafening eruption of applause broke out." Members of the audience rushed the stage amid tears of joy and kissing so general as to recall the Orthodox custom of ritual osculation at Easter. People were "rolling round in hysterics," says Stanislavsky, who himself celebrated by dancing a jig. After the remaining three acts had been received with comparable enthusiasm, Nemirovich-Danchenko sent an ecstatic telegram to Chekhov in Yalta. It recorded a colossal success with endless curtain calls and was signed "mad with joy." The shameful fiasco of the St. Petersburg first performance had been wiped out.

The links between Chekhov and the Art Theater became stronger still in the following year, when the company staged a showing specially for the author in an empty theater after the season had closed. But a slightly jarring note now appears. Though too polite to say so directly, Chekhov was downright disgusted by Stanislavsky's performance in the part of Trigorin. This serves to remind us that the Chekhov-Stanislavsky axis never developed into an idyll of cooperation. And famous though Stanislavsky's "method" has rightly become for sponsoring an ultra-naturalistic technique of acting, his procedures were never naturalistic enough for the exacting Chekhov. Rather were they too flamboyant and excessively "theatrical" in the traditional sense. Too tactful or too evasive, perhaps, Chekhov never succeeded in adequately putting across his own conception of the plays to those who produced and performed them. He was loath to tackle those responsible directly, preferring to express his dissatisfaction in scathing, sibylline asides to his intimates.

Meanwhile the Art Theater had enthusiastically put a second Chekhov play, *Uncle Vanya*, into production, and on October 26, 1899, it received its first Moscow performance. Once again the author was absent, and once again he was bombarded with congratulatory telegrams in his Yalta villa. As soon became evident, *Uncle Vanya* had not quite repeated *The Seagull's* success, but Chekhov was sufficiently encouraged to plan a new play to be called *Three Sisters*, the first of two great dramas that he was to write especially for Stanislavsky's company in the last years of his life. Chekhov was encouraged to press on with the work when, in April 1900, the Moscow Art Theater toured the Crimea, making it possible for him to see productions of *The Seagull* and *Uncle Vanya* before audiences on what was now his home territory.

By mid-October of the same year Chekhov had completed *Three Sisters* and taken the manuscript to Moscow. But when he read the long-awaited text to the Art Theater actors and producers it fell flat. It was unplayable, they found; it contained no proper parts, only hints.

Why did *Three Sisters* so disappoint its first interpreters? Like all Chekhov's serious drama it has the air of seeming to make, yet of never quite making, some statement about human life. One main theme is provincial frustration as it affects the three daughters and son of the deceased General Prozorov. Andrew Prozorov would have liked to be a professor in Moscow, but he works for the municipal council of which his wife's lover is chairman. The three girls are all disappointed in love: Olga regrets being an old maid, and Masha has married the wrong man; Irina's fiancé—unloved at that—is killed in a duel in Act Four. Olga dislikes being a schoolmistress, Masha dislikes being a schoolmaster's wife, Irina dislikes working in a post office. But all their problems would, they fervently believe, magically disappear if they could only fulfill their burning ambition to return to Moscow, their childhood home. These unhappy, ill-organized women are contrasted with their vulgar, insensitive, selfish sister-in-law Natasha. She intrudes on the ménage, marries the brother, fatuously dotes on her children, and converts the Prozorov family house into the opposite of a home.

But what do we learn from this? Is the play sad or funny? Does the tragedy reside in the characters' failure to rise to the level of tragedy? Or are they not tragic even in that restricted sense? Since these questions have never been fully resolved, we need not wonder that the first cast of *Three Sisters* was so baffled.

In December, Chekhov left Moscow, where the Art Theater was still wrestling with rehearsals of *Three Sisters*, and went to Nice. He was still revising and copying the text, and sent off improved versions of Acts Three and Four within a few days of his arrival. From Nice he also wrote polemical letters on the play, providing insights into his view of the theater. As usual, Stanislavsky as producer simply could not get anything right. "Four responsible female parts, four educated young women: I can't leave them to Stanislavsky with all my respect for his talent and understanding." Chekhov was anxious that the predicament of Masha, played by Olga Knipper, should not be falsified by overacting. Olga might therefore play Masha with feeling, "but not desperately." She must not look sad, because "people who have long been unhappy, and grown used to it, don't get beyond whistling and are often wrapped up in their thoughts." Nor should Masha be seen leading her equally unhappy sister Irina around by the arm in Act Three. That was inconsistent with the play's mood. "Don't you think Irina can get about on her own?" Then again, in Act Three, Natasha should not, Chekhov told Stanislavsky, wander about the stage putting out lights and looking for burglars under the furniture. She should cross the stage in a straight line without looking at anybody or anything, like Lady Macbeth with a candle. "It's quicker and more frightening that way."

It was, as always, Stanislavsky's exuberance that Chekhov most feared. How on earth could his drama of understatement be conveyed by such a dedicated apostle of overstatement? Why must Stanislavsky make such a cacophonous din with the offstage noises in Act Three? True, the town is supposed to be on fire at the time, the alarm is being rung on church bells, and fire engines are clattering about. But that was no reason to overdo things. "The noise is only in the distance: off stage, a vague, muffled sound." Nor, after Tuzenbakh's death in the off-stage duel of Act Four, need his body be solemnly borne across the stage, as Stanislavsky at one time proposed. So subtle an internal drama would be wrecked by these heavy-handed methods, Chekhov felt. But at one point he did require an actor to pull out all the stops: when denouncing the horrors of provincial life in Act Four Andrew Prozorov should be "very excited," and "just about ready to square up to the audience with his fists." Very excited! Though a quiet tone might often be appropriate with Chekhov, this instruction is a warning against *any* glib generalization about him or his work.

Primed with advice from Nice, the Moscow Art Theater presented its first performance of *Three Sisters* on January 31, 1901: the third Chekhov play to be launched by the same theater in the author's absence. Although the reception was somewhat disappointing, it was by no means disastrous, and the play was soon firmly established in the repertoire.

A few months after the first night of *Three Sisters*, Chekhov married the actress Olga Knipper, who had by now appeared in all three Art Theater productions of his plays. Naturally the bridegroom was soon under pressure from his leading lady and her colleagues to write a second play especially for their company. Chekhov was maddeningly slow to oblige, for he was increasingly suffering from ill health. But although he had now virtually abandoned narrative fiction, he was sufficiently master of his creative faculties to be mulling over a fruitful new dramatic theme. It was to become the most famous of all his works, and we meet the first recorded version of its title, *The Cherry Orchard*, in a letter of December 24, 1902. The new play had been conceived as "funny, very funny," and was to be a four-act farce. By February 1903 it was "already completed," but only in Chekhov's head. Not until the summer did he settle down to serious work, and by mid-October he was able to send the play to Moscow, where it had long been eagerly awaited. A few weeks later the author arrived in person, having decided—with the approval of his most recent medical adviser—that he would for once break his habit of wintering in the south.

The Cherry Orchard was now under intensive preparation at the Art Theater, and Chekhov attended rehearsals almost daily, yet without reaching any accord with Stanislavsky. The play was not flourishing, Stanislavsky complained. The main difficulty had arisen with earlier productions and stemmed from a fundamental difference of view between creator and interpreters. Were these plays, as Chekhov maintained, comedies? Did they even contain, as he said of *The Cherry Orchard*, elements of farce? Or were they "ponderous dramas of Russian life?" It was this last interpretation which Stanislavsky, and not he alone, insisted on imposing.

In firmly describing his plays, above all *The Cherry Orchard*, as comedies, Chekhov was perhaps confusing matters by dragging in a traditional theatrical term inapplicable to his new form of drama. What he was really appealing for was a lightness of touch, a throwaway casual style, an abandonment of the traditional over-theatricality of the Russian (and not only the Russian) theater. But here was Stanislavsky serving up a suet pudding instead of a soufflé, seeming hopelessly addicted to that heavy traditionalism of which he and his theater believed themselves to have sounded the death-knell. Meanwhile Chekhov was too resigned, too ill, too modest to thrash things out on first principles with his producer. Indeed, did he ever really probe into his concept of comedy in his own mind to find out exactly what he meant by it? Whatever the reasons, *The Cherry Orchard*'s first-night prospects seemed increasingly dim as rehearsal succeeded rehearsal. This was perhaps inevitable with a work so finely balanced between pathos and humor. Here is a plot hinging on the tragic loss, to an upstart businessman, of a family estate that its feckless genteel owners dearly love (insofar, that is, as they are capable of dearly loving anything). Yet the upstart is no vulgar *nouveau riche*, but a sensitive and compassionate man. And the tragic loss of the estate turns out neither a tragedy nor even much of a loss, once the blow has fallen. Even so grave a personal crisis as this can provoke no profound reaction in the charmingly superficial evicted proprietors, whom Chekhov gently ridicules, yet from whom he by no means withholds his sympathies. Nothing is quite what it seems, nor yet quite the opposite of what it seems, in a play that calls for rare delicacy of interpretation.

Even Chekhov's own works, in which the mirages of climaxes so deliciously melt into artistically contrived anticlimaxes, contain few examples of irony as poignant as that furnished in real life by *The Cherry Orchard*'s premiere. Here was a great writer's finest hour, the pinnacle of his career, the moment when he was to receive full and ecstatic recognition for a lifetime's achievement. But the great occasion so developed as to cause him acute suffering.

The ill-starred January 17, 1904, happened to be Chekhov's birthday: his forty-fourth and—as his thin, bowed, shrunken figure suggested—destined to be his last. What better occasion could there be for one of those jubilee celebrations so popular in the Russian literary world? Though his literary debut had occurred in 1880, making this at least one year premature, the decision was nevertheless taken to mark his twenty-fifth anniversary in the theater, at the first night of his new play. Chekhov himself utterly detested such "jubilees," as was well known. But the collective urge to dramatize the triumph of a dying genius took precedence over all real concern for his needs and feelings, the intermission between Acts Three and Four of *The Cherry Orchard* having been earmarked for elaborate speeches and presentations from the stage. Chekhov was not warned, for that would have been to risk the whole enterprise. Nor was he even present in the theater during the first two acts; he was therefore deliberately missing the fourth baptism of one of his plays at the Art Theater on the first occasion when his presence in Moscow would have made it possible for him to attend.

When the second act was over and tumultuous ovations seemed to assure the play's success, Nemirovich-Danchenko sent Chekhov a note begging him to come to the theater. Chekhov complied, still not realizing what was afoot when he appeared on stage in the intermission after Act Three and was greeted by fervent applause. He stood there, coughing and obviously ill. Some members of the audience called out that the sick Anton Pavlovich should at least face his ordeal seated.

The speeches and presentations seemed endless, and Chekhov stood it as best he could. When addressed as "dear and most honored author," he derived wry satisfaction from the coincidence with Gayev's line "dear and most honored bookcase" in Act One of his play. And though he did not enjoy himself, he at least endured his supreme triumph with characteristic stoicism and courtesy.

Six months later he died at Badenweiler in southern Germany.

What constitutes Chekhov's originality as a dramatist? And what are the special satisfactions that continue to attract audiences to performances of his plays in so many parts of the world? In an attempt to answer these questions certain features, common to the mature dramas and not yet touched on, will be presented and drawn together with themes already evoked in the above account of Chekhov's evolution as a dramatist.

From Chekhov's own early plays and from the bulk of pre-Chekhov drama in general the mature works differ, as already indicated, in the relatively slight emphasis placed on action. True, the occasional happening is to be observed, and there are even deeds of violence. Tuzenbakh of *Three Sisters* is killed in a duel; Uncle Vanya twice fires a revolver at his ludicrous brother-in-law. Yet we note that the former calamity takes place off stage, and that the briefly murderous Vanya predictably misses his target. Even *The Cherry Orchard*, last and most pacific of the plays, features a revolver: that carried by Yepikhodov in case he should feel the urge to commit suicide. But it is never fired, and if during the play's exquisite last scene the aged manservant, Firs, may be thought a victim of homicide, it is homicide by culpable negligence, not by direct action. With all this may be contrasted Chekhov's earliest play, *Platonov*, with its two attempted suicides, one attempted murder, one successful murder, and one lynching.

After the spectacular suicide at the end of his second full-length play, *Ivanov*, Chekhov abandoned the direct presentation of major catastrophes on stage; these were in any case becoming rarer, increasingly muted, more and more ironical. Nina's harrowing adventures in *The Seagull*, Tuzenbakh's death in *Three Sisters*, the seemingly fateful sale of the Cherry Orchard: none of these episodes is directly displayed to the audience. But though Greek tragedy observed a similar convention, and though Chekhov himself did reluctantly study the classics at school, there is no evidence whatever of any direct classical influence on his drama. That his avoidance of direct-action scenes differed radically from any Greek prototype is well emphasized by the complaint once made to him by Tolstoy. "Where does one get to with your heroes? From the sofa to the privy and from the privy back to the sofa." One can hardly say that of Sophocles.

Sparsely equipped with deeds of violence—and, indeed, with effective or even ineffective actions of any sort—the mature plays are not, as is sometimes suggested, entirely devoid of plot. But the plot is unobtrusive, being largely restricted to the bare minimum of suspense-inducing development without which even the characteristic Chekhovian letdown would be impossible; for even anticlimaxes, like climaxes, need their buildup. Thus, before he can shoot and miss, Uncle Vanya has to be set in motion by an expertly deployed family quarrel. Before the youngest of the three sisters can lose her fiancé in a duel, she must be brought to the point of agreeing, however unenthusiastically, to marry him in the first place. Then again, before the owners of the cherry orchard can be deprived of their beloved home, sympathy for their plight must be evoked—a necessary preliminary to the discovery that this plight is no plight at all for these feckless creatures. Nor, it turns out in the end, had that beloved orchard been so beloved that its annihilation could touch them in any profound sense. Once again Chekhov's audience has been gently led "down the garden path." But it has been led, not left standing in one spot.

If these are not plays of action, are they **perhaps plays of
ideas?** Is there some philosophical or instructional element
such as many great dramatists, from the Greeks onwards,
have incorporated in their work? That *Ivanov* contains such
an element has already been noted: it is both a play of action
and a drama with a message. The hero's character is painstak-
ingly analyzed (largely in his own long soliloquies) while the
audience is instructed—without necessarily being fully aware
of this—in the virtues of tolerance and the avoidance of facile
censoriousness. From its very different standpoint *The Wood
Demon* advocates these same virtues. But what of the mature
drama? The characters are indeed subtly delineated in various ways, yet without the analysis in depth to be found in
Ivanov and in the portraits of Trigorin and Treplev in *The
Seagull*. As for messages, critics have attempted to interpret
Nina's painfully pursued stage career, in *The Seagull*, as a call
to cultivate such admirable qualities as resilience, industry,
and persistence. Similar claims have even been made for the
"eternal student" Trofimov, that loser of galoshes in *The
Cherry Orchard*, whose pathetic harangues about a "new
life" have been invoked as an appeal by Chekhov to the
audience to build a different and better society.

Though such interpretations can be both ludicrous and
self-refuting, it by no means follows that the element of social
commentary should be dismissed out of hand. Does not *The
Cherry Orchard* indeed portray a dying and effete class in a
doomed society? May not these fruit trees and their owners,
as also the Prozorov and Voynitsky households in the two
other mature dramas, be legitimately interpreted as symbols
of the old Russia, which, for good or ill, was about to make
way for the new? Of course. But it could be dangerous to
overestimate this aspect. Socially significant as the mature
plays may be, valuable as they indeed are as a commentary
on their age, they were not written with that purpose primar-
ily in view. In the search for the plays' prime function, social
commentary is of only secondary importance.

Like most great writers for the theater, Chekhov seems
more interested in illuminating the human condition in general than in presenting the specific problems of his own
society. May the plays then claim the study of all mankind as
their fundamental concern? A rudimentary ethic can indeed
be deduced from the sympathy which the author lavishes by
implication on certain characters while sternly withholding it

from certain others. Serebryakov in *Uncle Vanya*, Yasha in *The Cherry Orchard*, above all Natasha in *Three Sisters:* these are hateful creatures, lacking any redeeming characteristic. Those who bask in their creator's approval include the unmarried young women, but also—as is known from the direct evidence of Chekhov's letters—Lopakhin in *The Cherry Orchard*. Selfishness and insensitivity are pilloried, while defenselessness and sensitivity are held up for admiration: a distinction undoubtedly reflecting Chekhov's personal taste. Yet it by no means follows that he wrote the plays chiefly to air these predilections, for which he could in any case claim no special originality. The problem of his sympathies and antipathies is significant, certainly, and would repay more systematic attention than it has received. But it is not absolutely crucial to the essence of his drama.

If Chekhov's plays are not dramas of action or of ideas, if they purvey neither entertainment nor instruction in any conventional sense, can they be helpfully defined as centered on the characters' emotions?

In his book *The Chekhov Play* (London, 1973), Harvey Pitcher ably argues that these are essentially plays of emotional content. It may seem churlish to quarrel with this thesis, which underpins an admirably original and sensitive evaluation of Chekhov's drama. Still, the plain fact is—and Pitcher himself shows full awareness of this—that emotions in the usual sense of the word are at least as conspicuous by their absence as by their presence. Love, hate, rage, jealousy— passions of one kind or another: these are in short supply, except in temporary or muted form. Rather are the prevailing moods low-key, desultory, inconsequential. One might call Chekhov's characters self-obsessed if "obsessed" were not, again, too positive a term to apply to them. Never embroiled in tempestuous passions, chiefly engaged in the desultory monitoring of their lives, they tend to offer from time to time torpid running commentaries on their own biographies. They regret misspent opportunities in the past, they voice their aspirations for the future. These hopes will never be "dashed"— again far too positive a term—but are sure to end in the inevitable metaphorical whimper.

One such plaint is to be found at the beginning of Andrew Prozorov's fine soliloquy in Act Four of *Three Sisters*. "Where is my past life, oh, what has become of it—when I was young, happy and intelligent, when I had such glorious thoughts and visions, and my present and future seemed so bright and promising?" Here is the ultimate distillation of Chekhovian hankering: the young man regretfully looks back to the time when he had—in vain, as he now knows—hopefully looked forward. This same passage has already been mentioned as emphasizing how difficult Chekhov can be to sum up; for as the speech develops, it acquires the momentum which led its author to describe it as "very excited."

Time, as Andrew Prozorov's speech indicates, is a crucial ingredient in the brewing of a Chekhovian mood, whether remembrance of things past, fears for the present, or concern for the future is involved. Time is invoked in any number of contexts. "It's exactly a year ago today since father died." "In twenty-five or thirty years' time everyone will work." Such are characteristic phrases from *Three Sisters*. Then there is the time-dominated *Cherry Orchard*, where the first page sets the key. "What time is it? . . . two o'clock . . . how late . . . a couple of hours . . . too late . . . living abroad for five years . . . I was a lad of fifteen . . . in those days."

The chief focuses for the futile regrets and aspirations of Chekhov's characters are those universal human preoccupations, work and love. In *The Seagull* artistic work, creative and performing, is the chief issue. Yet only one of the four characters involved—the egocentric actress Irina Arkadin—seems to derive satisfaction from her career: a reminder that in Chekhov only the insensitive and callous find fulfillment. Then again, one leading theme of *Uncle Vanya* is farm management as so laboriously undertaken by Vanya himself and his niece Sonya. This drudgery had once been rendered tolerable by being performed for a good cause, the financial support of an academic luminary, Professor Serebryakov. Then the Professor's pretensions are exposed, he is discredited in Vanya's eyes, a protest is attempted; but all in vain, and Vanya is still faced at the end with the same life of toil, now wholly unrewarding and stripped even of the comforting illusions that had once sustained it. Work is also a theme of *Three Sisters*, in which the concept is discussed at great length by Tuzenbakh on the basis of no personal experience whatever. Those who do engage in some form of toil in the same play—Andrew, Olga, Irina—are less inclined to theorize about it, but say enough to make it clear that none of them derives any satisfaction at all from his or her chosen employment.

Love, too, is inevitably frustrating—in the plays and in the stories. *The Seagull* strikes an untypically gloom-ridden note with its long chain of lugubrious love attachments. In *Uncle Vanya*, Sonya's hopeless love for Astrov is inadequately paralleled by his frustrated feelings for the beautiful Helen—feelings reciprocated only in being insufficiently passionate on both sides to lead even to any temporary and semi-serious attachment. As for the Prozorov family in *Three Sisters*, all the sisters and their brother present variations on the theme of failure in love. Then again, the most *The Cherry Orchard* can offer in the way of love is yet another low-key attachment, that between Varya and Lopakhin. This is portrayed as strong enough to arouse a feeling of pathos when their marriage, implied to be desirable from time to time in the course of the play, is silently dropped from the agenda.

To probe the nature of Chekhov's mature drama is to be forced more and more into negative statements. It has been easier to say what the plays are not than to say what they are: easier, also, to analyze what does not happen to the characters than what does. And we are now, alas, forced back to the supremely unoriginal and time-worn conclusion that Chekhov's drama is essentially a study in moods: moods desultory, sporadically inter-reacting, half-hearted, casual, yet somehow profoundly moving.

How depressing that familiar formula sounds; and how puzzling, too, when one remembers that the plays have had an exhilarating impact on successive generations of theater-goers. Through what mystery of art can these spectacles so apathetic, sluggish and pallid, these blurred and vaguely disturbing pictures of living and partly living, have aroused such universal enthusiasm, affection, and concern?

A dramatist will always provide stimulus if he effectively illuminates in a new way some aspect of the human condition neglected by his predecessors. And Chekhov did indeed have his own special view of mankind. To him—or so he appears to imply—human affairs were flatter, duller, less eventful, less heroic than they were to earlier playwrights. His outlook as a man was by no means so pessimistic, we know that. As a dramatist and short story writer, however, he certainly implies an acceptance of Henry Thoreau's thesis that "the mass of men lead lives of quiet desperation." Hence the vivid contrast between Chekhov and the many tragedians, from the tempestuous Aeschylus onwards, who have tended to portray larger-than-life heroes leading lives of noisy desperation. Other playwrights—the writers of comedy, from Aristophanes onwards—have tended to suggest, if only in their denouements, that cheerful and serene non-desperation might be the common human lot. In place of these familiar consolations provided by tragedy and comedy, in place of the delights purveyed by a Plautus, a Racine, a Goethe, a Schiller, by not a few pre-Chekhovian Russian dramatists and by many other playwrights great and small, Chekhov supplies something entirely different: the spectacle of characters palpably less vital, less heroic, less significant than the average theatergoer, however inclined to self-disparagement, might reasonably suppose himself to be.

Far from implying any view of life grandiose in the tragic manner, or ultimately harmonious in the spirit of comedy, Chekhov continually suggests the opposite: human existence is more pointless, more frustrating, less heroic, less satisfying than members of his audience may privately conceive. But this too may have its advantages. Harassed less by pestilence, famine, and foreign invaders than by the horrors of commuting, of parking his car, of filling in tax and other returns, of pacifying computers and bureaucrats—even harassed, perhaps, by the appalling misfortune of actually being a bureaucrat—a modern man may well find it more satisfyingly cathartic to be purged of Chekhovian boredom, despair, and *taedium vitae* than of the traditional Aristotelian pity and terror. Thus Chekhov admirably complements his great predecessors by catering to a different area of human need.

Hence the very special delight which he offers his audiences. First, they recognize Chekhov's world as "real" in a new and special sense (which does not necessarily invalidate the "reality" of other dramatists), and they have the aesthetic satisfaction that is experienced when obscurely discerned perceptions are exposed to view with supreme skill. And then, even better, the theatergoer can recognize at a second stage of perception that Chekhov's characters are even less decisive and effective than he probably considers himself. He or she who feels outclassed and overawed by an Oedipus or a Clytemnestra, or by an Antony or a Cleopatra, by a Faust or a Mephistopheles, can smile condescendingly and affectionately at the maneuvers of an Uncle Vanya, a Vershinin, a Lyuba Ranevsky.

In undergoing this new and blander form of dramatic purgation, Chekhov's first audiences were incidentally taught to savor the first major corpus of drama in Western literature that is the opposite of purpose-built. No longer were they presented with chains of episodes all designed to lead towards a predetermined goal. No longer were they expected to follow plots more purposive than life acted out by characters also purpose-directed beyond the common norm, a feature of pre-Chekhovian drama even when failure to achieve a purpose is a key theme. Shakespeare's Hamlet, like Chekhov's heroes, fails to take decisive action. But is not the main drive of *Hamlet* concentrated on eloquently demonstrating this very failure? Then again, just as Shakespeare manipulates Hamlet, so too do the Greek tragic poets manipulate their heroes—and also the very gods, whether to demonstrate their awesome and inscrutable power (as did Aeschylus) or to cast discreet doubt on some of their more outrageous proceedings (as did Euripides). Chekhov, by contrast, seems content to meander inconsequentially. He almost seems to allow his characters to take over, and rarely does he appear to manipulate them. In Chekhov nothing at all—not plot line, nor characters, nor even the very capacity to dither—is ever heroic, wholehearted, and concentrated. George Calderon, his early translator into English, was therefore right to call the plays "centrifugal," by contrast with other "centripetal" dramas. This discursive tendency was reinforced by Chekhov's abandonment, after *Ivanov*, of concentration on a single star part in favor of the more "democratic" approach whereby up to half a dozen of the main personages in a given play all seem to have roughly equal importance.

This muting of the characters harmonizes superbly with the concomitant muting of the emotions. Though the plays abound in suicidal moods, pessimistic utterances, unhappy love affairs, and frustrated careers, no producer should forget that most of this material is, in a very special sense, half-playful, and is balanced by other material—all the teasing, the badinage, the inconsequential backchat. Even if love always proves a failure, ordinary affection does not, and it is there in plenty. Moreover, virtually all the long complaints and self-disparaging soliloquies have a self-mocking, ironical seasoning: even those of the immature play *Ivanov*. The actor who declaims this material like a King Lear or newly blinded Oedipus will do Chekhov a gross and embarrassing disservice. The light touch, the throwaway manner—these will rarely come amiss, provided that the essential seriousness of the plays is never marred by flippancy. It is desirable, too, to stress the underlying harmony—of mood rather than of emotions—that usually unites the characters even when they manifest on the surface a total inability to communicate with each other over practicalities. In *The Cherry Orchard*, Gayev and Lyuba may drive Lopakhin nearly out of his mind with their hopelessness and refusal to listen to sensible advice; yet all the time the three remain firm friends, and are smiling or almost smiling at each other even as they seem to be quarreling or half-quarreling.

What of the many other satisfactions purveyed by Chekhov's drama? There is the exquisite evocation of atmosphere. Two settings in particular—the lake in *The Seagull* and the orchard in Chekhov's last play—cast an enchanted spell over all the proceedings. There is the subtle use of musical and other "noises off," not forgetting the shot that kills Tuzenbakh in *Three Sisters* and the "sound of a breaking string" in *The Cherry Orchard*. There is the humor. This takes in the broad farcical antics of a Telegin, a Ferapont, and a Simeonov-Pishchik. But it also runs to high subtlety: for example, in Uncle Vanya's superb accusation flung at his detested brother-in-law: "You have ruined my life. I might have been a Schopenhauer, a Dostoyevsky." And there is the deadly economy, also humorous in a sense, whereby that monstrous intruder, Natasha of *Three Sisters*, so ironically and unintentionally censures herself when she says of an aged servant that "there's no room for misfits in this house."

These are topics on which I have written elsewhere. And, believing in any case that art is essentially a mystery, I prefer now to leave that art to speak for itself. If these observations satisfactorily explain even a small part of the mystery I shall be content. But if they render it more creatively mysterious still, I shall be delighted indeed.

IVANOV

[Иванов]

A PLAY IN FOUR ACTS

(1887–1889)

CHARACTERS

NICHOLAS IVANOV, a local government official concerned with peasant affairs

ANNA, his wife, *née* Sarah Abramson

COUNT MATTHEW SHABELSKY, his uncle on his mother's side

PAUL LEBEDEV, chairman of the rural district council

ZINAIDA, his wife

SASHA, their daughter, aged 20

EUGENE LVOV, a young doctor on the council's panel

MARTHA BABAKIN, a young widow, estate-owner and daughter of a rich businessman

DMITRY KOSYKH, excise officer

MICHAEL BORKIN, a distant relative of Ivanov and manager of his estate

AVDOTYA, an old woman with no definite means of support

YEGORUSHKA, a dependent of the Lebedevs

FIRST GUEST

SECOND GUEST

THIRD GUEST

FOURTH GUEST

PETER, Ivanov's manservant

GABRIEL, a servant of the Lebedevs

Guests of both sexes, servants

The action takes place in the central Russian countryside

ACT ONE

The garden on IVANOV's *estate. Left, the front of the house, with terrace. One window is open. In front of the terrace is a broad semicircular area, with paths leading into the garden directly in front of the house and to its right. Garden seats, right, also tables, with a lighted lamp on one of them. Evening is drawing in. As the curtain rises there is the sound of a duet for piano and 'cello being practised indoors.*

SCENE I

[IVANOV *and* BORKIN. IVANOV *sits at a table reading a book.* BORKIN *is seen at the back of the garden carrying a shot-gun and wearing high boots. He is rather drunk. Seeing* IVANOV, *he tip-toes up to him and aims the gun at his face from close quarters.*]

IVANOV [*seeing* BORKIN, *starts and jumps up*]. Michael, what on earth—? You gave me a start. I've enough trouble already without your silly games. [*Sits down.*] Great fun, isn't it, frightening people?

BORKIN [*guffaws*]. All right, all right, I'm sorry. [*Sits beside him.*] All right, I won't do it again. [*Takes off his peaked cap.*] It's hot. You know, old boy, I've done over ten miles in about three hours and I'm dead beat. You feel my heart.

IVANOV [*reading*]. Very well, in a minute.

BORKIN. No, do it now. [*Takes* IVANOV's *hand and puts it to his chest.*] Well? Tick tock tick tock tick tock—something wrong with the old ticker, I might drop dead any moment. I say, would you care if I did?

IVANOV. I'm reading. Won't it keep?

BORKIN. But seriously, will you care if I drop dead? Nicholas, do you care if I die?

IVANOV. Leave me alone.

BORKIN. Just tell me if you'd mind, old boy.

IVANOV. What I mind is that smell of vodka. It's disgusting, Michael.

BORKIN [*laughs*]. Smell? That's funny. Actually, though, it isn't—I ran into the magistrate at Plesniki, and we did put away quite a few glasses. Drinking's really very bad for you. Bad for you, I say. Eh? Isn't it?

IVANOV. Look, this is altogether too much. You're behaving outrageously, my dear man.

BORKIN. All right, I'm sorry. Never mind, you take it easy. [*Gets up and moves off.*] Some people are funny, you can't even talk to them. [*Comes back.*] Oh yes, it nearly slipped my mind—I want eighty-two roubles from you.

IVANOV. Eighty-two roubles? What for?

BORKIN. To pay the men tomorrow.

IVANOV. I haven't got it.

BORKIN. Much obliged, I'm sure. [*Mimicking him.*] "Haven't got it." But the men have got to be paid. Or don't you think so?

IVANOV. I don't know. I've no money today. Wait till the first of the month when I get my salary.

BORKIN. What good is it bandying words with people like you? The men come for their wages tomorrow morning—not on the first of the month.

IVANOV. Well, what can I do now? Oh, go on, pester me—make my life a misery. But why you have to plague me so abominably just when I'm reading or writing or——

BORKIN. Do the men get paid or not? Yes or no. Oh, what's the good of talking to you? [*Makes a gesture of despair.*] Call yourself a farmer, a goddam landed proprietor? You and your scientific farming! Three thousand acres, and not a penny in his pocket! Owns a wine-cellar, but no cork-screw! I've a good mind to sell your carriage and horses tomorrow. Oh yes I will. I sold the oats before we cut them and tomorrow I'll damn well sell the rye. [*Strides about the stage.*] I'll make no bones about it either. What do you take me for?

SCENE II

[*The above,* SHABELSKY—*off-stage—and* ANNA.]

SHABELSKY [*off-stage, his voice heard through the window*]. It's no use us playing together. You've no more ear for music than a stuffed trout and you have an appalling touch.

ANNA [*seen through the open window*]. Who's talking out here? You, Michael? Why all the marching about?

BORKIN. Friend Nicholas is enough to make anyone's boots itch.

ANNA. I say, will you have some hay put on the croquet lawn?

BORKIN [*with a gesture of despair*]. Leave me alone, please.

ANNA. Really, what a way to talk, it doesn't suit you a bit. If you want women to like you, never let them see you being annoyed or stuffy. [*To her husband.*] Shall we have a romp in the hay, Nicholas?

IVANOV. Standing by an open window, Anna? It's bad for you, please move away. [*Shouts.*] Shut the window, Uncle.

[*The window is shut.*]

BORKIN. Lebedev's interest falls due in two days, don't forget.

IVANOV. I haven't. I'm going over this evening, I'll ask him to wait. [*Looks at his watch.*]

BORKIN. When are you leaving?

IVANOV. At once.

BORKIN [*eagerly*]. Hang on a minute, I do believe today's Sasha's birthday, eh? Tut, tut, tut. And I forgot. What a memory! [*Jumps up and down.*] I'm coming with you. [*Sings.*] Coming, coming. I'll have a bathe, chew some paper, and with three drops of ammonia I'll be a new man. Nicholas, old man, you're a bundle of nerves, dear boy, besides snivelling and being so depressed all the time.

Look, we two—hell knows what we couldn't pull off together! I'd do anything for you. Shall I marry Martha Babakin? And split the dowry with you? But no—you can have it all, take the lot.

IVANOV. Don't talk such rot.

BORKIN. No, seriously. Shall I marry Martha and give you half her dowry? But what am I saying? As if you could understand. [*Imitates him.*] "Don't talk such rot." You're a nice, clever fellow, but you lack flair, you know—a certain flamboyancy. You should let yourself go and to hell with the consequences. Why, you whining neurotic—if you were a normal man you could be a millionaire in a year. For instance, if I had twenty-three hundred roubles now, I could be twenty thousand in pocket inside a couple of weeks. You don't believe me? Think I'm still "talking rot"? Not a bit. Give me twenty-three hundred roubles, and I'll get you twenty thousand in a week. Ovsyanov's asking two thousand three hundred for a strip of land just across the river from us. If we buy it, we'll own both banks. Now, with both banks in our hands, we're entitled to dam the river, aren't we? We'll start building a mill, and as soon as we let it be known that we mean to make a dam, everyone down-stream will raise hell. We'll tell them straight—if they don't want a dam, let them come along here and cough up. See what I mean? The Zarevsky factory will pay five thousand, Korolkov three thousand, and the monastery will give five.

IVANOV. This is all very shady, Michael. Keep such things to yourself if you don't want us to quarrel.

BORKIN [*sits down at the table*]. Of course, I knew it! Won't lift a finger himself, and won't let me either.

SCENE III

[*The above,* SHABELSKY *and* LVOV.]

SHABELSKY [*coming out of the house with* LVOV]. Doctors are like lawyers, only lawyers just rob you, while doctors rob you and murder you as well. I'm not talking about present company. [*Sits down on the garden seat.*] They're so bogus, just out for what they can get. There may be some Utopia where there are exceptions to the rule, but—well, I've paid out twenty thousand odd in doctors' bills in my time and never met a doctor yet who didn't strike me as a licensed swindler.

BORKIN [*to* IVANOV]. Yes, won't lift a finger yourself, and won't let me either, which is why we've no money——

SHABELSKY. As I say, I'm not talking about present company. There may be exceptions, though actually—. [*Yawns.*]

IVANOV [*closing his book*]. Well, Doctor?

LVOV [*looking round at the window*]. As I said this morning, she must go to the Crimea straight away. [*Walks up and down the stage.*]

SHABELSKY [*gives a snort of laughter*]. The Crimea! Why don't you and I set up as doctors, Michael? It's so easy. If Mrs. So-and-so, or Miss Whatever-it-is, has a tickle in her throat and starts coughing out of boredom, just pick up a form and make out a proper medical prescription. Take one young doctor. Follow up with one trip to the Crimea, where some picturesque local lad may——

IVANOV [*to the* COUNT]. Oh, don't be such a bore. [*To* LVOV.] Trips to the Crimea cost money. All right, I might lay my hands on some, but you do know she's turned the idea down flat, don't you?

LVOV. Yes, I know. [*Pause.*]

BORKIN. Look, Doctor, can Anna really be so ill that she has to go to the Crimea?

LVOV [*looks round at the window*]. Yes, it's tuberculosis.

BORKIN. Phew! That's bad. She certainly looks as if she wouldn't last long, I've thought that for some time.

LVOV. But—keep your voice down. You can be heard indoors. [*Pause.*]

BORKIN [*sighing*]. Our life—. Man's life is like a bright flower blooming in a meadow. A goat comes along and eats it up. No more flower.

SHABELSKY. Nonsense, nonsense, nonsense. [*Yawns.*] Stuff and nonsense. [*Pause.*]

BORKIN. I say, everyone, I've been trying to show Nicholas how to make money. I gave him a gem of an idea, but the seed fell on stony ground as usual. You can't make him see sense. Look at the man—all that gloom, bad temper, wretchedness, moodiness, general misery——

SHABELSKY [*stands up and stretches*]. You're a great one for ingenious brain-waves and you're always giving advice. You might spare me a bit. Give me a lesson, if you're so clever. Show me some way out.

BORKIN [*stands up*]. I'm going for a swim. Good-bye, all. [*To the* COUNT.] There are at least twenty things you could do. If I were you I'd have twenty thousand in a week. [*Moves off.*]

SHABELSKY [*follows him*]. How? Come on, tell me.

BORKIN. There's nothing to tell, it's dead easy. [*Comes back.*] Lend me a rouble, Nicholas.

[IVANOV *gives him the money without speaking.*]

BORKIN. Thanks. [*To the* COUNT.] You've still a lot of cards up your sleeve.

SHABELSKY [*going after him*]. But what?

BORKIN. If I were you I'd have thirty thousand in a week. If not more. [*Goes out with the* COUNT.]

IVANOV [*after a pause*]. Futile people, futile words and silly questions to answer. Doctor, I'm so fed up with it all. I'm quite ill. I'm irritable, bad-tempered and rude these days, and so touchy, I hardly know myself. I have headaches for days on end, I can't sleep, and my ears buzz. But what can I do? Not a thing.

LVOV. I've a bone to pick with you, Ivanov.

IVANOV. Then pick it.

LVOV. It's your wife. [*Sits down.*] She refuses to go to the Crimea, but she'd go if you went.

IVANOV [*after some thought*]. The trip would cost quite a bit for two. Besides, I can't get much time off, I've already had one holiday this year.

LVOV. All right, I won't argue. Now then, the main cure for tuberculosis is absolute rest. But your wife never has a moment's peace, she's always worried about how you treat her. I'm rather excited, sorry, but I shan't mince my words. What you're doing is killing her. [*Pause.*] Let me think better of you, Ivanov.

IVANOV. It's only too true. I suppose I'm very much to blame, but I'm so mixed up, I feel paralysed, half dead or something. I don't know what I'm doing. I can't understand others, or myself either. [*Looks up at the window.*] We might be overheard, let's go for a stroll. [*They stand up.*] I'd start at the beginning and tell you the whole story, my dear fellow, but it's so long and involved, it would take all night. [*They move off.*] Anna's a splendid, wonderful woman. She gave up her religion for me—left her mother, father and wealthy home. If I'd asked her to give up a hundred more things, she'd have done it without thinking. Now I'm not in the least wonderful, and I've given up nothing. Anyway, it's a long story, but what it boils down to, my dear Doctor [*squirms*] is that—to put it briefly—I married because I was so much in love. I swore to love her for ever, but—well, that was five years ago, and she still loves me, while I—. [*Throws up his hands.*] Now you tell me she'll soon die, and I don't feel love or pity, just a sort of emptiness and exhaustion. I suppose anyone would think I'm behaving terribly, but I don't know myself what's going on inside me.

[*They go out down the garden path.*]

SCENE IV

[SHABELSKY *and, later,* ANNA.]

SHABELSKY [*comes in, laughing heartily*]. He's more than a petty crook, honestly—he's a virtuoso, a genius. We should put up a statue to him. He's every kind of modern rottenness mixed up together—lawyer, doctor, banker, gangster. [*Sits down on the bottom step of the terrace.*] And, you know, I don't think he's ever studied anywhere, that's what's so fantastic. What a master criminal he'd have made if he'd gone in for education and culture. "You can have twenty thousand in a week," says he. "And you also hold the ace of trumps—being a count." [*Laughs loudly*.] "Any girl with a dowry would marry you."

[ANNA *opens the window and looks down*.]

SHABELSKY. "Shall I marry you to Martha?" he asks. "Who's Martha?" "Oh, the Balabalkin woman. Martha Balabalkin, the one like a washerwoman."

ANNA. That you, Count?

SHABELSKY. What is it?

[ANNA *laughs*.]

SHABELSKY [*with a Jewish accent*]. Vy you are laughing, eh?

ANNA. I thought of something you said. Remember what you said at dinner? "Pardon a thief—." Something about a horse——

SHABELSKY. "Convert a Jew to Christian ways,
            Pardon a thief his life of crime,
            Or take a lame horse to the vet
            —these things are all a waste of time."

ANNA [*laughs*]. You can't make an ordinary joke without being nasty. You're a bad man. [*Seriously*.] Joking apart, Count, you're very spiteful. It's dull and rather unnerving living in the same house as you. You're always moaning and groaning, and to listen to you everyone's a frightful cad. Tell me frankly, have you ever said something nice about anyone?

SHABELSKY. Why the cross-examination?

ANNA. We've lived under one roof for five years and never once have I heard you talk about people calmly, without sneering and being spiteful. What harm have they done you? And do you really think you're better than everyone else?

SHABELSKY. I don't think so at all. I'm just as much a rotten swine on two legs as the next man. I'm in rotten bad taste, fit only for the rubbish dump. I'm always running myself down. Who am I? What am I? I was rich, free, quite

happy—but now I'm a parasite, a scrounger, a degraded
buffoon. If I express indignation or contempt, I only get
laughed at. And when I laugh they shake their heads sadly
and say the old man's a bit cracked. More often than not
they don't hear or notice me.

ANNA [*calmly*]. He's hooting again.

SHABELSKY. Who is?

ANNA. The owl. It hoots every evening.

SHABELSKY. Then let it hoot. Things couldn't be worse.
[*Stretches himself*.] Ah, my dear Sarah, if I won a few
hundred thousand roubles, I'd show you a thing or two. I'd
be out of here in no time, I'd leave this dump and my free
meals—wouldn't set foot here again till the crack of doom.

ANNA. What would you do if you won that money?

SHABELSKY [*after some thought*]. First thing, I'd go to Moscow to hear the gypsies. And then—then I'd be off to
Paris. I'd take lodgings there and go to the Russian church.

ANNA. What else?

SHABELSKY. I'd sit by my wife's grave and think for days on
end. I'd just sit there till I died. She's buried in Paris.
[*Pause.*]

ANNA. It's terribly boring. Shall we play another duet?

SHABELSKY. All right, get the music out.

SCENE V

[SHABELSKY, IVANOV *and* LVOV.]

IVANOV [*appears on a path with* LVOV]. You only left college
last year, my dear Lvov, and you're still young and full of
life, but I'm thirty-five, I have the right to advise you.
Don't you go marrying Jewesses, neurotics or blue-stockings,
but choose something nice and drab and ordinary. Don't
go in for bright colours or unnecessary fuss and bother. In
fact run your life on conventional lines. The greyer and
more monotonous your background the better. Don't take
on thousands of people single-handed, boy, don't fight

windmills or batter your head against brick walls. And may
God save you from things like scientific farming, cranky
schools and wild speeches. Crawl into your little shell, get
on with what little job God gave you to do. It's cosier,
healthier and more decent that way. But the life I've
lived—what a trying business, oh, how exhausting. So
many mistakes, so much unfairness and silliness. [*Spotting
the* COUNT, *irritatedly*.] Uncle, you're always popping up,
one can never talk in peace.

SHABELSKY [*tearfully*]. Damnation, you can't relax anywhere.
[*Jumps up and goes indoors*.]

IVANOV [*shouts after him*]. All right, I'm sorry. [*To* LVOV.]
Why was I rude to him? Oh, I really must be a bit
unhinged, I must do something about myself, I must——

LVOV [*agitated*]. I've heard you out, Ivanov, and—I'm sorry,
but I'm going to be blunt and call a spade a spade. Your
voice and tone, let alone your actual words, are so insensitive, selfish, cold and heartless that—. Someone who loves
you is dying just because she does love you. She hasn't
long to live, while you—you can be so callous and walk
about giving advice and striking attitudes. I can't put it
properly, I'm not much of a speaker, but—but I do most
thoroughly dislike you.

IVANOV. You may well be right, you can judge so much better,
not being involved. Very likely your idea of me is quite
right, and I daresay I'm very very much to blame. [*Listens*.] I think they've brought the carriage round, I'll go
and change. [*Moves towards the house and stops*.] You
dislike me, Doctor, and you don't mind saying so. That
does credit to your feelings. [*Goes indoors*.]

LVOV [*alone*]. Damn my feebleness! Again I missed a chance
to give him a piece of my mind. I can't speak to him
calmly. Hardly have I opened my mouth and uttered one
word when I start choking [*points to his chest*] and heaving
and I'm tongue-tied. I do most heartily loathe that hypocrite, that pretentious fraud! Now he's going out. His
wretched wife's only happy when he's around, she dotes on
him, begs him to spend one evening with her, but he—he
can't do it, because home cramps his style, don't you see?

If he spent an evening at home he'd get so bored he'd blow
his brains out. Poor man—he needs to branch out in some
new line of skulduggery. Oh, I know why you go to those
Lebedevs every evening, I'm under no illusions.

SCENE VI

[LVOV, IVANOV, *wearing hat and overcoat*, SHABELSKY *and* ANNA.]

SHABELSKY [*coming out of the house with* IVANOV *and* ANNA.]
Nicholas, you are a monster, I must say. Every night you
go out and leave us on our own, and we get so bored we go
to bed at eight. You can't call this living, it's monstrous. If
you can go, why can't we, eh?

ANNA. Leave him alone. Let him go, let him——

IVANOV [*to his wife*]. But how could you go when you're not
well? You're ill and you're not allowed out after dark—ask
the doctor here. You're not a child, Anna, you must be
sensible. [*To the* COUNT.] And why do you want to go?

SHABELSKY. I'd rather fry in hell or be eaten by crocodiles
than stay here. I'm bored, bored stiff. Everyone's sick of
me. You leave me here to keep her company, but she's
sick and tired of me and my nagging.

ANNA. Leave him alone, Count, let him go if he enjoys it.

IVANOV. Don't be like that about it, Anna. You know I'm not
going there to enjoy myself, I have to talk about the money
I owe them.

ANNA. I can't see why you make excuses. Just go, no one's
keeping you.

IVANOV. Can't we all stop annoying each other? There's surely
no need.

SHABELSKY [*tearfully*]. Nicholas, my boy—take me with you.
Please. It might be rather amusing just to have a look at
that lot of frauds and nit-wits. I haven't been anywhere
since Easter.

IVANOV [*irritatedly*]. All right, come then. I'm fed up with the
lot of you.

SHABELSKY. Yes? Oh, many, many thanks. [*Grasps him gaily by the arm and takes him on one side.*] Can I wear your straw hat?

IVANOV. Yes, but do hurry.

[*The* COUNT *runs indoors.*]

IVANOV. I'm fed up with you all. But—God, what am I saying? I've no right to talk to you like this, Anna. I never used to be this way. Ah well, good-bye, I'll be back by one.

ANNA. Nicholas, do stay at home, dear.

IVANOV [*agitated*]. My poor, precious darling, don't try and stop me going out at night, please. I'm cruel and unfair, but let me be unfair. It's such agony to stay in. At sunset things start to get me down, it's sheer hell. Don't ask me why, I don't know myself. I don't know, I tell you. You get fed up here, then you go on to the Lebedevs' where it's even worse. You come back, which means getting even more fed up and it goes on all night. I'm absolutely desperate.

ANNA. Then why not stay at home, dear? We'll talk as we used to. We'll have supper together and read. The old boy and I've learnt a lot of duets for you. [*Puts her arms round him.*] Do stay. [*Pause.*] I simply don't understand you, this has been going on a whole year. Why have you changed?

IVANOV. I don't know, I don't know.

ANNA. Why don't you want me to go out with you at night?

IVANOV. If you must know, I'd better tell you. It's rather a cruel thing to say, but it's better said. When I'm so depressed, I—I begin not to love you. I try to get away, even from you, at these times. In fact I just have to get out of the house.

ANNA. You're depressed, you say. That I understand. Look, Nicholas, why not try singing, laughing and losing your temper, as in the old days. You stay in. We'll laugh, drink home-made wine and cheer you up in no time. Shall I sing? Or shall we go and sit in your study in the dark as we used to, and you can tell me all about how depressed you are. Your eyes are so full of suffering. I'll look into them and cry, and we'll both feel better. [*Laughs and cries.*] What is it, Nicholas? Flowers come round every spring, but happiness doesn't—is that it? All right, go then.

IVANOV. Pray for me, Anna. [*Moves off, stops and thinks.*] No, it's too much! [*Goes out.*]

ANNA. Be off with you. [*Sits down near the table.*]

LVOV [*paces up and down the stage*]. Mrs. Ivanov, you must always come indoors on the stroke of six and stay in till morning. These damp nights are bad for you.

ANNA. Yes sir.

LVOV. "Yes sir"? I'm perfectly serious.

ANNA. But I don't want to be perfectly serious. [*Coughs.*]

LVOV. There, you see, you're coughing already.

SCENE VII

[LVOV, ANNA *and* SHABELSKY.]

SHABELSKY [*comes out of the house wearing hat and overcoat*]. Where's Nicholas? Is the carriage there? [*Quickly comes and kisses* ANNA's *hand.*] Good night, precious. [*Pulls a funny face.*] Vot can I do? Excuse, plis. [*Goes out quickly.*]

LVOV. Very funny.

[*Pause. The sound of an accordion far away.*]

ANNA. How boring. The coachmen and cooks are holding a dance and I—I feel forsaken. Doctor, why are you striding about there? Come and sit down here.

LVOV. I can't sit still. [*Pause.*]

ANNA. They're playing *Greenfinch* in the kitchen. [*Sings.*]
"Greenfinch, greenfinch, where have you been?
Drinking vodka on the green."

[*Pause.*] Are your mother and father alive, Doctor?

LVOV. My father's dead, but my mother's still alive.

ANNA. Do you miss her?

LVOV. I'm too busy to miss anyone.

ANNA [*laughs*]. Flowers come round every spring, but happiness doesn't. Who told me that? Now let me see, I think Nicholas himself said it. [*Pricks up her ears.*] The owl's hooting again.

LVOV. Let it.

ANNA. I'm beginning to think I've been unlucky, Doctor. There are lots of people, no better than me perhaps, who are happy and whose happiness costs them nothing. But I've paid for everything, every single thing. And so dearly. Why charge me such a shocking rate of interest? My dear, you're all so careful with me, so very tactful, you're afraid to tell me the truth, but do you think I don't know what's the matter with me? I know all right. Anyway, it's a boring subject. [*With a Jewish accent.*] Excuse, plis, can you tell funny chokes?

LVOV. No.

ANNA. Nicholas can. I've also started wondering why people are so unfair. Why can't they love those who love them? Why do they have to lie when they're told the truth? Tell me, when will my mother and father stop hating me? They live nearly forty miles away, but I feel their hatred all day and night, even in my sleep. And what am I to make of Nicholas being so depressed? He says it's only when he's bored stiff in the evenings that he doesn't love me. I understand that, I can accept it. But what if he stops loving me altogether? Of course that can't happen, but—what if it does? No, I mustn't even think of it. [*Sings.*] "Greenfinch, greenfinch, where have you been?" [*Shudders.*] What horrible thoughts I have. You're not married, Doctor, so there's a lot you can't understand.

LVOV. You're surprised—. [*Sits by her.*] No, it's I—I'm surprised at you. All right, tell me—make me see how you, a decent, intelligent woman, with a nature almost angelic, have let yourself be taken in so blatantly and hauled off to this haunt of owls? Why are you here? What have you in common with that callous, insensitive—but leave your husband out of it. Where do you fit into this whole futile, second-rate set-up? Ye gods! That fossilized maniac count with his non-stop grousing, and that twister Borkin—that frightful crook with his loathsome snout. Go on, tell me why you're here? How did you get here?

ANNA [*laughs*]. That's just how he used to speak, just like that. But his eyes are bigger and when he got excited about something they just blazed! Go on talking.

LVOV [*stands up and makes a gesture of despair*]. What can I say? Please go indoors.

ANNA. You say Nicholas is this and that and the other. What do you know about him? Can you get to know someone in six months? He's a wonderful man, Doctor, and I'm only sorry you didn't know him a year or two ago. Now he's rather under the weather and doesn't speak or do anything. But in the old days—oh, he was so charming, I fell in love at first sight. [*Laughs.*] I took one look and snap went the mousetrap! He said we should go away. I cut off everything, you know, like snipping off dead leaves with some scissors, and followed him. [*Pause.*] But now things are different. He visits the Lebedevs to enjoy other women's company now, while I—sit in the garden and listen to the owl hooting.

[*A watchman is heard tapping.*]

ANNA. Have you any brothers, Doctor?

LVOV. No.

[ANNA *sobs.*]

LVOV. What now? What's the matter?

ANNA [*stands up*]. I can't bear it, Doctor, I'm going over there.

LVOV. Where?

ANNA. Where he is. I'm going, tell them to harness the horses. [*Runs indoors.*]

LVOV. I flatly refuse to treat a patient in these conditions. It's bad enough not paying me, but they play hell with my feelings as well. Yes, I refuse, I've had enough. [*Goes indoors.*]

CURTAIN

ACT TWO

The ballroom in the LEBEDEVS' *house. Access to the garden, centre. Doors, right and left. Expensive antique furniture. A chandelier, candelabras and pictures, all under dust-covers.*

SCENE I

[ZINAIDA, KOSYKH, AVDOTYA, YEGORUSHKA, GABRIEL, *a* MAID, *elderly women guests, young ladies and* MRS. BABAKIN.

ZINAIDA *is sitting on the sofa, with old ladies in armchairs on each side. The young people are sitting on upright chairs. At the back of the stage near the door into the garden a game of cards is in progress, the players including* KOSYKH, AVDOTYA *and* YEGORUSHKA. GABRIEL *stands by the door, right. The* MAID *is handing round snacks on a tray. Throughout the act guests circulate from the garden through the door, right, and back.* MRS. BABAKIN *comes in through the door, right, and goes towards* ZINAIDA.]

ZINAIDA [*gaily*]. Martha, darling!

MRS. BABAKIN. Good evening, Zinaida. Best wishes for Sasha's birthday. [*They kiss.*] May God grant——

ZINAIDA. Thank you, darling, I'm so glad. Now how are you?

MRS. BABAKIN. Well, thanks. [*Sits beside her on the sofa.*] Good evening, young people.

[*The guests stand up and bow.*]

FIRST GUEST [*laughs*]. "Young people"! You don't call yourself old, do you?

MRS. BABAKIN [*sighing*]. I can't pretend to be all that young.

FIRST GUEST [*laughing respectfully*]. Oh, come, come. You

don't look like a widow—you put all the young girls in the shade.

[GABRIEL *brings* MRS. BABAKIN *tea*.]

ZINAIDA [*to* GABRIEL]. Hey, don't serve it like that. Get some jam, gooseberry or something.

MRS. BABAKIN. Don't bother, thanks. [*Pause*.]

FIRST GUEST. Did you come through Mushkino, Mrs. Babakin?

MRS. BABAKIN. No, on the Zaymishche road—it's a better one.

FIRST GUEST. Just so.

KOSYKH. Two spades.

YEGORUSHKA. Pass.

AVDOTYA. Pass.

SECOND GUEST. Pass.

MRS. BABAKIN. Lottery tickets are simply soaring again, darling. It's fantastic—they're up to two hundred and seventy roubles for the first draw and they're practically at two-fifty for the second. It's unheard of.

ZINAIDA [*sighs*]. Very nice for those who have lots of them.

MRS. BABAKIN. I'm not sure, darling. They may be worth a bit, but it doesn't pay to put money in them. They cost the earth to insure.

ZINAIDA. That's as may be, but one lives in hope, dear. [*Sighs*.] God is merciful.

THIRD GUEST. It's no use having capital these days, ladies, if you ask me. That's my view. Investments bring such small dividends, and lending money's a pretty risky business. The way I see it, ladies, a man with capital is in a worse fix these days than one who——

MRS. BABAKIN [*sighs*]. That's true.

[FIRST GUEST *yawns*]

MRS. BABAKIN. One doesn't yawn in front of ladies, surely.

FIRST GUEST. Sorry, ladies, I didn't mean to.

[ZINAIDA *gets up and goes out of the door, right. A long silence*]

YEGORUSHKA. Two diamonds.

AVDOTYA. Pass.

SECOND GUEST. Pass.

KOSYKH. Pass.

MRS. BABAKIN [*aside*]. Lord, I'm bored stiff.

SCENE II

[*The above,* ZINAIDA *and* LEBEDEV.]

ZINAIDA [*coming through door, right, with* LEBEDEV, *quietly*]. Why were you skulking in there? Who do you think you are? You sit with your guests. [*Sits in her former seat.*]

LEBEDEV [*yawns*]. Oh dear. [*Seeing* MRS. BABAKIN.] Heavens, there's sugar and spice and all things nice. [*Shakes hands.*] How are we feeling?

MRS. BABAKIN. Very well, thanks.

LEBEDEV. Thank God for that. [*Sits in an armchair.*] Ah well. Gabriel! [GABRIEL *brings him a glass of vodka and a tumbler of water. He drinks the vodka and chases it down with water.*]

FIRST GUEST. Your health.

LEBEDEV. My health, indeed! I'm only lucky I'm not pushing up the daisies. [*To his wife.*] Where's our birthday girl, Zizi?

KOSYKH [*tearfully*]. Hey, why didn't we win anything? [*Jumps up.*] Why did we lose, damn and blast it?

AVDOTYA [*jumps up, angrily*]. Why? If you don't know the game, don't play, man. What do you mean by leading one of their suits? Can you wonder you were left with the ace?

[*Both run forward from the table.*]

KOSYKH [*tearfully*]. Look here, everyone. I held a run—the ace, king, queen and seven small diamonds, the ace of

spades and one small heart, see? And she couldn't declare
a little slam, damn it! I bid no trumps.

AVDOTYA [*interrupting*]. It was I started bidding no trumps,
you went two no trumps——

KOSYKH. This is infuriating. Look here—you had—. I had—
you had—. [*To* LEBEDEV.] Judge for yourself, Lebedev. I
had the ace, king, queen and seven more diamonds——

LEBEDEV [*plugs his ears*.] Leave me alone, can't you?

AVDOTYA [*shouts*]. It was I bid no trumps.

KOSYKH [*furiously*]. Damn and blast me if I ever play cards
with that old trout again!

[*Hurries out into the garden. The* SECOND GUEST *follows
him out, leaving* YEGORUSHKA *at the table.*]

AVDOTYA. Phew, he's made me hot all over. Old trout! Trout
yourself!

MRS. BABAKIN. But you lost your temper too, old thing.

AVDOTYA [*seeing* MRS. BABAKIN, *throws up her hands*]. My
lovely darling. She's here and I don't even notice her, I
must be half blind. Darling! [*Kisses her shoulder and sits
by her*.] How delightful. Let me look at you, you beautiful
creature. But I mustn't say too many nice things or it'll
bring bad luck.

LEBEDEV. Why all the gush? Better find her a husband.

AVDOTYA. I will, I will. I won't lay my sinful old bones to rest
before I've found a husband for her and Sasha, that I
won't. [*Sighs*.] Only where do you find husbands these
days? Look at all our young men—there they sit preening
their feathers like a lot of wet hens.

THIRD GUEST. A most unhappy comparison. What I say, ladies,
is—if young men would rather stay single these days, that's
society's fault.

LEBEDEV. Oh, spare us the generalizations, I don't like them.

SCENE III

[The above and SASHA.*]*

SASHA *[comes in and goes to her father].* It's such glorious weather and you all sit stewing indoors.

ZINAIDA. Sasha, can't you see Mrs. Babakin's here?

SASHA. Oh, sorry. *[Goes up to* MRS. BABAKIN *and shakes hands.]*

MRS. BABAKIN. You're getting much too high and mighty, Sasha. You might come and see me once in a while. *[They kiss.]* Happy returns, darling.

SASHA. Thank you. *[Sits down by her father.]*

LEBEDEV. Yes, Avdotya, husbands are hard to find these days. You can't lay your hands on a decent best man, let alone an eligible groom. No offence meant, but young men are a pretty spineless, wishy-washy crew nowadays, God help them. Can't dance, can't talk, can't drink properly.

AVDOTYA. Can't drink? Oh yes they can, given the chance——

LEBEDEV. Drinking? There's nothing to it, even a horse can drink. No, the thing is to drink properly. Now, in our time you'd sweat away at your lectures all day long, then you'd make for the bright lights in the evening and buzz around till crack of dawn. You'd dance and amuse the girls and there'd be a bit of this business. *[Pretends to drink.]* Sometimes you'd jabber away nineteen to the dozen. But young men these days——. *[Makes a gesture of dismissal.]* I can't make them out, they're no use to man or beast. There's only one decent young fellow in the whole county, and he's married. *[Sighs.]* And I think he's going a bit off his head.

MRS. BABAKIN. Who's that?

LEBEDEV. Nicholas Ivanov.

MRS. BABAKIN. Yes, he's a nice man *[pulls a face]*, only he's so unhappy.

ZINAIDA. Can you wonder, darling? *[Sighs.]* The poor man made a ghastly mistake—marrying that wretched Jewess and thinking her parents would cough up a whacking great dowry. It didn't come off. When she changed her religion they cut her off and cursed her, so not a penny did he get. He's sorry now it's too late.

SASHA. That's not true, Mother.

MRS. BABAKIN [*heatedly*]. Not true, Sasha? But it's an open secret. Why marry a Jewess if there wasn't anything in it for him? Aren't there enough Russian girls to go round? He made a big mistake, darling. [*Eagerly*.] And now he gives her a terrible time, God knows—it's enough to make a cat laugh. The moment he gets home, he's on at her. "Your father and mother cheated me. Get out of my house!" But where can she go? Her parents won't take her back. She might get a job as a maid, but she's not trained. So he keeps on nagging till the count sticks up for her. If it wasn't for the count, he'd have been the end of her ages ago.

AVDOTYA. Or he locks her in the cellar. "Eat garlic, you so-and-so," he says. Eat and eat she does, till the stuff starts coming out of her ears.

[*Laughter*.]

SASHA. That's a lie, Father.

LEBEDEV. Well, what of it? Let them jabber away. [*Shouts*.] Gabriel!

[GABRIEL *gives him vodka and water*.]

ZINAIDA. That's why the poor man's ruined. He's in a bad way, darling. If Borkin didn't run the farm, he and his Jewess would have nothing to eat. [*Sighs*.] And what a fearful nuisance he's been, dear. God alone knows what we've had to put up with. My dear, do you know, he's owed us nine thousand roubles for the last three years?

MRS. BABAKIN [*horrified*]. Nine thousand!

ZINAIDA. Yes, my precious husband arranged to lend it him— he doesn't know who to lend money to and who not. I'm not talking about the loan itself—never mind that—but he might at least pay the interest on time.

SASHA [*heatedly*]. You've said all this thousands of times, Mother.

ZINAIDA. Why should you care? Why do you take his side?

SASHA [*stands up*]. How dare you talk like this about someone who never did you any harm? What harm did he ever do you?

THIRD GUEST. May I say a word, Miss Lebedev? I've a high opinion of Ivanov and have always been honoured to—. But between you and me I think the man's a rogue.

SASHA. Then I can only congratulate you on your insight.

THIRD GUEST. May I quote in evidence a communication made to me by his aide or general guide and philosopher, Borkin? During the cattle epidemic two years ago he bought a lot of cows, insured them——

ZINAIDA. Yes, yes, yes, I remember that business, I heard about it too.

THIRD GUEST. Insured them, mark my words—then infected them with cattle-disease and pocketed the insurance.

SASHA. Oh, that's all nonsense. Nonsense! No one bought cows or infected them, it was all Borkin's idea that he went round boasting about. When Ivanov heard of it he had Borkin going round for a couple of weeks apologizing. Ivanov's only fault is being weak and not having enough go in him to chuck out friend Borkin, and he's wrong to trust people too much. He's been robbed and fleeced left, right and centre—anyone who liked has made a packet out of Ivanov's idealistic plans.

LEBEDEV. Shut up, you little spitfire.

SASHA. Why must they talk such nonsense? Oh, how boring, boring, boring. Ivanov, Ivanov, Ivanov—is there nothing else to talk about? [*Goes towards the door and returns.*] I'm surprised. [*To the young men.*] I'm really surprised how long-suffering you all are. Don't you ever get tired of sitting round like this? The very air's stiff with boredom. Can't you say something, amuse the girls or move around a bit? All right, if you've nothing to talk about but Ivanov, then laugh or sing or dance or something.

LEBEDEV [*laughs*]. Yes, you jolly well pitch into them.

SASHA. Would you mind listening for a moment? If you don't want to dance or laugh or sing, if you're bored with that,

then please, please, just for once in your lives, if only for
the novelty or surprise or fun of the thing—join forces and
think up something brilliantly witty between you. Let it be
rude or vulgar if you like, but funny and original. Or else
do some small thing together which may not add up to all
that much, but does at least look vaguely enterprising and
might make the girls sit up and take notice for once in their
lives. Look, you all want to be liked, don't you? Then why
not try to be likeable? There's something wrong with you
all, and no mistake. The sight of you's enough to kill the
flies or start the lamps smoking. Yes, there's something
wrong—I've told you thousands of times and I'll go on
telling you—something wrong with you all, wrong, wrong,
wrong!

SCENE IV

[*The above*, IVANOV *and* SHABELSKY.]

SHABELSKY [*coming in with* IVANOV *through the door, right*].
Who's making the speeches round here? You, Sasha? [*Laughs
loudly and shakes hands with her.*] Happy returns, dear.
May you live to a ripe old age and not be born a second
time.

ZINAIDA [*gaily*]. Mr. Ivanov, Count Shabelsky.

LEBEDEV. Hey, who's this I see? The count. [*Goes to meet
them.*]

SHABELSKY [*spotting* ZINAIDA *and* MRS. BABAKIN, *stretches out
his arms towards them*]. Two money-boxes on one sofa.
What a lovely sight. [*Shakes hands. To* ZINAIDA.] Hallo
there, Zizi. [*To* MRS. BABAKIN.] Hallo, my little bit of fluff.

ZINAIDA. I'm so glad. You're such a rare visitor, Count. [*Shouts.*]
Tea, Gabriel! Won't you sit down?

[*Stands up, goes out of door, right, and returns immediately, looking extremely worried.* SASHA *sits in her former seat.* IVANOV *greets everyone without speaking.*]

LEBEDEV [*to* SHABELSKY]. Where did you spring from? What
brought you here? This is a surprise. [*Kisses him.*] What a
way to behave, you old pirate. [*Leads him by the hand*

towards the footlights.] Why do you never come and see us, are you angry or something?

SHABELSKY. How am I to get here? Ride on my walking-stick? I've no horses and Nicholas won't bring me—tells me to stay with Sarah and keep her company. Send me your horses and then I'll come.

LEBEDEV [*makes a gesture of resignation*]. That's a point— Zizi'd burst rather than send the horses. Dear old boy, you are my best friend, you know. You and I are the only two left over from the old days.
        "In you I love my former sufferings,
        In you I love my wasted youth."
Joking apart, I'm nearly crying. [*Kisses the* COUNT.]

SHABELSKY. Let me go, please, you smell like a distillery.

LEBEDEV. My dear man, you can't imagine how I miss my friends—I get bored to death. [*Quietly.*] Zizi's driven off all the nicer people by setting up as a moneylender, and as you see there are only monsters left—these Dudkins and Budkins. Anyway, have some tea.

[GABRIEL *brings the* COUNT *tea.*]

ZINAIDA [*to* GABRIEL, *worried*]. Hey, what a way to serve! Fetch some jam, gooseberry or something.

SHABELSKY [*laughs loudly, to* IVANOV]. There, what did I say? [*To* LEBEDEV.] We had a bet on the way over that Zizi would treat us to gooseberry jam the moment we got here.

ZINAIDA. You still like your little joke. [*Sits down.*]

LEBEDEV. Twenty barrels they've made and she doesn't know what to do with it.

SHABELSKY [*sitting near the table*]. Still hoarding money, Zizi? Run up your first million yet?

ZINAIDA [*with a sigh*]. Oh, we may look as if we're rolling in money, but where do you think it comes from? It's nothing but talk.

SHABELSKY. Quite, quite, we know all about that, we know what a poor hand you are at that game. [*To* LEBEDEV.] Tell me honestly, Paul—have you saved a million yet?

LEBEDEV. I don't know, better ask Zizi about that.

SHABELSKY [*to* MRS. BABAKIN]. And our plump little bit of fluff will soon have her million too. She gets prettier and plumper every hour of the day—that's what it means to be well-heeled.

MRS. BABAKIN. I'm most grateful, my Lord, but I don't particularly like being sneered at.

SHABELSKY. Call that sneering, my little pot of gold? It's just a cry from the heart—the fullness of my heart hath unsealed my lips. I just adore you and Zizi. [*Gaily*.] You're two visions of delight, I can't look at you unmoved.

ZINAIDA. You haven't changed a bit. [*To* YEGORUSHKA.] Put out the candles, Yegorushka. Why waste them if you're not playing? [YEGORUSHKA *starts, puts out the candles and sits down. To* IVANOV.] How's the wife, Nicholas?

IVANOV. Bad. The doctor told us today quite definitely that it's tuberculosis.

ZINAIDA. Oh, no! How awful. [*Sighs*.] And we're all so fond of her.

SHABELSKY. Stuff and nonsense. She hasn't got tuberculosis, that's just so much quackery and hocus-pocus. Our medical genius wants an excuse to hang about—so he makes out it's tuberculosis. It's lucky the husband's not jealous. [IVANOV *makes an impatient gesture*.] As for Sarah herself, I don't believe a thing she says or does. I've never trusted doctors, lawyers or women in my life, it's all stuff and nonsense, quackery and jiggery-pokery.

LEBEDEV [*to* SHABELSKY]. You're a pretty queer fish, Matthew, with this misanthropic pose you make such a parade of. You're no different from anyone else, but when you talk, you sound as if you were fed up to the back teeth.

SHABELSKY. You don't expect me to hobnob with all these rotten swine, do you?

LEBEDEV. What rotten swine? Where are they?

SHABELSKY. Not present company of course. But——

LEBEDEV. But me no buts, this is just a pose.

SHABELSKY. Oh, is it? It's a good job you've no principles.

LEBEDEV. What principles can I have? I sit here waiting to peg out, that's my principle. You and I've no time to think about our principles, old boy. No, indeed. [*Shouts*.] Gabriel!

SHABELSKY. There's been a sight too much of this "Gabriel" stuff, your nose is like a ruddy great beetroot.

LEBEDEV [*drinks*]. Never mind, old boy, it's not my wedding day.

ZINAIDA. It's ages since Dr. Lvov was here, he's quite forsaken us.

SASHA. My pet aversion. Oh, he's virtue incarnate, can't ask for a glass of water or light a cigarette without displaying his remarkable integrity. Walking or talking, he has "Honest Joe" written all over him. What a bore.

SHABELSKY. That shallow, narrow-minded medico. [*As if imitating him*.] "Make way for an honest, hard-working man!" Can't move an inch without squawking parrot-cries. Puts himself on a high moral pedestal and abuses everyone who doesn't squawk like him. His views are remarkably profound. Any peasant who's well-off and lives decently must be a scoundrel on the make. I wear a velvet coat and have a valet, so I'm a scoundrel and slave-driver. Oh, he's very honest, in fact he's bursting with it. And he can never relax. I'm actually afraid of him, I really am. You feel he'll punch you on the jaw any moment or call you a filthy swine—all from a sense of duty.

IVANOV. I find him terribly trying, but I do quite like him— he's so sincere.

SHABELSKY. A nice kind of sincerity. Last night he comes up to me completely out of the blue and says: "I thoroughly dislike you, Count." Thank you very much, I must say. And none of this is straightforward, there's always some twist to it. His voice shakes, his eyes flash, he's all of a dither. To hell with his phoney sincerity. Oh, he loathes me, finds me nauseating. It's only natural, I can see that, but why tell me so to my face? I may be no good, but my hair is going white, after all. It's a pretty cheap and uncharitable kind of honesty, his is.

LEBEDEV. Oh come, you've been young yourself, I imagine, and you can make allowances.

SHABELSKY. Yes, I've been young and foolish. I've been quite outspoken in my day and shown up all sorts of blackguards and bounders. But never in my life have I called anyone a thief to his face, nor have I ever plumbed the depths of sheer blatant tactlessness. I was properly brought up. But this dull quack would be tickled pink—he'd feel he'd attained his life's ambition—if he got the chance to bash my face in in public or hit me below the belt in the name of principles and humane ideals.

LEBEDEV. Young men always do have some bee in their bonnet. My uncle was a follower of Hegel. Used to collect a houseful of guests, have a drink and stand on a chair like this and start off. "You're ignorant! You're the forces of darkness! The dawn of a new life!" Blah blah blah blah. Yes, he let them have it all right.

SASHA. And what about his guests?

LEBEDEV. Oh, they didn't mind, they listened and carried on drinking. Actually, I once challenged him to a duel—my own uncle. It was about Bacon. Now let me think, I remember sitting just where Matthew is now, and Uncle and poor old Gerasim Nilovich were standing here, about where dear old Nicholas is. Then Gerasim Nilovich asks a question, old boy——

[BORKIN *comes in*.]

SCENE V

[*The above and* BORKIN *who comes in through door, right, in his best clothes, carrying a parcel, bobbing up and down and humming. A buzz of approval.*]

GIRLS. Michael!

LEBEDEV. Dear old Mike! Or do my ears deceive me?

SHABELSKY. The life and soul of the party.

BORKIN. Here I am. [*Runs up to* SASHA.] Noble signorina, I make bold to congratulate the universe on the birth of such a wondrous blossom. As a tribute to my joy, I venture to offer [*hands over the parcel*] some fireworks and bengal lights of my own manufacture. May they light up the night just as you make bright the shades in our realm of darkness. [*Gives a theatrical bow.*]

SASHA. Thank you.

LEBEDEV [*laughs loudly, to* IVANOV]. Why don't you get rid of that swine?

BORKIN [*to* LEBEDEV]. My dear Lebedev. [*To* IVANOV.] Respected patron. [*Sings.*] Nicholas *voilà*, ho-hi-ho! [*Goes round to all of them.*] Most revered Zinaida. Divine Martha. Most venerable Avdotya. Your Lordship.

SHABELSKY [*laughs loudly*]. The life and soul of the party. The moment he came in the tension lifted, did you notice?

BORKIN. I say, I am tired. I think I've said hallo to everyone. Well, what's the news, all of you? Is there some special item to shake us up a bit? [*To* ZINAIDA, *eagerly.*] Listen to this, old thing. On my way here just now—. [*To* GABRIEL.] Tea, please, Gabriel, but no gooseberry jam. [*To* ZINAIDA.] On my way here just now I saw some villagers stripping bark off the willows by your river. Why don't you let a dealer handle that?

LEBEDEV [*to* IVANOV]. Why don't you get rid of the swine?

ZINAIDA [*terrified*]. Do you know, I never even thought of it?

BORKIN [*does some arm exercises*]. I can't keep still. I say, couldn't we do something different, old thing? I'm on top of my form, Martha, I feel exalted. [*Sings.*] "Once more before you——"

ZINAIDA. Yes, do something, because we're all bored.

BORKIN. Really, why so downhearted anyway, all of you, sitting there like a lot of stuffed dummies? Let's play a game or something. What would you like? Forfeits, skipping, tag, dancing, fireworks?

GIRLS [*clapping their hands*]. Fireworks, fireworks. [*They run into the garden.*]

SHASHA [*to* IVANOV]. Why so depressed tonight?

IVANOV. My head aches, Sasha, and I'm bored.

SASHA. Come in the drawing-room. [*They go through the door, right. Everyone goes into the garden except* ZINAIDA *and* LEBEDEV.]

ZINAIDA. Now, that's a bit more like it, that young fellow— wasn't in here a minute before he'd cheered us all up. [*Turns down the large lamp.*] No point in wasting candles when everyone's in the garden. [*Puts out the candles.*]

LEBEDEV [*following her*]. We ought to give the guests some food, Zizi.

ZINAIDA. Lord, what a lot of candles—no wonder people think we're rich. [*Puts them out.*]

LEBEDEV [*following her*]. You might give them some food, Zizi. They're young folk, they must be starved, poor things. Zizi——

ZINAIDA. The count hasn't finished his tea. What a waste of sugar. [*Goes through door, left.*]

LEBEDEV. Ugh! [*Goes into the garden.*]

SCENE VI

[IVANOV *and* SASHA.]

SASHA [*coming in with* IVANOV *through door, right*]. They've all gone in the garden.

IVANOV. That's how things are, Sasha. I used to work hard and think hard, I never got tired. Now I do nothing and think of nothing, but I'm tired, body and soul. I feel so conscience-stricken all the time. I feel terribly guilty, but just where I went wrong I can't see. Now there's my wife's illness, my money troubles, this non-stop back-biting, gossip and idle chit-chat—and that ass Borkin. I'm sick and tired of my home, and living there's sheer hell. Frankly, Sasha, I can't even stand having my loving wife about. You're an old friend and won't be annoyed if I speak my mind. I came here to enjoy myself, but I'm bored here too, and feel like going back. Excuse me, I'll just slip away.

SASHA. I understand you, Nicholas. You're unhappy because you're lonely. You need someone near you that you love and who'll appreciate you. Only love can make a new man of you.

IVANOV. Now really, Sasha. For a bedraggled old wreck like me to start a new love affair, that would be the last straw. God save me from any such disaster. No, it's not love affairs I need, dear girl. God knows, I can stand all this—depression, neurosis, ruin, the loss of my wife, premature old age, being lonely. But despising myself—that's what I can't put up with. That a strong, healthy man like me should have turned into a sort of Hamlet, Manfred, odd-man-out or hell knows what—I could die of shame. Some wretched people are flattered to be called Hamlets or outsiders, but to me that's contemptible, it offends my pride, I'm overwhelmed with shame and I suffer agonies.

SASHA [*joking, through tears*]. Let's run away to America, Nicholas.

IVANOV. I'm too lazy to go as far as that door and you want to go to America. [*They go towards the exit to the garden.*] It's not much of a life for you here, Sasha, I must say. When I look at the people round you, it frightens me. Who can you marry here? The only hope is, some young subaltern or student may pass this way and run off with you.

SCENE VII

[ZINAIDA *comes through door, left, with a jar of jam.*]

IVANOV. Excuse me, Sasha, I'll catch you up.

[SASHA *goes into the garden.*]

IVANOV. Mrs. Lebedev, may I ask you a favour?

ZINAIDA. What is it, Mr. Ivanov?

IVANOV [*hesitates*]. Well, the thing is, you see, the interest on your loan falls due in two days' time. I'd be most obliged if you'd give me a bit longer or let me add the interest to the loan. At the moment I'm out of money.

ZINAIDA [*horrorstruck*]. Mr. Ivanov, what a shocking suggestion! Put it right out of your mind. And for God's sake don't bother me, I've troubles enough.

IVANOV. Sorry, sorry. [*Goes into the garden.*]

ZINAIDA. Heavens, how he upset me, I'm all of a tremble. [*Goes out of the door, right.*]

SCENE VIII

KOSYKH [*comes through door, left, and crosses the stage*]. I had the ace, king, queen and seven small diamonds, the ace of spades and one—one tiny heart, but she couldn't declare a little slam, damn her! [*Goes out of door, right.*]

SCENE IX

[AVDOTYA *and* FIRST GUEST.]

AVDOTYA [*coming out of the garden with the* FIRST GUEST]. Oh, I could tear her in pieces, the old skinflint—that I could. It's no joke. I've been here since five, and not one stale herring have we had to eat. What a house, and what a way to run it.

FIRST GUEST. This is all such a crashing bore, I feel like taking a running dive into a brick wall. God, what people! You get so bored and ravenous, like a howling, man-eating tiger.

AVDOTYA. I could tear her in pieces, God help me.

FIRST GUEST. I'll have a drink, old girl, and be off home. And I'm not interested in any of your marriageable young women. How the hell can a man think of love when he doesn't get a drink after dinner?

AVDOTYA. Let's go and find some, eh?

FIRST GUEST. Shush! There's some schnapps in the dining-room, I think, in the sideboard. We'll get hold of Yegorushka. Shush! [*They go out by door, left.*]

SCENE X

[ANNA *and* LVOV *come through the door, right.*]

ANNA. It's all right, they'll be pleased to see us. There's no one here, they must be in the garden.

LVOV. Why bring me to this vampires' lair, I wonder. This is no place for you and me, honest men shouldn't breathe this air.

ANNA. Listen to me, my honest friend. When you take a lady out, it's not very nice to keep on and on about how honest you are. Honest you may be, but you're also, to put it mildly, a bore. Never talk to a woman about your good points, let her see those for herself. At your age Nicholas only sang and told stories in ladies' company, but everyone could see what he was really like.

LVOV. Don't talk about friend Nicholas, I know his sort!

ANNA. You're a good man, but you don't understand anything. Let's go in the garden. He never said things like: "I'm honest, this air chokes me, vampires, owl's nest, crocodiles." He left out the zoology, and all I heard from him when he got annoyed was: "I was so unfair today," or "I'm sorry for that man, Anna". That's how he was, but you—. [*They go out.*]

SCENE XI

[AVDOTYA *and* FIRST GUEST.]

FIRST GUEST [*coming through door, left*]. It's not in the dining-room, so it must be in the larder somewhere. We must try Yegorushka. Let's go through the drawing-room.

AVDOTYA. I could tear her in pieces. [*They go out through door, right.*]

SCENE XII

[MRS. BABAKIN, BORKIN *and* SHABELSKY. MRS. BABAKIN *and* BORKIN *run in from the garden, laughing.* SHABELSKY *comes tripping after them, laughing and rubbing his hands.*]

MRS. BABAKIN. What a bore. [*Laughs loudly.*] Oh, what a bore, everyone walking about or sitting around like a lot of stuffed dummies. I'm so bored, I feel quite ossified. [*Jumps about.*] Must stretch my legs. [BORKIN *puts his arm round her waist and kisses her cheek.*]

SHABELSKY [*laughs loudly and snaps his fingers*]. Dash it all! [*Clears his throat.*] To some extent——

MRS. BABAKIN. Let me go, let go of my arms, you naughty man—or goodness knows what the count will think. Let me alone.

BORKIN. My angel, my heart's own little carbuncle. [*Kisses her.*] Lend me twenty-three hundred roubles.

MRS. BABAKIN. No, no. I'm sorry, but where money's concerned, the answer's no thank you——. No, no, no. Do let go of my arms.

SHABELSKY [*prances around*]. My little bit of fluff, delightful creature——

BORKIN [*seriously*]. Stop it. Let's come to the point, get down to brass tacks like businessmen. Tell me straight without beating about the bush—yes or no? Listen. [*Points to the* COUNT.] He needs money, three thousand a year at least. You need a husband. Want to be a countess?

SHABELSKY [*laughs loudly*]. How remarkably cynical.

BORKIN. Want to be a countess? Yes or no?

MRS. BABAKIN [*upset*]. Do think what you're saying, Michael. These things aren't managed in that slapdash way. The count can speak for himself if he wants, and—this is all so sudden, I don't know——

BORKIN. Cut out the funny stuff, it's a business deal. Yes or no?

SHABELSKY [*laughing and rubbing his hands*]. Well, I don't know. How about it? A damn shabby trick—but why not play it? My little bit of fluff. [*Kisses* MRS. BABAKIN *on the cheek.*] Tasty morsel!

MRS. BABAKIN. One moment, you've quite upset me. Go away, please. No, come back.

BORKIN. Hurry up. Yes or no? There's no time to waste.

MRS. BABAKIN. I tell you what, Count. Come and stay with me for a few days—you'll find it rather fun, not like this place. Come tomorrow. [*To* BORKIN.] You're joking, aren't you?

BORKIN [*angrily*]. What—joke about something so serious?

MRS. BABAKIN. One moment, please. I do feel awful, I feel faint. A countess—I'm fainting, I shall fall.

[BORKIN *and the* COUNT *laughingly take her by the arms and, kissing her cheeks, lead her off through the door, right.*]

SCENE XIII

[IVANOV *and* SASHA, *followed by* ANNA. IVANOV *and* SASHA *run in from the garden.*]

IVANOV [*clutching his head, in despair*]. That's impossible. Stop it, Sasha, you must stop.

SASHA [*carried away*]. I'm crazy about you—life has no meaning, no happiness, no joy without you. You're everything to me.

IVANOV. Oh, what's the use? God, nothing makes sense. Stop it, Sasha.

SASHA. When I was a little girl you were my only joy. I loved you and everything about you as I love myself, and now—I love you, Nicholas. I'll follow you to the ends of the earth, I'll go wherever you like, I'll die if need be, only for God's sake let it be soon, or I shall choke.

IVANOV [*with a peal of happy laughter*]. What does this all mean? Can I start a new life then, Sasha? My happiness! [*Draws her to him.*] My youth, my innocence!

[ANNA *comes in from the garden, sees her husband and* SASHA, *and stands rooted to the spot.*]

IVANOV. So I'm to live, then, am I? And start work again?

[*They kiss. After the kiss* IVANOV *and* SASHA *look round and see* ANNA.]

IVANOV [*in horror*]. Sarah!

CURTAIN

ACT THREE

IVANOV's *study. A desk on which papers, books, official packages, knick-knacks and revolvers are strewn around untidily. By the papers are a lamp, a decanter of vodka, a plate of herring, hunks of bread and cucumbers. On the walls hang maps, pictures, guns, pistols, sickles, whips and so on.*

Noon.

SCENE I

[SHABELSKY, LEBEDEV, BORKIN *and* PETER. SHABELSKY *and* LEBEDEV *sit, one on each side of the desk.* BORKIN *is astride a chair in the centre of the stage.* PETER *stands by the door.*]

LEBEDEV. France has a clear-cut, definite policy—the French know what they want. They only want to make mincemeat of Brother Fritz, but Germany's another cup of tea, old boy. Germany has other fish to fry besides France.

SHABELSKY. Nonsense. The Germans are cowards, if you ask me, and the French are no better. They're only bluffing each other, and that's as far as it'll go, believe you me. They won't fight.

BORKIN. Why should they, say I? Why all the armaments, congresses and expenses? Know what I'd do? I'd collect dogs from all over the country, give them a good dose of rabies and let them loose on enemy territory. I'd have the enemy all foaming at the mouth within a month.

LEBEDEV [*laughs*]. His head's quite small, isn't it, but it's fairly swarming with brain-waves, shoals of them.

SHABELSKY. The man's a genius.

LEBEDEV. God knows, you do entertain us, old man. [*Stops laughing.*] I say, we've fought quite a few armchair battles, but no one's mentioned vodka. Another dose. [*Pours out three glasses.*] Our very good health! [*They drink and eat.*] There's nothing to touch a spot of herring, old boy.

SHABELSKY. I don't know, cucumber's better. Wise men have cogitated since the dawn of history without hitting on anything smarter than salted cucumber. [*To* PETER.] Peter, go and get more cucumber, and tell them to cook four onion pasties in the kitchen. Make sure they're hot.

[PETER *goes out.*]

LEBEDEV. Caviare isn't bad with vodka, but the thing is to serve it properly. You need a quarter of a pound of pressed caviare, two spring onions and some olive oil. Mix the lot together, and then, you know—add the odd drop of lemon. Hell's bells, the mere smell will make you swoon!

BORKIN. Fried gudgeon also helps the vodka down—but fried properly. First clean. Then dip in toasted bread-crumbs and fry them so crisp, they crunch in your teeth. Crunch, crunch, crunch.

SHABELSKY. There was something good at Martha Babakin's yesterday—mushrooms.

LEBEDEV. Not half they were.

SHABELSKY. Cooked in some special way—with onion, you know, bay-leaves and spices. When they took the saucepan lid off and that steamy whiff came out—sheer ecstasy, it was.

LEBEDEV. What do you say? Another dose, everyone. [*They drink.*] Our good health! [*Looks at his watch.*] It looks as if I'll be gone before Nicholas gets back. Time I was off. You had mushrooms at Martha Babakin's, you say, but we haven't so much as smelt a mushroom round here yet. Will you please tell me why the blazes you're always popping over to Martha's place?

SHABELSKY [*nods at* BORKIN]. It's him—he wants to get me married.

LEBEDEV. Married? How old are you?

SHABELSKY. Sixty-two.

LEBEDEV. Just the age to marry. And Martha's just the wife for you.

BORKIN. Not Martha, Martha's money.

LEBEDEV. Martha's money—you're not asking for much! How about crying for the moon?

BORKIN. You wait till he's married and has his pockets nicely lined. You'll be all over him.

SHABELSKY. He's in earnest, you know. Our brainy friend's sure I'll do what he says and marry her.

BORKIN. Of course! Aren't you sure yourself?

SHABELSKY. What do you mean? When have I been sure of anything? Really!

BORKIN. Thank you, thank you very much. Let me down, would you? Now I'll marry, now I won't—what the hell does that mean? And after I gave my word of honour. You won't marry then?

SHABELSKY [*shrugs his shoulders*]. He's in real earnest. Extraordinary man.

BORKIN [*infuriated*]. In that case why upset a respectable woman? She's crazy to be a countess, can't sleep or eat— it's beyond a joke! Is this what you call honourable?

SHABELSKY [*snaps his fingers*]. It is a pretty foul trick, but how about it, eh? Just for the hell of it. I'll go ahead, honestly I will. What a lark.

[LVOV *comes in*.]

SCENE II

LEBEDEV. Our respects to the medical genius. [*Shakes hands with* LVOV *and sings*.]
      "Doctor, save me, save me, save me,
      I'm scared to death of being dead——"

LVOV. Ivanov not here yet?

LEBEDEV. No, he isn't, I've been waiting for over an hour.

[LVOV *paces impatiently up and down the stage*.]

LEBEDEV. How is Anna, old man?

LVOV. In a bad way.

LEBEDEV [*sighs*]. May one pay one's respects?

LVOV. Please don't, I think she's asleep. [*Pause*.]

LEBEDEV. Such a nice, charming woman. [*Sighs*.] When she fainted in our house on Sasha's birthday, I saw from her face that she hadn't long to live, poor thing. I don't know what gave her that turn. When I ran in and looked at her she was lying on the floor as white as a sheet with Nicholas kneeling by her, as white as she was, and Sasha in tears. Sasha and I felt quite shaken for a week after.

SHABELSKY [*to* LVOV]. Tell me, reverend high priest of science, what sage first discovered that ladies' chest complaints yield to frequent visits from a young doctor? A great discovery, great! Would you put it under the heading of homoeopathy or allopathy?

[LVOV *makes to answer, but gives a contemptuous gesture and goes out*.]

SHABELSKY. If looks could kill!

LEBEDEV. Why the blazes did you say that? Why insult him?

SHABELSKY [*irritably*]. Why must he talk such nonsense? "Tuberculosis, no hope, going to die." That's a lot of hot air, I hate that stuff.

LEBEDEV. What makes you think he doesn't mean it?

SHABELSKY [*stands up and walks about*]. I can't concede that a living person may suddenly drop dead for no reason. Let's change the subject.

SCENE III

KOSYKH [*runs in out of breath*]. Ivanov in? Good morning. [*Quickly shakes hands with everybody*.] Is he in?

BORKIN. No.

KOSYKH [*sits down and jumps up again*]. In that case goodbye. [*Drinks a glass of vodka and takes a quick bite of food*.] I must go on. So much to do. Worn out. Can hardly stand.

LEBEDEV. Where did you blow in from?

KOSYKH. From Barabanov's. We played bridge all night and we've only just finished. I've been cleaned out. That Barabanov's no good at cards. [*Tearfully.*] Listen, I was playing hearts all the time. [*Turns to* BORKIN, *who jumps away from him.*] He leads a diamond, I play another heart, he plays a diamond. I didn't make a trick. [*To* LEBEDEV.] We were trying to make four clubs. I held the ace, queen and five more clubs and the ace, ten and two more spades——

LEBEDEV [*shuts his ears*]. Spare us, for Christ's sake.

KOSYKH [*to the* COUNT]. See? The ace, queen and five more clubs and the ace, ten and two more spades.

SHABELSKY [*pushes him off*]. Go away, I won't listen.

KOSYKH. Then disaster struck. The ace of spades was the first to get it in the neck——

SHABELSKY [*picks up a revolver from the table*]. Go away or I shoot.

KOSYKH [*with a sweep of the arm*]. Can't one talk to anyone, dash it all? It's like Australia—no common interests or solidarity, each going his own way. Time I was off, though—high time. [*Picks up his peaked cap.*] Time's money. [*Shakes hand with* LEBEDEV.] I pass.

[*Laughter.* KOSYKH *goes out and bumps into* AVDOTYA *in the doorway.*]

SCENE IV

AVDOTYA [*shrieks*]. You nearly knocked me over, damn you.

ALL. Aha! She's everywhere at once.

AVDOTYA. So this is where they are, and me searching all over the house. Good morning, boys, and the best of jolly good appetites. [*Shakes hands.*]

LEBEDEV. What are you doing here?

AVDOTYA. Business, sir. [*To the* COUNT.] It concerns your Lordship. [*Bows.*] I was told to give you warmest regards and ask how you were. And the little darling says, if you don't come and see her this afternoon she'll cry her eyes out. "Take him aside, dear," says she, "and whisper it in his ear secretly." But why the mystery? We're all friends here, we're not planning to rob the hen-roost, it's all above board, a matter of love and mutual consent. I never touch a drop, God knows, but I'll have a glass to celebrate this.

LEBEDEV. So will I. [*Pours out.*] You look none the worse for wear, you old windbag. I remember you as an old woman thirty years ago.

AVDOTYA. I've lost count of the years. I've buried two husbands and I'd marry a third, but no one'll take me without a dowry. Eight children I've had. [*Takes a glass.*] Now we've made a good start, please God, and God grant we finish the job. They'll have their bit of fun and we'll enjoy watching them. May they live happily ever after. [*Drinks.*] A vodka to be reckoned with!

SHABELSKY [*laughing loudly, to* LEBEDEV]. The funny thing is, they seriously think I—. Fantastic! [*Stands up.*] It's a pretty shabby thing to do, but how about it, Paul? Just for the hell of it—the old dog up to his tricks again, eh?

LEBEDEV. You're raving, Count. We should both think of pushing up the daisies, old boy. Martha and her money aren't for us, our day's over.

SHABELSKY. Yes, I'll do it, honestly I will.

[IVANOV *and* LVOV *come in.*]

SCENE V

LVOV. Can you spare me just five minutes?

LEBEDEV. Nicholas! [*Goes up to* IVANOV *and kisses him.*] Good morning, old boy, I've been waiting a whole hour for you.

AVDOTYA [*bows*]. Good morning, sir.

IVANOV [*sadly*]. Oh, you've made a complete mess of my study again. I've asked you all not to thousands of times. [*Goes up to the desk.*] Look, you've spilt vodka on my papers, there are crumbs and cucumbers. It's disgusting.

LEBEDEV. I'm sorry, Nicholas, do forgive us. I've something important to discuss with you, old boy.

BORKIN. And so have I.

LVOV. I want a word with you, Ivanov.

IVANOV [*points to* LEBEDEV]. He wants a word as well. Please wait, I'll speak to you later. [*To* LEBEDEV.] What is it?

LEBEDEV. Gentlemen, I want this to be private. Please——

[*The* COUNT *goes out with* AVDOTYA, *followed by* BORKIN *and then by* LVOV.]

IVANOV. You drink as much as you like since you're that way afflicted, Paul, but please don't make my uncle drink. He never used to, and it's bad for him.

LEBEDEV [*alarmed*]. I didn't know, my dear chap, never even noticed.

IVANOV. If the old boy dies, which God forbid, it'll be me that suffers, not you. What do you want? [*Pause*.]

LEBEDEV. Look, old man, I don't know how to start—I don't want it to sound too outrageous. I'm so ashamed, Nicholas, I'm tongue-tied, I blush to speak, but put yourself in my shoes, old boy. I'm not free, you must see that, I'm more like a slave or something the cat brought in. I'm sorry——

IVANOV. What is this?

LEBEDEV. My wife sent me. Be a good chap and pay her that interest, please. She's nagged and pestered the life out of me, so for God's sake get out of her clutches.

IVANOV. You know I've no money just now, Paul.

LEBEDEV. I know, I know, but what can I do? She won't wait. If she takes you to court, how can Sasha and I ever face you again?

IVANOV. I'm sorry too, I could kick myself—but where am I to get it? Tell me, where? I can only wait till I sell the crops this autumn.

LEBEDEV [*shouts*]. She won't wait. [*Pause*.]

IVANOV. You're in a nasty, awkward spot—but I'm even worse off. [*Walks up and down, thinking*.] I'm clean out of ideas. There's nothing to sell——

LEBEDEV. Go and ask Milbakh—he does owe you sixteen thousand, you know.

[IVANOV *makes a hopeless gesture of despair*.]

LEBEDEV. I tell you what, Nicholas. I know you'll object, but—do the old soak a favour, between friends. Look on me as your friend. We've both been students, liberals—had the same ideals and interests, both went to Moscow University, the dear old *alma mater*. [*Takes out his pocket-book*.] This is my secret hoard, no one knows anything about it at home. Let me lend you it. [*Takes out money and puts it on the desk*.] Forget your pride, look on this as between friends. I'd take it from you, on my honour. [*Pause*.] Here it is on the table, eleven hundred roubles. Drive over today and hand it to her yourself. "There you are, Zinaida," say "and I hope it chokes you." But for God's sake don't let on you got it from me, or I'll be in hot water with old Gooseberry Jam. [*Stares at* IVANOV's *face*.] All right, never mind. [*Quickly takes the money from the desk and puts it in his pocket*.] Never mind, I was joking. Forgive me, for God's sake. [*Pause*.] Are you awfully fed up?

[IVANOV *makes a gesture of despair*.]

LEBEDEV. What a business. [*Sighs*.] Your trials and tribulations are just beginning. A man's like a samovar, old boy. He doesn't always stand on a cold shelf, there are times when he gets stoked up and starts fairly seething. The comparison's no damn good, but I can't think of anything better. [*Sighs*.] Troubles fortify the spirit. I'm not sorry for you, Nicholas, you'll get out of this mess, it'll come all right. But I'm fed up, old man—irritated with people. I'd like to know what started all the gossip. So many rumours are going round the county about you—you'll have the police in any moment. They call you murderer, vampire, robber.

IVANOV. That doesn't matter. I've a headache.

LEBEDEV. It comes from thinking too much.

IVANOV. I don't think at all.

LEBEDEV. Let it all go to hell, Nicholas, and move over to our

place. Sasha likes you—she appreciates and values you.
She's an honest, decent girl, I can't think who she takes
after—not her father or mother. Sometimes I look at her,
and I can't believe a bulbous-nosed old soak like me has
such a treasure. Go and have some intelligent conversation
with her, it'll make a change for you. She's a devoted,
sincere girl. [*Pause*.]

IVANOV. Leave me alone, Paul, please.

LEBEDEV. All right, I understand. [*Quickly looks at his watch*.]
I understand. [*Kisses* IVANOV.] Good-bye. I have to attend
the opening of a new school. [*Moves towards the door and
stops*.] Sasha's a bright girl. We were talking about gossip
yesterday. [*Laughs*.] She came out with quite a saying.
"Father," she says, "glow-worms shine at night to make it
easier for night birds to see them and eat them. And good
people are here to give slander and gossip something to
bite on." What price that? A genius, eh? Regular George
Sand.

IVANOV. Paul. [*Stops him*.] What's the matter with me?

LEBEDEV. I wanted to ask that myself, but I frankly didn't like
to. I don't know, old man. It did look to me as though your
various troubles had got you down, but then I know you're
not one to—it's not like you to knuckle under. It's something else, but just what—I've no idea.

IVANOV. I don't know either. I think, or rather—never mind.
[*Pause*.] Look, this is what I meant. I had a man working
here called Simon, remember? When we were threshing
once, he wanted to show the girls how strong he was, so he
heaved two sacks of rye on his back and broke under the
strain—he died soon after. I feel as if I'd broken my spine
too. There was school and university, and then farming,
village education, other plans—. I believed in different
things from other people, married a different sort of wife,
got excited, took risks, squandered money left, right and
centre, as you know, and was happier and unhappier than
anyone else in the county. Those things were my sacks, I
heaved a load on my back and it cracked. At twenty we're
all heroes, tackle anything, nothing's too much for us, but
by thirty we're tired and useless. How, how can you explain

this fatigue? Anyway, that's probably not the point, not at
all the point. Now off you go, Paul, and good luck to you.
I'm boring you.

LEBEDEV [*eagerly*]. You know what? Your environment's got
you down.

IVANOV. That's silly, and it's been said before. Off with you.

LEBEDEV. Yes, it really was silly, now I see how silly it was.
I'm off, I'm off. [*Goes.*]

SCENE VI

IVANOV [*alone*]. I'm just a nasty, miserable nobody. Only
another pathetic, bedraggled wreck like Paul could go on
liking and respecting me. God, how I despise myself. How
I loathe my own voice, footsteps, hands—these clothes, my
thoughts. Pretty ridiculous, isn't it? And pretty mortifying.
Less than a year ago I was strong and well, I was cheerful,
tireless and dynamic. I worked with my hands. My elo-
quence moved even ignorant louts to tears, I could weep
when I saw unhappiness and protest when I met evil. I
knew what inspiration meant, I knew the charm and magic
of quiet nights when you sit at your desk from dusk to
dawn or indulge in flights of fancy. I had faith, I looked at
the future as a child looks into its mother's eyes. But now,
oh God! I'm worn out, I've no faith, I spend days and
nights doing nothing. My brain doesn't obey me, nor do
my arms and legs. The estate's going to rack and ruin, the
woods fall before the axe. [*Weeps.*] My land seems to look
at me like a lost child. There's nothing I hope or care
about, and my spirit quails in fear of the morrow. Then
there's Sarah. I swore to love her for ever, told her how
happy we'd be, offered her a future beyond her wildest
dreams. She believed me. These five years I've watched
her giving way beneath the weight of her own sacrifices
and wilting in the struggle with her conscience, but God
knows she's never looked askance at me or uttered one
reproach. What then? I stopped loving her. How? Why?
What for? I can't understand. Now she's unhappy and her
days are numbered. And I'm low and cowardly enough to
run away from her pale face, sunken chest and pleading

eyes. How shameful. [*Pause*.] Little Sasha's touched by my misfortunes and tells me, at my age, that she loves me. It goes to my head, so I can't think of anything else. I'm spellbound, it's music in my ears. So I start shouting about being born again and being happy. But next day I believe in this new life and happiness about as much as I do in fairies. What's the matter with me? What depths have I sunk to? Where does my weakness come from? What's happened to my nerves? If my sick wife touches me on the raw, or a servant does something wrong, or my gun misfires—then I'm rude, bad-tempered and quite beside myself. [*Pause*.] I just don't understand. I might as well shoot myself and be done with it.

LVOV [*comes in*]. I want a word with you, Ivanov.

IVANOV. If you and I are to have words every day, Doctor, it'll be more than flesh and blood can stand.

LVOV. Do you mind if I have my say?

IVANOV. You have your say every day, but I still don't know what you're driving at.

LVOV. I speak clearly and precisely. Only a very callous person could miss the point.

IVANOV. That my wife's dying, I know. That I'm hopelessly to blame in my dealings with her, I also know. And that you're a blunt, honest man I am also aware. What more do you want?

LVOV. People are so cruel, that's what maddens me. A woman's dying. She has a father and mother that she loves and wants to see before her death. They know full well that she hasn't long to live, that she still loves them, but—damn them for being so cruel! Are they trying to show people how frightfully pious they are, or what? They still curse her. You, for whom she gave it all up—her home, her peace of mind—you drive off to see those Lebedevs every day quite blatantly and with your reasons for going there written all over you.

IVANOV. Look, I haven't been there for two weeks——

LVOV [*not listening*]. With your sort one has to go straight to the point and not mess around. If you don't choose to listen, don't. I call a spade a spade. You need her to die so you can move on to new escapades. All right, but couldn't you wait a bit? If you'd let her die naturally, and hadn't kept bullying her with such barefaced cynicism, would you really have lost the Lebedev girl and her dowry? You'd have had time to turn the girl's head a year or two later, you monstrous hypocrite, and pocket the dowry then. Why does it have to be now? Where's the great hurry? Why must your wife die now, and not in a month or a year?

IVANOV. This is agony. You're not much of a doctor if you think a man can hold himself in for ever. It's quite a strain to me to leave your insults unanswered.

LVOV. Really, who do you think you're fooling? Come off it.

IVANOV. Think a little, my clever friend. You think I'm an open book, don't you? I married Anna for her fortune. I didn't get it, and having slipped up then, I'm now getting rid of her so I can marry someone else and get *her* money. Right? How simple and straightforward. Man's such a simple, uncomplicated mechanism. No, Doctor, we all have too many wheels, screws and valves to judge each other on first impressions or one or two pointers. I don't understand you, you don't understand me and we don't understand ourselves. A man can be a very good doctor without having any idea what people are really like. So don't be too cocksure, but try and see what I mean.

LVOV. You can't really think you're so hard to see through, or that I'm too feeble-minded to tell good from evil.

IVANOV. You and I'll never agree, that's very clear. For the last time, I ask you—and please answer without a lot of mumbo jumbo—exactly what do you want from me? What are you driving at? [*Irritably*.] And to whom am I privileged to speak—a policeman or my wife's doctor?

LVOV. I'm a doctor. And as a doctor I insist you mend your ways—you're killing your wife.

IVANOV. But what can I do about it? What? If you know me better than I do myself, tell me exactly what to do.

LVOV. You might at least keep up appearances.

IVANOV. God, do you know what you're saying? [*Drinks some water.*] Leave me alone. I'm to blame a thousand times over, and I'll answer to God for it. But no one gave you the right to torment me every day.

LVOV. And who gave you the right to insult my sense of fair play? You've tortured me, poisoned me! Before I came to this part of the world I knew there were stupid, crazy people about, but I never believed there were people so criminal that they deliberately, consciously, wilfully chose evil. I respected and loved people, but when I saw you——

IVANOV. I've heard all this before.

LVOV. Oh, have you? [*Sees* SASHA *come in. She wears a riding habit.*] Anyway, I hope we understand each other now. [*Shrugs his shoulders and goes out.*]

SCENE VII

IVANOV [*frightened*]. Is it you, Sasha?

SASHA. Yes. Hallo. Surprised? Why haven't you been to see us for so long?

IVANOV. For God's sake, Sasha—this is most indiscreet. Your visit may have a very bad effect on my wife.

SASHA. She won't see me, I came round the back. I'm just going. I'm worried about how you are. Why haven't you been over for so long?

IVANOV. My wife's distressed as it is, she's almost dying—and you come here. It's a stupid, cruel thing to do, Sasha.

SASHA. I couldn't help it. You haven't been over for two weeks, or answered any letters. I was worried to death. I imagined you might be in a terrible way here—ill or dying. I haven't had one proper night's sleep. I'm just going. At least tell me if you're well.

IVANOV. Really, I've worn myself out and people never stop bothering me. I'm at the end of my tether. And now you turn up. What a morbid, neurotic thing to do! I'm so much to blame, Sasha, so very much.

SASHA. How you love these awful, tragic speeches. You're to

blame, you say, very much to blame? Then tell me what you've done.

IVANOV. I don't know, really.

SASHA. That's no answer. If you've done wrong you must know what you've done. Not forging bank-notes, I suppose?

IVANOV. That's not funny.

SASHA. Is it your fault you fell out of love with your wife? Perhaps, but one can't help one's feelings, and you didn't want your feelings to change. Is it your fault she saw me telling you I loved you? No, you didn't want her to.

IVANOV [interrupting]. And so on and so forth. In love, out of love, can't help one's feelings—that talk's so cheap and vulgar, it's no help.

SASHA. You are tiring to talk to. [Looks at a picture.] Isn't that dog drawn well? Was it done from life?

IVANOV. Yes. And this whole love affair of ours is cheap and vulgar. He loses heart, feels he has nothing to live for. Along comes She, strong and confident, and holds out a helping hand. All very romantic and convincing in a magazine story, but in real life——

SASHA. Life's no different.

IVANOV. You're a fine judge of life, I can see. My whining fills you with awe and you think you've found a second Hamlet, but to me my whole neurosis with all its trimmings is just plain farcical, and that's that. You should laugh yourself silly at my antics, not sound the alarm-bell! All this rescuing and crusading zeal! Oh, I'm so angry with myself today, I'm so tense, I feel something's bound to snap. I'll either smash something or——

SASHA. That's right—it's just what you need. Break something, smash things or start shouting. You're angry with me and it was silly of me to come here. All right, let off steam then, shout at me, stamp your feet. Come on, work up a rage. [Pause.] Come on then.

IVANOV. You're funny.

SASHA. Very well. We appear to be smiling. Kindly condescend to smile again.

IVANOV [*laughs*]. I've noticed that when you start rescuing me and giving me good advice, a look of sheer innocence comes over you, and your eyes grow huge, as if you were looking at a comet. Just a moment, there's dust on your shoulder. [*Brushes the dust off her shoulder.*] A naïve man's a fool, but you women have the art of being naïve and carrying it off with such charm, good sense and warm-heartedness—so it isn't as silly as it seems. But why must you all ignore a man so long as he's strong and well and happy—while the moment he starts sliding downhill and being sorry for himself, you throw yourselves round his neck? Is it really worse to be wife to a strong, brave man than nursemaid to a whining failure?

SASHA. Yes.

IVANOV. Why? [*Laughs loudly.*] It's a good job Darwin doesn't know, or he'd give you what for. You're ruining the race. All new babies will be snivelling neurotics, thanks to you.

SASHA. There's a great deal men don't understand. Any girl prefers a failure to a success because we're all fascinated by the idea of love in action. Active love, don't you see? Men are busy with their work, and love's very much in the background for them. You talk to your wife, stroll round the garden with her, pass the time of day nicely and have a little cry on her grave—and that's that. But love is our whole existence! I love you, and that means I long to cure your unhappiness and go with you to the ends of the earth. If you go up in the world, I'll be with you, and if you fall by the wayside, I'll fall too. For instance, I'd love to spend all night copying your papers or watching to see that no one woke you up. Or I'd walk a hundred miles with you. I remember once about three years ago, at threshing time. You came to see us covered with dust, sunburnt, tired out—and asked for a drink. By the time I brought you a glass, you were lying on the sofa, dead to the world. You slept about twelve hours in our house and I stood guard at the door all the time to stop anyone going in. And I felt so marvellous. The more effort you put into love, the better it is—I mean the more strongly it's felt, do you see?

IVANOV. Active love. I see. Is that a perversion of some kind? Or just a young girl's idea of things? Or is it perhaps the way things ought to be? [*Shrugs his shoulders.*] Who the hell knows? [*Gaily.*] Honestly, I'm not such a bad man, Sasha. Judge for yourself—I always liked generalizing, but I've never gone round saying things about our women being demoralized or "on the wrong track." I've just been grateful, that's all, there's no more to it. Dear child, how amusing you are. And I—what a silly ass I am, spreading general despondency and feeling sorry for myself for days on end. [*Laughs and quickly moves off.*] But you'd better go, Sasha, we're forgetting ourselves.

SASHA. Yes, it's time I went. Good-bye. I'm afraid our honest doctor might feel in duty bound to report my presence to Anna. Now listen. Go straight to your wife and stay with her, just stay put. If you have to stay a year, stay a year. If it has to be ten years, make it ten. Do your duty. Grieve for her, beg her forgiveness, weep—all as it should be. And above all, don't neglect your affairs.

IVANOV. I seem to have that horrible taste in my mouth again. Again!

SASHA. Well, may God preserve you. You can forget me completely. Just drop me a line every couple of weeks, and I'll think I'm lucky to get that. And I'll be writing to you.

[BORKIN *looks through the door.*]

SCENE VIII

BORKIN. Can I come in, Nicholas? [*Seeing* SASHA.] Sorry, I didn't see. [*Comes in.*] Bon jour. [*Bows.*]

SASHA [*embarrassed*]. Good morning.

BORKIN. You look plumper and prettier.

SASHA [*to* IVANOV]. Well, I'm leaving, Nicholas. I'm off. [*Goes.*]

BORKIN. What a vision of delight! I come looking for prose and walk slap into poetry. [*Sings.*] "Thou camest like a bird towards the light."

[IVANOV *walks up and down the stage, greatly upset.*]

BORKIN [*sits down*]. There's something about her, Nicholas, she has got something, eh? Something special, quite out of

this world. [*Sighs.*] She's the richest marriageable girl in the
county, actually, but her mother's such an old cow, no one'll
go near her. It'll all come to Sasha when the old girl dies, but
before that she'll give her a miserable ten thousand, a flat-
iron and some curling-tongs or something, and expect one to
get down on one's knees for that. [*Rummages in his pockets.*]
Cigars. Like one? [*Holds out his cigar-case.*] Quite smokable.

IVANOV [*goes up to* BORKIN, *choking with rage*]. Out of my
house this instant and don't set foot in it again! Do you hear?

[BORKIN *raises himself slightly and drops his cigar.*]

IVANOV. Get out this instant.

BORKIN. What does this mean, Nicholas? Why so angry?

IVANOV. Why? Where did you get those cigars? Think I don't
know where you take the old man every day, and what
you're after?

BORKIN [*shrugs his shoulders*]. What has that to do with you?

IVANOV. You low hound! The swindles you plot all over the
county, they've made my name mud. We've nothing in
common and I must ask you to leave my house this instant.
[*Walks quickly up and down.*]

BORKIN. You say that because you're annoyed, I know, so I'm
not angry. Insult away. [*Picks up his cigar.*] But it's time to
snap out of these depressions, you're not a schoolboy.

IVANOV. What did I say? [*Trembling.*] Trifle with me, would
you?

[ANNA *comes in.*]

SCENE IX

BORKIN. Look, Anna's here. I'll go.

[*Goes.* IVANOV *stops near the table and stands with bowed
head.*]

ANNA [*after a pause*]. Why did she come here? [*Pause.*] I ask
you—why did she come?

IVANOV. Don't ask me, Anna. [*Pause.*] I'm very much to

blame. I'll suffer any punishment you like, but—don't question me, I don't feel up to speaking.

ANNA [*angrily*]. What was she doing here? [*Pause*.] So this is what you're like! Now I understand—at last I see the kind of man you are, you rotten cad. Remember coming and telling me lies, saying how you loved me? I believed you, gave up my parents and my religion and married you. You lied about truth and goodness and your noble plans, and I believed every word.

IVANOV. I've never lied to you, Anna.

ANNA. I've lived with you five years, I've been depressed and ill, but I loved you and never left your side. I idolized you. And then what? All that time you were blatantly deceiving me.

IVANOV. Anna, don't tell untruths. I've made mistakes, it's true, but I never told a lie in my life. How dare you call me a liar?

ANNA. Now it all makes sense. You married me, thinking my parents would forgive me and give me money. That's what you thought.

IVANOV. God, to try one's patience like this, Anna—. [*Weeps*.]

ANNA. Shut up! Seeing there was no money in the offing, you started another little game. Now it all comes back, now I see. [*Weeps*.] You never loved me, were never faithful to me. Never!

IVANOV. Sarah, that's a lie. Say what you like, but don't insult me by lying.

ANNA. You rotten, contemptible creature. You're in debt to Lebedev, and now you try to wriggle out of paying by turning his daughter's head and deceiving her as you did me. Well, aren't you?

IVANOV [*choking*]. Hold your tongue, for God's sake, I won't answer for myself. I'm choking with rage and I—I might say something awful.

ANNA. You've always been a barefaced swindler, I'm not the only victim. You pretended all these frauds were Borkin's doing, but I know now who was behind them.

IVANOV. Sarah, stop this and go away or I'll say something I shouldn't. I feel driven to say something horribly insulting. [*Shouts.*] Shut up, you Jewish bitch!

ANNA. I will not shut up, you've made a fool of me too long, I won't be quiet any more.

IVANOV. Oh, won't you? [*Struggles with himself.*] For God's sake——

ANNA. Now go and make a fool of Sasha Lebedev.

IVANOV. Then you may as well know it—you'll soon be dead. The doctor told me you can't last long.

ANNA [*sits down, in a sinking voice*]. When did he say that? [*Pause.*]

IVANOV [*clutching his head*]. What a thing to do! God, I am a brute. [*Sobs.*]

CURTAIN

About a year passes between Act Three and Act Four

ACT FOUR

SCENE I

A drawing-room in LEBEDEV's *house. In the foreground an arch separating the drawing-room from the ball-room. Doors, right and left. Bronze antiques, family portraits, festive decorations. An upright piano with a violin on it, and a 'cello standing near by.*

Throughout the act guests in evening dress move about the ballroom.

LVOV [*comes in, looks at his watch*]. Gone four. They must be going to bless the bride, and after that they'll take her to church. Thus virtue and justice triumph! He didn't get Sarah's money, so he worried her into her grave. Now he has another victim, he'll play the same little game for her benefit till he gets his hands on the cash, when he'll dispatch her as he did poor Sarah. It's an old story—some people will do anything for money. [*Pause.*] He's in the seventh heaven now, he'll live happily to a ripe old age and die with a clear conscience. No, I'll show you up. I'll tear that damned mask off you so everyone sees what kind of customer you are, and then I'll pitch you out of your seventh heaven into a hell so deep, the devil himself won't get you out of it. As an honest man I'm bound to interfere and open people's eyes. I'll do my duty and leave this blasted neighbourhood tomorrow. [*Meditates.*] But what can I do? It's no use talking to the Lebedevs. Challenge him to a duel? Make a scene? God, I'm nervous as a kitten, I can't think any more. What can I do? A duel?

SCENE II

KOSYKH [*comes in, gaily to* LVOV]. Yesterday I declared a little slam in clubs and got a grand slam. But once again friend Barabanov cooked my goose. We sit down to play and I bid one no trump. He passes. I bid two clubs. He passes. I go on to two diamonds, three clubs and—it's beyond the bounds of credence! I declare a slam and he doesn't show his ace. If the swine had shown his ace I'd have declared a grand slam in no trumps.

LVOV. I'm sorry, I don't play cards and can't share your triumph. Will they bless the bride soon?

KOSYKH. I think so. They're trying to get some sense into Zizi. She's yelling her head off—can't bear to part with the dowry.

LVOV. What about parting with her daughter?

KOSYKH. The dowry, I said. And it is bad luck. Once married, he won't pay what he owes her, and you can't very well take your own son-in-law to court.

SCENE III

[MRS. BABAKIN, *dressed to kill, struts across the stage past* LVOV *and* KOSYKH. *The latter guffaws into his hand. She looks round.*]

MRS. BABAKIN. Don't be silly.

[KOSYKH *touches her waist with his finger and gives a loud laugh.*]

MRS. BABAKIN. Clumsy lout! [*Goes out.*]

KOSYKH [*laughs loudly*]. The woman's off her rocker. Before she set her sights on a title she wasn't a bad sort of female, but now you can't get near her. [*Imitates her.*] "Clumsy lout!"

LVOV [*upset*]. Look here, tell me frankly—what's your view of Ivanov?

KOSYKH. No good. Plays a rotten game of bridge. Take what happened just before last Easter. We sit down to play— me, the count, Borkin and Ivanov. I'm dealing——

LVOV [*interrupting*]. Is he a good man?

KOSYKH. Ivanov? Quite a snake in the grass, pretty slippery customer. He's been around a bit! He and the count are a precious pair, they've a pretty good eye for the main chance. He slipped up over his Jewess and found himself in queer street, so now he's after Zizi's moneybags. I bet you anything—and I'm damn sure I'm right—he'll turn Zizi out of house and home within the year. He'll handle Zizi and the count will deal with Martha Babakin. They'll pocket the takings and live off the fat of the land. Why so pale today, Doctor? You look ghastly.

LVOV. It's all right, I drank a bit too much yesterday.

SCENE IV

LEBEDEV [*coming in with* SASHA]. We can talk in here. [*To* LVOV *and* KOSYKH.] Clear out, monsters, and join the girls in the ballroom. We want a private talk.

KOSYKH [*passing* SASHA, *snaps his fingers triumphantly*]. Pretty as a picture, the queen of trumps.

LEBEDEV. Move along, caveman, move along.

[LVOV *and* KOSYKH *go out*.]

LEBEDEV. Sit down, Sasha, that's right. [*Sits down and looks round.*] Listen carefully and with due reverence. The fact is, your mother told me to give you a message. Do you see? It's not my idea, it's what your mother told me to say.

SASHA. Do cut it short, Father.

LEBEDEV. Your dowry's to be fifteen thousand roubles. Now look, we don't want arguments afterwards. No, don't speak, this is only the half of it, there are more treats in store. Your dowry's to be fifteen thousand, but as Nicholas owes your mother nine thousand, that's being deducted from the dowry. Now besides that——

SASHA. Why tell me this?

LEBEDEV. Your mother told me to.

SASHA. Can't you leave me alone? If you had any respect for either of us, you wouldn't let yourself talk like this. I don't want your dowry, I never asked for one and I'm not asking now.

LEBEDEV. Why pitch into me? Gogol's two rats had a sniff at each other and then left each other alone, but you're so much the emancipated woman, you lash out without even a sniff.

SASHA. Leave me alone, and don't insult my ears with your cheap calculations.

LEBEDEV [*flaring up*]. Really, you'll all have me stabbing myself or cutting someone's throat. One of you's for ever yelling blue murder, nagging, fussing and counting pennies, while this one's so intelligent, humane and goddam emancipated, she can't understand her own father. I insult her ears. Why—before coming here and insulting your ears I was being torn limb from limb out there. [*Points to the door.*] She can't understand! Oh, I don't know whether I'm on my head or my heels. Confound you all. [*Moves towards the door and stops.*] I don't like you, I don't like anything about any of you.

SASHA. What is it you dislike?

LEBEDEV. Everything, everything.

SASHA. Meaning what?

LEBEDEV. Well, I'm not going to sit back and spout about it. I hate the whole thing, I can't stand the idea of your wedding. [*Goes up to* SASHA *and speaks kindly.*] I'm sorry, Sasha, your marriage may be all very clever, noble, starry-eyed and high-principled, but there's something wrong with it, there really is. It's not like other marriages. You're young, pure, fresh as a spring morning, you're beautiful— and he's a shabby, frowsty widower. And I can't make sense of him, confound him. [*Kisses her.*] Sasha, I'm sorry, there's something not quite nice about it. There's a lot of talk about the way Sarah died and the way he was suddenly all set on marrying you because of this, that and the other. [*Briskly.*] I'm an old woman, anyway, I really am, a regular old grandmother. Don't listen to me, don't listen to anyone— listen only to yourself.

SASHA. I don't feel it's right myself, Father. It's wrong, all wrong. If you only knew how depressed I feel. I can't stand it. I feel awkward and afraid to admit it. Do cheer me up for God's sake, Father dear, and tell me what to do.

LEBEDEV. What do you mean, "what"?

SASHA. I was never so scared in my life. [*Looks round.*] I feel
I don't understand him and never will. Not once has he
smiled or looked me in the eye since we got engaged.
What with his never-ending complaints, vague remorse,
hints at some wrong he's done, his shudderings—I'm worn
out. Sometimes I even fancy I, er, don't love him as I
should. And when he comes here or talks to me it gets so
boring. What does it all mean, Father? I'm scared.

LEBEDEV. My darling, my only child, be guided by your old
father and call the thing off.

SASHA [*frightened*]. No, no, don't say that.

LEBEDEV. Yes, really, Sasha. There will be an awful scene and
it'll be the talk of the county, but better face a scandal than
ruin your life.

SASHA. Don't say that, Father, I won't listen to you. I mustn't
give way to such gloomy thoughts. He's a good, unhappy,
misunderstood man. I shall love and appreciate him and
put him on his feet. I'll do my job. That's settled.

LEBEDEV. It's no job, it's just plain hysteria.

SASHA. That'll do. I've told you things I wouldn't even admit
to myself. Don't tell anyone. Let's forget it.

LEBEDEV. I can't make sense of it. Either I'm old and dotty,
or else you've all grown far too clever. Anyway, I'm hanged
if I can make it out.

SCENE V

SHABELSKY [*coming in*]. To hell with everyone, myself included. It's infuriating.

LEBEDEV. What's up?

SHABELSKY. No, seriously, whatever happens, I must do something rotten and foul enough to make everyone else feel as
sick as I do. And I will too, honestly. I've told Borkin to
announce my engagement today. [*Laughs.*] They're all swine,
so let me be one too.

LEBEDEV. I'm fed up with you. Look here, Matthew, if you go on like this you'll be carted off to the madhouse, if you don't mind my saying so.

SHABELSKY. Is the madhouse worse than any other house? Carry on, take me there now if you want, I don't care. Rotten, trivial, worthless second-rate people! I'm disgusted with myself too, and I don't believe one word I say.

LEBEDEV. I tell you what, old man—you put some old rags in your mouth, light them and blow fire on people. Or better still, get your hat and go home. This is a wedding, everyone's enjoying themselves, but you go on like a dying duck in a thunderstorm. I must say——

[SHABELSKY *bends over the piano and sobs*.]

LEBEDEV. Good Lord above! Matthew! Count! What's up? Matthew, my dear good friend, have I offended you? Forgive a silly old man, forgive an old soak. Have some water.

SHABELSKY. I don't want it. [*Raises his head*.]

LEBEDEV. Why are you crying?

SHABELSKY. It's nothing really.

LEBEDEV. Come on, old man, don't tell lies. What's the reason?

SHABELSKY. I happened to look at that 'cello and—and I remembered poor little Sarah.

LEBEDEV. Hey, what a time for reminiscences! May she rest in peace, poor woman, but this is hardly the time to talk about her.

SHABELSKY. We used to play duets together. She was a wonderful, marvellous woman.

[SASHA *sobs*.]

LEBEDEV. What do you think you're doing? Give over. Good grief, they're both howling and I, er, I—. At least go somewhere else, the guests will see you.

SHABELSKY. Paul, you can be happy in a graveyard if the sun shines, and even old age is all right if you have hope. But I've no hope at all.

LEBEDEV. Yes, you really are in a rather bad way—no children, no money, nothing to do. Well, it can't be helped.
[*To* SASHA.] What set you off?

SHABELSKY. Lend me some money, Paul. We'll settle up in
the next world. I'll go to Paris and visit my wife's grave.
I've given a lot away in my time—I gave away half my
property, so I've the right to ask. What's more I ask as a
friend.

LEBEDEV [*at a loss*]. I haven't a penny, old boy. All right
then. I can't promise, that is, but you know—very well
then. [*Aside*.] They worry me to death.

SCENE VI

MRS. BABAKIN [*comes in*]. Where's my gentleman friend? How
dare you leave me on my own, Count? Oh, you horrid
man. [*Hits the* COUNT *on the arm with her fan*.]

SHABELSKY [*with loathing*]. Can't you leave me alone? I hate
you.

MRS. BABAKIN [*taken aback*]. What? What was that?

SHABELSKY. Go away.

MRS. BABAKIN [*falls into an armchair*]. Oh dear. [*Cries*.]

ZINAIDA [*comes in crying*]. Someone's just come—the best
man, I think. Time to bless the bride. [*Sobs*.]

SASHA [*imploringly*]. Mother!

LEBEDEV. Now they're all howling—quite a quartet. Do turn
off the waterworks. Matthew, Martha, this way you'll have
me—me crying too. [*Cries*.] Oh, Lord!

ZINAIDA. If you've no use for your mother and won't obey
her—oh well, I'll do as you wish and give you my blessing.

[IVANOV *comes in, wearing a tail-coat and gloves*.]

SCENE VII

LEBEDEV. This is the utter limit! What's going on?

SASHA. What are you doing here?

IVANOV. I'm sorry, but please can I talk to Sasha in private?

LEBEDEV. You shouldn't visit the bride before the wedding, you should be on your way to church.

IVANOV. Please, Paul.

[LEBEDEV *shrugs his shoulders. He,* ZINAIDA, *the* COUNT *and* MRS. BABAKIN *go out.*]

SCENE VIII

SASHA [*sternly*]. What do you want?

IVANOV. I'm in a rotten bad temper, but I can speak calmly. Listen. I was dressing for the wedding just now. I looked in the glass and saw grey hairs on my temples. It's all wrong, Sasha. We must end this senseless farce before it's too late. You're young and unspoilt, with your whole life before you, while I——

SASHA. That's not news, I've heard it thousands of times before and I'm sick of it. Go to church and don't keep people waiting.

IVANOV. I'm going straight home. Tell your family the wedding's off, give them some explanation. It's time we came to our senses. I've been acting like Hamlet, you've been the starry-eyed young heroine—and it's gone far enough.

SASHA [*flaring up*]. What a way to speak! I won't listen.

IVANOV. Well, I'm speaking and I shall go on speaking.

SASHA. Why did you come here? Your complaints sound more and more like sneers.

IVANOV. No, I'm not complaining this time. Sneers, you say? Oh yes, I'm sneering. If I could sneer at myself a thousand times harder and set the whole world laughing, then sneer I would. I looked at myself in the glass and something seemed to snap inside me. I laughed at myself and nearly went out of my mind with shame. [*Laughs.*] What price melancholia, noble grief, mysterious misery! The only thing left is for me to write poetry. Moaning and groaning, whining, making people's lives a misery and knowing that my vitality's gone beyond recall, that I've gone to seed, had my day, become weak-minded and am up to the neck in these sickening depressions—to feel all this in bright sunshine, when even an ant carries its load and is content! No, thank you very much! To see that some people think you're a fraud, others feel sorry for you, yet others hold out a helping hand, while a fourth lot—worst of all—listen to your sighs with reverence, looking on you as a great prophet and expecting you to preach a new religion! No, I still have some pride and conscience, thank God. I laughed at myself on my way here, and I felt as though the very birds were laughing at me, and the trees.

SASHA. This isn't anger, it's madness.

IVANOV. Think so? No, I'm not mad. I see things in their true light now, and my thoughts are as innocent as your own. We love each other, but our marriage is not to be. I can rant and fret to my heart's content, but I've no right to destroy anyone else. I poisoned the last year of my wife's life with my snivelling. Since we've been engaged you've forgotten how to laugh, and you look five years older. And your father, who once had a pretty sane outlook, can't make sense of people any more, thanks to me. When I attend meetings, go visiting or shooting—I carry boredom, gloom and despondency everywhere. No, don't interrupt. I'm being brutally frank, but I'm in a rotten temper, sorry, and this is the only way I can speak. I never used to lie or talk about how awful life is, but once I'd taken to grousing I started finding fault with things without meaning to or knowing what I was doing—started complaining and cursing fate, so that everyone who hears me gets infected with the same disgust for life and fault-finding. And what a way to speak—as if I was doing Nature a favour by being alive. To hell with me!

SASHA. Stop. What you've just said makes it clear that you're sick of complaining and it's time you started a new life. A good thing too.

IVANOV. I see nothing good about it. What is this "new life"? I'm absolutely done for—it's time we were both clear about that. New life indeed!

SASHA. Come off it, Nicholas—who says you're done for? Why

all the cynicism? No, I won't talk or listen to you. Go to church.

IVANOV. I'm done for!

SASHA. Don't shout like that or the guests will hear.

IVANOV. Once an intelligent, educated, healthy man begins feeling sorry for himself for no obvious reason and starts rolling down the slippery slope, he rolls on and on without stopping and nothing can save him. Well, where is there hope for me? What could it be? I can't drink, spirits make my head ache. I can't write bad verse, nor can I worship my own mental laziness and put it on a pedestal. Laziness is laziness, weakness is weakness—I can't find other names for them. I'm done for, I tell you, there's no more to be said. [*Looks round.*] We might be interrupted. Listen. If you love me, help me. You must break off the marriage without delay—this very instant. Hurry up——

SASHA. Nicholas, if you did but know how you've tired me out—you've really got me down. You're a kind, intelligent man, so judge for yourself—how can you tell people to do things like that? Every day you set some new task, each one harder than the last. I wanted active love, but our love's sheer martyrdom.

IVANOV. As my wife you'd find these tasks still more involved. So break it off. And get this clear—it's not love that makes you talk like this, it's a stubbornness that comes from your own integrity. You set yourself to rescue me at all costs and make a new man of me, and you liked to think you were being heroic. Now you're ready to back out, but sentimentality stands in your way, don't you see?

SASHA. What strange, mad logic! How can I break it off, how can I? You've no mother, sister or friends. You're ruined, your property's been ransacked, everyone says awful things about you——

IVANOV. I was a fool to come here, I should have done as I intended.

[LEBEDEV *comes in.*]

SCENE IX

SASHA [*runs to her father*]. For God's sake, Father—he rushed in here like a lunatic and he's been torturing me—insists I call it off, doesn't want to spoil my life. Tell him I don't need his generosity, I know what I'm doing.

LEBEDEV. This makes no sense to me. What generosity?

IVANOV. There won't be any wedding.

SASHA. There will be! Father, tell him the wedding's on.

LEBEDEV. Hey, just a moment—why won't you marry her?

IVANOV. I've told her why, but she refuses to see.

LEBEDEV. Don't tell her, tell me. And make it make sense. Nicholas, you've wrought such havoc in our lives, God forgive you—I feel I'm living in a chamber of horrors. I look round, but I can make nothing of it. It's more than flesh and blood can stand. What do you want an old man to do—challenge you to a duel, I suppose?

IVANOV. We don't need duels, we just need to keep our heads and understand plain language.

SASHA [*walks up and down the stage in agitation*]. This is awful, awful, he's just like a child.

LEBEDEV. One can only throw up one's hands in amazement. Listen, Nicholas. To you this is all very clever and subtle and follows the laws of psychology, but to me it's a fiasco, a disaster. Listen to an old man for the last time. What I want to say is—relax! Take the simple view of things like everyone else. Everything in the world's simple. The ceiling's white, boots are black, sugar's sweet. You love Sasha, she loves you. If you love her, stay with her. If you don't love her, go away and we won't hold it against you. What could be simpler? You're both healthy, intelligent, decent people. You have enough to eat, thank God, and you've clothes on your back. What more do you want? You may be hard up, but what matter? Money doesn't bring happiness. Of course, I know your estate's mortgaged and you can't afford to pay the interest, but I'm a father, I understand. Her mother can do what she likes, confound her. If she won't give you any money, never mind. Sasha says she doesn't need a dowry—something about principles, Schopenhauer and all that. Now that's a lot of nonsense. I've ten thousand roubles stowed away in the bank. [*Looks around.*] Not a soul knows about it at home—it was your grandmother's. It's for the two of you. Take it, only you must promise to let Matthew have a couple of thousand.

[*Guests gather in the ballroom.*]

IVANOV. There's nothing to be said, Paul. I'm doing as my conscience tells me.

SASHA. So am I doing as my conscience tells me. Say what you like, I won't let you go. I'm going to call Mother. [*Goes out.*]

SCENE X

LEBEDEV. I can't make sense of anything.

IVANOV. Listen, my poor man. I won't try and explain myself— whether I'm decent or rotten, sane or mad. You wouldn't understand. I used to be young, eager, sincere, intelligent. I loved, hated and believed differently from other people, I worked hard enough—I had hope enough—for ten men. I tilted at windmills and banged my head against brick walls. Without measuring my own strength, taking thought or knowing anything about life, I heaved a load on my back which promptly tore the muscles and cracked my spine. I was in a hurry to expend all my youthful energy, drank too much, got over-excited, worked, never did things by halves. But tell me, what else could you expect? We're so few, after all, and there's such a lot to be done, God knows. And now look how cruelly life, the life I challenged, is taking its revenge. I broke under the strain. I woke up to myself at the age of thirty, I'm like an old man in his dressing-gown and slippers. Heavy-headed, dull-witted, worn out, broken, shattered, without faith or love, with no aim in life, I moon around, more dead than alive, and don't know who I am, what I'm living for or what I want. Love's a fraud, or so I think, and any show of affection's just sloppy sentimentality, there's no point in working, songs and fiery speeches are cheap and stale. Wherever I go I carry misery, indifference, boredom, discontent and dis-

gust with life. I'm absolutely done for. You see a man
exhausted at the age of thirty-five, disillusioned, crushed
by his own pathetic efforts, bitterly ashamed of himself,
sneering at his own feebleness. How my pride rebels, I'm
choking with fury. [*Staggering.*] God, I'm on my last legs—
I'm so weak I can hardly stand. Where's Matthew? I want
him to take me home.

VOICES IN THE BALLROOM. The best man's here.

SCENE XI

SHABELSKY [*coming in*]. I borrowed these shabby tails, and
haven't any gloves, so of course I get all these sneering
looks, silly jokes and vulgar grins. Loathsome creatures.

BORKIN [*comes in quickly with a bunch of flowers, wearing
tails and the best man's buttonhole*]. Phew! Where is he?
[*To* IVANOV.] They've been waiting for you at church for
ages, and here you are making speeches. You are a scream,
honestly. Look, you mustn't go with your bride, but sepa-
rately with me and I'll come back from church and fetch
the bride. Can't you even get that into your head? You
really are funny.

LVOV [*comes in. To* IVANOV]. So you're here, are you? [*Loudly.*]
Nicholas Ivanov, I want everyone to hear this. *You are the
most unmitigated swine!*

IVANOV [*coldly*]. I'm very much obliged to you.

[*General confusion.*]

BORKIN [*to* LVOV]. That was a foul thing to say, sir. I challenge
you to a duel.

LVOV. Mr. Borkin, I consider it degrading even to exchange
words with you, let alone fight a duel. As for Mr. Ivanov,
he may receive satisfaction when he wishes.

SHABELSKY. I shall fight you, sir.

SASHA [*to* LVOV]. What is this? Why did you insult him? Just a
moment, everyone, let him tell me—why?

LVOV. I didn't insult him without good reason, Miss Lebedev.

I came here as an honest man to open your eyes. Please listen to me.

SASHA. What can you say? That you're an honest man? That's hardly a secret! You'd better tell me frankly whether you know what you're doing or not. You come in here with honest man written all over you, terribly insult him and nearly kill me. Before that you've dogged his footsteps and made his life a misery, quite convinced you were doing your duty as an honest man. You've meddled in his private life, made his name dirt and set yourself up to judge him. You took every chance to bombard me and all his friends with anonymous letters—thinking all the time what a very honest man you were. In the name of honesty you, a doctor, didn't spare even his sick wife, you pestered her with your suspicions. There's no outrageous, rotten, cruel trick you couldn't play while still thinking yourself an unusually honest and progressive man.

IVANOV [*laughing*]. This isn't a wedding, it's a public debate. Loud cheers!

SASHA [*to* LVOV]. Now think for a moment. Do you know what you're doing or don't you? Stupid, callous people. [*Takes* IVANOV *by the hand*.] Come away, Nicholas. Come on, Father!

IVANOV. What do you mean, come on? I'll put an end to all this here and now. I feel like a young man again, it's my old self that's speaking. [*Takes out his revolver*.]

SASHA [*shrieks*]. I know what he wants to do. Nicholas, for God's sake!

IVANOV. I've rolled downhill long enough, it's time to call a halt. I've outstayed my welcome. Go away. Thank you, Sasha.

SASHA [*shouts*]. Nicholas, for God's sake! Stop him!

IVANOV. Leave me alone! [*Runs to one side and shoots himself*.]

CURTAIN

THE SEAGULL

[Чайка]

A COMEDY IN FOUR ACTS

[1896]

CHARACTERS

IRINA ARKADIN [MRS. TREPLEV], an actress

CONSTANTINE TREPLEV, her son, a young man

PETER SORIN, her brother

NINA ZARECHNY, a young girl, daughter of a rich landowner

ILYA SHAMRAYEV, a retired army lieutenant, Sorin's manager

POLINA, his wife

MASHA, his daughter

BORIS TRIGORIN, a writer

EUGENE DORN, a doctor

SIMON MEDVEDENKO, a schoolmaster

JACOB, a labourer

A chef

A housemaid

The action takes place in Sorin's house and garden
There is an interval of two years between Acts Three and Four

ACT ONE

The park on SORIN's *estate. A wide path, leading away from the audience to a lake in the background, is blocked by a rough stage, put up for an amateur dramatic performance. It hides the lake from view. To left and right of this stage, bushes. A few chairs and a small table.*

The sun has just set. JACOB *and other workmen can be heard hammering and coughing on the stage behind the drawn curtain.* MASHA *and* MEDVEDENKO *come in, left, on their way back from a walk.*

MEDVEDENKO. Why do you wear black all the time?

MASHA. I'm in mourning for my life, I'm unhappy.

MEDVEDENKO. Why? [*Reflects.*] I don't understand. You're healthy and your father's quite well off, even if he's not rich. I'm much worse off than you—I'm only paid twenty-three roubles a month, and what with pension deductions I don't even get that. But I don't go round like someone at a funeral. [*They sit down.*]

MASHA. Money doesn't matter, even a poor man can be happy.

MEDVEDENKO. Yes—in theory. But look how it works out. There's me, my mother, my two sisters and my young brother. But I only earn twenty-three roubles and we need food and drink, don't we? Tea and sugar? And tobacco? We can hardly make ends meet.

MASHA [*looking back at the stage*]. The play will be on soon.

MEDVEDENKO. Yes. Nina Zarechny will act in it and Constantine Treplev wrote it. They're in love and this evening they'll be spiritually united in the effort to present a unified work of art. But you and I aren't soul-mates at all. I love you. I'm too wretched to stay at home and I walk over here every day, four miles each way, and it just doesn't mean a thing to you. And that's understandable. I've no money,

there are a lot of us at home, and anyway why marry a man
who doesn't get enough to eat?

MASHA. What rubbish. [*Takes snuff.*] Your loving me is all
very touching, but I can't love you back and that's that.
[*Offers him her snuff-box.*] Have some.

MEDVEDENKO. I don't feel like it. [*Pause.*]

MASHA. It's so close, it's sure to thunder tonight. You're
always holding forth about something or talking about money.
You think there's nothing worse than being poor, but if you
ask me it's a thousand times better to be a beggar and wear
rags than—. Oh, you can't understand.

[*Enter* SORIN *and* TREPLEV, *right.*]

SORIN [*leaning on a stick*]. Country life doesn't really suit me,
boy, and I shall never get used to this place, you can see
for yourself. I went to bed at ten o'clock last night and woke
at nine this morning, feeling as if all that sleep had glued my
brain to my skull or something. [*Laughs.*] Then I happened
to drop off again this afternoon, and now I feel more dead
than alive. It's a nightmare, that's what it comes to.

TREPLEV. Yes, you should really live in town. [*Seeing* MASHA
and MEDVEDENKO.] Look here, you'll be told when the
show begins, so don't hang round now. Go away, please.

SORIN [*to* MASHA]. Masha, would you mind asking your father
to have that dog let off its chain? It's always howling. My
sister couldn't sleep again last night.

MASHA. Speak to my father yourself, I shan't. Kindly leave me
out of this. [*To* MEDVEDENKO.] Come on.

MEDVEDENKO [*to* TREPLEV]. Let us know when it starts, will
you? [*Both go out.*]

SORIN. So that dog will howl again all night. Isn't it typical?
I've never done what I liked in the country. At one time
I'd take a month off and come down here for a break and so
on, but there'd be so much fuss and bother when you got
here—you felt like pushing off the moment you arrived.
[*Laughs.*] I was always glad to get away. Anyway, now I'm
retired I've nowhere else to go, that's what it comes to. I
have to live here, like it or not.

JACOB [*to* TREPLEV]. We're going for a swim, Mr. Treplev.

TREPLEV. All right, but mind you're in your places in ten minutes. [*Looks at his watch.*] It won't be long now.

JACOB. Very good, sir. [*Goes out.*]

TREPLEV [*looking round the stage*]. Well, this is our theatre. Just a curtain with the two wings and an empty space beyond. No scenery. There's an open view of the lake and horizon. We shall put up the curtain at exactly half past eight when the moon rises.

SORIN. Splendid.

TREPLEV. Of course the whole thing will fall flat if Nina Zarechny's late. It's time she was here. Her father and stepmother keep a sharp eye on her and she can't easily get away, she's pretty well a prisoner. [*Puts his uncle's tie straight.*] Your hair and beard *are* a mess. Shouldn't you get a trim?

SORIN [*combing his beard*]. It's the bane of my life. As a young man I always looked as if I had a hangover and so on. Women never liked me. [*Sitting down.*] Why is your mother in a bad mood?

TREPLEV. Well may you ask. She's bored. [*Sitting down beside* SORIN.] And jealous. She has it in for me—and for this performance and the play—because Nina's in it and she isn't. She knows nothing about the play, but she already loathes it.

SORIN [*laughs*]. What an idea——

TREPLEV. She's put out because Nina will be applauded on this little stage and she won't. [*Looks at his watch.*] She's a psychological freak, is Mother. Oh, she's brilliant enough. And clever. She can cry her eyes out over a book, reel off all Nekrasov's poems by heart, and when it comes to nursing the sick she's quite the ministering angel. But you try putting in a word for another actress—Duse, say. I wouldn't advise it, not while she's around. No one else must have a word of praise. The idea is that we write about her, make a great to-do and rave about her marvellous acting in *The Lady with the Camellias* or *It's a Mad Life*.

But out here in the country that drug isn't to be had, which is why she's so fed up and bad-tempered. That's why she thinks we're against her and that we're all to blame. What's more, she's superstitious, she thinks thirteen's an unlucky number and that sort of thing. She's stingy too. She has seventy thousand roubles in the bank in Odessa, I know that for a fact. But you ask her to lend you some and you'll have her in tears.

SORIN. You've got it in your head that your mother doesn't like your play and now you're upset and so on. Don't worry, your mother adores you.

TREPLEV [*pulling the petals off a flower*]. She loves me, she loves me not. She loves me, she loves me not. She loves me, she loves me not. [*Laughs.*] You see, Mother doesn't love me—to put it rather mildly. She likes excitement, romantic affairs, gay clothes—but I'm twenty-five years old and a constant reminder that she's not so young as she was. She's only thirty-two when I'm not around, but when I'm with her she's forty-three, and that's what she can't stand about me. Besides, she knows I've no use for the theatre. She adores the stage. Serving humanity in the sacred cause of art, that's how she thinks of it. But the theatre's in a rut nowadays, if you ask me—it's so one-sided. The curtain goes up and you see a room with three walls. It's evening, so the lights are on. And in the room you have these geniuses, these high priests of art, to show you how people eat, drink, love, walk about and wear their jackets. Out of mediocre scenes and lines they try to drag a moral, some commonplace that doesn't tax the brain and might come in useful about the house. When I'm offered a thousand different variations on the same old theme, I have to escape— run for it, as Maupassant ran from the Eiffel Tower because it was so vulgar he felt it was driving him crazy.

SORIN. But we must have a theatre.

TREPLEV. What we need's a new kind of theatre. New forms are what we need, and if we haven't got them we'd be a sight better off with nothing at all. [*Looks at his watch.*] I'm terribly fond of Mother. But she does lead such an idiotic life, for ever taken up with this author of hers, and her name's always being bandied about in the press—which is all very trying. Then sometimes I can't help being a bit selfish, as anyone would in my position, and I'm sorry to have a famous actress for my mother—feel I'd be better off if she was just an ordinary woman. Can you imagine anything more outrageous and idiotic, Uncle? Sometimes she'll have guests in the house—celebrities, every one of them, actors and writers. Only one nonentity in the whole bunch. Me. They only put up with me because I'm her son. Who am I? What am I? I left the university in my third year, "for reasons outside our control," as editors sometimes say. I'm no good at anything, I haven't a penny to my name and my passport description is "provincial shopkeeper, resident of Kiev." That, you see, was my father's official status, though he was well known on the stage himself. So when all these musicians, actors and writers deigned to notice me in her drawing-room, they looked as if they were wondering how anyone could be quite such a worm. I could tell what they thought—I suffered agonies of humiliation.

SORIN. By the way, tell me about this writer—this friend of your mother's. What's he like? He's a bit of a puzzle, he hardly speaks.

TREPLEV. He's intelligent and unassuming—a bit on the melancholy side, you know. Very decent sort. He's nowhere near forty yet, but he's already famous and thoroughly spoilt. As for his works, well, what shall I say? It's charming, clever stuff, but after Tolstoy or Zola you'd hardly care for Trigorin.

SORIN. You know, I'm rather fond of writers, my boy. I once wanted to get married and write books, those were my two great ambitions, but neither of them came off. Ah yes. Even being an obscure writer must be quite nice, come to think of it.

TREPLEV [*listens*]. I hear someone coming. [*Embraces his uncle.*] I can't live without her. The very sound of her footsteps is so beautiful. I'm wildly happy. [*Hurries towards* NINA ZARECHNY, *who now comes in.*] Entrancing creature, my vision of delight——

NINA [*upset*]. I'm not late am I? I can't be.

TREPLEV [*kissing her hands*]. No, no, of course not.

NINA. I've been worried all day, scared out of my wits. I was afraid Father wouldn't let me come, but he's just gone out with my stepmother. The sky was red, the moon was already rising and I rode over as fast as I could. [*Laughs.*] Oh, I'm so pleased. [*Shakes* SORIN *firmly by the hand.*]

SORIN [*laughs*]. You look as though you've been crying. Now that won't do, it really won't.

NINA. It's all right. I'm so out of breath, can't you see? I have to leave in half an hour, so we must be quick. No, no, don't try and keep me, for God's sake. My father doesn't know I'm here.

TREPLEV. It's time we started, anyway. We must go and call the others.

SORIN. I'll see to it and so on. At your service. [*Moves towards the right, singing.*] "There were once two French Grenadiers." [*Looks round.*] I once burst into song like that and a fellow in our legal department spoke up. "You've a mighty powerful voice, sir." Then he thought a bit and added, "And a pretty nasty one too." [*Laughs and goes out.*]

NINA. My father and stepmother won't let me come here. This place is wildly Bohemian according to them, and they're afraid of me going on the stage. But something seems to lure me to this lake like a seagull. My heart's full of my feelings for you. [*Looks round.*]

TREPLEV. We're alone.

NINA. I think there's someone over there.

TREPLEV. No, there isn't. [*They kiss.*]

NINA. What sort of tree is that?

TREPLEV. An elm.

NINA. Why is it so dark?

TREPLEV. Night's falling and everything's getting dark. Don't go home too early. Please.

NINA. I must.

TREPLEV. Then how about me coming over to your place, Nina? I'll stand in the garden all night gazing at your window.

NINA. You can't, the watchman would see you. Our dog doesn't know you yet and he'd bark.

TREPLEV. I love you.

NINA. Shush!

TREPLEV [*hearing footsteps*]. Who's there? Is it you, Jacob?

JACOB [*behind the stage*]. Yes sir.

TREPLEV. Get into position, it's time to start. Is the moon coming up?

JACOB. Yes sir.

TREPLEV. Have you the methylated spirits? And the sulphur? There must be a smell of sulphur when the red eyes appear. [*To* NINA.] Run along then—you'll find everything ready. Nervous?

NINA. Yes, terribly. I don't mind your mother, I'm not afraid of her, but Trigorin's here. To have him in the audience— I'm just a bundle of nerves. A famous writer! Is he young?

TREPLEV. Yes.

NINA. His stories are marvellous, aren't they?

TREPLEV [*coldly*]. I don't know, I've never read them.

NINA. Your play's hard to act, there are no living people in it.

TREPLEV. Living people! We should show life neither as it is nor as it ought to be, but as we see it in our dreams.

NINA. There's not much action, it's just a lot of speeches. I think a play really needs a love interest.

[*Both go behind the stage. Enter* POLINA *and* DORN.]

POLINA. It's getting damp. Go and put your galoshes on.

DORN. I'm hot.

POLINA. You don't take care of yourself, it's sheer pigheadedness. As a doctor you know very well that damp air's bad for you, but you want to make me suffer. And you spent the whole of yesterday evening out on the terrace to spite me.

DORN [*sings quietly*]. "Oh, tell me not your young life's ruined."

POLINA. You were so busy talking to Irina, you didn't notice the cold. You think she's attractive, don't you?

DORN. I'm fifty-five years old.

POLINA. Don't be silly, that's not old for a man. You're young for your age and still attractive to women.

DORN. Well, what do you want me to do about it?

POLINA. You men are all the same. When you see an actress you're ready to fall down and worship her.

DORN [*sings quietly*]. "Once more in thy presence—." That society makes a fuss of artists and doesn't treat them like tradesmen, say—it's only natural. It's a form of idealism.

POLINA. Women have always fallen in love with you and thrown themselves at you. That's idealism too, I suppose?

DORN [*shrugs his shoulders*]. What's wrong with it? There's a lot to be said for the way women have treated me. I'm a first-rate doctor, that's what they really liked about me. Ten or fifteen years ago, you remember, I was the only decent obstetrician in the county. And then I've always treated people fairly.

POLINA [*clutches his hand*]. My darling!

DORN. Take it easy, someone's coming.

[*Enter* IRINA *on* SORIN's *arm*, TRIGORIN, SHAMRAYEV, MEDVEDENKO *and* MASHA.]

SHAMRAYEV. I remember her acting superbly at the Poltava Trade Fair in 'seventy-three. Terrific, wonderful stuff! Then there was Paul Chadin, the comedian. You don't happen to know what became of him, I suppose? No one could touch his Rasplyuyev, it was better than Sadovsky's, believe me, dearest lady. Where is he now?

IRINA. You always want to hear about these old fossils. How on earth should I know? [*Sits down.*]

SHAMRAYEV [*with a sigh*]. Paul Chadin—you don't find his sort any more. The stage has gone downhill, Irina. Once we had giants, now we've only dwarfs.

DORN. There aren't many real stars these days, I grant you, but the average actor's come on a lot.

SHAMRAYEV. I can't agree, it's a matter of taste anyway. *De gustibus aut bene, aut nihil.*

[TREPLEV *appears from behind the stage.*]

IRINA [*to her son*]. When does the thing start, dear boy?

TREPLEV. In a minute, please be patient.

IRINA [*declaims from* Hamlet].
"O Hamlet, speak no more:
Thou turn'st mine eyes into my very soul;
And there I see such black and grained spots
As will not leave their tinct."

TREPLEV [*from* Hamlet].
"Nay, but to live
In the rank sweat of an enseamed bed,
Stew'd in corruption, honeying and making love
Over the nasty sty——"

[*A horn is sounded behind the stage.*]

TREPLEV. Ladies and gentlemen, we're starting. Attention, please. [*Pause.*] I'm starting now. [*Bangs his stick on the ground and speaks loudly.*] O ye ancient, hallowed shades that float above this lake at night, lull us to sleep, and may we dream of life in two hundred thousand years.

SORIN. In two hundred thousand years there won't be anything left.

TREPLEV. All right then, let them show us that.

IRINA. Let them, we're fast asleep anyway.

[*The curtain rises, opening on to the lake. The moon has risen above the horizon and is reflected in the water. NINA ZARECHNY, dressed in white, is sitting on a boulder.*]

NINA. Men, lions, eagles and partridges, horned deer, geese, spiders and silent fishes, denizens of the deep, starfishes and creatures invisible—that is, all life, all life, all life—has completed its melancholy cycle and died. For thousands of centuries Earth has not borne one living creature, and in vain does that poor moon light her lamp. No longer do cranes awake and call in the meadows and no may-beetles can be heard in the lime-groves. It is cold, cold, cold. Empty, empty, empty. Terrible, terrible, terrible. [*Pause.*] The bodies of living creatures have turned to dust, and eternal matter has converted them into stones, water, clouds. But their souls have all been fused into a single whole. That World Spirit am I. I. Within me is the soul of Alexander the Great, of Caesar, Shakespeare and Napoleon—and of the most miserable leech. In me the thoughts of men are mingled with the instincts of animals. I remember all, all, all, and I relive anew in my own being every other life.

[*Will-o'-the-wisps are seen.*]

IRINA [*quietly*]. This is something terribly modern.

TREPLEV [*imploringly and reproachfully*]. Mother!

NINA. I am lonely. Once in a hundred years I open my lips to speak and in this void with none to hear me my voice echoes mournfully. You too, pale lights, you hear me not. The foul marsh brings you forth before sunrise and you drift till daybreak, without thought, without will, without any quiver of life. The Devil, Father of Eternal Matter, fearing that you might bring forth new life, causes your atoms, and those of the stones and water, to change every second, and you are in a state of continual flux. Alone in the whole universe the Spirit remains one and the same. [*Pause.*] Like a prisoner flung into a deep, empty well, I know not where I am or what awaits me. All is hidden from me except that in the cruel, unrelenting struggle with the Devil, the principle of Material Force, I am destined to triumph. Then shall Spirit and Matter unite in wondrous harmony, then shall the reign of Cosmic Will commence. But that will only come about after a long, long succession of millennia, when Moon, bright Sirius and Earth shall gradually have turned to dust. Until then there shall be horror upon horror.

[*Pause. Two red spots appear over the lake.*]

NINA. But see—my mighty antagonist the Devil approaches. I see his awful blood-red eyes——

IRINA. There's a smell of sulphur. Was that really necessary?

TREPLEV. Yes.

IRINA [*laughs*]. Oh, a stage effect.

TREPLEV. Mother!

NINA. He is miserable without human beings——

POLINA [*to* DORN]. You've taken your hat off. Put it on before you catch cold.

IRINA. The doctor took his hat off to the Devil, Father of Eternal Matter.

TREPLEV [*losing his temper, in a loud voice*]. The play's over. Enough! Curtain!

IRINA. But why so annoyed?

TREPLEV. Enough! Curtain! Bring down that curtain! [*Stamping.*] Curtain! [*The curtain falls.*] I'm extremely sorry, I forgot that writing plays and acting are only for the chosen few, I'm poaching on other people's preserves, I—I—. [*Tries to add something, but makes a gesture of resignation and goes off, left.*]

IRINA. What's up with him?

SORIN. My dear Irina, that's hardly how to treat a touchy young man.

IRINA. Why, what did I do?

SORIN. You hurt his feelings.

IRINA. But he told us his play was a joke, and that's just how I treated it.

SORIN. All the same——

IRINA. Now he turns out to have written a masterpiece. Oh, for heaven's sake! I suppose he put on this performance, and choked us with sulphur, not as a joke, but to prove a point. He wanted to show us how to write and act. I've really had about enough of this! These constant outbursts and digs against me—well, say what you like, but they'd try anyone's patience. He's a selfish, spoilt little boy.

SORIN. He only wanted to give you pleasure.

IRINA. Oh, did he? But of course he couldn't choose an ordinary play, we have to sit through this experimental rubbish. Now, I don't mind listening to rubbish for a laugh, but doesn't this stuff claim to be a new art form, something epoch-making? Well, I don't see any new art form here, just a display of bad manners.

TRIGORIN. Everyone writes what he likes as best he can.

IRINA. Then let him write what he likes as best he can, but leave me out of it.

DORN. Jupiter, thou art angry——

IRINA. I'm not Jupiter, I'm a woman. [*Lights a cigarette.*] I'm not annoyed, I'm only sorry to see a young man spend his time so tediously. I didn't mean to hurt his feelings.

MEDVEDENKO. No one has the right to separate Spirit from Matter, since Spirit itself may well be a combination of material atoms. [*To* TRIGORIN, *eagerly.*] But you know, how about writing and staging a play based on the life of us schoolmasters? We have a pretty thin time.

IRINA. Quite right, but no more talk about plays or atoms. It's such a heavenly evening. I say, can you hear someone singing? [*Listens.*] Now isn't that nice?

POLINA. It's on the other side of the lake. [*Pause.*]

IRINA [*to* TRIGORIN]. Sit by me. Ten or fifteen years ago there was music and singing by this lake almost every night. There are six estates on the shore. There was so much laughter, fun and shooting, I remember, and so many, many love affairs. But who was the darling and idol of all six estates? I present [*nods towards* DORN] our doctor, Eugene Dorn. He's still charming, but in those days he was irresistible. Still, I'm beginning to feel rather guilty. Why did I hurt my poor boy's feelings? I'm worried. [*Loudly.*] Constantine, my dear! Constantine!

MASHA. I'll go and look for him.

IRINA. Please do, darling.

MASHA [*moving off, left*]. Hallo there! Constantine! Hallo there! [*Goes out.*]

NINA [*coming out from behind the stage*]. We obviously aren't going on, so I can come out. Good evening. [*Kisses* IRINA *and* POLINA.]

SORIN. Bravo, bravo!

IRINA. Bravo, bravo! We were quite fascinated. With those looks and that perfectly lovely voice you mustn't bury yourself in the country, it would be such a shame. I'm sure you have a real gift, do you hear me? Your duty is to go on the stage.

NINA. Oh, that's what I always dream of. [*With a sigh*.] But it can never be.

IRINA. Who knows? Now let me introduce—Boris Trigorin.

NINA. Oh, pleased to meet you—. [*With embarrassment*.] I always read what you——

IRINA [*giving* NINA *a seat next to her*]. Now don't be shy, darling. He's a famous man, but he's not at all stuffy. And he's a bit shy himself, you see.

DORN. I think we might raise the curtain now, it's a bit spooky like this.

SHAMRAYEV [*loudly*]. Jacob, be a good fellow and pull up the curtain.

[*The curtain goes up*.]

NINA [*to* TRIGORIN]. It's an odd play, isn't it?

TRIGORIN. I couldn't make sense of it. I enjoyed it, though. Your acting was so genuine, and the scenery was superb. [*Pause*.] There must be a lot of fish in that lake.

NINA. Yes.

TRIGORIN. I love angling. There's nothing I enjoy more than sitting on the water's edge in the late afternoon, watching my float.

NINA. After the joy of creative work I should have thought no other enjoyment would mean anything.

IRINA [*laughing*]. Oh, don't say that. Compliments always floor him completely.

SHAMRAYEV. I remember one evening at the Moscow Opera Theatre hearing the great Silva take a lower C. There was a bass from our parish choir sitting in the gallery, as it happened. Suddenly—we were quite flabbergasted, as you can imagine—we hear a voice from the gallery. "Bravo, Silva!" A whole octave lower. Like this. [*In a deep bass.*] "Bravo Silva!" You could have heard a pin drop in that theatre. [*Pause.*]

DORN. No one seems to have anything to say.

NINA. Well, I must be going. Good-bye.

IRINA. What! Where are you off to at this hour? We won't let you.

NINA. Father's expecting me.

IRINA. Well, I must say, he is a—. [*They kiss.*] Ah well, that's that, but I do so wish you could stay.

NINA. How I hate leaving, if you only knew.

IRINA. Someone ought to see you home, my pet.

NINA [*terrified*]. Oh, no, no!

SORIN [*to* NINA, *imploringly*]. Do stay.

NINA. I can't, Mr. Sorin.

SORIN. Just one hour and so on. Surely you can—

NINA [*after some thought, through tears*]. I can't. [*Shakes hands and hurries out.*]

IRINA. It really is bad luck on the girl. They say her mother left all her enormous fortune to her father when she died— every last bit of it—and now the child has nothing because the father's going to leave everything to his second wife. It's outrageous.

DORN. Yes, that dear father of hers is a pretty thoroughgoing swine, give him his due.

SORIN [*rubbing his cold hands*]. I think we might go in too, it's getting damp out here. My legs ache.

IRINA. They're so stiff, you can hardly walk. Well, come on, poor old thing. [*Takes his arm.*]

SHAMRAYEV [*offering his arm to his wife*]. Madam?

SORIN. I can hear that dog howling again. [*To* SHAMRAYEV.] Be a good fellow, Shamrayev, and have it let off its chain.

SHAMRAYEV. I can't, my dear sir. Thieves might get in the barn—I've millet in there. [*To* MEDVEDENKO, *who is walking beside him.*] Yes, a whole octave lower. "Bravo, Silva!" And no concert artist, mind you, just someone from the church choir.

MEDVEDENKO. What do they pay you in a church choir? [*All go out except* DORN.]

DORN [*alone*]. Well, I don't know. Perhaps it's all rather beyond me, perhaps I've gone mad, but I liked the play. It has something. When that child spoke about loneliness, and then afterwards when the Devil's red eyes appeared, my hands shook with excitement. It was all so fresh and innocent. Look, I think he's coming. I want to be as nice about it as I can.

TREPLEV [*coming in*]. They've all gone.

DORN. I'm here.

TREPLEV. Masha's looking for me all over the park. What a ghastly creature.

DORN. I liked your play enormously, Constantine. It's a bit odd in a way, and I haven't heard the end. Still, it made a great impression. You have a real bent that way and you mustn't give up.

[TREPLEV *shakes him firmly by the hand and embraces him impulsively.*]

DORN. Hey—a bit excitable, aren't you? Tears in your eyes—. Now, my point is this. You took your plot from the realm of abstract ideas, and quite right too, because a work of art simply must express some great idea. Nothing can be beautiful unless it's also serious. I say, you are pale.

TREPLEV. So you don't think I should give up?

DORN. No. But you must describe only the significant and the eternal. As you know, I've lived a varied life and enjoyed myself, I'm satisfied. But if I'd ever experienced the uplift that an artist feels when he's creating, I think I'd have scorned my material environment and all that goes with it, and I'd have taken wing and soared away into the sky.

TREPLEV. I'm sorry, where's Nina?

DORN. And then a work of art must express a clear, precise idea. You must know why you write, or else—if you take this picturesque path without knowing where you're going you'll lose your way and your gifts will destroy you.

TREPLEV [*impatiently*]. Where's Nina?

DORN. She's gone home.

TREPLEV [*in despair*]. What can I do? I want to see her, I *must* see her. I'm going over there.

[MASHA *comes in.*]

DORN [*to* TREPLEV]. Take it easy, my boy.

TREPLEV. But I'm going all the same. I must go.

MASHA. Come indoors, Constantine. Your mother wants you, she's worried.

TREPLEV. Tell her I've gone. And look here, can't you all leave me alone? Leave me alone, don't follow me around.

DORN. Come, come, dear boy, you can't go on like this. It's not right.

TREPLEV [*through tears*]. Good-bye, Doctor. Many thanks. [*Goes out.*]

DORN [*with a sigh*]. Ah, to be young!

MASHA. When people can't think what to say they always hold forth about the young. [*Takes some snuff.*]

DORN [*takes the snuff-box off her and hurls it into the bushes*]. That's disgusting. [*Pause.*] I think someone's playing the piano indoors. I must go in.

MASHA. Just a moment.

DORN. What is it?

MASHA. I must tell you again, I must speak. [*Excitedly.*] I don't care for my father, but I have a soft spot for you.

Somehow we have so much in common, I feel it with all my heart. So help me. Help me, or else I'll do something silly and make a mess of my life, ruin it. I can't go on.

DORN. Meaning what? How can I help you?

MASHA. I'm so unhappy. No one, no one knows how I suffer. [*Lays her head on his breast, softly*.] I love Constantine.

DORN. What a state they're all in. And what a lot of loving. Oh, magic lake! [*Tenderly*.] But what can I do, my child? What can I do?

CURTAIN

ACT TWO

*The croquet lawn. In the background, right, the house,
with a large terrace. To the left, a view of the lake with
sunlight sparkling on it. Flower beds. It is midday and
hot.* IRINA, DORN *and* MASHA *are sitting on a bench near
the lawn in the shade of an old lime-tree.* DORN *has an
open book on his lap.*

IRINA [*to* MASHA]. Let's stand up. [*Both stand up.*] Side by
side. You're twenty-two and I'm nearly twice as old. Now,
Dr. Dorn, which of us looks younger?

DORN. You, of course.

IRINA. Exactly. And why? Because I work, I feel, I'm always
on the go, while you just stay put—you're only half alive.
And I make it a rule not to look into the future, I never
think of growing old or dying. What is to be will be.

MASHA. I feel about a thousand years old. My life seems to
drag on and on endlessly, and I often think I'd rather be
dead. [*Sits down.*] That's silly, of course. I must pull myself
together and snap out of it.

DORN [*singing quietly*]. "Oh, speak to her, you flowers—"

IRINA. Then again I'm most particular, dear, like an Englishman.
I keep myself in trim and my clothes and hair are always
just right. Do I ever go out, even in the garden, with my
housecoat on, without doing my hair? No, I don't. That's
why I've lasted so well, because I've never been slovenly
and let myself go like some I could mention. [*Strolls up
and down the lawn, arms akimbo.*] See what I mean? Just
like a dear little robin. I could play a girl of fifteen.

DORN. Well, I'll carry on reading anyway. [*Picks up his book.*]
We stopped at the corn-dealer and the rats.

IRINA. "And the rats." You read. [*Sits down.*] Or rather let me
have it, I'll read, it's my turn. [*Takes the book and looks*

for the place.] "And the rats." Here we are. [*Reads*.] "For society people to encourage novelists and make a fuss of them is as obviously dangerous as for a corn-dealer to let rats breed in his storerooms. But you see, writers are very popular. So when a woman's marked one down for capture, she keeps on at him, flattering him, being nice to him and spoiling him." Well, the French may be like that, but we're different, we don't have things so cut and dried. Before a Russian woman tries to ensnare a writer she's usually head over heels in love with him, believe me. No need to look far—take me and Trigorin.

[*Enter* SORIN *leaning on a stick, with* NINA *at his side. Behind them* MEDVEDENKO *pushes an empty bath-chair*.]

SORIN [*kindly, as if to a child*]. Oh yes? Something nice has happened, has it? We're happy today, is that what it comes to? [*To his sister*.] Something nice has happened. Our father and stepmother have gone off to Tver, so we're free for three whole days.

NINA [*sits down beside* IRINA *and embraces her*]. I'm so happy, I belong to you now.

SORIN [*sits down in his bath-chair*]. And doesn't she look pretty this morning?

IRINA. Yes, and so nicely dressed and attractive—what a good little girl. [*Kisses* NINA.] But we mustn't be too nice, we'll bring her bad luck. Where's Boris Trigorin?

NINA. Down at the bathing place, fishing.

IRINA. I wonder he doesn't get bored. [*Is about to go on reading*.]

NINA. What's that?

IRINA. Maupassant's *On the Water*, darling. [*Reads a few lines to herself*.] Oh well, the rest's dull and unconvincing. [*Shuts the book*.] I'm rather worried. Tell me, what's wrong with my son? Why is he so terribly bored and depressed? He spends whole days out by the lake and I hardly ever see him.

MASHA. He's in rather a bad mood. [*To* NINA, timidly.] Please recite something from his play.

NINA [*shrugging her shoulders*]. Do you mean it? It's so boring.

MASHA [*restraining her enthusiasm*]. When he recites, his eyes blaze and he turns pale. He has a beautiful, sad voice, and he looks like a poet.

[SORIN *is heard snoring.*]

DORN. Happy dreams.

IRINA. Peter.

SORIN. Eh?

IRINA. Are you asleep?

SORIN. Not at all. [*Pause.*]

IRINA. You won't consult a doctor, dear, and that's very naughty of you.

SORIN. I wouldn't mind—it's the doctor here doesn't want me to.

DORN. What, dose yourself at the age of sixty!

SORIN. One wants to live, even at sixty.

DORN [*annoyed*]. Eh? Then take valerian drops.

IRINA. It would be good for him to go to a spa, I think.

DORN. Why not? Let him go. Or let him stay.

IRINA. What's that supposed to mean?

DORN. Nothing special. It's quite clear. [*Pause.*]

MEDVEDENKO. Mr. Sorin should give up smoking.

SORIN. Oh, rubbish.

DORN. No, it isn't. Drinking and smoking ruin your personality. After a cigar or glass of vodka you're not Peter Sorin any more, you're Peter Sorin plus something. Your ego dissolves and you start thinking of yourself as "him," in the third person.

SORIN [*laughs*]. It's all right for you to talk, you've enjoyed yourself. But what about me? Twenty-eight years I've worked for the Department of Justice, but I haven't lived yet, haven't experienced anything—that's what it comes to. So I want a bit of fun, it stands to reason. You've always had your own way and you don't care, which is why you're so given to idle chatter. But I want a bit of life, so I drink sherry at dinner and smoke cigars and so on. That's all there is to it.

DORN. One should take life seriously, but to go to your doctor when you're sixty and complain that you didn't enjoy yourself as a young man—well, I'm sorry, but that's just silly.

MASHA [*stands up*]. It must be lunch time. [*Walks in a lazy, drooping fashion.*] My foot's gone to sleep. [*Goes out.*]

DORN. She's off for a couple of quick ones before lunch.

SORIN. The poor child's unhappy.

DORN. Nonsense, sir.

SORIN. You've always had all you want, that's why you talk like this.

IRINA. Oh, could anything be duller than this charming country boredom—so hot and still, with you all lolling round airing your views? You're good company, my dears, and I like listening to you, but—I'd much rather sit in my hotel room learning a part.

NINA [*delightedly*]. Well said, I know what you mean.

SORIN. It's better in town, of course. You sit in your study, with a servant to stop anyone coming in unannounced, and there's a telephone. Then there are cabs in the street and so on.

DORN [*sings softly*]. "Oh, speak to her, you flowers—"

[SHAMRAYEV *comes in, followed by* POLINA.]

SHAMRAYEV. Here they are. Good morning. [*Kisses* IRINA's *hand, then* NINA's.] Nice to see you looking so well. [*To* IRINA.] My wife says you propose going to town together this afternoon. Is that so?

IRINA. Yes, that is the idea.

SHAMRAYEV. I see. Splendid. And how do you propose travelling, dearest lady? We're carting rye this afternoon and the men are all busy. So which horses are you taking? If you don't mind my asking.

IRINA. Horses? How on earth should I know?

SORIN. We do have some carriage horses.

SHAMRAYEV [*agitatedly*]. Carriage horses? And where am I to get collars? Yes, where am I to get collars? This baffles me, it passes the bounds of credence! Look, dear lady, I worship your genius and I'd give you ten years of my life, but horses I cannot provide.

IRINA. And what if I have to leave? This is most odd.

SHAMRAYEV. You've no idea what running a farm means, dear lady.

IRINA [*losing her temper*]. This is what we're always being told! Well, in that case I leave for Moscow this very afternoon. Hire me horses in the village, or I shall walk to the station.

SHAMRAYEV [*losing his temper*]. Then I resign, you can get yourself another manager. [*Goes out.*]

IRINA. This happens every summer. Every summer I come here to be insulted, I shan't set foot in this place again. [*Goes out, left, in the supposed direction of the bathing place off-stage. A minute later she can be seen going indoors, followed by* TRIGORIN *with fishing-lines and a pail.*]

SORIN [*flaring up*]. What insolence. What the hell *is* all this? I'm fed up, that's what it comes to. Bring all the horses here this instant.

NINA [*to* POLINA]. Fancy saying no to a famous actress like Miss Arkadin. Her slightest wish, her merest whim—surely they're more important than your entire farm. This is beyond belief.

POLINA [*in despair*]. What can I do? Put yourself in my place. What can I do?

SORIN [*to* NINA]. Let's go and find my sister. We'll all beg her to stay, how about it? [*Looking in the direction in which* SHAMRAYEV *disappeared.*] What an awful man. Tyrant!

NINA [*prevents him rising*]. Don't move, stay where you are. We'll wheel you. [*She and* MEDVEDENKO *push the bath-chair.*] Oh, isn't this awful!

SORIN. Yes, it certainly is. But he won't resign, I'll speak to him at once.

[*They go out. Only* DORN *and* POLINA *remain on stage.*]

DORN. Aren't people a bore? Your husband really deserves to be kicked out, but it'll end with that old woman Sorin and his sister apologizing to him, you'll see.

POLINA. He sent the carriage horses out on farm work. We have these mix-ups every day. If you only knew how it upsets me, it makes me ill—see how I'm shaking? I can't stand his rudeness. [*Imploringly.*] Eugene dear, let me come and live with you, darling. Our time's passing, we're not so young as we were. Can't we give up all the lying and pretence now we're getting on in life? [*Pause.*]

DORN. I'm fifty-five, it's too late for me to change my life.

POLINA. You say no because there are other women in your life besides me, I know that. You can't give them all a home, I see that. Sorry, I've been a nuisance.

[NINA *appears near the house, picking flowers.*]

DORN. It's all right.

POLINA. It's agony to me, being jealous. Of course, being a doctor you can't avoid women, I see that.

DORN [*to* NINA, *who comes up to them*]. What's happening?

NINA. Miss Arkadin's crying and Mr. Sorin has a touch of his asthma.

DORN [*stands up*]. I'd better go and give them both valerian drops.

NINA [*gives him some flowers*]. Please take these.

DORN. Thank you so much. [*Goes towards the house.*]

POLINA [*going with him*]. Aren't they nice? [*In a low voice, near the house.*] Give me those flowers, just you give me those flowers! [*Tears them up and throws them away. Both go indoors.*]

NINA [*alone*]. Isn't it funny to see a famous actress cry, and for such a silly reason? Another funny thing—a well-known writer, a celebrity with his name in all the papers, his picture on sale and translations coming out in foreign languages, but he spends all day fishing and is overjoyed when he catches a couple of chub. I thought famous people were proud and standoffish, I thought they despised the common herd, I thought they sort of used their glamour and brilliance to take revenge on people for making so much fuss over birth and wealth. But here they are crying, fishing, playing cards, laughing and losing their tempers like anyone else.

TREPLEV [*comes in without his hat on, carrying a sporting gun and a dead seagull*]. Are you alone?

NINA. Yes.

[TREPLEV *lays the seagull at her feet.*]

NINA. What does that signify?

TREPLEV. I meanly killed that seagull this morning. I lay it at your feet.

NINA. What's wrong with you? [*Picks up the seagull and looks at it.*]

TREPLEV [*after a pause*]. I shall soon kill myself in the same way.

NINA. You've changed so much.

TREPLEV. Yes, but who changed first? You did. You're so different to me now, you look at me coldly and you find me in the way.

NINA. You're touchy lately and you always talk so mysteriously, in symbols or something. This seagull's a symbol too, I suppose, but it makes no sense to me, sorry. [*Lays the seagull on the bench.*] I'm too simple to understand you.

TREPLEV. It all started that evening when my play was such a stupid flop. Women can't forgive failure. I've burnt the thing, every scrap of it. If you only knew how wretched I am. Your coldness terrifies me, I can't believe it, it's as if I'd woken up and found this lake had suddenly dried up or

soaked into the ground. You say you're too simple to
understand me, but what is there to understand? My play
failed, and you despise my inspiration and think me a
dreary nonentity like so many others. [*Stamping.*] All this
is only too clear. It's as if someone had banged a nail into
my brain, damn it—and damn the selfishness that seems to
suck my blood like a vampire. [*Spotting* TRIGORIN, *who
walks in reading a book.*] There's genius for you. Struts
about like Hamlet. Carries a book too. [*Sarcastically.*]
"Words, words, words." The great luminary hasn't come
near you yet, but you're smiling already, your whole expression has melted in his rays. I won't stand in your way.
[*Goes out quickly.*]

TRIGORIN [*making a note in his book*]. Takes snuff. Drinks
vodka. Always wears black. Loved by schoolmaster.

NINA. Good morning, Mr. Trigorin.

TRIGORIN. Good morning. Things took an unexpected turn and
I think we're leaving today. I don't suppose we'll meet
again. I'm sorry, I don't often run across young, attractive
girls, and I've forgotten how one feels at eighteen or
nineteen—can't picture it. That's why the girls in my stories don't usually come off. I'd love to be in your shoes for
an hour to find out how you think and what you're like.

NINA. And I'd like to be in your shoes.

TRIGORIN. Why?

NINA. To see how it feels to be a famous, gifted writer. How
does it feel? What's the sensation, being a celebrity?

TRIGORIN. Eh? I don't think there is a sensation, I never
thought of that. [*After reflection.*] Which means one of two
things—either I'm not so famous as you think, or else
being famous produces no sensation at all.

NINA. What about seeing your name in the papers?

TRIGORIN. That's all right when they're nice about you. When
they're not nice you go about in a bad temper for a day or
two.

NINA. What a wonderful world. If you knew how I envy you.
People's lives work out so differently. Some barely drag

out their days in drab obscurity. They're all alike and all miserable. But others, you for instance—you're one in a million—have fascinating, brilliant lives full of meaning. You're lucky.

TRIGORIN. What, me? [*Shrugging his shoulders.*] Well—. You speak of fame and happiness, and my fascinating, brilliant life. Sorry, but this nice talk only reminds me of boiled sweets—something I never eat. You're very young and kind.

NINA. Your life's marvellous.

TRIGORIN. What's so nice about it? [*Looks at his watch.*] I must go and write now. Sorry, I'm busy. [*Laughs.*] You've done what's called treading on my favourite corn and now I'm getting excited and a bit annoyed. Anyway, let me have my say. Let's talk about my wonderful, brilliant life. Right, where can we start? [*After a little thought.*] Some people have obsessions and can't help thinking day and night about something like the moon. Well, I'm a bit moonstruck too, haunted day and night by this writing obsession. I must write, I must—. Hardly have I ended one story when I somehow have to tackle another, then a third and fourth on top of that. I'm always writing, never stop, can't help it. What's wonderful and brilliant about that, eh? It's such a barbarous life. Here am I talking to you and getting quite excited, yet can't forget for a second that I've an unfinished novel waiting for me. Or I see a cloud over there like a grand piano. So I think it must go in a story. "A cloud like a grand piano sailed past." Or I smell heliotrope, and make a quick mental note. "Sickly scent. Flower. Sombre hue. Mention in description of summer evening." I try to catch every sentence, every word you and I say and quickly lock all these sentences and words away in my literary storehouse because they might come in handy. When I finish work, I rush off to the theatre or go fishing. That would be the time to relax and forget, but not a bit of it. I already have another great weight on my mind: a new plot. I feel I must go to my desk—hurry up and start writing, writing, writing all over again. This sort of thing goes on all the time, I can never relax, and I feel I'm wasting my life. I feel I'm taking pollen from my best flowers, tearing them up and stamping on the roots—all to make honey that goes to some vague, distant destination. I'm mad, I must be. Well, my friends and acquaintances don't exactly treat me as sane, do they? "What are you writing now? What have you got in store for us?" They keep on and on and on, and to me it's all so bogus—my friends' attention, praise and admiration. They deceive me, the way one does an invalid, and I'm sometimes afraid they're just waiting to creep up, grab me and cart me off to an asylum like the lunatic in Gogol. And in my young days, in my best years, when I was just beginning, this writing business was sheer agony. An obscure author feels clumsy, awkward, out of place—especially when things aren't going well. He's all on edge with nervous strain. He can't help hanging round literary and artistic people, unrecognized, unnoticed, afraid to look anyone in the face. He's like a gambling addict who has no money. I never saw any of my readers, but I somehow thought of them as hostile and sceptical. I was afraid of the public, scared stiff. When I put on a new play, I always felt the dark-haired people in the audience were against me, while the fair-haired ones didn't care either way. Isn't it awful? What agony it was.

NINA. Yes, but look—there is inspiration, the creative process. Doesn't that give you moments of ecstasy?

TRIGORIN. Yes. Writing's pleasant enough. I like reading proofs too, but as soon as the stuff's in print I can't stand it—I now see it was all wrong, all a mistake, and shouldn't have been written at all, and I feel annoyed and fed up. [*Laughing.*] The public reads it and says: "Yes. Oh, how nice. Oh, how clever. Very nice, but not a patch on Tolstoy." Or: "Marvellous stuff, but Turgenev's *Fathers and Children* is better." This way my work will go on being nice and clever, nice and clever till my dying day, that's all, and when I'm dead my friends will pass my grave and say: "Here lies Trigorin, a fine writer. But not as good as Turgenev."

NINA. Sorry, I don't understand. You're simply spoilt by success.

TRIGORIN. What success? I've never satisfied myself. I dislike my own work. I drift round in a trance and often can't make sense of what I write, that's what's so awful. I love this lake here, the trees and the sky, I've a feeling for nature—it inspires me, gives me a violent urge to write. But then I'm more than an artist, aren't I? I'm a citizen too. I love my country and its people. As a writer, I feel I must discuss ordinary people, their sufferings, their future—science, human rights, all that stuff. So I do discuss it, all in great haste, with everyone furiously hounding me in all directions, while I scurry about like a fox with the pack snapping at his heels. I seem to see life and learning vanishing into the distance, while I lag more and more behind, feeling like the village boy who missed the train, and end up believing that I can only do nature descriptions and that everything else I write is bogus through and through.

NINA. You've been overworking. You're too busy—and too unwilling—to see how important you are. You're not satisfied with yourself. Very well, but to others you're a great man, you're wonderful. If I was a great writer like you, I'd give my whole life to the people, knowing that their only happiness was to rise to my level, and they'd harness themselves to my chariot.

TRIGORIN. A chariot, eh? Who do you take me for—Agamemnon? [*Both smile*.]

NINA. If I was lucky enough to be a writer or actress, I wouldn't mind my family and friends disliking me, or being poor and disappointed. I'd live in a garret on black bread. I'd suffer, being dissatisfied with myself and knowing how imperfect I was. But I should insist on being a real celebrity, with all the tumult and the shouting that go with it. [*Covers her face with her hands*.] My head's swimming. Oh dear!

IRINA [*off-stage, speaking from inside the house*]. Boris!

TRIGORIN. I'm wanted. This means I have to pack. But I don't feel like leaving. [*Looks round at the lake*.] I say, isn't it superb! Wonderful!

NINA. You see the house and garden on the other side?

TRIGORIN. Yes.

NINA. That was poor Mother's place. I was born there, I've

spent my whole life near this lake and I know every little island on it.

TRIGORIN. It's a wonderful spot. [*Looking at the seagull.*] What's that?

NINA. A seagull. Constantine shot it.

TRIGORIN. A beautiful bird. I really don't feel like leaving. Can't you persuade Irina to stay? [*Makes a note in his book.*]

NINA. What are you writing?

TRIGORIN. Nothing, just a note. An idea for a plot. [*Putting his book away.*] A plot for a short story. A young girl like you has lived all her life by a lake. Like a seagull, she loves the lake, and she's happy and free like a seagull. But a man happens to come along and wrecks her life for want of anything better to do. As happened to this seagull.

[*Pause.* IRINA *appears at a window.*]

IRINA. Boris, where are you?

TRIGORIN. Coming. [*Moves off and looks back at* NINA. *Near the window, to* IRINA.] What is it?

IRINA. We're staying.

[TRIGORIN *goes indoors.*]

NINA [*comes to the front of the stage, after some reflection*]. It's all a dream.

CURTAIN

ACT THREE

The dining-room in SORIN's *house. Doors, right and left. A sideboard and medicine cupboard. A table in the middle of the room. A suitcase, cardboard boxes and other signs of an impending departure.* TRIGORIN *is having lunch and* MASHA *stands by the table.*

MASHA. I'm telling you all this because you're a writer and can use it. Quite honestly, if he'd wounded himself seriously I couldn't have gone on living one minute. I'm quite brave, though, so I simply decided to wrench this love out of my heart and uproot it.

TRIGORIN. But how?

MASHA. By getting married. To Medvedenko.

TRIGORIN. That schoolmaster?

MASHA. Yes.

TRIGORIN. I don't see the need.

MASHA. To be hopelessly in love, just waiting, waiting for years on end—. But when I'm married I shan't bother about love, new worries will drive out old, and anyway it'll make a change, won't it? Shall we have another?

TRIGORIN. Aren't you overdoing it a bit?

MASHA. Oh, come on. [*Fills two glasses.*] Don't look at me like that, women drink a lot more than you think. A few do it openly like me, but most keep quiet about it. Oh yes they do. And it's always vodka or brandy. [*Clinks glasses.*] All the best. You're a decent sort, I'm sorry we shan't see each other again. [*They drink.*]

TRIGORIN. I don't want to go, actually.

MASHA. Then ask her to stay.

TRIGORIN. No, she won't stay now. Her son's being very

tactless. First he tries to shoot himself, and now they say he means to challenge me to a duel. Why? He frets, fusses, crusades about new artistic forms—but there's plenty of room for both new and old, isn't there? Must we get in each other's way?

MASHA. He's just jealous. No business of mine, anyway.

[*Pause.* JACOB *crosses the stage from left to right, carrying a suitcase.* NINA *comes in and stands by the window.*]

MASHA. My schoolmaster's not all that bright, but he is kind. He's poor and very much in love with me. I'm sorry for him, and for his old mother too. Ah well, let me wish you all the best. Remember me kindly. [*Shakes him firmly by the hand.*] Thanks for being so nice. Send me your books, and mind you write something in them, not "with respects." Just put: "To Masha, who doesn't know where she comes from or what she's doing on this earth." Good-bye. [*Goes out.*]

NINA [*stretching one arm towards* TRIGORIN *with the fist clenched*]. Odd or even?

TRIGORIN. Even.

NINA [*with a sigh*]. Wrong, it's odd. I was trying to decide whether to go on the stage or not, I wish someone would advise me.

TRIGORIN. You can't give advice about that sort of thing. [*Pause.*]

NINA. We're parting, perhaps we'll never meet again. Please accept this little medallion to remember me by. I had your initials engraved on it, and there's the title of your book *Days and Nights* on the other side.

TRIGORIN. How charming. [*Kisses the medallion.*] A delightful present.

NINA. Think of me sometimes.

TRIGORIN. I shall indeed, I'll think of you as you were on that sunny day—remember?—a week ago, when you wore your light dress. We were talking and there was that white bird lying on the bench.

NINA [*thoughtfully*]. Yes, the seagull. [*Pause.*] We can't talk any more, someone's coming. Give me two minutes before you go—please. [*Goes out, left. At the same time* IRINA *comes in, right, with* SORIN, *who wears a tail-coat with the star of some decoration. He is followed by* JACOB, *who attends to the luggage.*]

IRINA. Stay at home, old boy. You shouldn't go gadding about, not with your rheumatism. [*To* TRIGORIN.] Who went out just then? Nina?

TRIGORIN. Yes.

IRINA. I'm sorry, we're intruding. [*Sits down.*] I think I've packed everything. I'm worn out.

TRIGORIN [*reads the inscription on the medallion*]. "Days and Nights, page 121, lines 11 and 12."

JACOB [*clearing the table*]. Shall I pack your fishing-rods too, sir?

TRIGORIN. Yes, I'll be needing them, but you can give away the books.

JACOB. Yes sir.

TRIGORIN [*to himself*]. "Page 121, lines 11 and 12." I wonder what those lines are. [*To* IRINA.] Are there any of my books in the house?

IRINA. Yes, in the corner bookcase in my brother's study.

TRIGORIN. "Page 121." [*Goes out.*]

IRINA. You really should stay indoors, Peter.

SORIN. You're leaving and I'll be miserable here without you.

IRINA. But what can you do in town?

SORIN. Nothing much, but still—. [*Laughs.*] They're laying the foundation stone of the new council building and so on. I just want to get out of this backwater for a couple of hours, I feel as stale as someone's old cigarette-holder. I've ordered my carriage for one o'clock, so we can leave together.

IRINA [*after a pause*]. Well, enjoy yourself here, don't get bored or catch cold. And do look after Constantine—take care of him and keep him in order. [*Pause*.] When I leave I still shan't know why Constantine tried to shoot himself. Jealousy was the main reason, I fancy, and the sooner I get Trigorin out of here the better.

SORIN. How can I put it? There was more to it than that. A clever young man, buried in the country, with no money, position or future, with nothing to do either—well, it stands to reason. He's afraid and ashamed to be so idle. I'm very fond of him, and he's devoted to me. Still, he feels he doesn't really belong here, that's what it comes to—feels like a hanger-on or poor relation. It's just a matter of pride, stands to reason.

IRINA. Oh, isn't he a nuisance! [*Thoughtfully*.] Why can't he get a job or something?

SORIN [*whistles, then speaks hesitantly*]. I think it would be best if you—well, let him have a bit of cash. He ought to dress decently for a start and so on. Well, look, he's been going round in that wretched jacket for the last three years and he has no overcoat. [*Laughs*.] It wouldn't hurt the boy to have a bit of fun, go abroad or something—it doesn't cost all that much, you know.

IRINA. Yes, but still—. I might run to a suit, but as for going abroad—. No, the way things are I can't afford even a suit. [*Decisively*.] I haven't any money.

[SORIN *laughs*.]

IRINA. I haven't!

SORIN [*whistles*]. Very well then. I'm sorry, dear, don't be angry. I believe you. You're a fine, generous woman.

IRINA [*through tears*]. I haven't any money.

SORIN. If I had some I'd give it him myself, stands to reason. But I haven't, I'm broke. [*Laughs*.] My manager takes all my pension and spends it on raising crops, cattle and bees, and my money's all wasted. The bees die, the cows die, and they won't let me use the horses.

IRINA. Well, I do have some money, but I am an actress, you know. My dresses alone have ruined me.

SORIN. You're a nice, kind woman. I think highly of you, indeed I do. But there's something wrong with me again. [*Staggers.*] I feel dizzy. [*Grips the table.*] I feel unwell and so on.

IRINA [*terrified*]. Peter! [*Trying to support him.*] Peter, darling! [*Shouts.*] Help me! Help!

[*Enter* TREPLEV, *with a bandage round his head, and* MEDVEDENKO.]

IRINA. He feels faint.

SORIN. Never mind, it's all right. [*Smiles and drinks some water.*] It's over now and so on.

TREPLEV [*to his mother*]. Don't be frightened, Mother, it's nothing serious. Uncle's been taken like this quite often lately. [*To his uncle.*] You should lie down, Uncle.

SORIN. For a bit, all right. But I'm still going to town. I'll lie down a bit and then go, stands to reason. [*Moves off, leaning on a stick.*]

MEDVEDENKO [*takes his arm*]. Do you know this riddle? "What walks on four legs in the morning, on two legs at noon and on three legs in the evening?"

SORIN [*laughs*]. Yes, I know. "And spends the night on its back." I can manage by myself, thanks very much.

MEDVEDENKO. Come, don't stand on ceremony. [*He and* SORIN *go out.*]

IRINA. How he did scare me.

TREPLEV. Country life's bad for him, it gets him down. Now, Mother, if you suddenly felt generous and lent him a thousand or two, he could spend a whole year in town.

IRINA. I haven't any money. I'm an actress, not a banker. [*Pause.*]

TREPLEV. Will you change my bandage, Mother? You do it so well.

IRINA [*gets some iodine and a box of bandages out of the medicine cupboard*]. The doctor's late.

TREPLEV. He said he'd be here by ten, and it's midday already.

IRINA. Sit down. [*Takes the bandage off his head.*] It looks like a turban. Yesterday there was some visitor in the kitchen asking what nationality you were. Well, it's almost healed up, there's not much wrong now. [*Kisses his head.*] You won't do anything naughty again after I've left, will you?

TREPLEV. No, Mother. That was an instant of wild despair when I couldn't control myself, it won't happen again. [*Kisses her hand.*] You have such wonderful hands. I remember long ago when you were still appearing in the State Theatres and I was a little boy—there was a fight in our yard and one of the tenants, a washerwoman, got hurt badly. She was picked up unconscious, remember? You used to visit her, take her medicine and bath her children in a tub. Don't you remember?

IRINA. No. [*Puts on a fresh bandage.*]

TREPLEV. There were two girls, ballet-dancers, living in the same house. They used to come and have coffee with you.

IRINA. That I do remember.

TREPLEV. They were frightfully pious. [*Pause.*] Just lately, these last few days, I find I love you as tenderly and devotedly as when I was a little boy. I've no one left but you now. But why, why do you give in to that man?

IRINA. You don't understand him, Constantine. He's a fine character.

TREPLEV. Still, when he heard I meant to challenge him to a duel, his fine character didn't save him from an attack of cold feet. He's leaving, running away with his tail between his legs.

IRINA. Don't be silly, I asked him to leave myself.

TREPLEV. A fine character! You and I nearly quarrel over him, while he's in the drawing-room or garden or somewhere, laughing at us, and—drawing Nina out, trying to make her see what a genius he is.

IRINA. You do so enjoy being disagreeable to me. I respect

Trigorin, so please don't be nasty about him when I'm around.

TREPLEV. Well, I don't respect him. You want me to think he's a genius too, but I'm no good at lying, sorry, and his books just make me sick.

IRINA. You're envious. Pretentious nobodies always run down really brilliant people, that's all they're good for. I only hope it makes you feel better.

TREPLEV [*ironically*]. Really brilliant people! [*Angrily.*] I'm more talented than all you lot put together, if it comes to that. [*Tears the bandage off his head.*] You hacks have a stranglehold on the arts. You don't recognize or put up with anything except what you do yourselves, everything else you sit on and crush. But I don't accept you! I don't accept either you or him.

IRINA. Miserable decadent!

TREPLEV. Run along to your precious theatre and act in your rotten feeble plays!

IRINA. I've never acted in such plays. Leave me alone! You couldn't even write a tenth-rate farce. Provincial shopkeeper! Scrounger!

TREPLEV. Miser!

IRINA. Tramp!

[TREPLEV *sits down and quietly cries.*]

IRINA. You nobody! [*Walking up and down excitedly.*] Don't cry. Stop crying. [*Cries.*] Do stop. [*Kisses his forehead, cheeks and head.*] My darling boy, I'm sorry. Forgive your wicked mother. Forgive me, I'm so unhappy.

TREPLEV [*puts his arms round her*]. Oh, if you did but know! I've nothing left. She doesn't love me and I can't write any more. My hopes have all come to nothing.

IRINA. Don't give up, it'll all come right. He's going away now and she'll love you again. [*Wipes away his tears.*] Don't cry. We're friends again.

TREPLEV [*kisses her hands*]. Yes, Mother.

IRINA [*tenderly*]. And you make it up with him too. We can't have a duel, can we?

TREPLEV. All right. But I don't want to meet him, Mother, do you mind? This business depresses me, I can't cope.

[TRIGORIN *comes in*.]

TREPLEV. Oh—I'll go. [*Quickly clears the first-aid material into the cupboard*.] The doctor can put my bandage on later.

TRIGORIN [*looking in a book*]. Page 121, lines 11 and 12. Ah. [*Reads*.] "If you should ever need my life, then come and take it."

[TREPLEV *picks the bandage off the floor and goes out*.]

IRINA [*glancing at her watch*]. The carriage will be here soon.

TRIGORIN [*to himself*]. "If you should ever need my life, then come and take it."

IRINA. I hope all your things are packed?

TRIGORIN [*impatiently*]. Yes, yes. [*Thoughtfully*.] This appeal from a pure, innocent girl—why does it sound so sad? Why does it wring my heart so painfully? "If you should ever need my life, then come and take it." [*To* IRINA.] Let's stay another day.

[IRINA *shakes her head*.]

TRIGORIN. Let's stay.

IRINA. I know why you want to stay, dear, but you must pull yourself together. You're a little intoxicated, so sober down.

TRIGORIN. Then you sober down as well—be reasonable and sensible, please. You must look on all this as a true friend. [*Presses her hand*.] You're capable of sacrifice. So be a friend and set me free.

IRINA [*greatly upset*]. Are you so infatuated?

TRIGORIN. She attracts me. Perhaps this is just what I need.

IRINA. The love of a little provincial miss? How little you know yourself.

TRIGORIN. You know how people sometimes sleep-walk? Talking to you now, I feel as if I was asleep, dreaming of her. I'm possessed by visions of delight. Do set me free.

IRINA [*trembling*]. No, no, no. You can't talk to me like that, I'm only an ordinary woman. Don't torture me, Boris. I'm terrified.

TRIGORIN. You can be extraordinary if you want. Young love, enchanting and magical love that sweeps you off your feet into a make-believe world—can anything else on this earth give one happiness? I've never known such love before— never had time for it as a young man because I was for ever hanging round editors' offices and trying to make ends meet. But now, you see, this love has come at last, it calls me on. Why should I run away from it?

IRINA [*angrily*]. You must be mad.

TRIGORIN. Perhaps I am.

IRINA. You're all conspiring to torment me today. [*Cries.*]

TRIGORIN [*clutches his head*]. She doesn't understand, she won't understand.

IRINA. Am I really so old and ugly that you don't mind talking to me about other women? [*Embraces and kisses him.*] Oh, you're mad. My marvellous, splendid man. You're the last page in my life. [*Kneels down.*] My delight, my pride, my joy! [*Embraces his knees.*] If you leave me for one hour I shan't survive, I shall go mad, my wonderful, splendid one. My master.

TRIGORIN. Someone might come in. [*Helps her to her feet.*]

IRINA. Let them, I'm not ashamed of loving you. [*Kisses his hands.*] My dear, reckless boy, you want to do something crazy, but I won't have it, I won't let you. [*Laughs.*] You're mine, mine. This forehead's mine, these eyes are mine, this lovely silky hair's mine too. You're mine, all of you. You're so brilliant, so clever, you're the best writer of our day—Russia's only hope, so sincere and natural, with your spontaneity and healthy humour. You can put over the essence of a person or landscape with one stroke of the pen. Your characters are so alive, one can't read you without being moved. Too much hero-worship, you think? Think I'm flattering you? Then look in my eyes, come on. Do I look like a liar? There, you see, I'm the only one who appreciates you, I'm the only one who tells you the truth, my wonderful darling. You will come, won't you? You won't desert me, will you?

TRIGORIN. I've no will of my own, never have had. I'm a flabby, spineless creature that always does what it's told— surely that's not what women like. Take me then, carry me off, but don't ever let me move one step from your side.

IRINA [*to herself*]. Now he's mine. [*Off-handedly and casually*]. Actually, you can stay on if you want. I'll leave on my own and you can come later, in a week's time. What's the hurry, after all?

TRIGORIN. No, we may as well go together.

IRINA. As you like. We'll go together if you say so.

[*Pause.* TRIGORIN *makes a note in his book.*]

IRINA. What's that?

TRIGORIN. I heard a good phrase this morning—"a virgin pine-wood." It might come in. [*Stretches.*] So we're going, are we? More railway carriages, stations, refreshment-rooms, mutton-chops and talk.

SHAMRAYEV [*comes in*]. I have the honour to announce with great regret that your carriage is ready. It's time to leave for the station, dearest lady, the train's due in at five past two. Now, would you do me a favour—remember to ask where the actor Suzdaltsev is these days? Is he alive and kicking? We're old drinking companions. He used to steal the show in *The Mail-Coach Robbery*. In those days, I remember, Izmaylov—another remarkable personality who played in tragedies—belonged to the same company in Yelizavetgrad. There's no hurry, dearest lady, you've another five minutes. They were playing the villains in a melo-drama once, when they were suddenly caught and Izmaylov was supposed to say: "We're caught in a trap." But he said: "We're trapped in a court." [*Laughs loudly.*] Trapped in a court!

[*While he is speaking,* JACOB *is busy with the suitcases. The* MAID *brings* IRINA *her hat, cloak, umbrella and gloves. All help* IRINA *into her clothes. The* CHEF *looks in through the door, left, and comes in after some hesitation.* POLINA *comes in, followed by* SORIN *and* MEDVE-DENKO.]

POLINA [*with a basket*]. Here are some plums for the journey—very sweet, you might feel like a bite.

IRINA. You're most kind, Polina.

POLINA. Good-bye, my dear. I'm sorry if there's been anything amiss. [*Cries.*]

IRINA [*embraces her*]. Everything's been wonderful, just wonderful—there's no need to cry.

POLINA. Our time is nearly over.

IRINA. That can't be helped.

SORIN [*comes in through the door, left, wearing a hooded coat and a hat, and carrying a stick. Passes through the room*]. It's time we left, Irina, or we may miss the train, that's what it comes to. I'll get in the carriage. [*Goes out.*]

MEDVEDENKO. I'll walk to the station and see them off. It won't take long. [*Goes out.*]

IRINA. Good-bye, darlings. We'll meet again next summer if we're alive and well. [*The* MAID, JACOB *and the* CHEF *kiss her hand.*] Now, don't forget me. [*Gives the* CHEF *a rouble.*] Here's a rouble for you three.

CHEF. Thank you kindly, madam. Have a good journey. Thank you for your kindness.

JACOB. God speed.

SHAMRAYEV. Do drop us a line. Good-bye, Trigorin.

IRINA. Where's Constantine? Will you tell him I'm leaving? I must say good-bye. Ah well, don't think too badly of me. [*To* JACOB.] I gave the cook a rouble. That's for the three of you.

[*All go out, right. The stage is empty. The sound of leave-taking off-stage. The* MAID *comes back to fetch the basket of plums from the table and goes out again.*]

TRIGORIN [*coming back*]. I forgot my stick, I think it's on the terrace there. [*Moves off and meets* NINA *as she comes in through the door, left*.] Ah, it's you. We're just off.

NINA. I was sure we'd meet again. [*Excitedly*.] Mr. Trigorin, I've made up my mind once and for all, I've burnt my boats and I'm going on the stage. I shan't be here tomorrow, I'm leaving Father and throwing everything up to start a new life. I'm going away, same as you—to Moscow. We'll meet there.

TRIGORIN [*looking round*]. Put up at the *Slav Fair*. Let me know at once, I'll be in Molchanov Street—Grokholsky House. I must hurry. [*Pause*.]

NINA. Just a moment——

TRIGORIN [*in an undertone*]. You're so lovely. What happiness to think we'll soon meet again! [*She leans her head on his chest*.] Once more I'll see your wonderful eyes, your tender smile, lovely beyond description. Your soft features, your look of angelic purity. My darling—. [*A lengthy kiss*.]

CURTAIN

There is an interval of two years between Acts Three and Four.

ACT FOUR

A drawing-room in SORIN's *house, which* TREPLEV *has turned into a study. Doors, right and left, leading into inner rooms. Facing the audience, a french window opening on a terrace. Besides the usual drawing-room furniture there is a desk in the corner, right. Near the door, left, an ottoman. A bookcase. Books on window-ledges and chairs.*

Evening. One shaded lamp is alight. It is rather dark. Sound of trees rustling and of wind howling in the chimneys. A watchman is banging. MEDVEDENKO *and* MASHA *come in.*

MASHA [*calling out*]. Constantine, Constantine! [*Looking round*]. No one about. The old man keeps asking for Constantine every minute of the day. He must have him around.

MEDVEDENKO. He's afraid of being lonely. [*Listening.*] What horrible weather, this is the second day of it.

MASHA [*turning up the lamp*]. The lake's very rough, there are huge waves.

MEDVEDENKO. It's dark in the garden. That stage out there— they should have had it knocked down. There it stands, bare and ugly as a skeleton, with the curtain banging in the wind. Going past last night I thought I heard someone crying there.

MASHA. Ah well. [*Pause.*]

MEDVEDENKO. Come home, Masha.

MASHA [*shakes her head*]. I'm staying here tonight.

MEDVEDENKO [*imploringly*]. Come on, Masha, baby must be hungry.

MASHA. I don't care, let Matryona feed it. [*Pause.*]

MEDVEDENKO. I'm sorry for him, this'll be three nights without his mother.

MASHA. You are a bore these days. You did have a little
general conversation once, but now it's all baby, baby,
baby, home, home, home. That's all you ever say.

MEDVEDENKO. Come on, Masha.

MASHA. You can go by yourself.

MEDVEDENKO. Your father won't give me a horse.

MASHA. Oh yes he will if you ask him.

MEDVEDENKO. Perhaps I will then. So you'll come tomorrow?

MASHA [*takes snuff*]. All right, tomorrow. Can't you leave me
alone?

[TREPLEV *and* POLINA *come in.* TREPLEV *carries pillows
and a blanket, and* POLINA *has some bed-linen. They put
them on the ottoman, after which* TREPLEV *sits at his
desk.*]

MASHA. Who's that for, Mother?

POLINA. Mr. Sorin asked to have a bed made up in Constantine's room.

MASHA. Let me do it. [*Makes the bed.*]

POLINA [*with a sigh*]. Old men are such children. [*Goes up to
the desk, leans her elbows on it and looks at a manuscript.
Pause.*]

MEDVEDENKO. I'll go then. Good night, Masha. [*Kisses his
wife's hand.*] Good night, Mother. [*Tries to kiss his mother-
in-law's hand.*]

POLINA [*annoyed*]. Well, go if you're going.

MEDVEDENKO. Good night, Constantine.

[TREPLEV *silently shakes hands.* MEDVEDENKO *goes out.*]

POLINA [*looking at the manuscript*]. No one ever dreamt
you'd be a real author, Constantine, but now the maga-
zines have started paying you, thank goodness. [*Strokes his
hair.*] You've become good-looking too. Please be a bit
nicer to my poor Masha, dear.

MASHA [*making up the bed*]. Leave him alone, Mother.

POLINA [*to* TREPLEV]. She's such a nice girl. [*Pause.*] A woman needs nothing, Constantine, just a few kind looks. I've learnt that.

[TREPLEV *gets up from the desk and goes out without speaking.*]

MASHA. Now you've annoyed him. Why go on at him?

POLINA. I'm sorry for you, Masha.

MASHA. A lot of use that is!

POLINA. My heart aches for you. I see everything, you know, I understand.

MASHA. Don't be so silly. Unhappy love affairs are only found in novels. What nonsense! The thing is, don't give way to it, and don't moon around waiting for the tide to turn. If love enters your heart, get rid of it. My husband's been promised a job in another part of the country. I'm going to forget all this when we move. I'll tear it from my heart.

[*A melancholy waltz is played in the next room but one.*]

POLINA. That's Constantine playing, he must be depressed.

MASHA [*silently does two or three waltz steps*]. The thing is not to keep seeing him, Mother. If only Simon gets that new job, I'll be over this in a month, take it from me. It's all so silly.

[*The door, left, opens.* DORN *and* MEDVEDENKO *push* SORIN *through in his bath-chair.*]

MEDVEDENKO. I've six mouths to feed now, and with flour at two copecks a pound.

DORN. He can hardly make ends meet.

MEDVEDENKO. All right, laugh—you're rolling in money.

DORN. Oh, am I? My friend, in thirty years of practice—a busy practice with hardly a moment to call my own, day or night—I managed to save only two thousand roubles and I just got through those on my trip abroad. I'm broke.

MASHA [*to her husband*]. Still here?

MEDVEDENKO [*guiltily*]. Can I help it if they won't give me a horse?

MASHA [*bitterly annoyed, in a low voice*]. Out of my sight!

[*The bath-chair comes to rest on stage left*. POLINA, MASHA *and* DORN *sit down near it*. MEDVEDENKO, *saddened, moves to one side*.]

DORN. You've made a lot of changes, though. You've turned the drawing-room into a study.

MASHA. It's better for Constantine's work, he can go in the garden and think when he wants to.

[*The watchman bangs*.]

SORIN. Where's my sister?

DORN. Gone to the station to meet Trigorin, she'll be back any moment.

SORIN. If you felt my sister had to be sent for, I really must be ill. [*After a short pause*.] It's a funny thing—I'm seriously ill, but I don't get any medicine.

DORN. What would you like? Valerian drops? Soda? Quinine?

SORIN. Oh, the speeches have started. This is the limit. [*Nods towards the sofa*.] Is that bed for me?

POLINA. Yes.

SORIN. Thank you.

DORN [*singing softly*]. "See the moon floating by in the evening sky."

SORIN. I'd like to give Constantine a plot for a novel. It ought to be called *The Man who Wanted—L'homme qui a voulu*. In youth I wanted to become a writer—I didn't. I wanted to speak well—I spoke atrociously. [*Mocks himself*.] "And all that sort, er, of thing, er, don't yer know." I'd be doing a summing-up sometimes, and find myself jawing on and on till I broke out in a sweat. I wanted to marry—I didn't. I wanted to live in town all the time—and here I am ending my days in the country and so on.

DORN. You wanted to become a senior civil servant—and did.

SORIN [*laughs*]. That's one thing I wasn't keen on, it just happened.

DORN. To talk about being fed up with life at the age of sixty-two—that's a bit cheap, wouldn't you say?

SORIN. Don't keep on about it, can't you see I want a bit of life?

DORN. That's just silly. All life must end, it's in the nature of things.

SORIN. You're spoilt, that's why you talk like this. You've always had what you wanted, so life doesn't matter to you, you just don't bother. But even you'll be afraid of dying.

DORN. Fear of death's an animal thing, you must get over it. It only makes sense to fear death if you believe in immortality and are scared because you've sinned. But you aren't a Christian for a start, and then—what sins have you committed? You've worked for the Department of Justice for twenty-five years, that's all.

SORIN [laughs]. Twenty-eight.

[TREPLEV *comes in and sits down on a stool at* SORIN's *feet.* MASHA *stares at him throughout.*]

DORN. We're stopping Constantine working.

TREPLEV. No, it's all right. [Pause.]

MEDVEDENKO. Doctor, which town did you like best abroad, may one ask?

DORN. Genoa.

TREPLEV. Why Genoa?

DORN. The street life is so wonderful. Leaving your hotel in the evening, you find the whole street jammed with people, and you drift round in the crowd, going any old where in any old direction. You share its life, enter into its spirit and begin to think there really could be such a thing as a World Spirit, like the one Nina Zarechny once acted in your play. By the way, where is Miss Zarechny these days? Where is she and how is she?

TREPLEV. She's well, I presume.

DORN. I heard she was leading a rather odd life. What's it all about?

TREPLEV. That's a long story, Doctor.

DORN. Then make it short. [*Pause.*]

TREPLEV. She ran away from home and had an affair with Trigorin. You knew that?

DORN. Yes.

TREPLEV. She had a baby. It died. Trigorin tired of her and returned to his former attachments, as could only be expected. He never really gave them up in point of fact, but somehow contrived in his feeble way to keep a foot in both camps. Nina's private life has been a disaster so far as I can see.

DORN. And her stage career?

TREPLEV. Even worse, I think. She started off in a theatre at a resort near Moscow somewhere, then went to the provinces. I kept her under observation at the time, followed her about for a while. She always took leading roles, but her acting was crude and inept, with lots of ranting and hamming. She had her moments when she screamed superbly and died superbly. But moments they remained.

DORN. Then she must be some good after all?

TREPLEV. It was hard to tell. I suppose so. I saw her, but she wouldn't see me and the hotel servants wouldn't let me in her room. I knew how she felt and didn't insist on a meeting. [*Pause.*] What else can I say? Back home afterwards I had some letters from her—bright, affectionate, interesting letters. She didn't complain, but I sensed that she was deeply unhappy. Every line seemed sick, like a frayed nerve, and her mind was slightly unhinged. She used to sign herself "Seagull." Like the miller who calls himself a raven in Pushkin's *Mermaid*, she kept calling herself a seagull in her letters. Now she's here.

DORN. Here? What do you mean?

TREPLEV. Staying at an inn in town, she's been there four or five days. I was going to visit her and Masha here went over, but she won't see anyone. Simon Medvedenko claims he saw her yesterday afternoon somewhere in the fields a couple of miles away.

MEDVEDENKO. Yes I did, she was walking away from here towards town. I bowed, asked why she didn't come over. She said she would.

TREPLEV. She won't. [*Pause.*] Her father and stepmother will have nothing to do with her, they've posted look-outs everywhere to stop her even going near the place. [*Moves towards the desk with the* DOCTOR.] It's easy enough to be a philosopher on paper, Doctor, but how hard to act like one!

SORIN. She was a delightful girl.

DORN. What?

SORIN. She was a delightful girl, I say. Mr. Senior Civil Servant Sorin was even in love with her for a bit.

DORN. Ah, you old dog.

[SHAMRAYEV's *laugh is heard from off-stage.*]

POLINA. I think the others have just got back from the station.

TREPLEV. Yes, I hear Mother.

[*Enter* IRINA *and* TRIGORIN, *followed by* SHAMRAYEV.]

SHAMRAYEV [*coming in*]. We don't get any younger, we're all a bit weather-beaten through exposure to the elements—but you're still as young as ever, dearest lady, in that gay blouse, so lively and graceful.

IRINA. You'll bring me bad luck again, you tiresome man.

TRIGORIN [*to* SORIN]. Good evening, Peter. Why are you always unwell? It's very wrong of you. [*Seeing* MASHA, *delightedly.*] Masha!

MASHA. So you do recognize me? [*Shakes hands.*]

TRIGORIN. Married?

MASHA. Ages ago.

TRIGORIN. Happy? [*Exchanges bows with* DORN *and* MEDVEDENKO, *then hesitantly approaches* TREPLEV.] Irina says you've forgotten the past and aren't angry any more.

[TREPLEV *holds out his hand.*]

IRINA [*to her son*]. Look, Boris brought the magazine with your new story.

TREPLEV [*taking the volume, to* TRIGORIN]. Thank you, most kind of you. [*They sit down.*]

TRIGORIN. Your admirers send their best wishes. There's great interest in you in St. Petersburg and Moscow, and I'm always being asked about you—what's he like, how old is he, is he dark or fair? Somehow everyone thinks you're not all that young. And you publish under a pseudonym, so no one knows your real name. You're an enigma like the Man in the Iron Mask.

TREPLEV. Are you staying long?

TRIGORIN. No, I intend to go back to Moscow tomorrow, I have to. There's a novel I must finish soon, and then I promised to do something for a collection of stories. Business as usual, in other words.

[*While they are speaking,* IRINA *and* POLINA *put a card-table in the middle of the room and open it.* SHAMRAYEV *lights candles and places chairs round it. They take a game of lotto out of the cupboard.*]

TRIGORIN. The weather's not being very kind, there's a nasty wind. If it drops by tomorrow morning, I'm going fishing by the lake. And I must look at the garden while I'm about it, and the place where your play was put on—remember? I've a subject for a story and I only need to refresh my memory of the scene.

MASHA [*to her father*]. Father, can Simon have a horse? He must get home.

SHAMRAYEV [*derisively*]. Horse? Must get home? [*Sternly.*] They've only just been to the station, you can see for yourself. We can hardly have them out again.

MASHA. There are other horses. [*As her father does not speak, makes a gesture of despair.*] Oh, you're impossible.

MEDVEDENKO. I can walk, Masha, really——

POLINA [*with a sigh*]. Walk in weather like this! [*Sits down at the card-table.*] Come on, all of you.

MEDVEDENKO. Well, it's only four miles. Good night. [*Kisses his wife's hand.*] Good night, Mother. [*His mother-in-law reluctantly holds out her hand for him to kiss.*] If it weren't for the baby I wouldn't have bothered anyone. [*Bows to everyone.*] Good night. [*Goes out, walking in an apologetic way.*]

SHAMRAYEV. He can walk, can't he? He's not all that high and mighty.

POLINA [*bangs the table*]. Come on, everyone. Let's not waste time, they'll be calling us for supper soon.

[SHAMRAYEV, MASHA *and* DORN *sit at the table.*]

IRINA [*to* TRIGORIN]. In the long autumn evenings one plays lotto in these parts—look, the same old lotto that my mother played with us as children. Won't you have a game before supper? [*Sits at the table with* TRIGORIN.] It's boring, but not bad when you get used to it. [*Deals everyone three cards.*]

TREPLEV [*turning the pages of the magazine*]. He read his own story, but didn't even cut the pages of mine. [*Puts the magazine on the desk, then moves towards the door, left. Passing his mother, he kisses her on the head.*]

IRINA. How about you, Constantine?

TREPLEV. Sorry, I don't feel much like it, I'm going for a stroll. [*Goes out.*]

IRINA. The stake's ten copecks. Will you put up ten copecks for me, Doctor?

DORN. All right.

MASHA. Have you all staked? I'll begin. Twenty-two.

IRINA. Yes.

MASHA. Three.

DORN. Right.

MASHA. Have you put down three? Eight. Eighty-one. Ten.

SHAMRAYEV. Don't go so fast.

IRINA. I had such a reception in Kharkov, dears, I'm still dizzy.

MASHA. Thirty-four.

[*A sad waltz is played off-stage.*]

IRINA. The students almost brought the house down. I had three baskets of flowers, two bouquets and this. [*Takes a brooch from her breast and throws it on the table.*]

SHAMRAYEV. Yes, that's quite something.

MASHA. Fifty.

DORN. You mean five-oh?

IRINA. I was superbly turned out—that's something I do know, how to dress.

POLINA. Constantine's playing the piano—he's depressed, poor boy.

SHAMRAYEV. They're so nasty about him in the newspapers.

MASHA. Seventy-seven.

IRINA. He's a fool to let that bother him.

TRIGORIN. Things aren't going too well, he still can't find his real level. There's something vaguely odd about his stuff, and some of it even seems rather wild. None of his characters is ever really alive.

MASHA. Eleven.

IRINA [*looking round at* SORIN]. Bored, Peter? [*Pause.*] He's asleep.

DORN. Our senior civil servant's asleep.

MASHA. Seven. Ninety.

TRIGORIN. You wouldn't catch me writing if I lived in a house by a lake like this. I'd get over the urge and do nothing but fish.

MASHA. Twenty-eight.

TRIGORIN. To catch a perch or a ruff—what bliss!

DORN. Well, I believe in Constantine. He's got something, I tell you. He thinks in images, his stories are bright and vivid and I find them very moving. I'm only sorry he has no definite aims. He produces an effect, that's all, and mere effects don't get you all that far, do they? Are you glad your son's an author, Irina?

IRINA. You know, I've never yet read his stuff, never have time.

MASHA. Twenty-six.

[TREPLEV *comes in quietly and goes to his desk*.]

SHAMRAYEV [*to* TRIGORIN]. We still have that thing of yours, Boris.

TRIGORIN. What thing?

SHAMRAYEV. Constantine shot a seagull that time and you asked me to have it stuffed.

TRIGORIN. I can't remember. [*Reflecting*.] I can't remember.

MASHA. Sixty-six. One.

TREPLEV [*throws open the window and listens*]. Isn't it dark! I'm terribly worried, I don't know why.

IRINA. Do close the window, Constantine, there's a draught.

[TREPLEV *closes the window*.]

MASHA. Eighty-eight.

TRIGORIN. I've won, everybody.

IRINA [*gaily*]. Well done, well done.

SHAMRAYEV. Well done.

IRINA. The man's always lucky. (*Stands up*.] Now let's go and have a bite of something. The great man missed his lunch today. We'll go on again after supper. [*To her son*.] Leave your manuscripts, Constantine, and let's have supper.

TREPLEV. I won't, Mother, I'm not hungry.

IRINA. As you wish. [*Wakes* SORIN.] Peter, supper time. [*Takes* SHAMRAYEV'*s arm*.] I'll tell you about my reception at Kharkov.

[POLINA *puts out the candles on the table. Then she and* DORN *wheel out the bath-chair. All go out by the door, left.* TREPLEV, *who is sitting at the desk, is left alone on the stage.*]

TREPLEV [*is intending to write and looks through what he has already written*]. I've talked so much about new techniques, but now I feel I'm gradually getting in the old rut. [*Reads.*] "The notice on the fence stated." "A pale face, framed in dark hair." "Stated," "framed." Very second-rate. [*Crosses it out.*] I'll start when my hero's woken up by the rain and cut out all the rest. The description of the moonlit evening is long and forced. Trigorin's worked out his methods, it's easy enough for him. He gives you the neck of a broken bottle glittering against a weir and the black shadow of a mill-wheel—and there's your moonlit night all cut and dried. But I have a quivering light and the silent twinkling of the stars and the distant sound of a piano dying on the calm, scented air. This is agony. [*Pause.*] Yes, I'm more and more convinced that old or new techniques are neither here nor there. The thing is to write without thinking about technique—write from the heart, because it all comes pouring out. [*Someone knocks on the window nearest to the table.*] What's that? [*Looks through the window.*] Can't see anything. [*Opens the french window and looks into the garden.*] Someone ran down the steps. [*Calls.*] Who's there? [*Goes out and can be heard walking quickly along the terrace. Half a minute later he comes back with* NINA.] Nina, Nina!

[NINA *lays her head on his breast and sobs quietly.*]

TREPLEV [*very moved*]. Nina, Nina! It's you—you. I thought you'd come somehow, I've been terribly overwrought all day. [*Takes off her hat and cape.*] Oh, my dear, my darling. She's come! There now, don't cry.

NINA. There's someone here.

TREPLEV. No.

NINA. Lock the doors or someone may come in.

TREPLEV. No one will come in.

NINA. I know Irina Arkadin's here. Lock the doors.

TREPLEV [*locks the door, right, and goes over to the door,* left]. This one doesn't lock, I'll put a chair against it. [*Puts an armchair against the door*.] Don't worry, no one will come in.

NINA [*stares into his face*]. Let me look at you. [*Looks round the room*.] It's nice and warm. This used to be the drawing-room. Am I very changed?

TREPLEV. Yes. You're thinner and your eyes are bigger. It's somehow strange to be seeing you, Nina. Why wouldn't you let me visit you, why didn't you come and see us before? You've been here nearly a week, I know. I've been over every day several times and stood by your window like a beggar.

NINA. I was afraid you hated me. Every night I dream you look at me and don't recognize me. Oh, if only you knew! Ever since I arrived I've been going for walks—by the lake. I've been near your house lots of times, but couldn't bring myself to go in. Shall we sit down? [*They sit down*.] Let's sit down and talk and talk. It's nice and warm here, very cosy. Do you hear the wind? There's a passage in Turgenev: "Lucky the man with a roof over his head and somewhere to be warm on a night like this." I'm a seagull. No, that's wrong. [*Wipes her forehead*.] What was I saying? Oh yes, Turgenev. "And may the Lord help all homeless wanderers." Never mind. [*Sobs*.]

TREPLEV. Nina, you're crying again. Nina!

NINA. It's all right, it does me good. I hadn't cried for two years. I went in the garden late last night to see if our stage was still standing. And there it still is. I cried for the first time in two years, and it was such a relief, it did me a lot of good. See, I'm not crying any more. [*Takes him by the hand*.] So you're a writer now, you're a writer and I'm an actress, we've got caught up in this hectic whirl. I used to be as happy as a child and woke up singing in the morning, I loved you and dreamed of being famous. But now—. I have to go to Yelets early tomorrow morning, third class, along with the peasants. And when I get there I shall be pestered with the attentions of the more educated local businessmen. It's a rough life.

TREPLEV. Why Yelets?

NINA. I've taken an engagement for the winter. It's time I went.

TREPLEV. Nina, I cursed you, hated you, tore up your letters and photographs, but all along I've known that my whole being is bound up with you for ever. I can't help loving you, Nina. Since I lost you and began having my work published, life's been unbearable, sheer agony. It's as if I'd suddenly stopped being young, I feel as if I was ninety. I call upon you, kiss the ground you have trodden on. Wherever I look I see your face—the gentle smile that brightened the best years of my life.

NINA [*taken aback*]. Why does he say this—why, why?

TREPLEV. I'm lonely, I haven't the warmth of anyone's devotion. I feel cold, as in a vault, and all I write is so dry, stale, dismal. Stay here, Nina, I beg you, or let me go with you.

[NINA *quickly puts on her hat and cape.*]

TREPLEV. But why, Nina? For God's sake, Nina. [*Watches her put on her clothes. Pause.*]

NINA. My carriage is at the gate. Don't see me off, I'll manage on my own. [*Through tears.*] Give me some water.

TREPLEV [*gives her some*]. Where are you going now?

NINA. To town. [*Pause.*] Is Irina Arkadin here?

TREPLEV. Yes. Uncle was taken worse on Thursday and we telegraphed for her.

NINA. Why do you say you kissed the ground I trod on? I'm not fit to live. [*Bends over the table.*] Oh, I'm so tired, I need a rest, a rest. [*Lifts up her head.*] I'm a seagull. No, that's wrong. I'm an actress. Ah, well. [*Hearing* IRINA *and* TRIGORIN *laughing, she listens, then runs to the door, left, and looks through the keyhole.*] He's here too. [*Going back to* TREPLEV.] Ah, well. It doesn't matter. Yes. He didn't believe in the stage, he always laughed at my dreams and I gradually stopped believing too and lost heart. Then there were all the cares of love, jealousy and constant fears for the baby. I became petty and small-minded and my acting made no sense. I didn't know what to do with my hands or know how to stand on the stage, and I couldn't control my voice. You've no idea what it feels like to know you're acting abominably. I'm a seagull. No, that's wrong. Remember you shot a seagull? A man happened to come along, saw it and killed it, just to pass the time. A plot for a short story. No, that's wrong. [*Wipes her forehead*.] What was I saying? I was talking about the stage. Oh, I'm different now, I'm a real actress. I enjoy acting, I adore it. I get madly excited on stage, I feel I'm beautiful. And since I've been here, I've kept going for walks, walking round and thinking—thinking and feeling my morale improving every day. Constantine, I know now, I've come to see, that in our work—no matter whether we're actors or writers—the great thing isn't fame or glory, it isn't what I used to dream of, but simply stamina. You must know how to bear your cross and have faith. I have faith and things don't hurt me so much now. And when I think of my vocation I'm not afraid of life.

TREPLEV [*sadly*]. You've found your road and you know where you're going, while I still drift about in a maze of dreams and images, not knowing who needs my stuff or why. I've no faith and I don't know what my vocation is.

NINA [*pricking up her ears*]. Shush! I must go. Good-bye. Come and see me when I'm a great actress. Promise? But now—. [*Presses his hand*.] It's late. I can hardly stand— I'm so exhausted and hungry.

TREPLEV. Stay, I'll get you some supper.

NINA. No, no. Don't see me off, I'll go on my own. My carriage is quite near. So she brought him with her, did she? Oh well, what of it? When you see Trigorin, don't say anything to him. I love him—love him even more than before. A plot for a short story. I love him, love him passionately, desperately. Wasn't it nice in the old days, Constantine? Do you remember? What a life it was—so serene and warm, so happy and innocent. What emotions we felt—like exquisite, delicate blossoms. Do you remember? [*Recites*.] "Men, lions, eagles and partridges, horned deer, geese, spiders and silent fishes, denizens of the deep, starfishes and creatures invisible—that is, all life, all life, all life—has completed its melancholy cycle and died.

For thousands of centuries Earth has not borne one living creature, and in vain does that poor moon light her lamp. No longer do cranes awake and call in the meadows and no may-beetles can be heard in the lime-groves." [*Embraces* TREPLEV *impulsively and runs out through the french window.*]

TREPLEV [*after a pause*]. It'll be a pity if anyone sees her in the garden and tells Mother. It might upset her. [*Spends two minutes silently tearing up all his manuscripts and throwing them under the desk, then unlocks the door, right, and goes out.*]

DORN [*trying to open the door, left*]. That's strange, the door seems to be locked. [*Comes in and puts the armchair back in its place.*] An obstacle race.

[IRINA *and* POLINA *come in, followed by* JACOB, *carrying some bottles, and* MASHA, *and finally by* SHAMRAYEV *and* TRIGORIN.]

IRINA. Put the claret and Mr. Trigorin's beer on the table here, we can have a drink with our game. Come on, everyone, sit down.

POLINA [*to* JACOB]. And please bring in the tea right away. [*Lights the candles and sits down at the card-table.*]

SHAMRAYEV [*takes* TRIGORIN *over to the cupboard*]. Here's the thing I was talking about just now. [*Takes the stuffed seagull from the cupboard.*] Your order, sir.

TRIGORIN [*looking at the seagull*]. I can't remember. [*After some thought.*] I can't remember.

[*A shot is heard from off-stage, right. Everyone gives a start.*]

IRINA [*terrified*]. What's that?

DORN. Don't worry. A bottle must have gone off inside my medical bag, don't worry. [*Goes out through door, right, and comes back half a minute later.*] As I said. A bottle of ether's exploded. [*Sings softly.*] "Once more enchanted I appear before thee."

IRINA [*sitting down at the table*]. Oh dear, I was frightened. It

reminded me of when—. [*Covers her face with her hands.*]
It made me feel quite ill.

DORN [*turning the pages of a magazine, to* TRIGORIN]. There
was an article in this thing about two months ago, a letter
from America, and I wanted to ask you, amongst other
things—. [*Takes* TRIGORIN *by the waist and leads him to the
front of the stage.*] Being extremely interested in this
matter—. [*Dropping his voice, in an undertone.*] Get Irina
out of here somehow. The fact is, Constantine has shot
himself.

CURTAIN

UNCLE VANYA

[Дядя Ваня]

SCENES FROM COUNTRY LIFE
IN FOUR ACTS

[1897]

CHARACTERS

ALEXANDER SEREBRYAKOV, a retired professor

HELEN, his wife, aged 27

SONYA, his daughter by his first wife

MRS. VOYNITSKY, the widow of a high official and mother of the professor's first wife

VANYA VOYNITSKY, her son

MICHAEL ASTROV, a doctor

ILYA TELEGIN, an impoverished landowner

MARINA, an old nurse

A labourer

The action takes place on Serebryakov's estate

ACT ONE

The garden. Part of the house and terrace can be seen.
A table, laid for tea, stands on a path under an old
poplar. Benches and chairs. There is a guitar on one of
the benches. Near the table is a swing. It is between
two and three o'clock in the afternoon. The sky is
overcast.

MARINA, *a stout, elderly woman, slow in her move-*
ments, sits by the samovar knitting a stocking. ASTROV
walks up and down near her.

MARINA [*pours out a glass of tea*]. Do have some tea, Doctor.

ASTROV [*reluctantly accepts the glass*]. I don't really feel like it.

MARINA. A little vodka then?

ASTROV. No, it's not every day I drink vodka. Besides it's so
stuffy today. [*Pause.*] Nanny, how long have we known
each other?

MARINA [*considering*]. How long? Lord, let me think. You
first came to these parts—when was it? It was when Sonya's
mother was still alive. You used to come and see us in her
day. Now that went on for two winters, so it must have
been about eleven years ago. [*After a moment's thought.*]
Maybe more.

ASTROV. Have I changed much since then?

MARINA. Yes, you have. You were young and good-looking
then, but you're beginning to show your age now and your
looks aren't what they were either. Another thing, you like
your drop of vodka.

ASTROV. Yes. In ten years I've become a different man. And
I'll tell you why. It's overwork, Nanny. On my feet from
morning to night with never a moment's peace, and then
lying under the bedclothes at night afraid of being dragged
out to a patient. All the time we've known each other I

haven't had one day off. It's enough to make anyone look old. And then life here is so dreary and stupid and sordid. It gets you down, this life does. You're surrounded by the oddest people, because that's what they all are—odd. Spend a couple of years among them, and you gradually turn into a freak yourself and don't even notice it. That's bound to happen. [*Twists his long moustache.*] Look at this, I've grown a huge moustache. An idiotic moustache. I've become a freak, Nanny. Not that I've grown stupid yet, thank God, I still have my wits about me. But somehow I don't feel things keenly any more. I don't want anything, I don't seem to need anything and there's no one I'm fond of. Except just you perhaps. [*Kisses her head.*] I had a nanny like you when I was a little boy.

MARINA. Would you care for something to eat?

ASTROV. No thank you. A few weeks before Easter I went to Malitskoye. They had an epidemic there. Typhus. There were village people lying around all over the place in their huts. Filth, stench, smoke everywhere and calves on the floor mixed up with patients—little pigs as well. I was on the go all day—didn't so much as sit down or have a bite to eat—and even when I got home there was no rest for me. They brought someone in from the railway, a switchman. I got him on the table to operate, and damned if he didn't have to die on me under chloroform. Then just at the worst possible moment my feelings did come to life and I felt as guilty as if I'd murdered the man. I sat down and closed my eyes like this. And I thought of the men and women who will be alive a hundred or a couple of hundred years after we've gone, those we're preparing the way for. Will they have a good word to say for us? You know, Nanny, they won't even remember us.

MARINA. Men may forget, but God will remember.

ASTROV. Thank you for saying that. You put it very well.

[*Enter* VOYNITSKY.]

VOYNITSKY [*coming out of the house. He has been taking a nap after lunch and looks dishevelled. He sits on a bench and straightens his smart tie*]. Yes. [*Pause.*] Yes.

ASTROV. Had a good sleep?

VOYNITSKY. Yes. Very. [*Yawns.*] Since the professor and his wife came to live here everything's been turned upside down. I sleep at the wrong times, eat all sorts of fancy things for lunch and dinner, drink wine. It's all very bad for me. Before they came I never had a minute to myself. Sonya and I were pretty busy, I can tell you that. But now only Sonya works and I just sleep, eat and drink. It's all wrong.

MARINA [*shaking her head*]. Disgraceful, I call it. The professor doesn't get up till midday, but the samovar's kept on the boil all morning waiting his pleasure. Before they came we always had dinner about half past twelve like everyone else, but now they're here we don't have it till nearly seven. The professor sits up at night reading and writing. Then all of a sudden, past one in the morning, the bell goes. Goodness gracious, whatever can it be? Wants some tea, if you please. So you have to wake up the servants and put the samovar on. Disgraceful, I call it.

ASTROV. Are they staying here much longer?

VOYNITSKY [*whistles*]. A hundred years. The professor's decided to make his home here.

MARINA. And now look what they've done. Two hours that samovar's been on the table, and they've gone for a walk.

VOYNITSKY. They're coming, they're coming. Don't get excited.

[*Voices are heard.* SEREBRYAKOV, HELEN, SONYA *and* TELEGIN *come in from the far end of the garden on the way back from their walk.*]

SEREBRYAKOV. Wonderful, wonderful. What scenery!

TELEGIN. Magnificent indeed, sir.

SONYA. We're going to the forest reservation tomorrow, Father. Like to come?

VOYNITSKY. Let's have tea, everybody.

SEREBRYAKOV. Would you good people send some tea into the study for me, please? I have some more work to do today.

SONYA. I'm sure you'll like it out at the reservation.

[HELEN, SEREBRYAKOV *and* SONYA *go into the house.* TELEGIN *goes towards the table and sits down by* MARINA.]

VOYNITSKY. It's hot and stuffy today, but the great sage is complete with overcoat, galoshes, umbrella and gloves.

ASTROV. Obviously takes good care of himself.

VOYNITSKY. But isn't she lovely? Lovely! She's the most beautiful woman I've ever seen.

TELEGIN. When I go for a country drive, Nanny, or stroll in the shade of the garden or just gaze at this table here, I experience bliss beyond compare. The weather is enchanting, the birds are singing and we all live in peace and harmony. What more could we ask for? [*Accepting a glass of tea.*] I'm uncommonly obliged to you.

VOYNITSKY [*dreamily*]. What eyes! A marvellous woman.

ASTROV. Come on, Voynitsky. Talk to us.

VOYNITSKY [*listlessly*]. What do you want me to say?

ASTROV. Have you nothing new to tell us?

VOYNITSKY. No, I haven't. It's the same old story. I'm no different—worse, I daresay, because I've grown lazy and don't do anything apart from grousing away like an old fogy. And my dear mother, the old chatterbox, still keeps burbling on about the emancipation of women. She's got one foot in the grave, but she still reads all those solemn pamphlets and thinks they'll lead her to a new life.

ASTROV. And the professor?

VOYNITSKY. And the professor still sits in his study writing from morning till last thing at night.

> "With harassed brain and furrowed brow
> We pen heroic lays.
> But neither we nor they till now
> Have had one word of praise."

I pity the paper he writes on. He'd do better to work on his autobiography. What a superb subject! A retired professor—an old fossil, if you see what I mean, a sort of academic stuffed trout. He suffers from gout, rheumatism, migraine and liver trouble, and he's almost bursting with envy and jealousy. The old fossil lives on his first wife's estate. Not that he wants to live here, but he can't afford to live in town. He's forever moaning about his misfortunes, though as a matter of fact he's been pretty lucky. [*Agitatedly*.] Just think what luck he's had. The son of an ordinary parish clerk and educated at a church school, he's collected academic degrees and a university chair, become a person of consequence, married a senator's daughter and so on and so forth. None of that matters, though. But you note my next point. For precisely twenty-five years the man's been lecturing and writing about art. And what does he understand about art? Nothing. For twenty-five years he's been chewing over other people's ideas on realism, naturalism and every other kind of tomfoolery. For twenty-five years he's been lecturing and writing about things which every intelligent person has known all along, and which don't interest fools anyway. In other words he's spent twenty-five years chasing his own shadow. And all the time what ghastly conceit! What presumption! Now he's retired and not a living soul knows who he is. He's totally obscure. In other words, for twenty-five years he's been in the wrong job. But you just watch him strut about as if he was God Almighty.

ASTROV. I think you're really a bit envious.

VOYNITSKY. I most certainly am. And what success with women! Casanova himself couldn't have done better. His first wife, my own sister—a beautiful, gentle creature as pure as the blue sky above us, a fine, generous girl who had more admirers than he had pupils—she loved him as only angels in heaven can love beings as pure and lovely as themselves. My own mother, his mother-in-law, still idolizes him, still goes in awe of him. His second wife—she just came through here—is a beautiful, intelligent woman, and she married him when he was already an old man and gave him her youth, her beauty, her freedom, her radiance. Whatever for? Why?

ASTROV. Is she faithful to him?

VOYNITSKY. Yes, I'm sorry to say.

ASTROV. Why sorry?

VOYNITSKY. Because she's faithful in a way that's so thoroughly bogus. Oh, it sounds impressive enough, but it just doesn't make sense. To be unfaithful to an elderly husband you can't stand, that's immoral. But if you make these pathetic efforts to stifle your own youth and the spark of life inside you, that isn't immoral at all.

TELEGIN [*in a tearful voice*]. Vanya, I hate it when you talk like that. Well, really. Anyone who betrays a wife or husband could easily be unreliable enough to betray his country as well.

VOYNITSKY [*with annoyance*]. Turn the tap off, Waffles.

TELEGIN. No, let me go on, Vanya. The day after we were married my wife ran away with another man because of my unprepossessing appearance. Since then I've always done my duty. I still love her, I'm still faithful to her, I help her as much as I can and I've spent all I had on educating her children by this other man. I've lost my happiness, but I've kept my pride. What about her, though? She's no longer young, she's lost her looks—as was bound to happen sooner or later—and her lover is dead. So what has she got left?

[SONYA *and* HELEN *come in. A little later* MRS. VOYNITSKY *comes in with a book. She sits down and reads. She is given some tea and drinks it without looking up.*]

SONYA [*rapidly, to the* NURSE]. Nanny dear, some people have turned up from the village. Go and see what they want, please, and I'll pour the tea. [*Pours the tea.*]

[*The* NURSE *goes out.* HELEN *takes her cup and drinks, sitting on the swing.*]

ASTROV [*to* HELEN]. I really came to see your husband, you know. You did write to say he was very ill with rheumatism and something else. But it seems he's as fit as a fiddle.

HELEN. He was in a bad way last night and complained of pains in his legs, but today he's all right.

ASTROV. And I've driven twenty miles at top speed to get here. Oh well, never mind, it's not the first time. Anyway,

I'll stay till tomorrow now I am here and at least have a good night's rest. Just what the doctor ordered.

SONYA. And a very good idea too. You stay here so seldom. I don't suppose you've eaten.

ASTROV. No, I haven't as a matter of fact.

SONYA. Good, you can eat with us then. We dine about half past six these days. [*Drinks.*] The tea's cold.

TELEGIN. The temperature in the samovar has indeed considerably diminished.

HELEN. Never mind, Mr. Galetin, we'll drink it cold.

TELEGIN. Pardon me, madam. My name is not Galetin, madam, it's Telegin. Ilya Telegin or, as some people call me because of my pock-marked face, Waffles. I happen to be Sonya's godfather and Professor Serebryakov, your husband, knows me very well. I'm now living here on your estate, madam. And as you may possibly have noticed, I have dinner with you every day.

SONYA. Mr. Telegin is a great help and support to us. [*Affectionately.*] Would you like some more tea, Godfather dear?

MRS. VOYNITSKY. Oh!

SONYA. What's the matter, Grandmother?

MRS. VOYNITSKY. I forgot to tell Alexander, it slipped my mind. I had a letter today from Kharkov, from Paul Alekseyevich. He sent his new pamphlet.

ASTROV. Is it interesting?

MRS. VOYNITSKY. Interesting, but rather odd. He attacks the very position he was defending seven years ago. That's dreadful.

VOYNITSKY. There's nothing dreadful about it. Drink your tea, Mother.

MRS. VOYNITSKY. But I want to talk.

VOYNITSKY. For fifty years we've talked and talked and read pamphlets. And it's about time we stopped.

MRS. VOYNITSKY. For some reason you dislike the sound of my

voice. I'm sorry, my boy, but this last year you've changed out of all recognition. You used to be a man of such firm principles, a shining example—

VOYNITSKY. Oh yes, I've been an example of something all right, but I haven't exactly shone. [*Pause.*] A shining example. That's a pretty poisonous sort of joke. I'm forty-seven. Until last year I was like you, I deliberately tried to befuddle myself with your brand of pedantic humbug so as not to see life as it really is. I thought I was doing the right thing, but now—if you only knew! I can't sleep at night for frustration and anger at the stupid way I've wasted time when I might have had everything I can't have now because I'm too old.

SONYA. Uncle Vanya, this is boring.

MRS. VOYNITSKY [*to her son*]. You seem to be blaming your former principles for something, but they're not to blame. You are. You're forgetting that principles on their own don't mean anything, they're just so much dead wood. You should have *done* something.

VOYNITSKY. "Done something?" We can't all be non-stop writing machines like the learned professor.

MRS. VOYNITSKY. What exactly do you mean by that?

SONYA [*beseechingly*]. Grandmother! Uncle Vanya! Please!

VOYNITSKY. I am silent. Silent and repentant.

[*Pause.*]

HELEN. It's a perfect day. Not too hot.

[*Pause.*]

VOYNITSKY. It's a perfect day. For a man to hang himself.

[TELEGIN *tunes the guitar.* MARINA *walks about near the house calling the hens.*]

MARINA. Chuck, chuck, chuck.

SONYA. Nanny, what did those village people want?

MARINA. Same thing as before, they're still on about that bit of waste land. Chuck, chuck, chuck.

SONYA. Which one are you calling?

MARINA. Old Speckles has gone off somewhere with her chicks. The crows might get them. (*Walks away.*)

[TELEGIN *plays a polka. All listen in silence. The* LABOURER *comes in.*]

LABOURER. Is the doctor here? [*To* ASTROV.] Will you come please, Dr. Astrov? You're wanted.

ASTROV. Who by?

LABOURER. The factory.

ASTROV [*irritated*]. Much obliged, I'm sure. Oh very well then, I'll have to go. [*Looks round for his cap.*] This is a damn nuisance.

SONYA. It really is too bad. But do come back to dinner when you're finished at the factory.

ASTROV. No, it'll be too late. Where could I—? Where on earth—? [*To the* LABOURER.] Look, be a good fellow, do, and fetch me a glass of vodka. [*The* LABOURER *goes out.*] Where could I—? Where on earth—? [*Finds his cap.*] In one of Ostrovsky's plays there's a character with more whiskers than sense. That's me. Well, I must bid you all good day. [*To* HELEN.] If you ever care to look me up, you and Miss Serebryakov here, I'll be delighted to see you. I've a small estate of eighty acres or so, but if you're interested there's an orchard that's something of a show-piece and a nursery such as you won't find for hundreds of miles around. Next to my place there's the government forest reservation. The forester is getting on and his health's none too good, so I pretty well run the whole thing.

HELEN. I've already heard how fond you are of forestry work. You can do a lot of good that way of course, but doesn't it interfere with your real business in life? You are a doctor after all.

ASTROV. God alone knows what our real business in life is.

HELEN. And is it interesting?

ASTROV. It's interesting work, yes.

VOYNITSKY [*ironically*]. Oh, very!

HELEN [*to* ASTROV]. You're still young, you don't look more than—well, thirty-six or seven—and you can't really find it as interesting as all that. Nothing but trees and more trees. It must be a bit monotonous, I should think.

SONYA. No, it's extremely interesting. Dr. Astrov plants new woods every year and he's already been given a bronze medal and a certificate. He's doing his best to save the old forests from destruction. If you'll listen to what he has to say you'll agree with him completely. He says that forests are the glory of our earth, that they teach man to appreciate beauty and give him a sense of grandeur. Forests alleviate a harsh climate. In countries with a mild climate less effort is spent on the struggle for existence, so that men and women are gentler and more affectionate. In such places people are handsome, adaptable and sensitive, their speech is elegant and their movements are graceful. Art and learning flourish among them, their philosophy is cheerful and they treat their womenfolk with great courtesy and chivalry.

VOYNITSKY [*laughing*]. Loud cheers! This is all very charming, but not in the least convincing, so [*to* ASTROV] allow me, my friend, to carry on burning logs in my stoves and building my barns of wood.

ASTROV. You can burn peat in your stoves and make your barns of stone. All right, I grant your point—cut the timber if you need it. But why ruin the forests? The forests of Russia are crashing down before the axe, millions upon millions of trees perish, the homes of birds and beasts are devastated, rivers grow shallow and dry up, wonderful scenery disappears without trace, and all because man's so lazy—hasn't the sense to bend down and take his fuel from the ground. [*To* HELEN.] Don't you agree, madam? Only an unreasoning brute could burn beauty like this in his stove, destroying what we cannot create. Man has been endowed with reason, with the power to create, so that he can add to what he's been given. But up to now he hasn't been a creator, only a destroyer. Forests keep disappearing, rivers dry up, wild life's become extinct, the climate's ruined and the land grows poorer and uglier every day. [*To* VOYNITSKY.] You look at me ironically. You don't take any of this seri-

ously, and—and perhaps I really have got a bee in my
bonnet. But when I walk past our village woodlands which
I've saved from the axe or hear the rustle of my own
saplings, planted with my own hands, I feel that I too have
some slight control over the climate and that if man is
happy a thousand years from now I'll have done a bit
towards it myself. When I plant a young birch and later see
it covered with green and swaying in the breeze, my heart
fills with pride and I—. [*Seeing the* LABOURER, *who has
brought a glass of vodka on a tray*.] However, [*drinks*] I
must go. Anyway, this is all a bee in my bonnet, I daresay.
I bid you good day. [*Makes for the house*.]

SONYA [*takes his arm and goes with him*]. But when are you
coming to see us again?

ASTROV. I don't know.

SONYA. Not for another month again?

[ASTROV *and* SONYA *go into the house*. MRS. VOYNITSKY *and*
TELEGIN *remain near the table*. HELEN *and* VOYNITSKY *go
towards the terrace*.]

HELEN. Once again you've behaved abominably, Vanya. Did
you have to annoy your mother with that stuff about non-
stop writing machines? And you had another quarrel with
Alexander at lunch today. That's a rather poor way to
behave.

VOYNITSKY. But what if I hate him?

HELEN. There's no reason to hate Alexander, he's just the
same as anyone else. No worse than you are, anyway.

VOYNITSKY. If you could only see your face and the way you
move. It's as if life was too much for you, altogether too
much.

HELEN. Dear me, it is, and I'm so bored too. They all run
down my husband and look at me as if they're sorry for me.
"Poor girl, she's married to an old man." This sympathy for
me, oh how well I understand it. It's just what Astrov was
saying a moment ago—you all wantonly destroy the forests,
and soon there won't be anything left on earth. You destroy
men and women too every bit as wantonly, and soon,

thanks to you, there will be no loyalty, integrity or unselfishness left on earth. Why does it upset you so much to see a woman who doesn't belong to you? Because—and the doctor's right—there's a demon of destruction in every one of you. You don't spare anything, whether it's the trees, the birds—or women or one another.

VOYNITSKY. I hate this sort of pretentious talk. [*Pause*.]

HELEN. The doctor looks tired and highly-strung. It's an attractive face. Sonya's obviously taken with him—she's in love with him, and I can understand that. He's been here three times since I arrived, but I'm rather shy, so we've never had a proper talk and I've never been really friendly to him. He doesn't think I'm very nice. Do you know why you and I are such good friends, Vanya? It must be because we're both such abysmal bores. Yes, bores! Don't look at me in that way, I don't like it.

VOYNITSKY. How else can I look at you when I love you? You are my happiness, my life, my youth. I know there's little or no chance of your loving me, but I don't want anything from you. Only let me look at you, listen to your voice—

HELEN. Sh! Someone might hear you. [*They move towards the house*.]

VOYNITSKY [*following her*]. Let me speak of my love. So long as you don't drive me away, that's all I need to be the happiest man on earth.

HELEN. This is really too much. [*Both go into the house*.]

[TELEGIN *plucks the strings and plays a polka*. MRS. VOYNITSKY *makes a note in the margin of her pamphlet*.]

CURTAIN

ACT TWO

The dining-room of SEREBRYAKOV's *house. Night time.
The watchman can be heard tapping his stick in the
garden.* SEREBRYAKOV *sits dozing in an armchair by an
open window while* HELEN, *also dozing, sits by his side.*

SEREBRYAKOV [*opening his eyes*]. Who's there? Sonya, is it
you?

HELEN. It's me.

SEREBRYAKOV. Oh, it's you, Helen. I'm in agony.

HELEN. Your rug's fallen on the floor. [*Wraps it round his
legs.*] I'd better shut the window.

SEREBRYAKOV. No, it's too stuffy. Just now I dozed off and
dreamed that my left leg didn't belong to me. I woke up
with an excruciating pain. It can't be gout, it's more like
rheumatism. What time is it?

HELEN. Twenty past twelve. [*Pause.*]

SEREBRYAKOV. You might look out Batyushkov's poems for me
in the library tomorrow. I think we have them.

HELEN. What's that?

SEREBRYAKOV. Find me a Batyushkov in the morning. I seem
to remember we had one. But why do I find it so hard to
breathe?

HELEN. You're tired. This is the second night you've had no
sleep.

SEREBRYAKOV. That's how Turgenev is supposed to have got
angina, from having gout. I'm afraid it might happen to
me. Old age, what a damnable, repulsive thing it is, confound it. Since I've aged so much I've even begun to
disgust myself. And obviously none of you can stand the
sight of me.

HELEN. The way you go on about your age, anyone would
think it was all our fault.

SEREBRYAKOV. You're the one who really can't stand me.

[HELEN *gets up and sits down farther away*.]

SEREBRYAKOV. You're right of course. I'm not such a fool I
can't see it. You're a good-looking, healthy young woman
and you want a bit of life. And I'm an old man more dead
than alive. Well? Do you really think I don't understand?
Stupid of me of course to go on living at all. But just wait a
bit, I'll soon set you all free. I shan't last much longer.

HELEN. I feel quite faint. For God's sake be quiet.

SEREBRYAKOV. What it comes to is that you're all faint and
weary and you're all wasting the best years of your lives on
my account. While I'm the only person who's happy and
enjoys life. Obvious, isn't it?

HELEN. Do stop it. You've completely worn me out.

SEREBRYAKOV. But then I've worn everybody out, haven't I?
Obviously.

HELEN [*through tears*]. I can't stand any more. Look here—
what do you want from me?

SEREBRYAKOV. Nothing.

HELEN. Well, in that case stop talking. Please.

SEREBRYAKOV. It's a curious thing, but if Vanya Voynitsky or
that imbecile old mother of his ever say anything, that's
perfectly in order and everyone listens. But I've only to
open my mouth and everyone starts feeling miserable.
Even my voice disgusts you. All right, I'm disgusting, I'm
selfish, I'm a tyrant. But haven't I the right to a little
selfishness in my old age? Haven't I earned it? I'm asking
you, have I really no right to a peaceful old age and a little
consideration from others?

HELEN. Nobody's disputing your rights. [*The window bangs
in the wind*.] There's a wind getting up, I'd better shut that
window. [*Shuts it*.] It's going to rain. Nobody's disputing
your rights.

[*Pause. The watchman in the garden is heard tapping his stick and singing a song.*]

SEREBRYAKOV. You give your whole life to scholarship, you get used to your study, your lecture-room and your distinguished colleagues. Then suddenly, God knows why, you turn up in this dead and alive hole where you can't get away from fools and their inane chatter. I want some life, I like success, I like to be well-known and make a bit of a stir. But here—I might just as well be exiled to the depths of Siberia. To spend every moment regretting one's past, watching others succeed and going in fear of death—I can't stand it. It's too much! And now they won't even forgive me for growing old.

HELEN. Just wait and be patient. In five or six years I'll be old too.

[SONYA *comes in*.]

SONYA. Father, it was you who told us to send for Dr. Astrov, but now he's here you won't see him. It's not very polite. We've troubled him for nothing.

SEREBRYAKOV. What do I want with this Astrov of yours? He knows as much about medicine as I do about astronomy.

SONYA. We can hardly bring an entire medical faculty out here to attend to your gout.

SEREBRYAKOV. I won't even talk to him, he's a complete crackpot.

SONYA. Have it your own way. [*Sits down*.] I don't care.

SEREBRYAKOV. What time is it?

HELEN. Past midnight.

SEREBRYAKOV. It's stuffy in here. Sonya, will you get me that medicine from the table?

SONYA. Here you are. [*Hands him the medicine*.]

SEREBRYAKOV [*irritably*]. Oh really, not that one! It's no use asking for anything.

SONYA. Please stop behaving like a child. It may appeal to some people, but don't treat me that way, thank you very much. I dislike that sort of thing. Besides I'm too busy, I must be up early tomorrow. There's haymaking to see to.

[*Enter* VOYNITSKY *wearing a dressing-gown and carrying a candle.*]

VOYNITSKY. There's going to be a storm. [*A flash of lightning.*] Did you see that! Helen and Sonya, you go to bed. I've come to relieve you.

SEREBRYAKOV [*terrified*]. No, no! Don't leave me alone with him. No! He'll talk my head off.

VOYNITSKY. But you must let them have some rest, they were up all last night.

SEREBRYAKOV. Let them go to bed, but you go away too, thank you very much. I implore you in the name of our past friendship, don't argue. We'll talk some other time.

VOYNITSKY [*with an ironical grin*]. Our past friendship—. Our *past* friendship——.

SONYA. Please be quiet, Uncle Vanya.

SEREBRYAKOV [*to his wife*]. My dear, don't leave me alone with him. He'll talk my head off.

VOYNITSKY. This is becoming quite ridiculous.

[MARINA *comes in carrying a candle.*]

SONYA. Why don't you go to bed, Nanny? It's late.

MARINA. I haven't cleared away the tea things. Much hope I have of getting to bed.

SEREBRYAKOV. None of you can sleep, you're all in a state of collapse. The only person who's enjoying himself is me.

MARINA [*approaching* SEREBRYAKOV, *affectionately*]. What is it, my dear? Have you got a pain? My own legs ache, they ache something terrible. [*Arranges his rug.*] It's your old trouble. Sonya's poor mother used to miss her sleep of a night worrying about it. Ever so fond of you she was. [*Pause.*] Old folks are like children, they want a bit of affection, but who feels sorry for old folks? [*Kisses* SEREBRYAKOV *on the shoulder.*] Come along to bed, my dear.

Come on, my lamb, I'll give you some lime-flower tea and warm your poor feet. I'll say a prayer for you.

SEREBRYAKOV [*very touched*]. Come on then, Marina.

MARINA. My own legs ache and ache something terrible. [*Leading him with* SONYA's *help*.] Sonya's mother used to take on so, crying all the time. You were just a little child then, Sonya, didn't understand. Come on, come on, my dear.

[SEREBRYAKOV, SONYA *and* MARINA *go out*.]

HELEN. He's completely worn me out, I can hardly stand.

VOYNITSKY. He wears you out and I wear myself out. This is the third night I've had no sleep.

HELEN. We are in a bad way in this house. Your mother hates everything except her pamphlets and the professor. The professor's overwrought, he doesn't trust me and he's afraid of you. Sonya's annoyed with her father and with me too. She hasn't spoken to me for a fortnight. You loathe my husband and openly sneer at your mother, and I'm so much on edge I've been on the verge of tears a dozen times today. We are in a bad way, aren't we?

VOYNITSKY. We can do without the moralizing, thank you.

HELEN. You're an intelligent and civilized man, Vanya. I should have thought you could see why the world's heading for disaster. It's not fire and sword we have to blame, it's hatred, malice and all these sordid little squabbles. You ought to stop grousing and try to make peace here.

VOYNITSKY. First help me make peace with my own self. My darling—. [*Bends down and kisses her hand*.]

HELEN. Leave me alone. [*Removes her hand*.] Go away.

VOYNITSKY. Soon the rain will be over. All living things will revive and breathe more freely. Except me. The storm won't revive me. Day and night my thoughts choke me, haunt me with the spectre of a life hopelessly wasted. I've never lived. My past life has been thrown away on stupid trivialities and the present is so futile, it appals me. My life and my love—well, there you have it. What can I do with them? What can I make of them? My feelings are wasted like a ray of sunlight falling in a well, and I'm running to waste too.

HELEN. When you talk about love I somehow can't think or feel—words fail me. I'm sorry, but I've nothing to say to you. [*Makes to leave.*] Good night.

VOYNITSKY [*barring her way*]. And if you only knew how it hurts me to think that in this very house another life is wasting away besides my own. I mean yours. What are you waiting for? What's stopping you, dammit? Some wretched theory or other? Do, do get it into your head that——

HELEN [*stares at him*]. Vanya, you're drunk.

VOYNITSKY. Possibly, very possibly.

HELEN. Where's the doctor?

VOYNITSKY. In there. He's sleeping in my room tonight. Possibly, very possibly. Anything's possible.

HELEN. So you've been drinking again today, have you? What do you do it for?

VOYNITSKY. It at least gives one the illusion of being alive. Don't try and stop me, Helen.

HELEN. You never used to drink. You never used to talk so much either. Go to bed. You bore me.

VOYNITSKY [*bending down to kiss her hand*]. My darling. Wonderful woman!

HELEN [*with annoyance*]. Leave me alone. This is becoming quite disgusting. [*Goes out.*]

VOYNITSKY [*alone*]. She's gone. [*Pause.*] To think that ten years ago I used to meet her at my sister's when she was only seventeen and I was thirty-seven. Why didn't I fall in love then and ask her to marry me? It would have been the most natural thing in the world. And she'd be my wife now. Yes. And tonight the storm would have woken us both. She'd be scared of the thunder and I'd hold her in my arms and whisper, "Don't be afraid. I'm here." Oh, what wonderful thoughts, I could laugh for sheer joy. But oh God, my head's in such a whirl. Why am I so old? Why can't she understand me? The affected way she talks, her languid moralizing, those trivial, tired ideas about the world heading for disaster—how utterly I loathe it all. [*Pause.*] Oh, I've made such a fool of myself. I used to idolize that miserable, gout-ridden professor—worked my fingers to the bone for him. Sonya and I've squeezed every drop we could out of this estate and we've haggled over our linseed oil and peas and cream cheese like a couple of miserly peasants. We've gone short ourselves so we could scrape odd savings together and send him thousands of roubles. I was proud of him and his great learning. He was the very breath of life to me. Everything he wrote or uttered seemed to me inspired. But ye gods, what does it look like now? Now he's retired you can see exactly what his life is worth. Not a page of his work will survive him. He's totally obscure, a nonentity. A soap bubble! And I've made a fool of myself, I see it now, a complete fool.

[ASTROV *comes in. He wears a frock-coat, but no waistcoat or tie. He is a bit tipsy.* TELEGIN *follows him carrying a guitar.*]

ASTROV. Play something.

TELEGIN. But everyone's asleep.

ASTROV. Play.

[TELEGIN *strums softly.*]

ASTROV [*to* VOYNITSKY]. Here on your own? None of the ladies about? [*Puts his hands on his hips and sings softly.*]

"Come dance, my stove, come dance, my shed.
The master has nowhere to lay his head."

The storm woke me up. Quite a shower. What time is it?

VOYNITSKY. How the hell should I know?

ASTROV. I thought I heard Mrs. Serebryakov speaking.

VOYNITSKY. She was in here a moment ago.

ASTROV. Gorgeous creature. [*Looks at the medicine bottles on the table.*] Medicine, eh? Prescriptions from everywhere under the sun. From Moscow, Kharkov, Tula. Every town

in Russia has been plagued with his gout. Is he really ill or
just putting it on?

VOYNITSKY. He's ill. [*Pause*.]

ASTROV. Why so mournful tonight? Feeling sorry for the
professor or something?

VOYNITSKY. Leave me alone.

ASTROV. Or could it be that you're in love with Mrs. Professor?

VOYNITSKY. She's a friend of mine.

ASTROV. Already?

VOYNITSKY. What do you mean, "already"?

ASTROV. A woman can become a man's friend only in the
following stages—first an acquaintance, next a mistress,
and only then a friend.

VOYNITSKY. That's a pretty cheap line of talk.

ASTROV. Eh? Oh, yes. But then I'm becoming a pretty cheap
kind of person. Drunk too, you see. As a rule I only drink
this much once a month. When I'm in this state I get
terribly bumptious and impudent. I feel equal to anything.
I take on the most difficult operations and do them perfectly. Draw up the most sweeping plans for the future. At
such times I no longer think of myself as a freak and I
believe I'm bringing humanity enormous benefits. Enormous. And at such times I have my own philosophical
system and all of you, my lads, are no more than a lot of
insects so far as I'm concerned. Microbes. [*To* TELEGIN.]
Waffles, play on.

TELEGIN. Only too pleased to oblige, old man, but people are
trying to sleep, you know.

ASTROV. Play.

[TELEGIN *strums softly*.]

ASTROV. We need a drink. Come on, I think we still have
some brandy left in the other room. And as soon as it's
light we'll drive over to my place. Wodger say? I have an
assistant who can't say "what do you," always says "wodger."
A frightful rogue. So wodger say? [*Seeing* SONYA, *who is*

coming in.] Excuse me, I haven't got a tie on. [*Goes out quickly*. TELEGIN *follows him*.]

SONYA. So you've been drinking with the doctor again, Uncle Vanya. The boys *have* been getting together, haven't they? All right then, he's always that way inclined, but what's got into you? It doesn't suit you at your time of life.

VOYNITSKY. My time of life is neither here nor there. When people aren't really alive they live on illusions. It's better than nothing anyway.

SONYA. The hay's all cut, there's rain every day, and it's all rotting. And you spend your time on illusions. You've completely abandoned the farm. I do all the work myself and I'm about at the end of my tether. [*Alarmed*.] Uncle, you have tears in your eyes.

VOYNITSKY. What do you mean, tears? Nothing of the sort. Rubbish. The way you looked at me just now, your poor dear mother used to look like that. My darling—. [*Eagerly kisses her hands and face*.] My sister, my darling sister—. Where is she now? If she only knew! Oh, if she only knew!

SONYA. Knew what? What do you mean, Uncle?

VOYNITSKY. It's so painful, such a wretched business. Never mind, I'll tell you later. It doesn't matter—I'll go. [*Goes*.]

SONYA [*knocks at the door*]. Dr. Astrov! You aren't asleep, are you? May I see you a moment?

ASTROV [*through the door*]. Coming. [*Comes in after a short delay. He now has his waistcoat and tie on*.] Can I help you?

SONYA. You drink as much as you like if you don't find it disgusting, but for goodness' sake don't let my uncle drink. It's bad for him.

ASTROV. All right. We won't drink any more. [*Pause*.] I'll be off home now, so that's all well and truly settled. By the time the horses are harnessed it will be light.

SONYA. It's still raining. Why not wait till morning?

ASTROV. The storm's passing over, we shall pretty well miss it. I'll be off. And please don't ask me to attend your father again. I tell him it's gout, he says it's rheumatism, and if I ask him to lie down he sits up. And today he wouldn't talk to me at all.

SONYA. He's spoilt. [*Looks in the sideboard*.] Do you want something to eat?

ASTROV. Well, yes perhaps.

SONYA. I like eating in the middle of the night. We have some food in the sideboard, I think. Father's said to have been a great ladies' man in his day. Women have spoilt him. Here, have some cheese. [*Both stand by the sideboard and eat*.]

ASTROV. I haven't eaten all day, done nothing but drink. Your father's a very difficult man. [*Takes a bottle from the sideboard*.] May I? [*Drinks a glassful*.] There's no one else here, so I can speak freely. You know, I don't think I should survive a single month in your house, this air would choke me. Your father, so obsessed with his gout and his books, Uncle Vanya with his depressions, your grandmother, and then your step-mother——

SONYA. What about my step-mother?

ASTROV. People should be beautiful in every way—in their faces, in the way they dress, in their thoughts and in their innermost selves. She *is* beautiful, there's no question about that, but—let's face it, she does nothing but eat, sleep, go for walks and enchant us with her beauty. That's all. She has no responsibilities, and other people work for her. That's so, isn't it? But there's something wrong about a life of idleness. [*Pause*.] Well, perhaps I'm a bit harsh. I'm disappointed with life like your Uncle Vanya. He and I are turning into a couple of old grousers.

SONYA. Aren't you satisfied with life then?

ASTROV. I do like life in general, but the kind of provincial, parochial life we get in Russia—that I simply can't stand, in fact I heartily despise it. As for my own private life, well, heaven knows there's absolutely nothing good about that. You know, sometimes when you walk in a wood on a dark night there's a glimmer of light shining in the distance, isn't there? Then you don't notice how tired you are or how dark it is or how the thorns and twigs hit you in the face. As you well know, I work harder than anyone else round here, the most awful things are always happening to me and there are times when the whole business really gets me down. But for me there's no light shining in the distance. I don't expect anything for myself any more and I don't care for other people either. It's ages since I was really fond of anyone.

SONYA. You're not fond of anyone at all then?

ASTROV. No, I'm not, though I do have a soft spot for your nanny just for old time's sake. The peasants are all the same. They're uncivilized and they live in filth. And it's hard to get on with educated people. They make me so tired. These good friends of ours all think their shallow little thoughts and have their shallow little feelings, but not one of them can see farther than the end of his own nose. In fact they're just plain stupid. And the brighter ones who have a bit more to them, well, they're hysterical and go in for all this brooding and morbid introspection, all this whining, hating and slandering. They come crawling up to you, look at you sideways on and then proclaim, "Oh, he's a psychopath," or, "He talks a lot of hot air." And when they don't know how to label me they say, "He's an odd fellow, odd." I like forests. So that's odd. I don't eat meat, so that's odd too. They don't have straightforward, decent, free relationships any more either with nature or with other people. That's gone entirely. [*Is about to have a drink.*]

SONYA [*stops him*]. Please, I implore you, don't drink any more.

ASTROV. And why not?

SONYA. Because you're not that kind of person. You're so distinguished, you have such a gentle voice. And then again, you're so different from everyone else I know. You're a really fine man. So why ever should you want to be like ordinary people, the sort who drink and play cards? Oh don't be like that. Please! You're always saying that man doesn't create anything, that he only destroys what God has given him. Then why, oh why, destroy your own self? Don't do it, don't do it, I beg you, I implore you.

ASTROV [*holds out his hand to her*]. I'll stop drinking then.

SONYA. Give me your word.

ASTROV. My word of honour.

SONYA [*clasps his hand firmly*]. Thank you.

ASTROV. Right, that's settled. Now I'm sober. Yes, as you see, I'm now quite sober, and sober I shall remain till the end of my days. [*Looks at his watch.*] Right, let's go on. The fact is, my time's run out and I'm rather past it all. I feel so old, I've worked myself to a standstill and become thoroughly second-rate. I don't feel things keenly any more and I don't think I could grow fond of anyone any more. There's no one I love, or ever shall love now. One thing still thrills me—beauty. That does affect me very much. I think if Helen Serebryakov wanted to for instance, she could turn my head in a day. But then that wouldn't be love or affection. [*Covers his eyes with his hand and shudders.*]

SONYA. What's the matter?

ASTROV. Nothing. Just before Easter one of my patients died under chloroform.

SONYA. It's time you forgot about that. [*Pause.*] Tell me, Dr. Astrov, suppose I had a friend or a younger sister and you found out that she—well, let's say she loved you. What would be your attitude?

ASTROV [*shrugging his shoulders*]. I don't know. I don't suppose I'd have an attitude. I should make it clear to her I couldn't love her. After all I do have other things to think about. Anyway, if I'm to go it's time I went. I'll say good-bye, my dear, or else we shan't be finished till the sun's up. [*Shakes hands with her.*] I'll go out through the drawing-room if I may, otherwise your uncle might keep me back. [*Goes out.*]

SONYA [*alone*]. He didn't say anything to me. I still don't know what his real feelings are, but why, why do I feel so happy? [*Laughs happily.*] I told him, "You're so distin-

guished, such a fine man, you have such a gentle voice."
Surely that didn't sound out of place. His voice vibrates so
tenderly, I can still hear it ringing in the air. But when I
spoke about a younger sister he didn't understand. [*Wringing her hands.*] Oh, how dreadful not to be beautiful. It's
dreadful. And I know I'm not beautiful, I know, I know, I
know. Coming out of church last Sunday I heard some
people talking about me and one woman said, "She's such
a nice, kind girl. What a pity she's so plain." So plain.

[HELEN *comes in.*]

HELEN [*opens the windows*]. The storm's over. What wonderful air. [*Pause.*] Where's the doctor?

SONYA. Gone home. [*Pause.*]

HELEN. Sonya.

SONYA. What?

HELEN. When are you going to stop sulking? We've done
each other no harm, so why should we be enemies? Can't
we make it up?

SONYA. I've wanted to myself. [*Embraces her.*] Let's not be
angry any more.

HELEN. That's splendid. [*Both are very moved.*]

SONYA. Has Father gone to bed?

HELEN. No, he's in the drawing-room. We don't speak to
each other for weeks on end and heaven knows why.
[*Noticing that the sideboard is open.*] What's this?

SONYA. Dr. Astrov has been having some supper.

HELEN. There's wine too. Let's drink to our friendship.

SONYA. Yes, let's.

HELEN. From the same glass. [*Fills it.*] That's better. So
we're friends now, Sonya?

SONYA. Friends, Helen. [*They drink and kiss each other.*]
I've wanted to make it up for ages, but I felt too embarrassed somehow. [*Cries.*]

HELEN. But why are you crying?

SONYA. Never mind, it's nothing.

HELEN. There, there, that'll do. [*Cries.*] You silly girl, now I'm crying too. [*Pause.*] You're angry with me because you think I married your father for selfish reasons. I give you my word of honour, if that means anything to you, that I married him for love. He attracted me as a scholar and public figure. It wasn't real love, it was quite artificial, but it seemed real enough at the time. It wasn't my fault. But since the day we were married you've been tormenting me by looking as if you knew what I was up to and didn't much like it.

SONYA. Please, please, remember we're friends now. Let's forget all that.

HELEN. You shouldn't look at people like that, it doesn't suit you. One must trust people or life becomes impossible. [*Pause.*]

SONYA. Tell me honestly as a friend. Are you happy?

HELEN. No.

SONYA. I knew it. Another question. Tell me frankly, do you wish you were married to somebody younger?

HELEN. What a child you are. Of course I do. [*Laughs.*] All right, ask me something else, go on.

SONYA. Do you like the doctor?

HELEN. Yes I do, very much.

SONYA [*laughs*]. I have a foolish expression on my face, haven't I? He's just left, but I can still hear his voice and footsteps. And if I look into a dark window I seem to see his face in it. Let me finish what I have to say. But I can't say it out loud like this, I feel too embarrassed. Let's go to my room and talk there. Do you think I'm silly? You do, don't you? Tell me something about him.

HELEN. All right.

SONYA. He's so intelligent. He can do anything, he's so clever. He practises medicine, plants trees——

HELEN. There's a bit more to it than medicine and trees.

Don't you see, my dear? He's a brilliant man. And you know what that means? It means he has courage, flair, tremendous vision. When he plants a tree he's already working out what the result will be in a thousand years' time, already glimpsing man's future happiness. People like that are rare and should be cherished. He drinks and is sometimes a bit rude, but never mind that. In Russia a brilliant man can't exactly be a saint. Just think what the doctor's life is like. Roads deep in mud, freezing cold, blizzards, enormous distances, coarse, brutal peasants, poverty and sickness on all sides. If a man does his job and battles on day in day out in conditions like these, you can't expect that at the age of forty he'll still be a good little boy who doesn't drink. [*Kisses her.*] I wish you happiness with all my heart. You deserve it. [*Stands up.*] As for me, I'm just a tiresome character and not a very important one. In my music, in my husband's house, in all my romantic affairs—in everything, that is—I've always played a minor role. Come to think of it, Sonya, I'm really very, very unhappy. [*Walks agitatedly up and down the stage.*] There's no happiness for me in this world. None at all. What are you laughing at?

SONYA [*laughing and hiding her face*]. I'm so happy. So happy.

HELEN. I feel like playing the piano. I'd like to play something now.

SONYA. Yes, do. [*Embraces her.*] I can't sleep. Do play something.

HELEN. Just a minute, your father's still awake. Music annoys him when he's unwell. Go and ask him and I'll play something if he doesn't mind. Go on.

SONYA. All right. [*Goes out.*]

[*The watchman is heard tapping his stick in the garden.*]

HELEN. It's ages since I played anything. I'll play and cry, cry my eyes out like a silly girl. [*Through the window.*] Is that you knocking, Yefim?

WATCHMAN [*off stage*]. Yes madam.

HELEN. Stop it then. The master's unwell.

WATCHMAN [*off stage*]. I'm just going. [*Whistles under his breath.*] Hey there, good dogs. Come, boy! Good dog! [*Pause.*]

SONYA [*returning*]. He says no.

CURTAIN

ACT THREE

The drawing-room of SEREBRYAKOV'*s house. Three doors, right, left and centre. It is early afternoon.*

VOYNITSKY and SONYA *are seated.* HELEN *walks up and down, deep in thought.*

VOYNITSKY. The learned professor has graciously desired us all to assemble in the drawing-room here at one o'clock today. [*Looks at his watch.*] It's a quarter to. He has some message for the world.

HELEN. It's more likely a business matter.

VOYNITSKY. He never deals in such things. All he ever does is write nonsense, grumble and feel jealous.

SONYA [*reproachfully*]. Uncle!

VOYNITSKY. All right, all right. I'm sorry. [*Points to* HELEN.] Look at the way she goes around, nearly falling over from sheer laziness. A charming sight, I must say.

HELEN. Really, you do keep on and on so the whole day. Don't you ever get tired? [*Miserably.*] I'm bored to death, I don't know what to do.

SONYA [*shrugging her shoulders*]. There's plenty to do if you wanted to.

HELEN. Well, what for example?

SONYA. You could help to run the farm. You could do some teaching or nursing, there's plenty to do. For instance, before you and Father lived here Uncle Vanya and I used to go to market and sell our own flour.

HELEN. I'm no good at that sort of thing, and besides I'm not interested. It's only in a certain kind of earnest novel that people go in for teaching and dosing peasants. And do you really see me suddenly dropping everything to run round nursing and teaching?

SONYA. What I don't understand is how you can help wanting to go and teach. You'd get used to it after a bit. [*Embraces her.*] Don't be bored, dear. [*Laughing.*] You're bored, you don't know what to do with yourself and boredom and idleness are infectious. Look—Uncle Vanya does nothing but trail round after you like a shadow. I've left my work and rushed along here to talk to you. And I've grown so impossibly lazy. Then Dr. Astrov used to come here very seldom, once a month—it was hard to get him here at all—but now he visits us every day and he's quite abandoned his trees and his patients. You must be a witch.

VOYNITSKY. Why so downhearted? [*Vigorously.*] No really, my dear, splendid creature, do be sensible. There's mermaid's blood flowing in your veins. So go on, be a mermaid. Let yourself go for once in your life and fall madly in love with a river-god, dive head first into deep water and leave the learned professor and the rest of us gasping on the shore.

HELEN [*angrily*]. Leave me alone. How can you be so cruel? [*Makes to leave.*]

VOYNITSKY [*preventing her*]. Very well, my dear, forgive me. I'm sorry. [*Kisses her hand.*] Let's be friends.

HELEN. You'd try the patience of a saint, you know.

VOYNITSKY. I'll fetch you a bunch of roses as a peace offering. I got them for you this morning. Autumn roses, beautiful and sad—. [*Goes out.*]

SONYA. Autumn roses, beautiful and sad—. [*Both look out of the window.*]

HELEN. September already. How ever shall we get through the winter here? [*Pause.*] Where's the doctor?

SONYA. In Uncle Vanya's room, writing. I'm glad Uncle went out, I must talk to you.

HELEN. What about?

SONYA. What about? [*Puts her head on* HELEN's *breast.*]

HELEN. There there, that'll do. [*Strokes her hair.*] There now.

SONYA. I'm not beautiful.

HELEN. You have lovely hair.

SONYA. No. [*Turns round and looks in the mirror.*] No. When a woman isn't beautiful, people always say, "You have lovely eyes, you have lovely hair." I've loved him for six years. I love him more than I loved my own mother. Every moment I seem to hear his voice or feel his hand in mine. I keep looking at the door, expecting him, thinking he's just going to come in and now, as you see, I'm always coming to you to talk about him. He visits us every day now, but he doesn't look at me, doesn't even see me. It's breaking my heart. There's no hope for me, no hope at all. [*Desperately.*] God, give me strength. I spent the whole night praying. I often go up to him, start talking to him, look into his eyes. I've no pride left, no self-control. Yesterday I couldn't help telling Uncle Vanya I was in love, and all the servants know. Everyone knows.

HELEN. Does he know?

SONYA. No. He doesn't even notice me.

HELEN [*thoughtfully*]. He's a strange man. I tell you what, let me talk to him. I'll be most discreet, I'll only drop a hint or two. [*Pause.*] Really, how much longer is this uncertainty to go on? Do let me.

[SONYA *nods.*]

HELEN. Well, that's settled. It won't be hard to find out whether he loves you or not. Now don't be embarrassed, my dear, don't worry, I'll question him so carefully he won't even notice. We only need to find out whether it's yes or no. [*Pause.*] If it's no he'd better stop coming here, don't you think?

[SONYA *nods.*]

HELEN. It'll be easier for you if you don't see him. Now we won't keep putting it off, we'll question him straight away. He was going to show me some maps. You go and tell him I want to see him.

SONYA [*very agitated*]. You will tell me the whole truth, won't you?

HELEN. Of course I will. It's always better to know the truth, however bad, or that's what I think. Better than not knowing, anyway. Depend on me, dear.

SONYA. Yes, yes, I'll say you want to see his maps. [*Starts to leave, then stops by the door.*] No, not knowing *is* better. At least there's still hope.

HELEN. What did you say?

SONYA. It doesn't matter. [*Goes out.*]

HELEN [*alone*]. There's nothing worse than knowing someone else's secret and not being able to help. [*Meditatively.*] He's not in love with her, that's obvious, but why shouldn't he marry her? She isn't beautiful, but for a country doctor at his time of life she'd make an excellent wife. She's such a clever girl, so kind and unspoilt. But no, that's not really the point at all. [*Pause.*] I understand the poor child so well. In the middle of all this ghastly boredom, where there are no real people, but just dim, grey shapes drifting round, where you hear nothing but vulgar trivialities, where no one does anything but eat, drink and sleep—h̬ appears from time to time, so different from the others, so handsome, charming and fascinating, like a bright moon rising in the darkness. To fall under the spell of such a man, to forget everything—. I do believe I'm a little attracted myself. Yes, I'm bored when he's not about and here I am smiling as I think of him. And Uncle Vanya says I've mermaid's blood in my veins. "Let yourself go for once in your life." Well, and why not? Perhaps that would be the thing. Oh to fly away, free as a bird, away from you all, away from your sleepy faces and your talk, to forget that you so much as exist! But I'm such a coward, I'm so shy. My conscience would torment me. He comes here every day now. I can guess why, and I already feel guilty. I want to kneel down and cry and ask Sonya to forgive me.

ASTROV [*entering with map*]. Good afternoon. [*Shakes hands.*] You wanted to see these works of art?

HELEN. You did promise yesterday to show me some of your work. Can you spare the time?

ASTROV. Why, of course. [*Spreads the map on a card table and fixes it with drawing-pins.*] Where were you born?

HELEN [*helping him*]. In St. Petersburg.

ASTROV. And where were you educated?

HELEN. At the College of Music.

ASTROV. Then I don't suppose this will interest you.

HELEN. Why not? It's true I know nothing about country life, but I've read a great deal.

ASTROV. I have my own table in this house, in Voynitsky's room. When I'm worn out, absolutely dead beat, I drop everything, run along here and spend an hour or two amusing myself with this stuff. Voynitsky and Miss Serebryakov click away on their counting frame while I sit near by at my table messing about with my paints. It's warm and peaceful and the cricket chirps. But I don't allow myself this pleasure very often, only once a month. [*Pointing to the map.*] Now look at this. This gives a picture of our district as it was fifty years ago. Dark green and light green stand for woodlands, and half the entire area was wooded. Where I have this red cross-hatching over the green, that was the home of elk and wild goat. I show both flora and fauna. This lake here was the home of swans, geese and wild duck, and they made "a powerful lot of birds," as the old peasants say, no end of them—whole clouds swarming overhead. Besides the villages and larger settlements there were, as you see, isolated hamlets all over the place, odd farmsteads, hermitages and watermills. There were lots of cattle and horses. Those are shown in blue. Do you see this area where there's such a lot of blue? There were any number of horses here, an average of three per household. [*Pause.*] Now let's look lower down and see what things were like twenty-five years ago. Here only a third of the area's under timber. There are no more wild goats, but there are still some elk. The green and blue colouring is less in evidence. And so it goes on, so it goes on. Now let's move on to part three, a picture of the district as it is today. There are odd bits of green here and there in patches, but no continuous stretches. The elk, swans and wood-grouse are no more. The old hamlets, farmsteads, hermitages and mills have vanished without trace. The general picture is one of a gradual and unmistakable decline, and it obviously needs only another ten or fifteen years to become complete. You'll tell me it's the influence of civilization, that the old life obviously had to make way for the new. All right, I see what you mean. If roads and railways had been built in place of the ravaged woodlands, if we had factories, workshops and schools, the peasants would have become healthier, better off and more intelligent. But you see, nothing of the sort has happened. Our district still has the same old swamps and mosquitoes, the same terrible roads, the same poverty, typhus, diphtheria, the same fires breaking out all over the place. The point is, everything's gone downhill because people have found the struggle for existence too much for them, because they're backward and ignorant, because they haven't the faintest idea what they're doing. Shivering with cold, hungry and ill, man wants to hang on to what's left of his life, wants to protect his children, and so he clutches instinctively and blindly at anything that might fill his belly and keep him warm. He destroys everything with no thought for the morrow. And now pretty well everything has been destroyed, but so far nothing new has been put in its place. [*Coldly.*] I can see this bores you.

HELEN. But I understand so little about these things.

ASTROV. It's not a question of understanding, you're just not interested.

HELEN. To be perfectly honest, I was thinking about something else. I'm sorry, I have to put you through a sort of cross-examination and I feel a bit embarrassed. I don't know how to begin.

ASTROV. A cross-examination?

HELEN. Yes, but—a fairly harmless one. Let's sit down. [*They sit down.*] It concerns a certain young person. Let's be honest with each other like good friends and come straight to the point. We'll talk it over and then forget about it. All right?

ASTROV. All right then.

HELEN. It's about my step-daughter Sonya. Do you like her?

ASTROV. Yes I do, I think very highly of her.

HELEN. Does she attract you as a woman?

ASTROV [*after a short pause*]. No.

HELEN. I've very nearly finished. Haven't you noticed anything?

ASTROV. No.

HELEN [*taking him by the arm*]. You don't love her, I can see it in your eyes. She's so unhappy. Do understand that and—stop coming here.

ASTROV [*standing up*]. I'm a bit past all that. I have too much to do anyway. [*Shrugs his shoulders.*] You know how busy I am. [*Is embarrassed.*]

HELEN. Really, what a disagreeable conversation. I'm so upset, I feel as if I'd been dragging a ton weight about. Anyway, thank heavens it's over. Let's forget it, let's pretend nothing's been said, and you—you go away. You're a sensible man, you can understand. [*Pause.*] It's even made me blush.

ASTROV. If you'd told me a month or two ago I might perhaps have considered it, but now—. [*Shrugs his shoulders.*] But if she's unhappy, then of course—. There is one thing I don't understand, though—why did you bring this business up at all? [*Looks into her eyes and wags a finger at her.*] You're quite a little box of tricks, aren't you?

HELEN. What do you mean?

ASTROV [*laughing*]. You've got it all worked out, haven't you? All right, Sonya may be unhappy, I'll grant you that—but why interrogate me? [*Vigorously, preventing her from speaking.*] Now don't try and look so surprised. You know perfectly well why I come here every day. Why I come and who I come to see, that you know perfectly well. Don't look at me like that, you little vampire, I'm not exactly new to this game.

HELEN [*bewildered*]. Vampire? I don't understand at all.

ASTROV. You beautiful furry little weasel. You must have your prey. For a whole month I do nothing at all, let everything slide because I simply have to see you. And you like that, don't you, oh yes you like that very much indeed. Well now, what am I to say? I'm conquered, as you very well knew without cross-examining me at all. [*Folding his arms and bowing his head.*] I surrender. Come on, eat me.

HELEN. You must be out of your mind.

ASTROV [*laughing through clenched teeth*]. Quite standoffish, aren't you?

HELEN. Oh, I'm not quite so bad or so despicable as you think, I can tell you. [*Makes to leave.*]

ASTROV [*barring her way*]. I'll go away today, I won't come here any more, but—. [*Takes her by the hand and looks around.*] Where can I see you? Tell me quickly, where? Someone may come in, tell me quickly. [*Passionately.*] You splendid, glorious creature. One kiss—just let me kiss your hair, your fragrant hair.

HELEN. I do assure you that——

ASTROV [*preventing her from speaking*]. You assure me, do you? No need for that. No need to say anything either. Oh, how beautiful you are. What lovely hands! [*Kisses her hands.*]

HELEN. That's quite enough. Really! Go away. [*Withdraws her hands.*] You're forgetting yourself.

ASTROV. But tell me, tell me, where can we meet tomorrow? [*Puts his arm round her waist.*] You see, Helen, there's no getting away from it, we must meet. [*Kisses her just as* VOYNITSKY *comes in with a bunch of roses and stops near the door.*]

HELEN [*not seeing* VOYNITSKY]. Please let me go. Leave me alone. [*Lays her head on* ASTROV'S *chest.*] No! [*Tries to get away.*]

ASTROV [*holding her by the waist*]. Come to the forest reservation tomorrow. Be there by two o'clock. You will come, won't you? For God's sake say you'll come.

HELEN [*seeing* VOYNITSKY]. Let me go. [*Goes towards the window in great agitation.*] This is dreadful.

VOYNITSKY [*puts the roses on a chair, then agitatedly wipes his face and neck with a handkerchief*]. Never mind, that is—. It doesn't matter.

ASTROV [*inwardly fuming*]. Today's weather, my dear Voynitsky, isn't bad at all. It was dull and looked like rain this morning, but now the sun's come out. It certainly has been a splendid autumn, and the winter corn isn't doing too badly. [*Rolls up the map.*] The trouble is, though, the days are drawing in. [*Goes out.*]

HELEN [*going quickly up to* VOYNITSKY]. You must do everything you can, everything in your power, to get my husband and me away from this place. And it must be today. Do you hear? Today!

VOYNITSKY [*wiping his face*]. What? Oh, yes—of course. Helen, I saw what happened, I——

HELEN [*excitedly*]. Do you hear what I say? I must get away from this place today.

[*Enter* SEREBRYAKOV, SONYA, TELEGIN *and* MARINA.]

TELEGIN. I'm a bit out of sorts myself, Professor, been poorly these last two days. Something the matter with my head, er——

SEREBRYAKOV. But where are the others? I hate this house. It's such a labyrinth, twenty-six enormous rooms with people wandering off in all directions so you can never find anyone. [*Rings.*] Ask my mother-in-law and my wife to come here.

HELEN. I *am* here.

SEREBRYAKOV. Ladies and gentlemen, pray be seated.

SONYA [*going up to* HELEN, *impatiently*]. What did he say?

HELEN. I'll tell you later.

SONYA. You're trembling, aren't you? You're quite upset. [*Looks inquiringly into her face.*] I see. He said he wouldn't be coming here again. Is that it? [*Pause.*] Tell me, is it that?

[HELEN *nods.*]

SEREBRYAKOV [*to* TELEGIN]. One can put up with ill health.

What does it matter anyway? But what I can't stand is the whole pattern of country life. I feel as if I'd left the earth entirely and got stuck on some strange planet. Do sit down, everyone, please. Sonya! [SONYA *does not hear him, but stands sadly hanging her head.*] Sonya! [*Pause.*] She doesn't hear. [*To* MARINA.] And you sit down too, Nanny. [MARINA *sits down and knits a stocking.*] Now! Friends, ladies, gentlemen, lend me your ears, as the saying goes. [*Laughs.*]

VOYNITSKY [*agitated*]. You don't need me, do you? Do you mind if I go?

SEREBRYAKOV. Yes, I need you more than anyone else.

VOYNITSKY. What exactly do you require of me?

SEREBRYAKOV. "Require of you?" But why are you so upset? [*Pause.*] If I've offended you somehow, please forgive me.

VOYNITSKY. Oh, don't be so pompous and let's get down to business. What do you want?

[MRS. VOYNITSKY *comes in.*]

SEREBRYAKOV. Ah, here is Mother. Ladies and gentlemen, I'll begin. [*Pause.*] Ladies and gentlemen, I have invited you here to announce that a government inspector is on his way. Actually, joking apart, I do have something serious to say. I have gathered you all here to ask for your help and advice. And, aware as I am of your unfailing kindness, I trust I shall receive the same. I'm an academic person, a man of books, and I've always been out of my depth in practical affairs. I cannot manage without the guidance of competent persons, so I appeal to you, Vanya, to you, Mr. Telegin, and to you, Mother. The thing is that *manet omnes una nox*. In other words none of us is going to live for ever. I'm old and ill, so it seems to me high time to put my property and affairs in order in so far as they affect my family. My own life is over and I'm not thinking of myself, but I do have a young wife and an unmarried daughter. [*Pause.*] I simply cannot go on living in the country. We are not cut out for country life. But we can't live in town either on the income from this estate. Let's say we sell some of the timber—well, that's an abnormal measure which can't be repeated every year. We must find some procedure that guarantees us a constant, more or less stable income. Such a procedure has occurred to me and I have the honour to submit it for your consideration. I'll leave out the details and explain it in general terms. Our estate gives an average return of no more than two percent on its capital value. I propose we sell it. If we invest the proceeds in securities we should get from four to five per cent on them and there may even be a few thousand roubles to spare, so that we can buy a cottage near St. Petersburg.

VOYNITSKY. Just a moment. My ears must be deceiving me. Say that again.

SEREBRYAKOV. Invest the money in securities and buy a cottage near St. Petersburg with what's left over.

VOYNITSKY. No, it wasn't the bit about St. Petersburg. It was something else you said.

SEREBRYAKOV. I propose selling the estate.

VOYNITSKY. Ah, that was it. You're going to sell the estate. Wonderful. A very bright idea. And what do you suggest my old mother and I should do with ourselves? And what about Sonya here?

SEREBRYAKOV. We'll discuss that all in good time. One can't do everything at once.

VOYNITSKY. Just a moment. It looks as if I've never had a scrap of ordinary common sense. Till now I've been stupid enough to think this estate belonged to Sonya. This estate was bought by my father as a dowry for my sister. So far I've been simple-minded enough to imagine that our laws weren't made in Turkey and I thought the estate had passed from my sister to Sonya.

SEREBRYAKOV. Yes, the estate does belong to Sonya. Nobody denies that. Without Sonya's consent I shouldn't venture to sell it. Besides, it's in the girl's own best interests that I propose to do so.

VOYNITSKY. But this is fantastic, utterly fantastic. Either I've gone stark, staring mad or—. Or else——

MRS. VOYNITSKY. Vanya dear, don't contradict Alexander. He

knows better than we do what's right and what's wrong, believe me.

VOYNITSKY. Oh, give me some water. [*Drinks water*.] Say what you like then, I give up.

SEREBRYAKOV. I don't know why you're so worked up. I'm not claiming my scheme is ideal. If you all decide it's no good I shan't insist on it. [*Pause*.]

TELEGIN [*embarrassed*]. I revere scholarship, Professor, and even have a kind of family feeling for it. My brother Gregory's wife's brother, a Mr. Konstantin Lakedemonov— you may possibly know him—was a Master of Arts.

VOYNITSKY. One moment, Waffles, this is serious. Wait a bit, you can tell us later. [*To* SEREBRYAKOV.] Here, ask him. This estate was bought from his uncle.

SEREBRYAKOV. Oh indeed, and why should I ask him? Where would that lead us?

VOYNITSKY. This estate was bought for ninety-five thousand roubles as prices went in those days. My father paid only seventy thousand down and left twenty-five thousand on mortgage. Now listen to me. The estate would never have been bought at all if I hadn't given up my own share of the inheritance to my sister, whom I loved dearly. What's more, I slaved away for ten years and paid off the whole mortgage.

SEREBRYAKOV. I'm sorry I ever started this conversation.

VOYNITSKY. This estate is free from debt and in good order solely through my own personal efforts. And now I've grown old I'm to be pitched out of it neck and crop!

SEREBRYAKOV. I don't know what you're getting at.

VOYNITSKY. For twenty-five years I've run this estate. I've worked and sent the money to you. The best manager in the world couldn't have done more. And all this time you haven't thanked me once. All this time, when I was young and just the same today, I've been getting a salary of five hundred roubles a year from you—a miserable pittance! And not once has it occurred to you to give me a single extra rouble.

SEREBRYAKOV. But how was I to know, my dear man? I'm not a practical person, I don't understand these things. You could have helped yourself to as much as you liked, couldn't you?

VOYNITSKY. Why didn't I steal, you mean? Why don't you all despise me for not stealing? It would have been only fair if I had and I shouldn't be a pauper now.

MRS. VOYNITSKY [*sternly*]. Vanya!

TELEGIN [*agitatedly*]. Vanya, my dear chap, don't talk like this, for heaven's sake. I'm trembling all over. Why spoil good relations? [*Kisses him.*] Please don't.

VOYNITSKY. For twenty-five years I've been cooped up in this place like a mole with this mother of mine. All our thoughts and feelings were for you alone. In the daytime we talked of you and your writings, we were proud of you and worshipped the very sound of your name. And we wasted our nights reading books and journals that I now utterly despise.

TELEGIN. Oh stop it, Vanya, please, I can't stand this.

SEREBRYAKOV [*angrily*]. What are you driving at? That's what I don't see.

VOYNITSKY. We thought of you as a superior being and we knew your articles by heart. But now my eyes have been opened. Everything's perfectly clear. You write about art, but you haven't the faintest idea what art is all about. Your entire works, which once meant so much to me, aren't worth a brass farthing. You've made fools of us all.

SEREBRYAKOV. My friends, can't you stop him? Really! I'll go away.

HELEN. Vanya, I insist you keep quiet. Do you hear me?

VOYNITSKY. I will not keep quiet. [*Barring* SEREBRYAKOV'*s way.*] Wait, I haven't finished yet. You've ruined my life! I've not lived, not lived, I tell you. Thanks to you the best years of my life have been thrown down the drain. You are my worst enemy!

TELEGIN. I can't stand this, I really can't. I'm going. [*Goes out in terrible agitation.*]

SEREBRYAKOV. What do you want from me? And what right have you to talk to me like that? Nonentity! If the estate is yours take it. I don't want it.

HELEN. I'm getting out of this madhouse this instant. [*Shouting.*] I've had about as much as I can stand.

VOYNITSKY. My life's ruined. I'm gifted, intelligent, courageous. If I'd had a normal life I might have been a Schopenhauer or a Dostoyevsky. But I'm talking nonsense, I'm going mad. Mother dear, I'm desperate. Mother!

MRS. VOYNITSKY [*sternly*]. Do as Alexander says.

SONYA [*kneeling down in front of* MARINA *and pressing close to her*]. Nanny! Nanny, darling!

VOYNITSKY. Mother! What am I to do? Never mind, don't tell me. I know what to do all right. [*To* SEREBRYAKOV.] I'll give you something to remember me by! [*Goes out through centre door.*]

[MRS. VOYNITSKY *follows him.*]

SEREBRYAKOV. Really, everybody, what on earth is all this? Rid me of this maniac! I cannot live under the same roof with him. His room is here [*points to centre door*], almost next to mine. Let him move into the village, into a cottage in the grounds, or I'll move out myself, but I cannot stay in the same house.

HELEN [*to her husband*]. We're leaving this place today. We must arrange it at once.

SEREBRYAKOV. Utter nonentity!

SONYA [*kneeling, addresses her father excitedly through her tears*]. Do show some understanding, Father. Uncle Vanya and I are so unhappy. [*Trying to hold back her despair.*] You must be charitable. Remember, when you were younger Uncle Vanya and Grandmother used to translate books for you at night, copy out your papers—every night, every single night. Uncle Vanya and I worked without a moment's rest, afraid to spend anything on ourselves, and sent everything to you. We did earn our keep, you know. Oh, I'm not putting it the right way at all, but you've got to understand us, Father. You must show some sympathy.

HELEN [*very upset, to her husband*]. Alexander, for heaven's sake sort the thing out with him. Please!

SEREBRYAKOV. Very well, I'll talk to him then. I am not accusing him of anything and I am not angry, but you must admit his conduct is, to put it mildly, odd. All right then, I'll go and see him. [*Goes out through centre door.*]

HELEN. Be gentle with him, calm him down. [*Follows him out.*]

SONYA [*nestling up to* MARINA]. Nanny! Nanny, darling!

MARINA. It's all right, my child. The geese will cackle for a while and then they'll stop. They'll cackle a bit and then they'll stop their cackling.

SONYA. Nanny!

MARINA [*stroking her hair*]. You're shivering as if you'd been out in the cold. There there, my darling, God is merciful. A drink of lime-flower tea or some raspberry juice and it'll pass off. Don't grieve, my poor darling. [*Looking at the centre door, angrily.*] Dear me, the feathers are flying. A plague on those geese!

[*A shot off stage.* HELEN *is heard to scream.* SONYA *shudders.*]

MARINA. Oh, a curse upon you!

SEREBRYAKOV [*runs in, staggering and terrified*]. Stop him, stop him! He's gone mad!

[HELEN *and* VOYNITSKY *are seen struggling in the doorway.*]

HELEN [*trying to take the revolver from him*]. Give it to me. Give it to me, I tell you!

VOYNITSKY. Let me go, Helen. Let go of me. [*Frees himself, runs in and looks round for* SEREBRYAKOV.] Where is he? Ah, there he is. [*Fires at him.*] Bang! [*Pause.*] Missed him, did I? Missed him again, eh? [*Angrily.*] Oh, hell, hell! Hell and damnation! [*Bangs the revolver on the floor and sinks exhausted in a chair.* SEREBRYAKOV *looks stunned.* HELEN *leans against a wall almost fainting.*]

HELEN. Get me away from here. Take me away, I don't care if you kill me, but I can't stay here. I can't.

VOYNITSKY [*desperately*]. Oh, what am I doing? What am I doing?

SONYA [*quietly*]. Nanny darling! Nanny!

CURTAIN

ACT FOUR

VOYNITSKY's *room, which serves as his bedroom and the estate office. Near the window is a large table covered with ledgers and various papers, also a bureau, cupboards and a pair of scales. There is a smaller table for* ASTROV *with drawing materials and paints on it. Near them a portfolio. A cage containing a starling. On the wall hangs a map of Africa which is obviously quite out of place here. A huge sofa upholstered in American cloth. A door, left, leading to the rest of the house. A door, right, into the hall. Near the door, right, is a mat for the peasants to wipe their boots on.*

It is an autumn evening and very quiet.

TELEGIN *and* MARINA *sit facing each other, winding wool.*

TELEGIN. Hurry up, Marina, they'll be calling us to say good-bye soon. They've already ordered their carriage.

MARINA [*tries to wind more quickly*]. There's not much wool left.

TELEGIN. They're going to Kharkov, going to live there.

MARINA. A good thing too.

TELEGIN. They've properly got the wind up. There's Mrs. Serebryakov. "I won't spend another hour in this place," says she. "We'll go away altogether," she says. "We'll go to Kharkov for a bit and have a look round, then send for our things." They're not taking much with them. So they're not going to live here after all, Marina, so that's how things have worked out. Such are the dictates of destiny.

MARINA. And a good thing too. The row they made this afternoon and all that shooting, a thorough disgrace I call it.

TELEGIN. Yes, it was a subject worthy of the brush of Ayvazovsky.

MARINA. It was no sight for my old eyes. [*Pause.*] We'll go back to our old way of doing things, with breakfast at eight o'clock and dinner at one. And we'll sit down to supper in the evenings. We'll do everything properly like other self-respecting people, in a decent Christian manner. [*With a sigh.*] I haven't tasted noodles for ages, old sinner that I am.

TELEGIN. Yes, it's quite a while since noodles were cooked in this house. [*Pause.*] Quite a while. I was going through the village this morning, Marina, and a shopkeeper shouted after me, "Hey there, you useless scrounger!" It quite upset me, I can tell you.

MARINA. Don't take any notice, my dear. In God's eyes we're all scroungers. You and Sonya and Mr. Voynitsky are all the same. You none of you sit around doing nothing. All of us work. Where's Sonya?

TELEGIN. In the garden with the doctor. They're looking for Vanya, they're afraid he might do himself an injury.

MARINA. But where's his pistol?

TELEGIN [*in a whisper*]. I hid it in the cellar.

MARINA [*with a grin*]. What a business!

[VOYNITSKY *and* ASTROV *come in from outside.*]

VOYNITSKY. Leave me alone. [*To* MARINA *and* TELEGIN.] Go away. Can't you leave me alone for a single hour? I'm fed up with people watching me.

TELEGIN. All right then, Vanya. [*Creeps away.*]

MARINA. You old gander. Cackle, cackle, cackle! [*Picks up her wool and goes out.*]

VOYNITSKY. Leave me alone.

ASTROV. With the greatest pleasure. I ought to have gone long ago, but I tell you once more, I shan't leave till you give me back what you took from me.

VOYNITSKY. I haven't taken anything from you.

ASTROV. I mean what I say. Don't keep me waiting, please. I should have left ages ago.

VOYNITSKY. I didn't take anything from you. [*Both sit down*.]

ASTROV. Oh no? Right, I'll give you a bit longer, and then I'm sorry, but we'll have to use force. We shall tie you up and search you. I mean what I say, I can tell you.

VOYNITSKY. Have it your own way. [*Pause*.] How could I be such a fool—fire twice and miss both times? I'll never forgive myself.

ASTROV. If you were so keen on shooting someone why didn't you blow your own brains out?

VOYNITSKY [*shrugging his shoulders*]. It's very funny. I've just tried to murder somebody, but no one thinks of arresting me or putting me on trial. So they must think I'm mad. [*Laughs unpleasantly*.] I'm a madman. But those who dress themselves up as professors and learned pundits, so people can't see how cheap, stupid and utterly callous they are— they aren't mad at all. And women who marry old men and openly deceive them, they aren't mad either. I saw you. I saw you kissing her.

ASTROV. Yes. I did kiss her, and my answer to you, sir, is this. [*Thumbs his nose*.]

VOYNITSKY [*looking at the door*]. No, it's the earth itself which must be mad for still putting up with you.

ASTROV. That's a stupid thing to say.

VOYNITSKY. What of it? I'm mad, aren't I? I'm not responsible for my actions, so I have the right to say stupid things.

ASTROV. That line's as old as the hills. You're no madman, you just have no sense. You're an old clown. I used to think anyone like that was ill and abnormal, but my view now is that having no sense is man's normal condition. You're perfectly normal.

VOYNITSKY [*hiding his head in his hands*]. I'm ashamed of myself, so ashamed, if you did but know. This feeling of shame, it hurts so much. It's worse than any pain. [*With anguish*.] I can't stand it. [*Bends over the table*.] What am I to do? What am I to do?

ASTROV. Nothing.

VOYNITSKY. Give me some medicine or something. Oh my God, I'm forty-seven. Suppose I live to be sixty, that means I have still thirteen years to go. It's too long. How am I to get through those thirteen years? What am I to do? How do I fill the time? Oh, can you think—? [*Feverishly clutches* ASTROV's *arm.*] Can you think what it would be like to live the rest of one's life in a new way? Oh, to wake up some fine, clear morning feeling as if you'd started living all over again, as if the past was all forgotten, gone like a puff of smoke. [*Weeps.*] To begin a new life—. Tell me, how should I begin? Where do I start?

ASTROV [*annoyed*]. Oh, get away with you. New life indeed. Our situation's hopeless, yours and mine.

VOYNITSKY. Is it?

ASTROV. I'm perfectly certain of it.

VOYNITSKY. Please give me something. [*Pointing to his heart.*] I've a burning feeling here.

ASTROV [*shouts angrily*]. Oh, shut up! [*More gently.*] Those who live a century or two after us and despise us for leading lives so stupid and tasteless, perhaps they'll find a way to be happy, but as for us—. There's only one hope for you and me, that when we're resting in our graves we may have visions. Even pleasant ones perhaps. [*Sighs.*] Yes, my dear fellow. In our whole district there were only two decent, civilized people—you and I. But ten years or so of this contemptible, parochial existence have completely got us down. This filthy atmosphere has poisoned our blood and we've become as second-rate as the rest of them. [*Vigorously.*] Anyhow, don't you try and talk your way out of it. You give me back what you took.

VOYNITSKY. I didn't take anything.

ASTROV. You took a small bottle of morphia out of my medical case. [*Pause.*] Look here, if you're so terribly keen on doing yourself in, why not go into the woods and blow your brains out there? But do give me back that morphia or people will start talking and putting two and two together and they'll end up thinking I gave it you. It'll be quite bad enough having to do the post mortem. You don't suppose that will be exactly fun, do you?

[SONYA *comes in.*]

VOYNITSKY. Leave me alone.

ASTROV [*to* SONYA]. Sonya, your uncle has taken a bottle of morphia from my case and he won't give it back. Tell him that this is—well, not particularly bright of him. Besides, I'm in a hurry, I ought to be off.

SONYA. Uncle Vanya, did you take the morphia? [*Pause.*]

ASTROV. He took it all right.

SONYA. Give it back. Why frighten us like this? [*Affectionately.*] Give it back, Uncle Vanya. I daresay I'm no less unhappy than you, but I don't give way to despair. I put up with things patiently and that's how I mean to go on till my life comes to its natural end. You must be patient as well. [*Pause.*] Give it back. [*Kisses his hands.*] Uncle, darling Uncle, do give it back. [*Weeps.*] You're kind, you'll have pity on us and give it back. You must be patient, Uncle. Please.

VOYNITSKY [*gets the bottle from the table drawer and gives it to* ASTROV]. There you are, take it. [*To* SONYA.] But we must hurry up and start work, we must do something quickly, or else I just can't carry on.

SONYA. Yes, yes, we'll do some work. As soon as we've seen the others off we'll get down to work. [*Agitatedly moves some papers about on the table.*] We've let everything go here.

ASTROV [*puts the bottle in his case and tightens the straps*]. Now I can be on my way.

HELEN [*comes in*]. Vanya, are you here? We're just leaving. Go and see Alexander, he wants a word with you.

SONYA. Come on, Uncle Vanya. [*Takes* VOYNITSKY *by the arm.*] Come with me. You and Father must make it up and be friends, you really must.

[SONYA *and* VOYNITSKY *go out.*]

HELEN. I'm just leaving. [*Gives her hand to* ASTROV.] Goodbye.

ASTROV. So soon?

HELEN. The carriage is at the door.

ASTROV. Good-bye then.

HELEN. This afternoon you promised me you'd go away.

ASTROV. I haven't forgotten. And I'm just off. [*Pause.*] Got cold feet, have you? [*Takes her by the hand.*] Are you really quite so scared?

HELEN. Yes, I am.

ASTROV. Why not stay on after all? How about it? Tomorrow at the forest reservation——

HELEN. No. It's all settled. And that's why I can look you in the face now, just because we definitely *are* leaving. One thing I do ask you, don't think too badly of me. I'd like to feel you respected me.

ASTROV. Oh, really! [*Makes an impatient gesture.*] Do stay, please. You have nothing in the world to do, you may as well admit it—no object in life, nothing to occupy your mind—and sooner or later your feelings are going to be too much for you, that's bound to happen. Well, it would be a lot better for it to happen here in the depths of the country than in Kharkov or Kursk or somewhere like that. At least this is a romantic sort of place and it's even beautiful in autumn. We've the forest reservation and tumble-down country houses and gardens like those in Turgenev.

HELEN. You really are absurd. I'm angry with you, but all the same—I shall remember you with pleasure. You're an interesting man, you're different somehow. We shall never meet again, you and I, so—I may as well admit it—I did find you rather attractive, actually. Let's shake hands then and part as friends. No hard feelings.

ASTROV [*after shaking hands*]. Yes, you'd better leave. [*Thoughtfully.*] You're quite a decent, sensitive person in your way, but everything about you seems odd somehow. No sooner do you and your husband turn up in this place than people here who were getting on with their work, all busy creating something, have to drop everything and do nothing all summer but attend to you and your husband's gout. You two have infected us all with your idleness. I've been under your spell and I've done nothing for a whole month while all the time people have been falling ill and the villagers have been grazing their cattle in my newly-planted woods. So you see, you and your husband bring havoc wherever you go. I'm joking of course, but still—it is odd. And I'm quite sure of this. If you'd stayed on here we'd have had a full-scale disaster on our hands. It would have been the end of me and you wouldn't have come out of it too well either. All right then, off with you. The show is over.

HELEN [*takes a pencil from his table and quickly hides it*]. I'm taking this pencil to remember you by.

ASTROV. It's strange somehow. We've been friends and now suddenly for no good reason we shall never meet again. It's the way things happen in this world. Before anyone comes in, before Uncle Vanya turns up with his bunch of flowers, allow me—to kiss you good-bye. May I? [*Kisses her cheek*.] Well, there you are. And very nice too.

HELEN. I wish you every happiness. [*Looks round*.] Oh, all right then, just for once in a lifetime. [*Embraces him impulsively, after which they quickly move away from each other*.] I must go.

ASTROV. Hurry up and go then. If the carriage is ready you'd better be off.

HELEN. I think someone's coming. [*Both listen*.]

ASTROV. The show is over.

[*Enter* SEREBRYAKOV, VOYNITSKY, MRS. VOYNITSKY *carrying a book*, TELEGIN *and* SONYA.]

SEREBRYAKOV [*to* VOYNITSKY]. We'll let bygones be bygones. So much has happened and I've been through so much and thought so many thoughts these last few hours, I could probably write a whole treatise on the art of living for the benefit of posterity. I gladly accept your apologies and beg you to accept mine. Good-bye. [*He and* VOYNITSKY *kiss each other three times*.]

VOYNITSKY. You'll be receiving a regular amount as before. Everything will be just as it was.

[HELEN *embraces* SONYA.]

SEREBRYAKOV [*kissing* MRS. VOYNITSKY's *hand*]. Mother——.

MRS. VOYNITSKY [*kissing him*]. Do have your photograph taken again, Alexander, and send me it. You know how fond I am of you.

TELEGIN. Good-bye, sir. Think of us sometimes.

SEREBRYAKOV [*kisses his daughter*]. Good-bye. Good-bye, all. [*Shaking hands with* ASTROV.] Thank you for the pleasure of your company. I respect your way of thinking, your enthusiasm and your eager impulses, but permit an old man to include one suggestion among his farewell wishes. You should get down to work, gentlemen. What we need is a bit of action. [*Everyone bows*.] I wish you all the best. [*Goes out followed by* MRS. VOYNITSKY *and* SONYA.]

VOYNITSKY [*kisses* HELEN's *hand with great feeling*]. Good-bye. Forgive me. We shall never meet again.

HELEN [*very touched*]. Good-bye, Vanya. [*Kisses him on the head and goes out*.]

ASTROV [*to* TELEGIN]. Waffles, would you mind telling them to bring my carriage round as well while they're about it?

TELEGIN. At your service, old man. [*Goes out*.]

[*Only* ASTROV *and* VOYNITSKY *are left*.]

ASTROV [*removes his paints from the table and puts them in a suitcase*]. Why don't you go and see them off?

VOYNITSKY. Let them go, I—. It's all a bit too much for me. I feel so depressed. I must get down to work quickly. To work then. Must work. [*Rummages among the papers on the table*.]

[*Pause. Harness bells can be heard*.]

ASTROV. They've gone. I bet the professor's pleased. You won't catch him coming back here in a hurry.

MARINA [*coming in*]. They've gone. [*Sits in an armchair and knits a sock*.]

SONYA [*coming in*]. They've gone. [*Wipes her eyes*.] I hope to

God they'll be all right. [*To her uncle*.] Well, Uncle Vanya, how about getting down to something?

VOYNITSKY. Work—must work.

SONYA. It's ages since we sat at this table together. [*Lights the lamp on the table*.] There doesn't seem to be any ink. [*Takes the inkstand, goes to the cupboard and fills it with ink*.] I feel so sad now they've gone.

MRS. VOYNITSKY [*coming in slowly*]. They've gone. [*Sits down and becomes absorbed in her reading*.]

SONYA [*sitting down at the table and turning the leaves of a ledger*]. First we'll make out the accounts, Uncle Vanya. We really have let things slide. Today someone sent for his account again. Start writing. You do one lot and I'll do another.

VOYNITSKY [*writing*]. To the account—of Mr. —. [*Both write silently*.]

MARINA [*yawning*]. Well, I'm ready for bed.

ASTROV. How quiet it is. Pens scratching, the cricket chirping. It's warm and cosy, I don't feel like leaving. [*Harness bells can be heard*.] Ah, there's my carriage. So it remains for me to say good-bye to you, my friends, to say good-bye to my table and—be off. [*Puts his maps in the portfolio*.]

MARINA. What's the great rush? Why not stay on a bit longer?

ASTROV. I can't.

VOYNITSKY [*writing*]. And two roubles seventy-five brought forward from your previous account——

[*The* LABOURER *comes in*.]

LABOURER. Your carriage is ready, Doctor.

ASTROV. I heard it. [*Hands him the medicine case, suitcase and portfolio*.] Here, take these things. And mind you don't squash the portfolio.

LABOURER. Very good, sir. [*Goes out*.]

ASTROV. Well now—. [*Comes forward to say good-bye*.]

SONYA. When shall we see you again?

ASTROV. Probably not before next summer. Not this winter, I imagine. If anything happens of course, let me know and I'll come over. [*Shakes hands.*] Thanks for all your hospitality and kindness—for everything in fact. [*Goes up to* MARINA *and kisses her on the head.*] Good-bye, old girl.

MARINA. You're not going off without any tea?

ASTROV. I don't want any, Nanny.

MARINA. A little vodka then?

ASTROV [*hesitantly*]. Well, perhaps——.

[MARINA *goes out.*]

ASTROV [*after a pause*]. My trace horse has gone a bit lame. I noticed it yesterday when Petrushka was taking him to water.

VOYNITSKY. You'll have to get him reshod.

ASTROV. I'd better call at the blacksmith's in Rozhdestvennoye. There's nothing else for it. [*Goes up to the map of Africa and looks at it.*] Down there in Africa the heat must be quite something. Terrific!

VOYNITSKY. Very probably.

MARINA [*returning with a glass of vodka and a piece of bread on a tray*]. Here you are.

[ASTROV *drinks the vodka.*]

MARINA. Your health, my dear. [*Bows low.*] Why not have a little bread with it?

ASTROV. No, it'll do as it is. All the best to you then. [*To* MARINA.] Don't bother to see me to the door, Nanny, there's no need.

[*He goes out.* SONYA *goes after him with a candle to see him off.* MARINA *sits down in her armchair.*]

VOYNITSKY [*writing*]. February second, three gallons of linseed oil——. February sixteenth, another three gallons of linseed oil——. Buckwheat——. [*Pause.*]

[*Harness bells are heard.*]

MARINA. He's gone.

[*Pause*.]

SONYA [*returning, puts the candle on the table*]. He's gone.

VOYNITSKY [*making a calculation on the counting frame and writing it down*]. That makes—fifteen—twenty-five.

[SONYA *sits down and writes*.]

MARINA [*yawns*]. Oh dearie me.

[TELEGIN *comes in on tip-toe, sits down near the door and quietly tunes his guitar*.]

VOYNITSKY [*to* SONYA, *running his hand over her hair*]. I'm so depressed, Sonya, you can't think how depressed I feel.

SONYA. Well, it can't be helped. Life must go on. [*Pause*.] And our life will go on, Uncle Vanya. We shall live through a long succession of days and endless evenings. We shall bear patiently the trials fate has in store for us. We shall work for others—now and in our old age—never knowing any peace. And when our time comes we shall die without complaining. In the world beyond the grave we shall say that we wept and suffered, that our lot was harsh and bitter, and God will have pity on us. And you and I, Uncle dear, shall behold a life which is bright and beautiful and splendid. We shall rejoice and look back on our present misfortunes with feelings of tenderness, with a smile. And we shall find peace. We shall, Uncle, I believe it with all my heart and soul. [*Kneels down in front of him and places her head on his hands, continuing in a tired voice*.] We shall find peace.

[TELEGIN *quietly plays the guitar*.]

SONYA. We shall find peace. We shall hear the angels, we shall see the sky sparkling with diamonds. We shall see all the evils of this life, all our own sufferings, vanish in the flood of mercy which will fill the whole world. And then our life will be calm and gentle, sweet as a caress. I believe that, I do believe it. [*Wipes away his tears with a handkerchief*.] Poor, poor Uncle Vanya, you're crying. [*Through tears*.] There's been no happiness in your life, but wait,

Uncle Vanya, wait. We shall find peace. [*Embraces him.*] We shall find peace.

[*The watchman taps.*]

[TELEGIN *quietly strums.* MRS. VOYNITSKY *writes something in the margin of her pamphlet.* MARINA *knits her stocking.*]

SONYA. We shall find peace.

THE CURTAIN SLOWLY FALLS

THREE SISTERS

[Три сестры]

A DRAMA IN FOUR ACTS

(1900–1901)

CHARACTERS

ANDREW PROZOROV

NATASHA, his fiancée, later his wife

OLGA
MASHA } his sisters
IRINA

THEODORE KULYGIN, a schoolmaster, Masha's husband

ALEXANDER VERSHININ, a lieutenant-colonel and battery commander

BARON NICHOLAS TUZENBAKH, a lieutenant

CAPTAIN VASILY SOLYONY

IVAN CHEBUTYKIN, an army doctor

ALEKSEY FEDOTIK, a second lieutenant

VLADIMIR RODÉ, a second lieutenant

FERAPONT, a caretaker at the county council offices, an old man

ANFISA, an old nurse, aged 80

The action takes place in a county town

ACT ONE

The PROZOROVS' *house. A drawing-room with columns beyond which a ballroom can be seen. Midday. Outside the sun is shining cheerfully. A table in the ballroom is being laid for lunch.*

OLGA, *wearing the regulation dark-blue dress of a high-school teacher, carries on correcting her pupils' exercise books, standing up or walking about the room.* MASHA, *in a black dress, sits with her hat on her lap reading a book.* IRINA, *in a white dress, stands lost in thought.*

OLGA. It's exactly a year ago today since Father died—on the fifth of May, your name-day, Irina. It was very cold then, and snowing. I thought I'd never get over it and you actually passed out, fainted right away. But now a year's gone by and we don't mind talking about it any more. You're wearing white again and you look radiant. [*The clock strikes twelve.*] The clock struck twelve then too. [*Pause.*] I remember the band playing when they took Father to the cemetery, and they fired a salute. He was a general, commanded a brigade. All the same, not many people came—it was a wet day of course, with heavy rain and sleet.

IRINA. Why bring up old memories?

[BARON TUZENBAKH, CHEBUTYKIN *and* SOLYONY *appear beyond the columns near the table in the ballroom.*]

OLGA. It's warm today and we can have the windows wide open, but the birch trees aren't in leaf yet. It's eleven years now since Father got his brigade and we all left Moscow. I remember it so well. It was early May, as it is now, and in Moscow everything was in blossom, it was warm and there was sunshine everywhere. Eleven years ago, but I remember it all as though we'd only left yesterday. Heavens, how marvellous! When I woke up this morning and saw the great blaze of light and knew that spring had come—I felt so happy and excited, I felt I just had to go back home to Moscow.

CHEBUTYKIN [*to* SOLYONY *and* TUZENBAKH]. Not a chance in hell.

TUZENBAKH. Absolute nonsense of course.

[MASHA, *absorbed in her reading, softly whistles a tune.*]

OLGA. Do stop whistling, Masha. Really! [*Pause.*] Being at school every day and then giving lessons till late in the evening, I'm always having headaches and the things that run through my mind—why, I might be an old woman already. And it's true that these four years I've been at the high school, I've felt my youth and energy draining away drop by drop each day. Only one thing grows stronger and stronger, a certain longing——

IRINA. To go to Moscow, to sell the house, have done with everything here and go to Moscow.

OLGA. Yes, to Moscow! As soon as we can.

[CHEBUTYKIN *and* TUZENBAKH *laugh.*]

IRINA. Andrew's probably going to be a professor and he won't live here anyway. There's nothing stopping us except poor Masha here.

OLGA. Masha can come and spend the whole summer in Moscow every year.

[MASHA *softly whistles a tune.*]

IRINA. I only pray it will work out all right. [*Looks out of the window.*] What a marvellous day! I'm in such a good mood, I don't know why. This morning I remembered it was my name-day and I suddenly felt happy, I remembered when we were children and Mother was still alive. And such wonderful thoughts passed through my head, I felt so excited.

OLGA. You're perfectly radiant today, I've never seen you look so beautiful. Masha's beautiful too. Andrew wouldn't be bad-looking either, only he's put on so much weight and it doesn't suit him. But I've aged and grown terribly thin—

because I'm always losing my temper with the girls at school, I suppose. Now I have the day off, I'm here at home, my headache's gone and I feel younger than I did yesterday. I'm twenty-eight, that's all. God's in his heaven, all's right with the world, but I think if I got married and stayed at home all day it might be even better. [*Pause*.] I'd love my husband.

TUZENBAKH [*to* SOLYONY]. You talk such nonsense, I'm tired of listening to you. [*Comes into the drawing-room*.] Oh, I forgot to tell you—do you know who's going to call on you today? Our new battery commander, Vershinin. [*Sits down at the piano*.]

OLGA. Oh, is he? How nice.

IRINA. Is he old?

TUZENBAKH. No, not really. Forty or forty-five at the most. [*Plays softly*.] Seems a good chap. He's no fool, you can take my word for it, only he does talk rather a lot.

IRINA. Is he an interesting man?

TUZENBAKH. Oh, he's all right, but he has a wife and mother-in-law and two little girls—his second wife, by the way. He goes round calling on people and tells everyone he has a wife and two little girls. He'll tell you the same thing. His wife's not quite all there, she has a long pigtail like a school-girl and her conversation's rather up in the air, lot of philosophical stuff. And then she tries to commit suicide every so often, obviously just to annoy her husband. I'd have left a woman like that long ago, but he puts up with it and just goes round feeling sorry for himself.

SOLYONY [*comes into the drawing-room from the ballroom with* CHEBUTYKIN]. With one hand I can only lift half a hundredweight, but if I use both hands I can lift two or even two-and-a-half hundredweight. From which I conclude that two men aren't just twice as strong as one, but three times as strong, if not more.

CHEBUTYKIN [*reading a newspaper as he comes in*]. If your hair starts falling out, take two drams of naphthalene to half a bottle of spirit. To be dissolved and applied daily—. [*Writes in his notebook*.] Must note that down. [*To* SOLYONY.]

Well, as I was saying, you cork up the bottle and you have a little glass tube running through it. Then you take a pinch of ordinary, common-or-garden powdered alum——

IRINA. Doctor, Doctor, dearest Doctor!

CHEBUTYKIN. What is it, my precious?

IRINA. Tell me, why am I so happy today? I feel as if I was sailing along with a great blue sky above me and huge white birds soaring about. Tell me, why?

CHEBUTYKIN [*kisses both her hands, tenderly*]. You're like a white bird yourself, my dear.

IRINA. Today I woke up, got out of bed and had a wash. And then I suddenly felt as if everything in the world made sense, I seemed to know how to live. I know everything, dearest Doctor. Man should work and toil by the sweat of his brow, whoever he is—that's the whole purpose and meaning of his life, his happiness and his joy. How wonderful to be a workman who gets up at dawn and breaks stones in the road, or a shepherd, or a schoolmaster who teaches children or an engine-driver. Heavens, better not be a human being at all—better be an ox or just a horse, so long as you can work, rather than the kind of young woman who wakes up at noon, has her coffee in bed and then spends two hours getting dressed. Oh, that's so awful. You know how you sometimes long for a drink on a hot day—well that's how I long to work. And if I don't start getting up early and working you must stop being my friend, Doctor.

CHEBUTYKIN [*affectionately*]. I will, I will.

OLGA. Father taught us to get up at seven o'clock. Now Irina wakes at seven and lies in bed at least till nine, just thinking. And looks so serious too. [*Laughs.*]

IRINA. You're so used to seeing me as a little girl, you think it's funny when I look serious. I am twenty, you know.

TUZENBAKH. This great urge to work, heavens, how well I understand it. I've never done a hand's turn all my life. I was born in St. Petersburg—that bleak, idle place—and grew up in a family that never knew the meaning of work or worry. I remember how I used to come home from my cadet school. The footman would pull off my boots while I'd make a thorough nuisance of myself, watched by my mother who thought I was just wonderful and couldn't see why others took a rather different view. They tried to protect me from work. Only I doubt if their protection is going to prove all that effective. I doubt it. The time has come, an avalanche is moving down on us and a great storm's brewing that'll do us all a power of good. It's practically on top of us already and soon it's going to blast out of our society all the laziness, complacency, contempt for work, rottenness and boredom. I'm going to work and in twenty-five or thirty years' time everyone will work. Everyone.

CHEBUTYKIN. Well, I shan't for one.

TUZENBAKH. You don't count.

SOLYONY. In twenty-five years you won't be here at all, thank God. In a couple of years or so you'll have a stroke and die or I'll lose my temper and put a bullet through your head, my good friend. [*Takes a bottle of scent from his pocket and sprinkles his chest and hands*.]

CHEBUTYKIN [*laughs*]. You know, I've never done a thing and that's a fact. Since I left the university I haven't lifted a finger, I've never even read a book. I've read nothing but newspapers. [*Takes another newspaper out of his pocket*.] See what I mean? I know from newspapers that there was someone called Dobrolyubov, for instance, but what the fellow wrote I've no idea. I can't say I greatly care either. [*There is a banging on the floor from below*.] Aha! They want me down there, someone must have come to see me. I'll be with you in a moment. Just a second. [*Hurries out combing his beard*.]

IRINA. He's up to something.

TUZENBAKH. That's right. He went out looking terribly solemn, he's obviously going to bring you a present.

IRINA. How dreadful.

OLGA. Yes, isn't it awful? He's always playing these stupid tricks.

MASHA.   "A green oak by a curving shore,
                And on that oak a chain of gold—
                And on that oak a chain of gold."

               [*Stands up and hums quietly.*]

OLGA. You're not very cheerful today, Masha.

               [MASHA, *humming, puts on her hat.*]

OLGA. Where are you going?

MASHA. Home.

IRINA. That's a bit odd, isn't it?

TUZENBAKH. What! Leaving your sister's party?

MASHA. It doesn't matter, I'll be back this evening. Good-bye,
    darling. [*Kisses* IRINA.] Once again, many happy returns. In
    the old days when Father was alive there'd be thirty or
    forty officers at our parties and it was all great fun, but
    today there's only one man and a boy and the place is like a
    graveyard. I must go—I'm down in the dumps today, I feel
    so depressed, so don't you listen to me. [*Laughing through
    her tears.*] We'll talk later, but good-bye for now, darling.
    I'll go out somewhere.

IRINA [*displeased*]. Why, what's the matter with you?

OLGA [*crying*]. I know how you feel, Masha.

SOLYONY. When a man starts philosophizing that's what's termed
    philosophistics or just plain sophistics, but when a woman
    or a couple of women start doing it then it's just a case of
    them talking through their hats.

MASHA. What do you mean by that, you terrible, terrible
    man?

SOLYONY. Never mind.

               "Before he'd time to turn a hair
                He'd been knocked over by a bear." [*Pause.*]

MASHA [*to* OLGA, *angrily*]. Oh, stop that crying!

               [*Enter* ANFISA *and* FERAPONT *with a large cake.*]

ANFISA. In here, old fellow. Come in, your boots aren't dirty.

[*To* IRINA.] This is from the county council offices. Mr. Michael Protopopov sent it. A cake.

IRINA. Thank you. Please thank him. [*Accepts the cake.*]

FERAPONT. Eh?

IRINA [*in a louder voice*]. Will you please thank him?

OLGA. Nanny dear, give him some cake. You can go, Ferapont, you'll get a piece of cake out there.

FERAPONT. Eh?

ANFISA. Come on, Ferapont. Come on, old fellow.

[*Goes out with* FERAPONT.]

MASHA. I don't like that Protopopov—Michael or Matthew or whatever he calls himself. We shouldn't ask him here.

IRINA. I didn't ask him.

MASHA. Well, I'm glad to hear that.

[CHEBUTYKIN *comes in followed by a* SOLDIER *carrying a silver samovar. There is a buzz of astonishment and displeasure.*]

OLGA [*covers her face with her hands*]. A samovar! How frightful!

[*Goes off towards the table in the ballroom.*]

IRINA. My dear good Dr. Chebutykin, how could you?

TUZENBAKH [*laughs*]. What did I say?

MASHA. You ought to be thoroughly ashamed of yourself.

CHEBUTYKIN. My darling girls, I've no one else but you, you're more precious to me than anything in the world. I'll soon be sixty and I'm an old man, a lonely, insignificant old man. My love for you is the only good thing about me and if it wasn't for you I'd have departed this life long ago. [*To* IRINA.] I've known you since the day you were born, dear child, I used to hold you in my arms. And I loved your mother, God rest her soul.

IRINA. But why these expensive presents?

CHEBUTYKIN [*through tears, angrily*]. Expensive presents! Oh, get away with you! [*To the* SOLDIER.] Take the samovar in there. [*Mocking her.*] Expensive presents! [*The* SOLDIER *takes the samovar into the ballroom.*]

ANFISA [*on her way through the drawing-room*]. My dears, a colonel's just arrived, someone we don't know. He's taken his coat off, girls, and he's on his way in here. Irina dear, mind you're nice and polite to him. [*Going out.*] You should have started lunch long ago, goodness me you should.

TUZENBAKH. Must be Vershinin.

[VERSHININ *comes in.*]

TUZENBAKH. Lieutenant-Colonel Vershinin.

VERSHININ [*to* MASHA *and* IRINA]. May I introduce myself? I'm Vershinin. Delighted, absolutely delighted to be here at last. Well, you *have* grown up and no mistake.

IRINA. Please sit down. This is a great pleasure.

VERSHININ [*gaily*]. I'm more pleased than I can say, I really am. But there should be three of you sisters. I remember three little girls. Can't remember your faces, but that your father, Colonel Prozorov, had three little girls I remember quite clearly, saw you with my own eyes. How time flies, dear me, how time does fly.

TUZENBAKH. The Colonel comes from Moscow.

IRINA. From Moscow? You come from Moscow?

VERSHININ. Yes, I do. Your father was battery commander there and I served in the same brigade. [*To* MASHA.] Now I think I do just remember your face.

MASHA. I don't remember you, I'm afraid.

IRINA. Olga! Olga! [*Shouts into the ballroom.*] Olga, do come here.

[OLGA *comes into the drawing-room from the ballroom.*]

IRINA. We've just heard that Colonel Vershinin comes from Moscow.

VERSHININ. You must be Olga Prozorov, the eldest. You're Masha. And you'll be Irina, the youngest.

OLGA. Do you come from Moscow?

VERSHININ. Yes. I was at school in Moscow and that's where I joined the service. I was stationed there for a long time and ended up getting a battery here and moving here, as you see. I don't really remember you actually, I only remember there were three sisters. I remember your father all right, I only have to close my eyes to see him just as he was. I used to visit you in Moscow.

OLGA. I thought I remembered everyone, and now suddenly——

VERSHININ. My name is Vershinin.

IRINA. Colonel Vershinin, you're from Moscow. That really is a surprise.

OLGA. You see, we're moving to Moscow.

IRINA. We hope to be there by autumn. It's our home town. We were born there, in the Old Basmanny Road. [*Both laugh happily*.]

MASHA. Fancy meeting someone from home. [*Eagerly*.] Now I remember. Olga, you remember how we used to talk about "the lovesick major." You were a lieutenant then and you were in love, and everyone teased you and called you a major for some reason.

VERSHININ [*laughs*]. Oh yes, the lovesick major. You're quite right.

MASHA. You only had a moustache in those days. Oh, you look so much older. [*Through tears*.] So much older.

VERSHININ. Yes, when I was known as the lovesick major I was young and in love. Things have changed since then.

OLGA. But you haven't a single grey hair. You may look older, but no one could call you old.

VERSHININ. I'm nearly forty-three all the same. Is it long since you left Moscow?

IRINA. Eleven years. But why are you crying, Masha, you silly girl? [*Through tears*.] You'll have me crying too.

MASHA. Never mind me. Do tell me, what street did you live in?

VERSHININ. The Old Basmanny Road.

OLGA. But that's where we lived!

VERSHININ. I lived in Nemetsky Street at one time. Used to walk to the Red Barracks from there. You cross a gloomy-looking bridge on the way and you can hear the water rushing underneath it—a depressing place when you're on your own. [*Pause.*] But what a magnificent wide river you have here. It's a splendid river.

OLGA. Yes, but it's so cold. It's cold here and there are mosquitoes.

VERSHININ. Oh, you mustn't say that. You have a good healthy climate, what I call a real Russian climate. There are the woods and the river, and you've silver birches too. Charming, modest birches, they're my favourite tree. This is a good place to live. Only what's so odd is, the railway station's twelve miles out of town and nobody knows why.

SOLYONY. Well, I know why. [*Everyone looks at him.*] Because if the station was near it wouldn't be far away. And if it's far away it can't be near, can it?

[*An awkward pause.*]

TUZENBAKH. Captain Solyony likes his little joke.

OLGA. Now I do remember you. Yes, I do.

VERSHININ. I knew your mother.

CHEBUTYKIN. She was a wonderful woman, may she rest in peace.

IRINA. Mother's buried in Moscow.

OLGA. In the Novo-Devichy cemetery.

MASHA. Do you know, I'm already beginning to forget her face? Not that anyone will remember us either. We'll be forgotten too.

VERSHININ. Yes, we'll all be forgotten. Such is our fate and we can't do anything about it. And the things that strike us as so very serious and important, they'll all be forgotten one day or won't seem to matter. [*Pause.*] The curious thing is, we can't possibly know now just what will be thought significant and important, or what will seem pathetic and absurd. Take the discoveries of Copernicus or Columbus, say. Didn't they look pointless and absurd at first? While the crazy rubbish put out by some nonentity seemed a great revelation. And it may turn out the same with our present way of life—it suits us all right, but one day it may look odd, inconvenient, foolish, and not' all that reputable either. It may even seem terribly sinful.

TUZENBAKH. Who can say? Or perhaps people will think our life was lofty and sublime, and remember it with respect. There are no tortures, public executions or invasions nowadays, but there's a lot of suffering for all that.

SOLYONY [*in a high-pitched voice, as if calling chickens*]. Chuck, chuck, chuck. The baron wouldn't mind starving so long as you let him say his little piece.

TUZENBAKH. Kindly leave me alone, Solyony. [*Sits down in another chair.*] It gets a bit boring, you know.

SOLYONY [*in a high-pitched voice*]. Chuck, chuck, chuck.

TUZENBAKH [*to* VERSHININ]. The suffering we see around us these days—and there's plenty of it—is at least a sign that society has reached a certain moral level.

VERSHININ. Yes, yes of course.

CHEBUTYKIN. Baron, you just said that people would think of our life as something lofty. But people are a pretty lowdown lot all the same. [*Stands up.*] Look what a low fellow I am. It's only to console me that my life has to be called lofty, that's quite plain.

[*A violin is played off stage.*]

MASHA. That's Andrew playing, our brother.

IRINA. He's the clever one of the family. He's bound to become a professor. Father was a soldier, but his son's chosen an academic career.

MASHA. Which was what Father wanted.

OLGA. We did tease him terribly today. We think he's a bit in love.

IRINA. With one of the local young ladies. She'll be visiting us today, very likely.

MASHA. Oh dear, the way she dresses. It's not merely ugly and unfashionable, it's downright pathetic. She wears a weird skirt in a kind of bright yellow with such a vulgar fringe, my dear, and a red blouse. And her cheeks always look as if they've been scrubbed and scrubbed. Andrew isn't in love, that I just won't believe. I mean to say, he has got some taste. He's only having us on, it's just his little game. Yesterday I heard she's going to marry Protopopov, the chairman of the local council. And a good thing too. [*Speaking into the side door.*] Andrew, come here. Come here a moment, dear.

[ANDREW *comes in.*]

OLGA. This is my brother Andrew.

VERSHININ. My name's Vershinin.

ANDREW. I'm Prozorov. [*Wipes the sweat off his face.*] You're the new battery commander here, aren't you?

OLGA. Colonel Vershinin comes from Moscow, believe it or not.

ANDREW. Really? Then I must congratulate you. Now my dear sisters won't give you a moment's peace.

VERSHININ. I'm afraid your sisters must be rather bored with me already.

IRINA. Look what Andrew gave me today, this little picture frame. [*Shows him the frame.*] He made it himself.

VERSHININ [*looking at the frame and not knowing what to say*]. Yes. Quite something, isn't it?

IRINA. And you see that frame above the piano? That's his work too.

[ANDREW *makes an impatient gesture and moves away.*]

OLGA. He's the clever one of the family, he plays the violin and does all this fretwork—in fact he's good at everything. Don't go away, Andrew. He's always going off like this. You come back.

[MASHA *and* IRINA *take him by the arms and bring him back, laughing.*]

MASHA. Now just you come here.

ANDREW. Leave me alone, please.

MASHA. Isn't he a funny boy? They used to call Colonel Vershinin the lovesick major and he didn't mind a bit.

VERSHININ. No, not a bit.

MASHA. And I want to call you the lovesick fiddler.

IRINA. Or the lovesick professor.

OLGA. He's in love. Andrew's in love.

IRINA [*clapping her hands*]. Three cheers for Andrew! Encore! He's in love!

CHEBUTYKIN [*coming up behind* ANDREW *and putting both arms round his waist*].
        "That love alone might rule the earth,
        Kind nature gave us mortals birth." [*Laughs loudly. He keeps his newspaper with him all the time.*]

ANDREW. All right, that's enough of that. [*Wipes his face.*] I couldn't get to sleep last night and now I don't feel too grand, as they say. I was reading till four o'clock, then I went to bed, but it was no use. I kept thinking about one thing and another—then it gets light so early and the sun comes streaming right into my room. There's an English book I want to translate while I'm here this summer.

VERSHININ. So you know English, do you?

ANDREW. Oh yes. Our father, God rest his soul, inflicted education on us. It's a funny thing, sounds silly in fact, but I must confess that since he died I've started putting on weight and in one year I've filled out like this, just as if my body had shaken off some kind of burden. Thanks to Father, my sisters and I know French, German and English, and Irina knows Italian too. But what an effort!

MASHA. Knowing three languages is a useless luxury in this town. It's not even a luxury, but a sort of unwanted appendage like having a sixth finger. We know much too much.

VERSHININ. Oh, what a thing to say! [*Laughs.*] You know much too much. I don't think there exists, or ever could exist, a town so dull and dreary that it has no place for intelligent, educated men and women. Let's suppose that among the hundred thousand inhabitants of this town—oh, I know it's a backward, rough sort of place—there's no one else like you three. Well, you obviously can't hope to prevail against the forces of ignorance around you. As you go on living you'll have to give way bit by bit to these hundred thousand people and be swallowed up in the crowd. You'll go under, but that doesn't mean you'll sink without trace—you will have some effect. Perhaps when you're gone there will be six people like you, then twelve and so on, and in the end your kind will be the majority. In two or three hundred years life on this earth will be beautiful beyond our dreams, it will be marvellous. Man needs a life like that, and if he hasn't yet got it he must feel he's going to get it, he must look forward to it, dream about it, prepare for it. That means he must have more vision and more knowledge than his father or grandfather ever had. [*Laughs.*] And here are you complaining you know much too much.

MASHA [*takes off her hat*]. I'm staying to lunch.

IRINA [*with a sigh*]. You know, what you've just said ought really to be written down.

[ANDREW *has slipped away unobserved.*]

TUZENBAKH. Many years from now, you tell us, life on this earth will be beautiful and marvellous. That's quite true. But if we're to play a part in it now, even at this distance, we must get ready for it and work for it.

VERSHININ [*stands up*]. Yes. I say, what a lot of flowers you have. [*Looking round.*] And what a splendid house! How I envy you. All my life I've been knocking round from one lot of rooms to another, with a couple of chairs and a sofa and stoves smoking all the time. Why, they're just what I've been missing all my life, flowers like these. [*Rubs his hands.*] Ah well, never mind.

TUZENBAKH. Yes, we must work. I'm sure you think that's a bit of sloppy German sentimentality, but I'm a Russian, you can take my word for it, and I can't even speak a word of German. My father belonged to the Orthodox Church. [*Pause.*]

VERSHININ [*walking up and down*]. I often wonder what it would be like if we could start living all over again, knowing exactly what we were doing. Suppose our past life could be just the rough draft, so to speak, and we could start the new one on a fresh sheet of paper. Then we'd all try hard not to repeat ourselves, I imagine. We'd create different surroundings for ourselves anyway, and see we had somewhere to live like this with these flowers and all this light. I have a wife and two little girls, my wife is in poor health and so on and so forth—and, well, if I could start my life again, I wouldn't get married. No, I would not.

[*Enter* KULYGIN *wearing a teacher's uniform.*]

KULYGIN [*goes up to* IRINA]. Permit me, Irina dear, to wish you many happy returns, and to add from the bottom of my heart sincere wishes for your good health and everything else one may wish a girl of your age. And now may I present you with this little book? [*Hands over a book.*] The history of our high school during the last fifty years. I wrote it myself. A trifling work, written because I had nothing better to do, but do read it all the same. Good morning to you all. [*To* VERSHININ.] My name is Kulygin and I teach at the local high school, I'm a senior assistant master. [*To* IRINA.] In this book you'll find a list of all the pupils who've been through our school in the last fifty years. *Feci quod potui, faciant meliora potentes.* [*Kisses* MASHA.]

IRINA. But you've given me this book before, last Easter.

KULYGIN [*laughs*]. Oh, surely not. In that case give it back. Or better still, give it to the colonel here. Here you are, Colonel. You can read it some time when you're at a loose end.

VERSHININ. I thank you. [*Prepares to leave.*] I really am glad to have met you.

OLGA. You aren't going, are you? We can't allow that.

IRINA. You must stay to luncheon. Please do.

OLGA. Yes, do stay.

VERSHININ [*with a bow*]. I believe I've intruded on a family occasion. Please excuse me. I didn't know, so I haven't offered my good wishes. [*Goes into the ballroom with* OLGA.]

KULYGIN. My friends, today is Sunday, the day of rest. Let us therefore relax and enjoy ourselves, each in the manner befitting his age and station. We'll have to take the carpets up for the summer and put them away till winter. We'll need some insect powder or mothballs. The Romans were healthy because they knew how to work *and* how to relax, what they had was a *mens sana in corpore sano*. Their life followed a definite pattern. Our headmaster says the important thing about life is its pattern or shape. A thing that loses its shape is finished, and that's true of our everyday life as well. [*Puts his arm round* MASHA's *waist, laughing*.] Masha loves me, my wife loves me. We must put the curtains away as well, along with the carpets. I'm happy today, I'm on top of the world. We're due at the headmaster's at four this afternoon, Masha. An outing has been fixed up for the teachers and their families.

MASHA. I'm not going.

KULYGIN [*dismayed*]. My dear, why ever not?

MASHA. I'll tell you later. [*Angrily*.] All right then, I'll go, but please leave me alone. [*Moves away*.]

KULYGIN. And after that we're to spend the evening at the headmaster's. In spite of poor health our head does do his best to be sociable. What a wonderful inspiration to us all—a thoroughly first-rate chap. After the staff meeting yesterday he said to me, "I'm tired, Kulygin. Tired." [*Looks at the clock, then at his watch*.] Your clock's seven minutes fast. "Yes," he said. "I'm tired!"

[*The sound of a violin is heard from off stage*.]

OLGA. Come along please, everyone, let's start luncheon. There's a pie.

KULYGIN. Ah, Olga my dear! Last night I worked right up to

eleven o'clock and got very tired, and today I feel happy. [*Goes to the table in the ballroom.*] My dear——

CHEBUTYKIN [*puts his newspaper in his pocket and combs his beard*]. Did somebody say pie? Splendid.

MASHA [*to* CHEBUTYKIN, *sternly*]. You mind you don't drink today, do you hear? It's bad for you.

CHEBUTYKIN. Oh, stuff and nonsense! That's a thing of the past. It's two years since I really pushed the boat out. [*Impatiently.*] Anyway, old girl, what does it matter?

MASHA. All the same, don't you dare drink. Don't you dare. [*Angrily, but making sure that her husband cannot hear.*] This means another dismal evening at the headmaster's, damn it.

TUZENBAKH. I wouldn't go if I were you, it's perfectly simple.

CHEBUTYKIN. Just don't go, my dear.

MASHA. Don't go, indeed. Oh, damn this life, it's the absolute limit. [*Goes into the ballroom.*]

CHEBUTYKIN [*going up to her*]. There, there.

SOLYONY [*going through to the ballroom*]. Chuck, chuck, chuck.

TUZENBAKH. That'll do, Solyony. Give it a rest.

SOLYONY. Chuck, chuck, chuck.

KULYGIN [*gaily*]. Your health, Colonel. I'm a schoolmaster and quite one of the family here, being Masha's husband. She's a good, kind girl.

VERSHININ. I think I'll have a little of this dark vodka. [*Drinks.*] Your health. [*To* OLGA.] It's so good to be here. [*Only* IRINA *and* TUZENBAKH *are left in the drawing-room.*]

IRINA. Masha's in a bad mood today. She got married at eighteen when she thought him the wisest of men. Now things have changed. He's the kindest of men, but hardly the wisest.

OLGA [*impatiently*]. Andrew, when are you coming?

ANDREW [*off stage*]. Coming. [*Comes in and goes up to the table.*]

TUZENBAKH. What are you thinking about?

IRINA. Oh, nothing much. I don't like your friend Solyony, he frightens me. He says such stupid things.

TUZENBAKH. He's a strange man. I'm sorry for him—he annoys me too, but I feel more sorry than annoyed. I think he's shy. He's always sensible and friendly when we're alone together, but in company he's rude and throws his weight about. Don't go in just yet, let's wait till they've all sat down. Just let me be with you for a bit. What are you thinking about? [*Pause.*] You're twenty and I'm not yet thirty. What a lot of years we have ahead of us—so many, many days, all full of my love for you.

IRINA. Don't talk to me about love, Nicholas dear.

TUZENBAKH [*not listening*]. I feel such a tremendous zest for life. I want to work and struggle, and this urge has become part of my love for you, Irina. And just because you're so beautiful I find life beautiful too. What are you thinking about?

IRINA. You say life is beautiful. But what if it only seems so? As far as we three girls are concerned there hasn't been any beauty in our lives so far, life has been choking us like weeds in a garden. I'm crying. I mustn't. [*Quickly dries her eyes and smiles.*] We must work, work, work. That's why we're so miserable and take such a gloomy view of things—because we don't know the meaning of work. We're descended from people who despised it.

[NATASHA *comes in wearing a pink dress with a green sash.*]

NATASHA. They've gone into lunch already. I'm late. [*Glances at the mirror and tidies herself.*] My hair looks all right. [*Seeing* IRINA.] Many happy returns, Irina dear. [*Gives her a vigorous and prolonged kiss.*] You've got so many guests, I feel quite shy, really. Good morning, Baron.

OLGA [*coming into the drawing-room*]. Oh, here's Natasha. How are you, dear? [*They kiss.*]

NATASHA. Many happy returns. You have so many people here, I feel awfully nervous.

OLGA. Don't worry, they're all old friends. [*In a horrified undertone*.] You're wearing a green sash. That's quite wrong, my dear.

NATASHA. Why? You mean it's unlucky?

OLGA. No, but it just doesn't go with your dress, it looks odd somehow.

NATASHA [*in a tearful voice*]. Does it? But it isn't really green, you know, it's more a sort of dull colour. [*Follows* OLGA *into the ballroom*.]

[*They all sit down to luncheon in the ballroom. The drawing-room is empty*.]

KULYGIN. You know, I wish you'd find yourself a nice young man, Irina. It's high time you were married.

CHEBUTYKIN. And I wish you the same, Natasha.

KULYGIN. Natasha already has a young man.

MASHA. I'm going to have a little glass of something. Eat, drink and be merry—after all, we only live once.

KULYGIN. Take a black mark for conduct.

VERSHININ. I say, this wine is good. What's it made of?

SOLYONY. Black-beetles.

IRINA [*in a tearful voice*]. Oh! How disgusting!

OLGA. We're having roast turkey and apple pie for dinner tonight. Thank goodness I'll be home all day today, and this evening too. Do come and see us this evening, all of you.

VERSHININ. Am I invited too?

IRINA. Yes, please do come.

NATASHA. It's ever so informal here.

CHEBUTYKIN. "That love alone might rule this earth,
　　　　　　Kind nature gave us mortals birth." [*Laughs*.]

ANDREW [*angrily*]. Oh, can't you all stop it? I wonder you don't get tired.

[FEDOTIK *and* RODÉ *come in with a large basket of flowers*.]

FEDOTIK. I say, they've already started.

RODÉ [*speaks in a loud voice and pronounces the letter "r" in his throat in the manner affected by some Russian cavalry regiments.*] Started lunch already, have they? Yes, they have.

FEDOTIK. Half a second! [*Takes a snapshot.*] One. Half a second again. [*Takes another snapshot.*] Two. Now that's done.

[*They take the basket and go into the ballroom where they are greeted noisily.*]

RODÉ [*in a loud voice*]. Many happy returns and all possible good wishes. Marvellous weather today, simply magnificent. I've been out walking with the boys all morning. I teach gymnastics at the high school here.

FEDOTIK. You can move now if you want to, Irina. [*Takes another snapshot.*] You do look nice today. [*Takes a humming-top from his pocket.*] By the way, here's a top. It's got a wonderful hum.

IRINA. Oh, how lovely!

MASHA.   "A green oak by a curving shore,
                    And on that oak a chain of gold—
                    And on that oak a chain of gold."

[*Tearfully.*] But why do I keep saying that? Those words have been going through my head all day.

KULYGIN. Thirteen at table!

RODÉ [*in a loud voice*]. I say, you surely aren't superstitious, are you? [*Laughter.*]

KULYGIN. When there are thirteen at table it means someone's in love. I suppose it wouldn't be you by any chance, Chebutykin? [*Laughter.*]

CHEBUTYKIN. Oh, I'm an old sinner, but why Natasha looks so embarrassed I really can't imagine.

[*Loud laughter.* NATASHA *runs from the ballroom into the drawing-room followed by* ANDREW.]

ANDREW. Please—don't take any notice of them. Stop. Wait a moment, please.

NATASHA. I feel so ashamed. I don't know what's the matter with me and they keep making fun of me. It was awful of me, getting up like that, but I couldn't help it, I really couldn't. [*Covers her face with her hands.*]

ANDREW. Please don't be upset, Natasha. Please. Believe me, they're only joking, it's all meant kindly. Natasha, darling, they're all kind, good-hearted people and they're fond of you and me. Come over to the window here where they can't see us. [*Looks round.*]

NATASHA. I'm just not used to meeting people.

ANDREW. Oh, how young you are, Natasha, how marvellously, splendidly young! My dearest, my darling, don't be so upset. Believe me, trust me. I feel so wonderful, my heart is full of love and joy. Oh, they can't see us, they really can't. How, oh how did I come to fall in love with you and when did it happen? Oh, I don't understand at all. My dear, innocent darling, I want you to be my wife. I love you, I love you. I've never loved anyone like this before. [*They kiss.*]

[*Two officers come in and, seeing* NATASHA *and* ANDREW *kissing, stand and stare in amazement.*]

CURTAIN

ACT TWO

The scene is the same as in Act One.

It is eight o'clock in the evening. From the street comes the faint sound of an accordion. The stage is unlit. NATASHA *comes in wearing a dressing-gown and carrying a candle. She crosses the stage and stops by the door leading into* ANDREW's *room.*

NATASHA. What are you doing, Andrew? Reading, are you? It's all right, I only wondered. [*Goes and opens another door, glances through the doorway, then closes it.*] I thought someone might have left a light burning.

ANDREW [*comes in carrying a book*]. What's that, Natasha?

NATASHA. I was seeing if there were any lights on. It's carnival week and the servants are in such a state anything might happen—you need eyes in the back of your head. Last night I went through the dining-room about midnight and found a candle burning. But who lit it? That's what I couldn't find out. [*Puts down the candle.*] What time is it?

ANDREW [*with a glance at his watch*]. A quarter past eight.

NATASHA. Olga and Irina aren't here yet. They're still not back from work, poor things. Olga's at a staff meeting and Irina's at the post office. [*Sighs.*] I was telling that sister of yours only this morning. "You look after yourself, Irina dear," I said. But she won't listen. A quarter past eight, you say? I'm afraid little Bobik isn't at all well. Why does he get so chilly? Yesterday he had a temperature and today he's cold all over. I'm so worried.

ANDREW. It's all right, Natasha, the child's well enough.

NATASHA. Still, he'd be better on a special diet. I'm so worried. And I'm told there are some people calling here about half past nine, a fancy dress party from the carnival. I'd much rather they didn't come, dear.

ANDREW. I don't quite know what to say. After all, they were asked.

NATASHA. The sweet little thing woke up this morning and looked at me, and suddenly he smiled. He knew who I was, you see. "Good morning, Bobik," I said. "Good morning, darling." And he laughed. Babies do understand, oh yes, they understand very well. All right then, dear, I'll say those carnival people aren't to be asked in.

ANDREW [*indecisively*]. Isn't that rather up to my sisters? It is their house, you know.

NATASHA. Yes, it's their house too. I'll have a word with them, they're so kind. [*Moves off.*] I've ordered some yogurt for supper. The doctor says you shouldn't eat anything but yogurt or you'll never lose weight. [*Stops.*] Bobik gets so chilly. I'm afraid his room may be too cold. We ought to put him somewhere else, at least till the weather's warmer. Irina's room, for instance, is just right for a baby, it's not damp and it gets the sun all day. We must have a word with her, she can go in with Olga for the time being. She's never at home during the day anyway, she only sleeps here. [*Pause.*] Andrew, sweetie-pie, why don't you say something?

ANDREW. I was thinking. There's nothing to say anyway.

NATASHA. Now I had something to tell you. Oh yes, Ferapont's here from the council offices, he wants to see you.

ANDREW [*yawns*]. Ask him to come in, please.

[NATASHA *goes out.* ANDREW *bends over the candle, which she has left behind, and starts reading his book.* FERAPONT *comes in wearing a shabby old overcoat with the collar up and a scarf round his ears.*]

ANDREW. Hallo, my good fellow. What is it?

FERAPONT. A book and some papers from the chairman. Here. [*Hands over a book and a packet.*]

ANDREW. Thank you. Good. But why so late? It's getting on for nine o'clock.

FERAPONT. Eh?

ANDREW [*raising his voice*]. You're late, I tell you. It's nearly nine.

FERAPONT. As you say, sir. I did get here before dark, but they wouldn't let me in. The master's busy, they told me. Ah well, if you were busy you were busy. I wasn't in a hurry. [*Thinking* ANDREW *is asking him something*.] Eh?

ANDREW. Nothing. [*Examining the book*.] Tomorrow's Friday and the office will be closed, but I'll go in and work anyway. I get so bored at home. [*Pause*.] Isn't it funny, my dear old fellow, how things change? And isn't life a swindle? Today I was bored and at a loose end, so I picked up this book, my old university lecture notes, and couldn't help laughing. God, I'm secretary of the county council and the chairman's Protopopov. I'm secretary, and the most I can ever hope for is to get on the council myself. Me—stuck here as a councillor, when every night I dream I'm a professor at Moscow University, a distinguished scholar, the pride of all Russia.

FERAPONT. I don't know, sir, I'm a bit hard of hearing.

ANDREW. If you could hear properly I don't suppose I'd talk to you at all. I must talk to someone, but my wife doesn't understand me and I'm somehow afraid of my sisters, afraid they'll laugh at me and make me look a complete fool. I don't drink and I don't like going into bars, but if I could drop in at Testov's in Moscow right now, or the Great Muscovite Hotel—why, it would suit me down to the ground, old boy.

FERAPONT. There was a contractor at the office a few days back telling us about some businessmen in Moscow. They were eating pancakes, and one of them ate forty and died, or so he said. It was either forty or fifty, I don't rightly remember.

ANDREW. When you sit down in a big Moscow restaurant you don't know anyone and nobody knows you, but you still don't feel out of things. Now here you know everybody and everybody knows you, but you don't seem to belong at all. You're the odd man out all right.

FERAPONT. What's that? [*Pause*.] The same man was saying— he may have been having me on of course—that there's an enormous rope stretched right across Moscow.

ANDREW. What for?

FERAPONT. I don't know, sir. It's what the man said.

ANDREW. Nonsense. [*Reads the book.*] Have you ever been to Moscow?

FERAPONT [*after a pause*]. No, the chance never came my way. [*Pause.*] Shall I go now?

ANDREW. Yes, you can go. Good night. [FERAPONT *goes.*] Good night. [*Reading.*] You might come and fetch some papers tomorrow morning. Off with you then. [*Pause.*] He's gone. [*A bell rings.*] Oh, what a life. [*Stretches himself and goes off slowly to his own room.*]

[*Singing is heard off stage—the nanny is rocking the baby to sleep.* MASHA *and* VERSHININ *come in. While they talk to each other the* MAID *lights the lamp and candles.*]

MASHA. I don't know. [*Pause.*] I don't know. A lot depends on habit of course. After Father's death for instance it was ages before we got used to having no orderlies about the place. But quite apart from what one's used to, I still think what I'm saying's perfectly fair. Other places may be different, but in this town the most decent, the most civilized and cultivated people are the military.

VERSHININ. I'm a bit thirsty, I could do with some tea.

MASHA [*glancing at her watch*]. They'll be bringing some in a minute. I got married when I was eighteen, and I was scared of my husband because he was a schoolmaster and I'd only just left school myself. I thought he was terribly clever, and oh so learned and important. But things have changed since then, I'm sorry to say.

VERSHININ. Yes, I see.

MASHA. Anyway, I'm not talking about my husband. I'm used to him. But civilians in general are often so rude, disagreeable and bad-mannered. Rudeness bothers me, really upsets me. It's painful to meet people who aren't as considerate, or as kind and polite, as they might be. As for schoolteachers, my husband's colleagues, I find their company sheer torture.

VERSHININ. Yes. Though I should have thought there was nothing to choose between civilians and soldiers, at least in this town. It's six of one and half a dozen of the other. Listen to any educated person in this place—soldier or civilian, it makes no difference—and you'll find he's fed up with his wife, fed up with his house, fed up with his estate and fed up with his horses. A Russian feels so much at home when his thoughts are up in the clouds, but tell me—why is his everyday life so very earthbound? Why?

MASHA. Why?

VERSHININ. Why is he fed up with his children and fed up with his wife? Why are his wife and children fed up with him?

MASHA. You're in rather a bad mood today.

VERSHININ. Perhaps I am. I missed lunch, had nothing to eat since breakfast. One of the girls is a bit unwell, and when my children are ill I always get worried and feel so guilty because their mother's the way she is. Oh, if you could have seen her this morning, she really is beneath contempt. We started quarrelling at seven o'clock, and at nine I walked out and slammed the door. [*Pause.*] I never talk about it, the funny thing is I never complain to anyone but you. [*Kisses her hand.*] Don't be angry with me. Apart from you I have no one, no one in the world. [*Pause.*]

MASHA. What a noise the stove's making. The wind howled in the chimney before Father died, made a noise just like that.

VERSHININ. Are you superstitious then?

MASHA. Yes.

VERSHININ. How strange. [*Kisses her hand.*] You're a wonderful, marvellous woman. You're wonderful, marvellous. It's dark in here, but I can see your eyes shining.

MASHA [*moving to another chair*]. There's more light over here.

VERSHININ. I love you, love you, love you. I love your eyes, I love the way you move, I dream about you. You're a wonderful, marvellous woman.

MASHA [*laughing softly*]. When you talk like this it somehow makes me laugh, though it frightens me as well. Please don't talk that way again. [*In an undertone.*] No, it's all right, go on, I don't care. [*Covers her face with her hands.*] I don't care. There's somebody coming, you'd better talk about something else. [IRINA *and* TUZENBAKH *come in through the ballroom.*]

TUZENBAKH. I have a triple-barrelled name, Baron Tuzenbakh-Krone-Altschauer, but I'm just as much of a Russian as you are. There's not much trace of any German ancestry about me, except perhaps that I'm so persistent and stubborn about inflicting myself on you. I walk home with you every evening.

IRINA. I'm so tired.

TUZENBAKH. And I shall go on calling for you at the post office and bringing you home every evening. I'll keep it up for the next ten or twenty years if you don't tell me to go away. [*Noticing* MASHA *and* VERSHININ, *delightedly.*] Oh, it's you. Hallo.

IRINA. Well, here I am, home at last. [*To* MASHA.] Just now a woman came into the post office and wanted to send a telegram to her brother in Saratov to tell him her son died today, but couldn't remember the address. So she sent it without a proper address, just sent it to Saratov. She was crying. And I was rude to her for no reason at all, told her I'd no time to waste. Wasn't that stupid of me? Are those carnival people calling tonight?

MASHA. Yes.

IRINA [*sitting down in an armchair*]. Must have a rest. I'm so tired.

TUZENBAKH [*with a smile*]. When you come back from work you always look so young and pathetic somehow. [*Pause.*]

IRINA. I'm tired. Oh dear, I don't like working at the post office, I really don't.

MASHA. You've got thin. [*Whistles.*] You seem younger too and you've begun to look like a little boy.

TUZENBAKH. It's the way you do your hair.

IRINA. I must find another job because this one doesn't suit me. The things I'd hoped for and wanted so much—they're just what it doesn't give me. It's sheer drudgery with nothing romantic or intellectual about it. [*There is a knock on the floor from below*.] That's the doctor banging. [*To* TUZENBAKH.] Would you give him a knock, Nicholas? I can't, I'm too tired.

[TUZENBAKH *knocks on the floor*.]

IRINA. He'll be up here in a moment. Something ought to be done about this business. The doctor went to the club with Andrew yesterday and they lost again. I heard Andrew was two hundred roubles down.

MASHA [*apathetically*]. It's a bit late to do anything about that now.

IRINA. He lost money a fortnight ago and also in December. The sooner he loses the lot the better, it might mean we'd leave this place. My God, do you know, I dream about Moscow every night? I feel as if I'd gone out of my mind. [*Laughs*.] We're moving there in June, but it's, let me see—February, March, April, May—almost six months till June.

MASHA. The only thing is, Natasha mustn't find out about his gambling.

IRINA. I shouldn't think she'd care.

[CHEBUTYKIN, *who has just got out of bed after an afternoon nap, comes into the ballroom and combs his beard, then sits down at the table and takes a newspaper out of his pocket*.]

MASHA. Oh, look who's come. Has he paid his rent?

IRINA [*laughing*]. No. We haven't had a thing from him for eight months. He's obviously forgotten.

MASHA [*laughing*]. He looks so pompous sitting there.

[*Everyone laughs. Pause*.]

IRINA. Why don't you say anything, Colonel?

VERSHININ. I don't know. I'd like some tea. My kingdom for a glass of tea! I've had nothing since breakfast.

CHEBUTYKIN. Irina.

IRINA. What is it?

CHEBUTYKIN. Please come here. *Venez ici.* [IRINA *goes over and sits at the table.*] I can't do without you. [IRINA *lays out the cards for a game of patience.*]

VERSHININ. Ah well, if there's not going to be any tea we may as well have a bit of a discussion.

TUZENBAKH. All right then, what about?

VERSHININ. Let me see. Well, for instance, let's try and imagine life after we're dead and buried, in two or three hundred years, say.

TUZENBAKH. Very well then. When we're dead people will fly around in balloons, there will be a new style in men's jackets and a sixth sense may be discovered and developed, but life itself won't change, it will still be as difficult and full of mystery and happiness as it is now. Even in a thousand years men will still be moaning away about life being a burden. What's more, they'll still be as scared of death as they are now. And as keen on avoiding it.

VERSHININ [*after some thought*]. Now how can I put it? I think everything on earth is bound to change bit by bit, in fact already is changing before our very eyes. Two or three hundred years, or a thousand years if you like—it doesn't really matter how long—will bring in a new and happy life. We'll have no part in it of course, but it is what we're now living for, working for, yes and suffering for. We're creating it, and that's what gives our life its meaning, and its happiness too if you want to put it that way.

[MASHA *laughs quietly.*]

TUZENBAKH. What's the matter?

MASHA. I don't know. I've been laughing all day.

VERSHININ. I went to the same cadet school as you, though I didn't go on to staff college. I do a lot of reading, but I'm not much good at choosing books and I daresay I read all the wrong things. But the longer I live the more I want to know. My hair's going grey now and I'm growing old, but the trouble is I know so precious little. Still, when it comes to the things that really matter, there I do know my stuff pretty well, I think. And I only wish I could make you see that happiness—well, we haven't got it, we've no right to it, in fact it isn't meant for us at all. Our business is to work and go on working, and our distant descendants will have any happiness that's going. [*Pause.*] I won't have it, but my children's children may.

[FEDOTIK *and* RODÉ *appear in the ballroom. They sit down and sing quietly, one of them strumming on a guitar.*]

TUZENBAKH. You seem to think we shouldn't even dream of happiness, but what if I'm happy already?

VERSHININ. You're not.

TUZENBAKH [*throwing up his arms and laughing*]. We obviously don't speak the same language. Now how can I convince you?

[MASHA *laughs quietly.*]

TUZENBAKH [*holding up a finger to her*]. Laugh at that then. [*To* VERSHININ.] Forget your two or three hundred years, because even in a million years life will still be just the same as ever. It doesn't change, it always goes on the same and follows its own laws. And those laws are none of our business. Or at least you'll never understand them. Think of the birds flying south for the winter, cranes for instance. They fly on and on and on, and it doesn't matter what ideas, big or small, they may have buzzing about inside their heads, they'll still keep on flying without ever knowing why they do it or where they're going. They fly on and on, and what if they do throw up a few philosophers? Let them keep their philosophy so long as they don't stop flying.

MASHA. But what's the point of it all?

TUZENBAKH. The point? Look, it's snowing out there. What's the point of that? [*Pause.*]

MASHA. I feel that man should have a faith or be trying to find one, otherwise his life just doesn't make sense. Think of living without knowing why cranes fly, why children are born or why there are stars in the sky. Either you know what you're living for, or else the whole thing's a waste of time and means less than nothing. [*Pause.*]

VERSHININ. Still, I'm sorry I'm not young any more.

MASHA. As Gogol said, "Life on this earth is no end of a bore, my friends."

TUZENBAKH. What I say is, arguing with you is no end of a job, my friends. Oh, I give up.

CHEBUTYKIN [*reading the newspaper*]. Balzac got married in Berdichev.

[IRINA *sings softly.*]

CHEBUTYKIN. I really must put that down in my little book. [*Makes a note.*] Balzac got married in Berdichev. [*Carries on reading the newspaper.*]

IRINA [*playing patience, thoughtfully*]. Balzac got married in Berdichev.

TUZENBAKH. Well, I've burnt my boats. Did you know I'd resigned my commission, Masha?

MASHA. So I'd heard, but what's so good about that? I don't like civilians.

TUZENBAKH. Never mind. [*Gets up.*] I'm not handsome, so what business have I got in the army? And what does it matter anyway? I'm going to get a job. For once in my life I'd like to put in a hard day's work that would bring me home in the evening ready to drop down on my bed dead tired and fall straight asleep. [*Going into the ballroom.*] I'm sure labourers must sleep well.

FEDOTIK [*to* IRINA]. I've just bought you some crayons at Pyzhikov's in the Moscow Road. And this pen-knife.

IRINA. You always treat me like a child, but I am grown up, you know. [*Takes the crayons and pen-knife, delightedly.*] Oh, aren't they lovely!

FEDOTIK. And I bought a knife for myself. Just take a look at this. One blade, two blades, three blades, and here's a thing to clean your ears out with. These are some little scissors and this is a sort of nail-file.

RODÉ [*in a loud voice*]. Doctor, how old are you?

CHEBUTYKIN. Me? Thirty-two. [*Laughter*.]

FEDOTIK. Now let me show you another kind of patience. [*Lays out the cards*.]

[*The samovar is brought in and* ANFISA *attends to it. A little later* NATASHA *comes in and also busies herself at the table.* SOLYONY *comes in, greets everybody and sits down at the table.*]

VERSHININ. I say, there's quite a wind.

MASHA. Isn't there? I'm fed up with winter, I've forgotten what summer's like.

IRINA. It's going to come out, this game of patience. So we shall go to Moscow.

FEDOTIK. No it isn't. You see, that eight's on top of the two of spades. [*Laughs*.] Which means no Moscow for you.

CHEBUTYKIN [*reads his newspaper*]. "Tsitsihar. A smallpox epidemic is raging here."

ANFISA [*going up to* MASHA]. Tea's ready, Masha dear. [*To* VERSHININ.] Come and have tea, Colonel. I'm sorry, I've forgotten your name.

MASHA. Bring some here please, Nanny, I'm not going in there.

IRINA. Nanny!

ANFISA. Coming, coming.

NATASHA [*to* SOLYONY]. Tiny babies understand very well. "Hallo Bobik," I said. "Hallo, dear." And he gave me a special kind of look. You think I only say that because I'm his mother, but that's not it, you know, it really isn't. He's no ordinary baby.

SOLYONY. If that child was mine I'd fry it up in a frying-pan and eat it. [*Takes his glass of tea into the drawing-room and sits in a corner*.]

NATASHA [*covering her face with her hands*]. What a rude, ill-bred man!

MASHA. People don't notice whether it's winter or summer when they're happy. If I lived in Moscow I don't think I'd care what the weather was like.

VERSHININ. The other day I was reading the diary of a French minister written in prison—he'd been sentenced over the Panama swindle. He gets quite carried away with enthusiasm writing about the birds he sees from his cell window, the birds he'd never even noticed when he was a minister. Now he's been let out and of course he takes no more notice of birds than he did before. Just as you won't notice Moscow when you live there. We have no happiness. There's no such thing. It's only something we long for.

TUZENBAKH [*takes a chocolate box from the table*]. I say, what happened to the chocolates?

IRINA. Solyony ate them.

TUZENBAKH. What, the whole lot?

ANFISA [*handing round tea*]. A letter for you, sir.

VERSHININ. For me? [*Takes the letter.*] It's from my daughter. [*Reads it.*] Of course, in that case. I'm sorry, Masha, I must slip away quietly, I won't have tea. [*Stands up in agitation.*] It's the same old story again.

MASHA. What's the matter? Or is it something private?

VERSHININ [*quietly*]. My wife's taken poison again. I must go, I'll slip out so nobody notices. How frightfully unpleasant. [*Kisses MASHA's hand.*] My darling, you splendid, marvellous woman. I'll slip out quietly this way. [*Goes out.*]

ANFISA. Where's he off to? And I'd just poured him some tea. A fine way to behave.

MASHA [*losing her temper*]. Oh, be quiet. You're on at people all the time—why can't you leave anyone in peace? [*Goes towards the table carrying her cup.*] I'm fed up with you, wretched old woman.

ANFISA. But what have I done wrong, dear?

ANDREW [*off stage*]. Anfisa!

ANFISA [*mimicking him*]. Anfisa! Sits in there—. [*Goes out.*]

MASHA [*by the table in the ballroom, angrily*]. Well, do let me sit down. [*Jumbles up the cards on the table.*] Playing cards all over the place. Drink your tea.

IRINA. You *are* in a bad temper, Masha.

MASHA. Don't talk to me then, if I'm so bad-tempered. You leave me alone.

CHEBUTYKIN [*laughing*]. Leave her alone, mind you leave her alone.

MASHA. You're sixty years old, but you might just as well be a schoolboy with your incessant jabber about absolutely damn all.

NATASHA [*sighs*]. Need you really use such language, Masha? A nice-looking girl like you, why, you could appear in the very best society—yes, I really mean it—and be thought quite charming if only you didn't use words like that. *Je vous prie, pardonnez-moi, Marie, mais vous avez des manières un peu grossières.*

TUZENBAKH [*trying not to laugh*]. Please, give me some—. I think there's some brandy somewhere.

NATASHA. *Il paraît que mon Bobik déjà ne dort pas*, the little chap's woken up. He's a bit off colour today. I must see to him, excuse me. [*Goes out.*]

IRINA. Where did Colonel Vershinin go?

MASHA. Home. There's been another of those peculiar episodes with his wife.

TUZENBAKH [*approaches* SOLYONY *carrying a decanter of brandy*]. You always sit by yourself brooding about something, heaven knows what. Come on, let's make it up and be friends. Let's have a brandy. [*They drink.*] I suppose I'll have to play a lot of rubbish on the piano all night. Oh, what does it matter?

SOLYONY. Why should we make it up? We haven't quarrelled.

TUZENBAKH. You always give me the feeling there's something wrong between us. You are an odd specimen and no mistake.

SOLYONY [*reciting*]. "I may be odd, but who is not?" Aleko, be not angry.

TUZENBAKH. What has Aleko got to do with it? [*Pause.*]

SOLYONY. When I'm alone with someone I'm perfectly all right, I'm no different from anyone else, but in a group of people I feel unhappy and awkward and—talk a lot of rubbish. For all that I'm a sight more honest and decent than many other people. What's more, I can prove it.

TUZENBAKH. You often make me angry and you keep picking on me in company, but somehow I like you all the same. Oh, what does it matter? I'm going to get drunk tonight. Drink up.

SOLYONY. All right. [*They drink.*] I've never had anything against you, Baron, but I'm rather the Lermontov type. [*Quietly.*] I even look a bit like Lermontov, or so people say. [*Takes a bottle of scent from his pocket and puts some on his hands.*]

TUZENBAKH. I'm resigning my commission and that's the end of that. I've been thinking of doing it for five years and at last I've taken the plunge. I'm going to get a job.

SOLYONY [*declaiming*]. Aleko, be not angry. Forget, forget your dreams. [*While they are speaking* ANDREW *comes in quietly with a book and sits down near a candle.*]

TUZENBAKH. I'm going to get a job.

CHEBUTYKIN [*coming into the drawing-room with* IRINA]. They gave us real Caucasian food too—onion soup followed by a meat dish, a kind of *escalope.*

SOLYONY. A shallot isn't meat at all, it's a plant rather like an onion.

CHEBUTYKIN. You're wrong, my dear man. *Escalope* isn't an onion, it's a sort of grilled meat.

SOLYONY. Well, I'm telling you a shallot is an onion.

CHEBUTYKIN. Well, I'm telling you *escalope* is meat.

SOLYONY. Well, I'm telling you a shallot is an onion.

CHEBUTYKIN. Why should I argue with you? You've never been to the Caucasus or eaten *escalope.*

SOLYONY. I've never eaten them because I can't stand them. Shallots smell just like garlic.

ANDREW [*imploringly*]. That's enough, you two, please.

TUZENBAKH. When's the carnival party coming?

IRINA. About nine, they said, so they'll be here any moment.

TUZENBAKH [*embracing* ANDREW]. "Oh, my porch, my nice new porch——"

ANDREW [*dancing and singing*]. "My nice new porch of maple wood——"

CHEBUTYKIN [*dancing*]. "With fancy carving everywhere!" [*Laughter*.]

TUZENBAKH [*kisses* ANDREW]. Damn it, let's have a drink. Let's drink to our friendship, Andrew. And I'll go to Moscow University with you, Andrew my boy.

SOLYONY. Which university? Moscow's got two.

ANDREW. Moscow has only one university.

SOLYONY. Well, I'm telling you it has two.

ANDREW. Why not make it three while you're about it? The more the merrier.

SOLYONY. Moscow has two universities. [*Sounds of protest and murmurs of* "hush."] Moscow has two universities, one old and one new. And if you don't choose to listen, if what I say irritates you, I can keep my mouth shut. In fact I can go into another room. [*Goes out through one of the doors*.]

TUZENBAKH. And a very good thing too. [*Laughs*.] Ladies and gentlemen, take your partners, I'll play you something. He's a funny chap is friend Solyony. [*Sits down at the piano and starts playing a waltz*.]

MASHA [*waltzing without a partner*]. The baron is drunk, is drunk, is drunk.

[NATASHA *comes in*.]

NATASHA [*to* CHEBUTYKIN]. Doctor! [*Says something to* CHEBUTYKIN, *then goes out quietly*. CHEBUTYKIN *touches* TUZENBAKH *on the shoulder and whispers to him*.]

IRINA. What's the matter?

CHEBUTYKIN. It's time we were going. Good-night.

TUZENBAKH. Good-night. Time to go.

IRINA. But look here, what about the carnival party?

ANDREW [*embarrassed*]. There won't be any carnival party. The fact is, my dear, Natasha says Bobik's not very well and so—oh really, I don't know and I certainly don't care either.

IRINA [*shrugging her shoulders*]. Bobik's unwell.

MASHA. Oh, what's the odds! If we're being chucked out we'd better go. [*To* IRINA.] It isn't Bobik that's ill, it's his mother. In the upper storey. [*Taps her forehead.*] Vulgar creature.

[ANDREW *goes off through the door, right, to his own room, followed by* CHEBUTYKIN. *In the ballroom everyone is saying good-bye.*]

FEDOTIK. What a shame. I was looking forward to a pleasant evening, but if the baby's ill, then of course—. I'll bring him some toys tomorrow.

RODÉ [*in a loud voice*]. I took a nap after lunch today specially— thought I'd be dancing all night. Why, it's only nine o'clock.

MASHA. Let's go out in the street and talk it over. We can decide what to do there.

[*Voices are heard saying,* "Good-bye, take care of yourself." TUZENBAKH *is heard laughing happily. Everyone goes out.* ANFISA *and the* MAID *clear the table and put the lights out. The nanny can be heard singing off stage.* ANDREW, *wearing an overcoat and hat, and* CHEBUTYKIN *come in quietly.*]

CHEBUTYKIN. I never got round to marrying because my life has just flashed past like lightning, and besides I was madly in love with your mother and she was married already.

ANDREW. One shouldn't get married, indeed one shouldn't. It's a bore.

CHEBUTYKIN. Yes, yes, that's a point of view, but there is such a thing as loneliness. You can argue about it as much as you like, my boy, but loneliness is a terrible thing. Though actually of course it doesn't matter a damn.

ANDREW. Let's hurry up and get out of here.

CHEBUTYKIN. What's the great rush? There's plenty of time.

ANDREW. I'm afraid my wife might stop me.

CHEBUTYKIN. Oh, I see.

ANDREW. I shan't play cards tonight, I'll just sit and watch. I feel a bit unwell. I get so out of breath, is there anything I can do for it, Doctor?

CHEBUTYKIN. Why ask me? I don't know, dear boy. Don't remember.

ANDREW. Let's go through the kitchen. [*They go out*.]

[*The door-bell rings. There is a pause and then it rings again. Voices and laughter are heard*.]

IRINA [*comes in*]. What's that?

ANFISA [*in a whisper*]. The carnival party. [*The bell rings again*.]

IRINA. Tell them there's no one at home, Nanny. They'll have to excuse us.

[ANFISA *goes out*. IRINA *walks up and down the room, deep in thought. She is upset. Enter* SOLYONY.]

SOLYONY [*in amazement*]. No one here. But where is everybody?

IRINA. They've gone home.

SOLYONY. That's funny. Are you on your own then?

IRINA. Yes. [*Pause*.] Good-night.

SOLYONY. I rather let myself go just now and was a bit tactless. But you're different from the rest, you're such a fine, decent person, and you have so much insight. You're the only one who really understands me, no one else can. I love you so profoundly, so infinitely much——

IRINA. Good-bye. Do please go.

SOLYONY. I can't live without you. [*Following her.*] My happiness! [*Through tears.*] My joy! Your glorious, wonderful, dazzling eyes, I've never seen another woman with eyes like yours.

IRINA [*coldly*]. Please stop, Captain Solyony.

SOLYONY. It's the first time I've ever told you how I love you, and I feel like a being on another planet. [*Rubs his forehead.*] Oh, what does it matter anyway? I can't make you love me of course. But I'm not having any successful rivals, let that be quite clear. And by God I mean it, if there's anybody else I'll kill him. Oh, you are so marvellous!

[NATASHA *starts to cross the stage, carrying a candle.*]

NATASHA [*looks through one door, then another, and goes past the door leading to her husband's room*]. Andrew's in there. He may as well go on reading. Excuse me, Captain Solyony, I didn't know you were here. I'm not dressed for visitors.

SOLYONY. I don't care. Good-night. [*Goes out.*]

NATASHA. Oh, you are tired, poor child. [*Kisses* IRINA.] You should go to bed a bit earlier.

IRINA. Is Bobik asleep?

NATASHA. Yes, but he's rather restless. By the way, dear, I keep meaning to ask you, but either you've been out or I've been too busy. I think Bobik's nursery's too cold and damp. But your room's just right for a baby. Darling, would you mind moving in with Olga for a bit?

IRINA [*not understanding*]. Move in where?

[*A troika with bells is heard driving up to the house.*]

NATASHA. You can share Olga's room for the time being and Bobik can have yours. He's such a sweet little fellow. This morning I said to him, "Bobik, you're mine, my very own." And he just looked at me with his dear little eyes. [*The door-bell rings.*] That must be Olga. Isn't she late!

[*The* MAID *comes in and whispers in* NATASHA's *ear.*]

NATASHA. Protopopov? Oh, isn't he a scream? Protopopov's turned up, wants to know if he can take me for a drive.

[*Laughs.*] Aren't men funny! [*The door-bell rings again.*] And there's someone else. Perhaps I might go for a little spin just for a quarter of an hour. [*To the* MAID.] Tell him I'm coming. [*The door-bell rings.*] There goes the bell again, it must be Olga. [*Goes out.*]

[*The* MAID *runs out.* IRINA *sits deep in thought.* KULYGIN *and* OLGA *come in followed by* VERSHININ.]

KULYGIN. Well, this is a surprise. They said they were having a party.

VERSHININ. It's very funny. I only left half an hour ago, and they were expecting some people from the carnival then.

IRINA. They've all gone away.

KULYGIN. Has Masha gone too? Where did she go? And what is Protopopov doing outside in a carriage? Who's he waiting for?

IRINA. Don't ask questions. I'm tired.

KULYGIN. Oh dear, isn't she a naughty little girl!

OLGA. The meeting's only just ended. I'm absolutely worn out. Our headmistress is ill and I have to take her place. My head, my head, my poor, poor head, how it aches. [*Sits down.*] Andrew lost two hundred roubles at cards last night, the whole town's talking about it.

KULYGIN. Yes, I got tired at the meeting too. [*Sits down.*]

VERSHININ. My wife has just decided to give me a little scare and almost managed to poison herself. It's all right now, thank goodness, and I can relax. So we've got to go, have we? Very well, I wish you all good evening. Shall we go somewhere together, Kulygin? I can't sit at home, I really can't. What do you say?

KULYGIN. I'm tired, you'd better count me out. [*Stands up.*] I'm so tired. Has my wife gone home?

IRINA. She must have.

KULYGIN [*kisses* IRINA's *hand*]. Good-night. For the next two days we can take it easy. All the best then. [*Moves off.*] I would have liked some tea. I was looking forward to a pleasant social evening, but *o, fallacem hominum spem!* Accusative of exclamation.

VERSHININ. I'll have to go off on my own then. [*Goes out with* KULYGIN, *whistling.*]

OLGA. How my head does ache. Andrew lost at cards, the whole town's talking about it. I'll go to bed. [*Moves off.*] I've got the day off tomorrow. My goodness, isn't that nice! I have the day off tomorrow and the day after too. How my head does ache. [*Goes out.*]

IRINA [*alone*]. Everyone's gone away. There's nobody left.

[*There is the sound of an accordion in the street and of the nanny singing a song.*]

NATASHA [*crosses the ballroom wearing a fur coat and a fur hat. She is followed by the* MAID]. I'll be back in half an hour, I'm just going for a little airing. [*Goes out.*]

IRINA [*alone on the stage, with intense longing*]. Moscow, Moscow, Moscow!

CURTAIN

ACT THREE

The bedroom shared by OLGA *and* IRINA. *There are beds, left and right, with screens round them. It is between two and three o'clock in the morning. Off stage church bells are ringing the alarm, a fire having broken out some time previously. Obviously no one in the house has gone to bed yet.* MASHA *is lying on a sofa wearing a black dress as usual.* OLGA *and* ANFISA *come in.*

ANFISA. They're sitting down there under the stairs now. "Please come upstairs," I tell them. "We can't have this, can we?" They're crying. "We don't know where Father is," they say. "He might have been burnt to death." What an idea! Then there are those other people out in the yard as well, they're in their nightclothes too.

OLGA [*takes some dresses out of a wardrobe*]. Take this grey one. And this one too. And the blouse. And take this skirt as well, Nanny. Oh heavens, what a business! Kirsanovsky Street must be burnt to the ground. Take this. And this. [*Throws the clothes into* ANFISA's *arms.*] The Vershinins had a fright, poor things, their house only just escaped. They'd better spend the night here, we can't let them go home. And poor Fedotik's lost everything, it's all gone up in smoke.

ANFISA. You'd better call Ferapont, dearie, I can't manage all this.

OLGA [*rings*]. They don't come when you ring. [*Calls through the door.*] Come here, please. Is anyone there? [*The red glare of a window is seen through the open door. A fire engine is heard passing the house.*] How horrible. And how thoroughly tiresome too.

[FERAPONT *comes in.*]

OLGA. Here, take all this down, please. The Kolotilin girls are down there under the stairs, give it to them. And give them this too.

FERAPONT. Very well, miss. Moscow had a fire as well, in 1812. Dear oh dear, the French did get a surprise.

OLGA. Run along now, be off with you.

FERAPONT. Very well, madam. [*Goes out*.]

OLGA. Give them everything we have, Nanny dear. We don't need it, give it all away. I'm so tired, I can hardly stand. We can't possibly let the Vershinins go home. The little girls can sleep in the drawing-room, and the colonel had better go in with Baron Tuzenbakh downstairs. Fedotik can go in with the baron as well or have the dining-room if he likes. The doctor has to go and get hopelessly drunk at this of all times, so we can't put anyone in with him. And Vershinin's wife had better go in the drawing-room too.

ANFISA [*in a tired voice*]. Don't send me away, Miss Olga, please don't send me away.

OLGA. That's silly talk, Nanny. There's no question of sending you away.

ANFISA [*resting her head on* OLGA's *breast*]. I do work hard, Miss Olga, my precious, I really do. If I grow too weak to manage I'll be told to go. But where can I go, you tell me that. I'm over eighty. Eighty-one I am——

OLGA. Sit down a bit, Nanny. You're worn out, poor thing. [*Helps her to sit down*.] Have a rest, dear, you look so pale.

[NATASHA *comes in*.]

NATASHA. They're saying we ought to set up a relief committee at once for the fire victims. You know, that's not a bad idea. In fact we should always be ready to help the poor. It's up to the rich, isn't it? Bobik and little Sophie are sound asleep in bed just as if nothing had happened. There's such a crowd in the house, with people everywhere whichever way you turn. And now there's 'flu about in town I'm afraid the children might catch it.

OLGA [*not listening to her*]. You can't see the fire from this room, it's peaceful here.

NATASHA. Isn't it? I must look a sight. [*Stands in front of the mirror.*] People say I've put on weight. But it's not true, not a bit of it. Masha's asleep—tired out, poor girl. [*To* ANFISA, *coldly.*] How dare you be seated in my presence? Stand up! Be off with you! [ANFISA *goes out. Pause.*] Why you keep that old woman I don't understand.

OLGA [*taken aback*]. I'm sorry, I don't quite understand either.

NATASHA. There's no place for her here. She came from a village and she should go back to her village. This is sheer extravagance. I like to see a house run properly, there's no room for misfits in this house. [*Strokes* OLGA's *cheek.*] Poor thing, you're tired out. Our headmistress is tired. You know, when little Sophie grows up and goes to school I'll be quite scared of you.

OLGA. I shan't be a headmistress.

NATASHA. But they're appointing you, dear, it's all settled.

OLGA. I shall turn it down. I can't do it, it's more than I can manage. [*Drinks some water.*] A few moments ago you were very rude to Nanny. I'm sorry, I can't stand that kind of thing, it made me feel quite faint.

NATASHA [*very upset*]. Forgive me, Olga, forgive me. I didn't mean to upset you.

[MASHA *stands up, takes a pillow and goes out angrily.*]

OLGA. Try to understand, my dear. It may be the strange way we were brought up, but I can't stand that attitude. It really depresses me, actually makes me ill. I feel simply awful about it.

NATASHA. Forgive me, please. [*Kisses her.*]

OLGA. The least rudeness, a single word spoken unkindly—and I get upset.

NATASHA. I often say the wrong thing, I admit, but you must agree, dear, she could go and live in her village.

OLGA. She's been with our family for thirty years.

NATASHA. But the point is she can't work any more. Either I don't understand you or you've made up your mind not to understand me. She can't do a proper job, all she does is sleep or sit around.

OLGA. Then let her sit around.

NATASHA [*astonished*]. What? Let her sit around! She's a servant, isn't she? [*Through tears.*] I can't make you out, Olga. I keep a nanny myself and a wet nurse for the baby, and we have a maid and a cook. But what do we need that old woman for? That's what I don't see.

[*The fire-alarm is sounded off stage.*]

OLGA. Tonight seems to have put ten years on my life.

NATASHA. We must get this straight once and for all, Olga. Your place is the school, mine is the home. You teach. I run the house. And if I happen to pass a remark about the servants I know what I'm talking about. And the sooner you get that into your head the better. So you mind that thieving old hag gets her marching orders for tomorrow. [*Stamps her feet.*] The old bitch! How dare you exasperate me like this, how dare you? [*Regaining her self-control.*] Really, if you don't move downstairs we'll never stop quarrelling. It's perfectly horrible.

[KULYGIN *comes in.*]

KULYGIN. Where's Masha? It really is time we went home. I'm told the fire's dying out. [*Stretches himself.*] Only one row of houses burnt down, but there was a wind, you know, and it looked at one time as if the whole town was on fire. [*Sits down.*] I'm tired out. Dear Olga, I often think, if it hadn't been for Masha I'd have married you, dear. You're a wonderful person. I'm all in. [*Listens.*]

OLGA. What is it?

KULYGIN. The doctor has to pick a time like this to get roaring drunk. A time like this. [*Gets up.*] I think he's coming up here. Can you hear anything? Yes, he is. [*Laughs.*] Really, what a character. I'm going to hide. [*Goes towards the cupboard and stands in the corner.*] The old pirate.

OLGA. He hasn't touched a drop for two years and now he has to go and get drunk. [*Moves to the back of the room with* NATASHA.]

[CHEBUTYKIN *comes in. He walks across the room as steadily as if he was sober, stops, stares, then goes to the washstand and begins to wash his hands.*]

CHEBUTYKIN [*morosely*]. Damn the whole lot of them. To hell with them. They think I'm a doctor and can cure diseases, but I know absolutely nothing. What I did know I've forgotten, I don't remember a thing, my mind's a blank. [OLGA *and* NATASHA *go out, unnoticed by him.*] To hell with them. I had a patient at Zasyp last Wednesday, a woman. She died, and it was all my fault. Yes indeed. I did know a thing or two about twenty-five years ago, but now I've forgotten it all, it's all gone. Perhaps I'm not even a human being, perhaps I only pretend to have arms and legs and a head, perhaps I don't even exist at all, and only imagine I walk about and eat and sleep. [*Weeps.*] Oh, how nice not to exist. [*Stops weeping, morosely.*] Who the hell cares? A couple of days ago at the club they were talking about Shakespeare and Voltaire. I've never read them, never read a word of them, but I managed to look as if I had and everyone else did the same. Could anything be more vulgar? Or more sordid? Then I suddenly remembered the woman I killed on Wednesday, it all came back to me and I felt rotten, dirty, twisted inside. So I went and got drunk.

[IRINA, VERSHININ *and* TUZENBAKH *come in.* TUZENBAKH *is wearing a new and fashionable suit.*]

IRINA. Let's sit here a bit. No one will come in here.

VERSHININ. If it hadn't been for the troops the whole town would have gone up in flames. Good for them! [*Rubs his hands with pleasure.*] What a grand lot of chaps! Absolutely splendid!

KULYGIN [*going up to them*]. I say, what's the time?

TUZENBAKH. Well after three. It's starting to get light.

IRINA. They're all sitting in the dining-room, nobody seems to be going. Your friend Solyony's there as well. [*To* CHEBUTYKIN.] Why don't you go to bed, Doctor?

CHEBUTYKIN. I'm all right. Thanking you very much. [*Combs his beard.*]

KULYGIN [*laughs*]. Thoroughly plastered, aren't you, Doctor? [*Claps him on the shoulder.*] Well done, my boy. *In vino veritas*, as the ancients used to say.

TUZENBAKH. Everyone's asking me to get up a concert in aid of the fire victims.

IRINA. Oh, I shouldn't have thought anyone would——

TUZENBAKH. We could do it if we wanted. Masha for instance plays the piano beautifully.

KULYGIN. Indeed she does. Beautifully.

IRINA. She's forgotten how to. She hasn't played for three or four years.

TUZENBAKH. Nobody in this town appreciates music, nobody at all. But I do, I really do, and believe me, Masha plays magnificently. Brilliantly almost.

KULYGIN. Quite right, Baron. I'm so fond of Masha. She's wonderful.

TUZENBAKH. Imagine being able to play so gloriously, knowing all the time that not one living soul appreciates you.

KULYGIN [*sighs*]. True enough. But would it be quite the thing for her to play in a concert? [*Pause.*] Of course I'm a child in these matters, you know. I daresay it's quite all right. But to be perfectly honest, though our head's a decent enough chap—first rate in fact, quite outstanding— still he does hold certain views. This is nothing to do with him of course, but still I could have a word with him if you liked.

[CHEBUTYKIN *picks up a porcelain clock and examines it.*]

VERSHININ. I got terribly dirty at the fire, must look like

nothing on earth. [*Pause*.] Yesterday I heard a rumour that our brigade's in for a transfer to the back of beyond. Some say it's Poland. Others reckon it's the far side of Siberia.

TUZENBAKH. I heard the same. Ah well, the town will be deserted and no mistake.

IRINA. We're going away as well.

CHEBUTYKIN [*drops the clock and breaks it*]. Smashed to smithereens.

    [*Pause. Everyone is distressed and embarrassed.*]

KULYGIN [*picking up the pieces*]. A valuable object like that— good heavens, Doctor, whatever next! Take nought out of ten for conduct.

IRINA. That clock belonged to Mother.

CHEBUTYKIN. Very possibly. No doubt it was your mother's if you say so, but what if I didn't really break it, what if we only think I did? What if we only think we exist and aren't really here at all? I know nothing and nobody else knows anything either. [*Stands by the door*.] What are you all staring at? Natasha's carrying on with Protopopov and a lot of notice you take. You sit around as if you'd lost the use of your eyes while Natasha carries on with Protopopov. [*Sings*.] "Be so good as to accept one of these dates." [*Goes out*.]

VERSHININ. Well, well. [*Laughs*.] A funny business all this, it really is. [*Pause*.] When the fire broke out I ran home as fast as I could. I reached the house and saw it was quite all right, not in any danger or anything. My two little girls were standing by the front door in their nightclothes, their mother wasn't there, people were rushing about, horses and dogs were charging around, and you should have seen the children's faces. They looked frightened out of their wits, terribly pathetic and goodness knows what else. When I saw those faces my heart sank. My God, I thought, how much more have the children got to live through before they're finished? I grabbed them and rushed off, and I could think only of one thing—how much more will they have to put up with in this world? [*The alarm sounds.*

Pause.] I arrive here and find their mother shouting and in a filthy temper.

[MASHA *comes in with a pillow and sits down on the sofa*.]

VERSHININ. The children were standing by the front door in their nightclothes, the street was all red with flames, there was a most appalling din. It struck me that it must have been rather like this in the old days of sudden enemy invasions, with all the looting and burning. But what a difference between then and now, come to think of it. Before very long—in two or three hundred years, say—people will look back on our way of life with the same horror and contempt, they'll regard our times as tough, hard, strange and most uncomfortable. Why, life is going to be absolutely wonderful, it really is. [*Laughs*.] Sorry, I'm laying down the law again. Does anyone mind if I go on? I'm in just the mood to air my views at the moment, I can't help it. [*Pause*.] Everyone seems to be asleep. Well, as I say, life is going to be wonderful. Just imagine it. The point is, just now there are only three people like you in this town, but in future generations there will be more and more of them. Things will change in course of time and everything will be done your way. People will live your way too and after that you'll become back numbers in your turn, and a new and better breed will arise. [*Laughs*.] I'm in a funny sort of mood tonight, I feel ready to take on anything. [*Sings*.]
"As everyone has always found,
 It's love that makes the world go round." [*Laughs*.]

MASHA. Ti tum ti tum ti——

VERSHININ. Tum tum tum——

MASHA. Tara tarara.

VERSHININ. Tum ti tum. [*Laughs*.]

[FEDOTIK *comes in*.]

FEDOTIK [*dances about*]. Burnt to a cinder. Not a thing left! [*Laughter*.]

IRINA. It isn't exactly funny. Have you really lost everything?

FEDOTIK [*laughs*]. The whole lot. The cupboard's bare. My guitar, my photographic stuff, my letters—all gone up in smoke. I was going to give you a little notebook, but that went up as well.

[SOLYONY *comes in.*]

IRINA. Oh, please go away, Captain Solyony. You can't come in here.

SOLYONY. No? And why is the baron allowed in here when I'm not?

VERSHININ. We really should be going. What news of the fire?

SOLYONY. I was told it's dying down. I must say it's decidedly odd that the baron can come in here when I can't. [*Takes out a bottle of scent and sprinkles himself with it.*]

VERSHININ. Ti tum ti tum.

MASHA. Tum Tum.

VERSHININ [*laughing, to* SOLYONY]. Let's go into the dining-room.

SOLYONY. Very well, I'll take a note of it.
          "I could develop my idea,
          But might annoy the geese, I fear."

[*Looking at* TUZENBAKH.] Chuck, chuck, chuck. [*Goes out with* VERSHININ *and* FEDOTIK.]

IRINA. That beastly Solyony's filled the place with scent. [*Bewildered.*] The baron's gone to sleep. Hey, Baron!

TUZENBAKH [*opening his eyes*]. I say, I am tired. A brick-works. No, I'm not talking in my sleep, I'm actually going to a brick-works very shortly, going to do a job there. I've already spoken to them. [*To* IRINA, *tenderly.*] You look so pale and beautiful, so enchanting. Your pale face seems to light up the darkness around you. You're depressed and dissatisfied with life. Oh, why not come with me? We'll go away and get a job together.

MASHA. Oh Nicholas, I wish you would go away.

TUZENBAKH [*laughing*]. So you're here, are you? I can't see.

[*Kisses* IRINA's *hand*.] Good-bye then, I'll be off. Looking at you now, I remember a long time ago—it was on your name-day—when you spoke about the thrill of doing a real job of work. You were so cheerful and confident then and I seemed to see a happy future ahead of me. Where's all that gone now? [*Kisses her hand*.] There are tears in your eyes. You'd better go to bed, it's already getting light. It's almost morning. How I wish I could give my life for you.

MASHA. Do go, Nicholas. This really is too much.

TUZENBAKH. I'm going. [*Goes*.]

MASHA [*lying down*]. Theodore, are you asleep?

KULYGIN. Eh?

MASHA. Why don't you go home?

KULYGIN. Darling Masha, Masha my dear one——

IRINA. She's tired out. Better let her rest, Theodore.

KULYGIN. All right, I'll go. My splendid, wonderful wife—I love you, I love no one but you.

MASHA [*angrily*]. *Amo, amas, amat, amamus, amatis, amant.*

KULYGIN [*laughs*]. Oh, isn't she marvellous! You and I've been man and wife for seven years, but I feel as if we were married only yesterday, I do honestly. You really are a marvellous creature. I'm happy, happy, oh so happy.

MASHA. I'm bored, bored, oh so bored. [*Sits up*.] And there's something else I can't get out of my mind, something quite revolting. It's become an obsession, I can't keep it to myself any longer. It's about Andrew. He's mortgaged this house to the bank and his wife's pocketed the money. But the point is the house isn't his alone, it belongs to all four of us. He must surely realize that if he has any decency at all.

KULYGIN. Steady on, Masha. Why bring all that up? Andrew's in debt all round, so leave the poor fellow alone.

MASHA. Well, anyway, it's revolting. [*Lies down*.]

KULYGIN. You and I aren't poor. I have my job at the high school and I give private lessons as well. I'm a plain straightforward chap. *Omnia mea mecum porto*, as the saying goes.

MASHA. It's not that I want anything for myself. It's so unfair, that's what infuriates me. [*Pause.*] Theodore, why don't you go home?

KULYGIN [*kisses her*]. You're tired. Have half an hour's rest, and I'll just sit and wait. Go to sleep. [*Moves off.*] I'm happy, happy, oh so happy. [*Goes out.*]

IRINA. I must say, poor old Andrew has gone to seed. Living with that wretched woman has put years on his life and knocked all the stuffing out of him. At one time he was aiming to be a professor, and there he was yesterday boasting he'd got on the county council at long last. He's on the council and Protopopov's the chairman. The whole town's talking about it, everyone's laughing at him and he's the only one who doesn't know or see what's going on. And when everyone rushed off to the fire just now, there was he sitting in his room not taking the slightest notice and just playing his violin. [*Upset.*] Oh, it's frightful, absolutely frightful. [*Cries.*] I've had as much as I can take, I just can't stand any more.

[OLGA *comes in and starts tidying her bedside table.*]

IRINA [*sobs loudly*]. Why don't you get rid of me, throw me out? I can't stand it any more.

OLGA [*frightened*]. But what's the matter, darling?

IRINA [*sobbing*]. What's become of everything, where's it all gone? Where is it? Oh my God, I've forgotten, forgotten everything, my head's in such a whirl. I can't remember the Italian for "window"—or "ceiling" either. I'm always forgetting things, I forget something every day. And life is slipping away, it will never, never come back again, and we shall never go to Moscow either, I just know we shan't.

OLGA. Don't, dear, don't.

IRINA [*trying to control herself*]. Oh, I'm so miserable. I can't,

I won't, I will not work. I've had enough. I used to be at the post office and now I work for the town council, and I loathe and despise everything they give me to do. I'm twenty-three, I've been working all this time and my brain's shrivelled up. I've grown thin and ugly and old and I've nothing to show for it, nothing, no satisfaction of any kind, while time passes by and I feel I'm losing touch with everything fine and genuine in life. It's like sinking down, down into a bottomless pit. I'm desperate. Why am I still alive, why haven't I done away with myself? I don't know.

OLGA. Don't cry, child, please, it upsets me so.

IRINA. I'm not crying, I'm not. I won't. Look, I've stopped now. I must stop, I really must.

OLGA. My dear, let me tell you something as your sister and your friend. If you want my advice, marry the baron.

[IRINA *cries quietly*.]

OLGA. After all you do respect him, you think so much of him. He may not be all that good-looking, but he's a fine, decent man. One doesn't marry for love, you know, it's only a matter of doing one's duty. That's what I think anyway, and I'd marry without love. I'd marry the first man who came along provided it was someone honest and decent. I'd even marry an old man.

IRINA. I've been waiting for us to move to Moscow all this time, thinking I'd meet my true love there. I've dreamed about him, loved him, but that was sheer foolishness as it's turned out.

OLGA [*embraces her sister*]. I understand, Irina darling, I do understand. When the baron resigned his commission and came to see us in his civilian suit, he looked so ugly it actually brought tears to my eyes. He asked me why I was crying. How could I tell him? But if he did marry you, if such was God's will, I'd be happy. That's an altogether different thing, you see.

[NATASHA *comes in through the door, right, carrying a candle, crosses the stage and goes out through the door, left, without saying anything*.]

MASHA [*sits up*]. The way she goes about you'd think it was she who started the fire.

OLGA. Masha, you're silly. You're the silliest person in the whole family. Forgive me saying so. [*Pause.*]

MASHA. My dears, I've a confession to make. I feel I must get it off my chest. I'll tell you two and then never breathe another word about it to anyone, I'll tell you right away. [*Quietly.*] It's my secret, but I want you to know it, I can't keep it to myself. [*Pause.*] I'm in love, in love with that man. He was in here just now. Oh, what's the use? What I'm saying is, I love Vershinin.

OLGA [*goes behind her screen*]. That's enough of that. I'm not listening anyway.

MASHA. It's hopeless. [*Clutches her head.*] I found him strange at first, then felt sorry for him, then fell in love with him—with him, with his voice, his conversation, his misfortunes and his two little girls.

OLGA [*from behind the screen*]. Anyway, I'm not listening. I don't care what rubbish you talk, I'm just not listening.

MASHA. Oh, you are funny, Olga. Since I love him it must be my fate, it must be my destiny. And he loves me. It's terrifying, isn't it? Isn't it? [*Takes IRINA by the hand and draws her towards herself.*] Oh darling, how shall we spend the rest of our lives, and what's to become of us? When you read a novel this sort of thing all seems so trite and obvious, but when you fall in love yourself you see that nobody knows anything and we all have to decide these things for ourselves. My dears, now I've confessed I'll say no more. Now I'll be like the madman in Gogol's story. I'll keep quiet and say nothing.

[ANDREW *comes in followed by* FERAPONT.]

ANDREW [*angrily*]. What do you want? I don't understand.

FERAPONT [*standing in the doorway, impatiently*]. I must have told you ten times already, Mr. Andrew.

ANDREW. Well, don't call me Mr. Andrew for a start. Call me sir.

FERAPONT. It's the firemen, sir, they say can they please go to the river through your garden. They've been going the long way round all this time and it's more than flesh and blood can stand.

ANDREW. All right. Tell them it's all right. [FERAPONT *goes out*.] Confound them. Where's Olga? [OLGA *comes out from behind the screen*.] It's you I wanted to see. Would you mind giving me the key of the cupboard? I've lost mine. You know that little key you've got. [OLGA *silently hands him the key*. IRINA *goes behind her screen. Pause*.]

ANDREW. Well, it's been quite a fire, hasn't it? It is dying down now. That wretched Ferapont made me lose my temper, dammit, and say something silly. I told him to call me sir. [*Pause*.] Why don't you speak, Olga? [*Pause*.] Isn't it time you stopped being so silly, there's nothing to sulk about. You're here, Masha, and Irina's here. Well, that's fine, we can clear the air once and for all. What have you all got against me, eh?

OLGA. Don't start that, Andrew. We can talk about it tomorrow. [*With feeling*.] What a dreadful night.

ANDREW [*greatly put out*]. There's no need to get excited. I'm asking you quite calmly what it is you have against me, and I want a straight answer.

VERSHININ [*off stage*]. Tum ti ti.

MASHA [*getting up, in a loud voice*]. Tum tum tum. [*To* OLGA.] Goodnight, Olga, look after yourself. [*Goes behind the screen and kisses* IRINA.] Pleasant dreams. Good-night, Andrew. Do go away, they're worn out. You can sort this all out tomorrow. [*Goes out*.]

OLGA. Yes, really, Andrew, let's leave it till tomorrow. [*Goes behind her screen*.] It's time we were in bed.

ANDREW. I'll say what's on my mind and go. Right. In the first place, you all seem to have it in for Natasha. Oh yes, I've noticed it since the day we were married. My wife, in case you want to know, is a fine, decent, straight-forward, honourable woman. Or that's what I think. I love my wife and respect her. I respect her, I tell you, and I require others to do the same. I repeat—she's a decent, honourable woman, and you'll forgive my saying that all your objections to her are sheer childishness. [*Pause.*] And in the second place, you seem annoyed with me because I'm not a professor and don't do academic work. But I happen to work for the county council. I'm a county councillor and I consider that work every bit as honourable and worth-while as any academic job. I'm on the county council and proud of it, in case you're interested. [*Pause.*] And in the third place I've something else to say. I know I mortgaged this house without getting your permission. That was wrong, I admit, and I apologize. I had to do it because of all that money I owed, thirty-five thousand roubles of it. I don't gamble any more, I gave that up long ago, but the main point in my defence is that you girls have an annuity, whereas I've had no such source of—income, so to speak. [*Pause.*]

KULYGIN [*through the door*]. Isn't Masha here? [*Agitated.*] Where can she have got to? This is all very odd. [*Goes out.*]

ANDREW. They won't listen. Natasha's a fine, decent woman, I tell you. [*Walks silently up and down the stage, then stops.*] When we got married I thought we were going to be happy, all of us. But oh my God! [*Cries.*] My dear sisters, my darling sisters, don't believe what I've been saying, don't believe a word of it. [*Goes out.*]

KULYGIN [*through the door, agitatedly*]. Where's Masha? Isn't she here? This is most peculiar. [*Goes away.*]

[*The alarm sounds. The stage is empty.*]

IRINA [*from behind the screen*]. Olga, who's that knocking on the floor?

OLGA. The doctor. He's drunk.

IRINA. It's been one thing after another all night. [*Pause.*] Olga! [*Looks out from behind the screen.*] Have you heard? They're moving our brigade, posting it somewhere far away.

OLGA. That's only a rumour.

IRINA. Then we'll be all on our own. Olga!

OLGA. Yes?

IRINA. I respect the baron, Olga darling, I think very highly of
him, he is a very good man and I will marry him, I will, I
will, only do let's go to Moscow. We must go. Please!
There's nowhere in the world like Moscow. Let's go, Olga,
do let's go!

CURTAIN

ACT FOUR

The old garden belonging to the PROZOROVS' *house. A long avenue of firs with a view of the river at the end. A wood on the far side of the river. On the right the terrace of the house. On it a table with bottles and glasses—someone has obviously just been drinking champagne. Midday. From time to time people from the street go through the garden towards the river. Five or six soldiers march briskly past.*

CHEBUTYKIN, who remains in a genial mood throughout the Act, is sitting in an armchair in the garden waiting for someone to call him. He has his army cap on and holds a stick. IRINA, KULYGIN—*who wears a decoration on a ribbon round his neck and has shaved off his moustache—and* TUZENBAKH *are standing on the terrace saying good-bye to* FEDOTIK *and* RODÉ, *who are coming down the steps. Both officers are in service dress.*

TUZENBAKH [*embraces* FEDOTIK]. You're a good fellow, we've always got on well together. [*Embraces* RODÉ.] Once more then. Good-bye, my dear fellow.

IRINA. *Au revoir.*

FEDOTIK. It isn't *au revoir*, it's good-bye. We'll never see each other again.

KULYGIN. Who knows? [*Wipes his eyes and smiles.*] Now I'm crying too.

IRINA. We'll meet again some time.

FEDOTIK. You mean in ten or fifteen years? By then we'll hardly know each other, we'll meet as strangers. Stand still, please. [*Takes a snapshot.*] Now, just once more.

RODÉ [*embraces* TUZENBAKH]. This is the last time we'll see each other. [*Kisses* IRINA's *hand.*] Thank you for all you've done.

FEDOTIK [*annoyed*]. Oh, can't you stand still a moment?

TUZENBAKH. We shall meet again with luck. And be sure to write to us, don't forget.

RODÉ [*looking round the garden*]. Good-bye, trees. [*Shouts*.] Halloo-oo! [*Pause*.] Good-bye, echo.

KULYGIN. You'll get married over in Poland, very likely. Your wife will put her arms round you and call you "darling" in Polish. [*Laughs*.]

FEDOTIK [*with a glance at his watch*]. There's less than an hour to go. Solyony's the only one from our battery on the barge party, the rest of us go with the marching column. There's a unit of three batteries leaving today and three more going tomorrow, and then the town will have a bit of peace and quiet.

TUZENBAKH. And an awful dose of boredom.

RODÉ. I say, where's Masha?

KULYGIN. In the garden somewhere.

FEDOTIK. We must say good-bye to her.

RODÉ. Good-bye. I must go or I'll start crying. [*Quickly embraces* TUZENBAKH *and* KULYGIN, *kisses* IRINA's *hand*.] We've had a wonderful time here.

FEDOTIK [*to* KULYGIN]. Here's something to remember me by, a note-book and pencil. We'll take this way down to the river. [FEDOTIK *and* RODÉ *move off, glancing back*.]

RODÉ [*shouts*]. Halloo-oo!

KULYGIN [*shouts*]. Good-bye.

[FEDOTIK *and* RODÉ *meet* MASHA *at the back of the stage and say good-bye to her. She goes off with them*.]

IRINA. They've gone. [*Sits down on the bottom step of the terrace*.]

CHEBUTYKIN. And forgotten to say good-bye to me.

IRINA. Well, what about you?

CHEBUTYKIN. That's true, I forgot to myself. Still, I'll be seeing them again before long. I'm off tomorrow. Yes. I have just one day left. A year from now I'll be on the retired list and I'll come back here and spend the rest of my life with you. Only a year now till I get my pension. [*Puts his newspaper in his pocket and takes out another*.] I'll come back here and turn over a new leaf. I'll be a good little boy, very considerate, and oh so well behaved.

IRINA. It's high time you did mend your ways somehow, my dear, it really is.

CHEBUTYKIN. Quite. That's how I feel. [*Sings quietly*.] Tararaboomdeay, let's have a tune today.

KULYGIN. You're incorrigible, Doctor, incorrigible.

CHEBUTYKIN. You should have taken me in hand then, you might have put me on the right lines.

IRINA. Theodore's shaved off his moustache. I can't bear to look at him.

KULYGIN. Why, what's wrong?

CHEBUTYKIN. I might tell you what your face puts me in mind of, but I'd better not.

KULYGIN. Why all the fuss? It's quite the thing these days, *modus vivendi* and all that. The head's clean shaven, so when I became second master I followed suit. No one likes it, but I don't care. I'm perfectly happy. Moustache or no moustache, I'm happy either way. [*Sits down*.]

[ANDREW *crosses the back of the stage pushing a pram with a sleeping baby in it*.]

IRINA. Doctor, be an angel—I'm awfully worried. You were in town last night. Tell me, what was this affair on the boulevard?

CHEBUTYKIN. What affair? It was nothing. Lot of poppycock. [*Reads his paper*.] Nothing that matters anyway.

KULYGIN. What I heard is, Solyony and the baron met on the boulevard outside the theatre yesterday——

TUZENBAKH. Please stop. Oh, what's the use—? [*Makes a gesture as if to dismiss the subject and goes into the house*.]

KULYGIN. It happened outside the theatre. Solyony started

picking on the baron and the baron lost his temper and insulted him.

CHEBUTYKIN. I don't know anything about it. It's a lot of bunkum.

KULYGIN. A schoolmaster once wrote "bunkum" on a pupil's essay and the boy thought it was Latin and started declining it. *Bunkum, bunkum, bunkum, bunki, bunko, bunko.* [*Laughs.*] Terribly funny that. Solyony's said to be in love with Irina and he seems to have got it in for the baron. Well, that's only natural. Irina's a very nice girl, she's even a bit like Masha, always wrapped up in her own thoughts. But you're more easy-going than Masha, Irina. Though actually Masha's very good-natured too. Oh, I do love Masha.

[*From off stage at the back comes a cry:* Hallo there! Halloooo!]

IRINA [*shudders*]. The least thing seems to frighten me today. [*Pause.*] I've packed everything and I'm sending my stuff on after luncheon. The baron and I are getting married tomorrow, then we're going straight off to that brick-works. Next day I start work at school and a new life begins, God willing. When I sat for my teacher's diploma I was actually crying for joy. [*Pause.*] The carter will be here for our things in a minute.

KULYGIN. This is all very well, but it doesn't add up to much, does it? It's just a lot of hot air, there's precious little sense in it. Anyway I wish you luck, I really do.

CHEBUTYKIN [*deeply moved*]. My darling child, my splendid little girl, you're so far ahead of me I'll never catch up with you now. I've been left behind like a bird that's too old to fly away with the flock. Fly away, my dears, fly away and the best of luck to you. [*Pause.*] It's a pity you shaved your moustache off, Kulygin.

KULYGIN. That's quite enough of that. [*Sighs.*] Well, the army's leaving today and we'll be back where we were. They can say what they like, but Masha's a good, loyal little woman, I love her very much and I thank my lucky stars. It's all the luck of the game, you know. There's a clerk in the tax

office here, fellow called Kozyrev. We were at school together, but when he was in the fifth form he was expelled
because he just couldn't grasp the construction of *ut* and
the subjunctive. He's ill these days and terribly hard up,
and when I run across him I always say, "Hallo there, *ut*
and the subjunctive." "Yes," he always says. "That's just my
trouble, *ut* and the subjunctive." Then he starts coughing.
Now I've been lucky all my life, I'm very fortunate, I even
have the Order of St. Stanislaus second class. And now I
teach other people this *ut* and the subjunctive business. Of
course I'm no fool, I am brighter than average. But there's
more to happiness than that.

[*The* Maiden's Prayer *is played on a piano in the house*.]

IRINA. Tomorrow night I shan't have to hear that *Maiden's
Prayer* any more or keep meeting Protopopov. [*Pause*.] Do
you know, Protopopov's in the drawing-room. He's even
turned up today.

KULYGIN. Isn't our headmistress here yet?

IRINA. No. We've sent for her. You can't imagine what a bore
I find it living here on my own without Olga. Now she's
headmistress, she lives in at school and she's on the go all
day, while I'm lonely and depressed with nothing to do
and I hate my room in this house. But I've made up my
mind. If I can't go to Moscow, well, I can't, and that's that.
It's just the way things have turned out. It can't be helped,
it's all God's will and that's the truth. Nicholas asked me to
marry him. Well, I thought it over and decided to say yes.
He's a good man, he really is—unbelievably good. I suddenly felt as if I'd grown wings. I cheered up and felt so
much easier in my mind, and the old urge came over me to
work, work, work. But then there was this incident yesterday, whatever it was, and I feel as if something awful's
going to happen to me.

CHEBUTYKIN. Stuff and nonsense. *Bunki, bunko, bunko*.

NATASHA [*through a window*]. The headmistress.

KULYGIN. The headmistress has come. Let's go in.

[*Goes indoors with* IRINA.]

CHEBUTYKIN [*reads the paper and sings softly*]. Tararaboomdeay, let's have a tune today.

[MASHA *comes up to him.* ANDREW *crosses the back of the stage pushing the pram.*]

MASHA. Taking it nice and easy, aren't you?

CHEBUTYKIN. What's wrong with that?

MASHA [*sits down*]. Oh, nothing. [*Pause.*] Were you in love with my mother?

CHEBUTYKIN. Very much so.

MASHA. Did she love you?

CHEBUTYKIN [*after a pause*]. That I don't recall.

MASHA. Is my man here? That's what our cook Martha used to call her policeman—"my man." Is my man here?

CHEBUTYKIN. Not yet.

MASHA. When you have to snatch what crumbs of happiness you can and then lose it all, as is happening to me, you gradually grow hard and bad-tempered. [*Points at her breast.*] I feel I'm going to burst. [*Looking at* ANDREW *as he pushes the pram.*] There goes brother Andrew. All our hopes have come to nothing. Imagine thousands of people hoisting up a huge bell. Then after all the effort and money spent on it, it suddenly falls and is smashed to pieces. Suddenly, for no reason at all. That's how it's been with Andrew.

ANDREW. I say, when are we going to have some quiet round here? What an awful row.

CHEBUTYKIN. It won't be long now. [*Looks at his watch.*] I've got an old-fashioned watch, a repeater. [*Winds the watch. It rings.*] One, Two and Five Battery are leaving at one o'clock sharp. [*Pause.*] And I'm off tomorrow.

ANDREW. Will you ever come back?

CHEBUTYKIN. I don't know, I may be back next year. Damned if I know. Or care either.

[*There is the sound of a harp and violin somewhere far away.*]

ANDREW. This town will be quite dead, it'll be like living in a museum. [*Pause*.] Something happened outside the theatre yesterday, I've no idea what, but everyone's talking about it.

CHEBUTYKIN. Oh, it was nothing. Lot of nonsense. Solyony started annoying the baron, the baron lost his temper and insulted him, and the upshot was Solyony had to challenge him to a duel. [*Looks at his watch*.] It must be pretty well time. It's to be at half past twelve in that bit of crown forest over there on the other side of the river. Bang, bang! [*Laughs*.] Solyony sees himself as a Lermontov. Even writes poetry. Joking apart though, this is his third duel.

MASHA. Whose?

CHEBUTYKIN. Solyony's.

MASHA. What about the baron?

CHEBUTYKIN. What about the baron? [*Pause*.]

MASHA. I'm in a complete daze. I still say they shouldn't be allowed to fight. He might wound the baron or even kill him.

CHEBUTYKIN. The baron's a nice enough fellow, but one baron more or less in the world—what does that matter? Let them get on with it. Who cares? [*Shouts are heard from the other side of the garden*: "Yoo-hoo! Halloo-oo!"] You can just wait a minute. That's Skvortsov shouting, one of the seconds. He's there in a boat. [*Pause*.]

ANDREW. If you ask me, duelling or attending a duel, even as a doctor, is downright immoral.

CHEBUTYKIN. That's only the way you see it. We're not real, neither is anything else in the world. We aren't here at all actually, we only think we are. And who cares anyway?

MASHA. Talk, talk, talk. Nothing but talk the whole blessed day. [*Moves off*.] As if this climate wasn't quite enough, with snow liable to fall any minute, there has to be all this chit-chat as well. [*Stops*.] I'm not going indoors, I can't bear it there. Please let me know when Vershinin gets here. [*Moves off down the avenue*.] Look, the birds are flying off already. [*Looks up.*] They're swans or geese. Dear, happy birds. [*Goes off.*]

ANDREW. Our house is going to seem awfully empty. The officers are going, you're going, Irina's getting married, and I'll be all on my own here.

CHEBUTYKIN. What about your wife?

[FERAPONT *comes in with some papers.*]

ANDREW. My wife is—well, she's my wife. She's loyal and decent—kind too, if you like—but there's something degrading about her too, as if she was some kind of blind, groping, scruffy little animal. She's not a human being anyway. I'm speaking to you as a friend. There's no one else I can really talk to. I love Natasha, yes I do, but there are times when I find her thoroughly vulgar, and then I don't know what to think and I've no idea why I do love her so much—or anyway used to.

CHEBUTYKIN [*stands up*]. I'm leaving tomorrow, old boy, and we may never meet again, so here's a word of advice. You just put your hat on, pick up a walking stick and go. Go on and on and on, and don't ever look back. And the further you go the better.

[SOLYONY *crosses the back of the stage with two officers. Seeing* CHEBUTYKIN, *he turns towards him while the officers walk on.*]

SOLYONY. It's time, Doctor. Half past twelve. [*Greets* ANDREW.]

CHEBUTYKIN. All right then, confound you all. [*To* ANDREW.] If anyone wants me, Andrew, would you mind saying I'll be back in a minute? [*Sighs.*] Ah me!

SOLYONY. "Before he'd time to turn a hair
        He'd been knocked over by a bear." [*Moves off with* CHEBUTYKIN.] What are you moaning about, Grandad?

CHEBUTYKIN. Oh, go away.

SOLYONY. How are you feeling?

CHEBUTYKIN [*angrily.*] Don't ask silly questions and you won't get silly answers.

SOLYONY. The old boy needn't get hot under the collar. I

shan't overdo it, I'll only wing him like a woodcock. [*Takes out a bottle and sprinkles scent on his hands*.] I've used up a whole bottle today, but my hands still smell. They smell like a corpse. [*Pause*.] Yes indeed. Do you remember those lines of Lermontov's?

> "Restless, he seeks the raging storm,
> As if the storm could give him rest."

CHEBUTYKIN. Yes.
> "Before he'd time to turn a hair
> He'd been knocked over by a bear." [*Goes out with* SOLYONY.]

[*Shouts are heard*: "Halloo-oo! Yoo-hoo!" ANDREW *and* FERAPONT *come in*.]

FERAPONT. Some papers to sign——

ANDREW [*irritably*]. Leave me alone for heaven's sake, do leave me alone. [*Goes out with pram*.]

FERAPONT. But that's what papers are for, isn't it? To be signed. [*Goes to the back of the stage*.]

[*Enter* IRINA *and* TUZENBAKH, *who is wearing a straw hat*. KULYGIN *crosses the stage shouting*, "Hallo there, Masha, hallo!"]

TUZENBAKH. He must be the only person in town who's glad the army's leaving.

IRINA. That's only natural. [*Pause*.] The town will be half dead now.

TUZENBAKH. I'll be back in a minute, my dear.

IRINA. Where are you going?

TUZENBAKH. I must go into town and—see some of my friends off.

IRINA. That isn't true. Your thoughts seem far away this morning, Nicholas. Why? [*Pause*.] What did happen outside the theatre last night?

TUZENBAKH [*with an impatient gesture*.] I'll be back in an hour, back with you again. [*Kisses her hands*.] Darling. [*Gazes into her eyes*.] It's five years since I first fell in love with you and I still can't get used to it, I find you more beautiful every day. You have such marvellous, wonderful hair, such lovely eyes. I'll take you away tomorrow, we'll work, we'll be rich and all my dreams will come true. And you'll be happy. There is just one thing wrong though. You don't love me.

IRINA. I can't help that. I'll be your wife, I'll honour and obey you, but I don't love you and I can't help it. [*Cries.*] I've never been in love, never. Oh, I've longed for love, dreamed about it so much day and night, but my heart is like a wonderful grand piano that can't be used because it's locked up and the key's lost. [*Pause.*] You look worried.

TUZENBAKH. I couldn't sleep last night. Not that there's anything alarming or particularly frightening in my life, but the thought of that lost key torments me and keeps me awake. Say something to me. [*Pause.*] Say something.

IRINA. Why, what am I to say?

TUZENBAKH. Anything.

IRINA. Oh, please don't talk like that. [*Pause.*]

TUZENBAKH. It's funny the way stupid, trivial little things sometimes loom up out of the blue and affect one's life. You still laugh at them, still think of them as trivial, but you somehow get carried away by them and don't seem able to stop yourself. Anyway let's not talk about that. I feel marvellous. I feel as if I'm seeing all these fir-trees, maples and silver birches for the first time. All these things seem to be watching me as if wondering what was going to happen next. What beautiful trees. And when you come to think of it, what a beautiful thing life ought to be with trees like this around. [*Shouts of*: "Yoo-hoo! Halloo-oo!"] I have to go now. Look at that dead tree. It's withered, but it still sways in the breeze with all the others. It's the same with me, I feel I'll still be part of life somehow or other even if I die. Good-bye, Irina. [*Kisses* IRINA's *hands.*] I've put those papers you gave me under a calendar on my table.

IRINA. I'm coming with you.

TUZENBAKH [*alarmed*]. Oh no, no! [*Moves off quickly and stops some way down the avenue.*] Irina!

IRINA. What?

TUZENBAKH [*not knowing what to say*]. I haven't had any coffee this morning. Would you ask them to make me some? [*Goes off quickly.*]

[IRINA *stands lost in thought, then goes to the back of the stage and sits on the swing.* ANDREW *comes in pushing the pram.* FERAPONT *appears.*]

FERAPONT. Mr. Andrew, these papers aren't mine, you know, they're official documents. I didn't invent them.

ANDREW. Where is my past life, oh what has become of it—when I was young, happy and intelligent, when I had such glorious thoughts and visions, and my present and future seemed so bright and promising? Why is it we've hardly started living before we all become dull, drab, boring, lazy, complacent, useless and miserable? This town's two hundred years old and we've a hundred thousand people living here, but the trouble is, every man jack of them's exactly like every other one, and no one here does anything really worth while. Or ever has. We've never produced a single scholar or artist or anyone else with a touch of originality to make us envy him, or decide we were damn well going to go one better ourselves. All these people do is eat, drink and sleep till they drop down dead. Then new ones are born to carry on the eating, drinking and sleeping. And to save themselves getting bored to tears and put a bit of spice in their lives, they go in for all this sickening gossip, vodka, gambling, litigation. Wives deceive their husbands and husbands tell lies and pretend they're deaf and blind to what's going on, and all the time the children are crushed by vulgarity, lose any spark of inspiration they might ever have had, and—like their fathers and mothers before them—turn into a lot of miserable living corpses, each one exactly like his neighbour. [*To* FERAPONT, *angrily.*] What do *you* want?

FERAPONT. Eh? Papers for you to sign.

ANDREW. You're a nuisance.

FERAPONT [*handing over the papers*]. The porter at the tax office was on about something just now, says they had two hundred degrees of frost in St. Petersburg last winter.

ANDREW. I loathe our present life, but thinking about the future makes me feel really good. I feel so easy and relaxed, I see a light glimmering in the distance, I have a vision of freedom. I see myself and my children freed from idleness and drinking kvass and stuffing ourselves with goose and cabbage, freed from our after-dinner naps 'and this vile habit of trying to get something for nothing.

FERAPONT. Two thousand people froze to death, he says. He says everyone was scared stiff. It was either St. Petersburg or Moscow, I don't rightly remember.

ANDREW [*in a sudden access of tenderness*]. My dear sisters, my wonderful sisters. [*Through tears.*] Masha, my sister——

NATASHA [*appearing in a window*]. Who's making all that noise? Is that you, Andrew? You'll wake up little Sophie. *Il ne faut pas faire du bruit, la Sophie est dormée déjà. Vous êtes un ours.* [*Flaring up.*] If you can't keep your mouth shut you'd better give the pram to someone else. Ferapont, take that pram from Mr. Prozorov.

FERAPONT. Very well, madam. [*Takes the pram.*]

ANDREW [*embarrassed*]. I wasn't making much noise.

NATASHA [*from behind the window, speaking lovingly to her little boy*]. Bobik! Naughty Bobik! Bad, bad Bobik!

ANDREW [*glancing over the papers*]. All right, I'll look through this lot and sign the ones that need signing, and you can take them back to the office. [*Goes indoors reading the papers.* FERAPONT *wheels the pram off into the garden.*]

NATASHA [*from behind the window*]. Bobik! What's Mummy's name? Oh, isn't he sweet? And who's this? It's Aunty Olga. Say, "Hallo, Aunty Olly."

[*Two street musicians, a man and a girl, come in playing a violin and a harp.* VERSHININ *comes out of the house with* OLGA *and* ANFISA. *They listen for a while in silence.* IRINA *goes up to them.*]

OLGA. Our garden's like a public highway with people coming and going all the time. Nanny, give these people something.

ANFISA [*gives the musicians money*]. Run along then and God be with you, my dears. [*The musicians bow and go off.*] Poor things, they must be half starved. Why else would they do it? Good morning, Irina dear. [*Kisses her.*] I'm having a lovely time, child, I really am. I'm living with Olga at the high-school in a school flat. The good Lord's found me a little place of my own in my old age and I'm having the time of my life, old sinner that I am. It's a great big flat belonging to the school, and I've a little room of my own and my own little bed, all rent free. I sometimes wake up in the middle of the night and think—Lord and Holy Mother of God, I'm the happiest woman in the world.

VERSHININ [*with a glance at his watch*]. We're just leaving, Olga. I have to go. [*Pause.*] I wish you every, every—. Where's Masha?

IRINA. Somewhere in the garden. I'll go and find her.

VERSHININ. That's very kind, I am in rather a hurry.

ANFISA. I'll go and look as well. [*Shouts.*] Masha, are you there? [*Goes off into the garden with* IRINA.] Hallo there, hallo!

VERSHININ. Everything comes to an end some time, and here we are saying good-bye. [*Looks at his watch.*] The town gave us a sort of farewell lunch, we had champagne and the mayor made a speech. I ate my lunch and listened to the mayor, but I was here with you in spirit. [*Glances round the garden.*] I've grown so fond of you all.

OLGA. Shall we ever meet again?

VERSHININ. I shouldn't think so. [*Pause.*] My wife and the girls are staying on here for a couple of months. If anything should happen or they need anything, please——

OLGA. Yes, yes of course, set your mind at rest. [*Pause.*] Tomorrow there won't be a single soldier left in town. We shall stay behind with our memories, and of course things will be very different for us now. [*Pause.*] Nothing ever works out as we want it. I never wanted to be a headmistress, but I am one. So it's obvious I'll never get to Moscow now.

VERSHININ. Ah well, thank you for everything. And if there's been anything at all amiss, please forgive me. I've talked much too much. Please forgive that too. Don't think too badly of me.

OLGA [*wiping her eyes*]. Why doesn't Masha come?

VERSHININ. What else is there to say before I go? Shouldn't I hold forth about something? [*Laughs.*] Life isn't a bed of roses. A lot of us think it's a hopeless dead end. Still, you must admit things are getting brighter and better all the time, and it does look as if we'll see a real break in the clouds before very long. [*Looks at his watch.*] It really is time for me to go. In the old days people were always fighting wars and their lives were one long round of campaigns, invasions and victories, but those things are all past history now. They've left a great gap behind them and so far there's been nothing to put in their place, but people are desperately trying to find something and in the end they're bound to succeed. Oh, if that could only happen soon. [*Pause.*] If we could only combine education with hard work, you know, and hard work with education. [*Looks at his watch.*] Well, I really must be on my way——

OLGA. Here she is.

[MASHA *comes in.*]

VERSHININ. I came to say good-bye. [OLGA *moves a little to one side so that they can say good-bye.*]

MASHA [*looking into his eyes*]. Good-bye, dear. [*A long kiss.*]

OLGA. Don't, don't, please.

[MASHA *sobs loudly.*]

VERSHININ. Write to me, darling. Don't forget me. Now let me go, I must go——. You take her, Olga, I really—have to go. I'm late. [*Deeply moved, kisses* OLGA's *hands, then embraces* MASHA *again and quickly leaves.*]

OLGA. Don't cry, Masha. Do stop, dear.

[KULYGIN *comes in.*]

KULYGIN [*embarrassed*]. Never mind, let her cry, let her. Dear Masha, good, kind Masha, you're my wife, and I'm still happy in spite of everything. I'm not complaining or

blaming you at all, as Olga here can witness. Let's go back
to living as we used to, and I won't breathe so much as a
word or hint——

MASHA [*choking back her sobs*].
       "A green oak by a curving shore,
        And on that oak a chain of gold—
        And on that oak a chain of gold."
I'm going crazy. A green oak—by a curving shore.

OLGA. There, there, Masha. Calm yourself. Get her some
water.

MASHA. I've stopped crying now.

KULYGIN. She's stopped crying. She's a good girl.

[*The muffled sound of a distant shot is heard.*]

MASHA.   "A green oak by a curving shore,
            And on that oak a chain of gold."
A green cat. A green oak. I've got it all mixed up. [*Drinks
some water.*] I've made a mess of my life. I don't want
anything now. I'll be all right in a moment—. It doesn't
matter. What does it mean, "by a curving shore?" Why can't
I get those words out of my head? Oh, my thoughts are in
such a whirl.

[IRINA *comes in.*]

OLGA. Calm yourself, Masha. That's right, there's a sensible
girl. Let's go indoors.

MASHA [*angrily*]. I'm not going in there. [*Starts sobbing again,
but stops at once.*] I don't go in that house any more. I'm
not going in now.

IRINA. Let's all sit here for a bit, there's no need to talk. I'm
leaving tomorrow, you know. [*Pause.*]

KULYGIN. Yesterday I took this false beard and moustache off a
boy in the third form. [*Puts on the beard and moustache.*]
I look like our German master. [*Laughs.*] I do, don't I?
Those boys are really priceless.

MASHA. I say, you really do look like the German master.

OLGA [*laughs*]. Yes, he does.

[MASHA *cries.*]

IRINA. Please don't, Masha.

KULYGIN. A striking resemblance.

[NATASHA *comes in.*]

NATASHA [*to the* MAID]. Now what was it? Oh yes. Mr. Protopopov's going to keep an eye on Sophie and my husband may as well push Bobik's pram. Children do make such a lot of work. [*To* IRINA.] What a shame you're leaving tomorrow, Irina. Why don't you stay on another week? [*Sees* KULYGIN *and shrieks. He laughs and removes the beard and moustache*.] Oh, you awful man, you did give me a shock. [*To* IRINA.] I'm used to having you around and I'll find it quite a wrench, you know, now you're leaving. I'll move Andrew into your room along with his violin. He can scrape away in there as much as he likes and we'll put Sophie in his room. What a heavenly little girl. Isn't she a wonderful child? She gave me such a sweet look today and said "Mummy."

KULYGIN. She is a lovely baby, no doubt about it.

NATASHA. So I'll be all on my own here tomorrow. [*Sighs.*] The first thing I'll do is have that avenue of firs cut down and that maple-tree. It looks so hideous in the evening. [*To* IRINA.] That sash doesn't suit you at all, dear, in fact it's in very poor taste. You need something nice and bright. And I'll have lots and lots of nice flowers planted all over the place, and they'll make ever such a lovely perfume. [*Sternly.*] What's this fork doing on the bench here? [*Going indoors, to the* MAID.] I asked what this fork was doing on the bench. [*Shouts.*] You dare answer me back!

KULYGIN. She's off again.

[*A band is heard playing a march off stage. Everyone listens.*]

OLGA. They're leaving.

[CHEBUTYKIN *comes in.*]

MASHA. Our friends are leaving. Oh well, may they have a happy journey. [*To her husband.*] We'd better go home. Where's my hat and coat?

KULYGIN. I took them indoors. I'll go and get them.

OLGA. Yes, now we can all go off home. It's high time.

CHEBUTYKIN. Olga!

OLGA. What is it? [*Pause*.] What's happened?

CHEBUTYKIN. Nothing. I don't know how to tell you. [*Whispers in her ear*.]

OLGA [*aghast*]. No, no, it can't be true.

CHEBUTYKIN. Yes. What a business! I'm tired out, absolutely done in, I don't want to say another word. [*Annoyed*.] Anyway, what does it all matter?

MASHA. What happened?

OLGA [*embraces* IRINA]. This has been a terrible day. Darling, I don't know how to tell you——

IRINA. What is it? Tell me at once, for God's sake—what is it? [*Cries*.]

CHEBUTYKIN. The baron's just been killed in a duel.

IRINA [*weeps quietly*]. I knew it, I knew it.

CHEBUTYKIN [*sits down on a bench at the back of the stage*]. I'm worn out. [*Takes a newspaper out of his pocket*.] They may as well have a cry. [*Sings softly*.] Tararaboomdeay, let's have a tune today. Anyway, what does it all matter?

[*The three sisters stand close together*.]

MASHA. Oh, listen to the band. They're all leaving us, and one has gone right away and will never, never come back, and we shall be left alone to begin our lives again. We must go on living, we must.

IRINA [*puts her head on* OLGA'*s breast*]. What is all this for? Why all this suffering? The answer will be known one day, and then there will be no more mysteries left, but till then life must go on, we must work and work and think of nothing else. I'll go off alone tomorrow to teach at a school and spend my whole life serving those who may need me. It's autumn now and it will soon be winter, with everything buried in snow, and I shall work, work, work.

OLGA [*embraces both her sisters*]. Listen to the band. What a splendid, rousing tune, it puts new heart into you, doesn't it? Oh, my God! In time we shall pass on for ever and be forgotten. Our faces will be forgotten and our voices and how many of us there were. But our sufferings will bring happiness to those who come after us, peace and joy will reign on earth, and there will be kind words and kind thoughts for us and our times. We still have our lives ahead of us, my dears, so let's make the most of them. The band's playing such cheerful, happy music, it feels as if we might find out before long what our lives and sufferings are for. If we could only know! If we could only know!

[*The music becomes fainter and fainter.* KULYGIN, *smiling cheerfully, brings the hat and coat, while* ANDREW *pushes the pram with* BOBIK *sitting in it.*]

CHEBUTYKIN [*singing softly*]. Tararaboomdeay, let's have a tune today. [*Reads the newspaper.*] None of it matters. Nothing matters.

OLGA. If we could only know, oh if we could only know!

CURTAIN

THE CHERRY ORCHARD

[Вишнёвый сад]

A COMEDY IN FOUR ACTS

(1903–1904)

CHARACTERS

MRS. LYUBA RANEVSKY, an estate-owner

ANYA, her daughter, aged 17

VARYA, her adopted daughter, aged 24

LEONID GAYEV, Mrs. Ranevsky's brother

YERMOLAY LOPAKHIN, a businessman

PETER TROFIMOV, a student

BORIS SIMEONOV-PISHCHIK, an estate-owner

CHARLOTTE, a governess

SIMON YEPIKHODOV, a clerk

DUNYASHA, a maid

FIRS, a manservant, aged 87

YASHA, a young manservant

A passer-by

A stationmaster

A post office clerk

Guests and servants

The action takes place on Mrs. Ranevsky's estate

ACT ONE

A room which is still known as "the nursery." One of the doors leads to ANYA's *room. Dawn is breaking and the sun will soon be up. It is May. The cherry trees are in bloom, but it is cold and frosty in the orchard. The windows of the room are shut.*

Enter DUNYASHA *carrying a candle, and* LOPAKHIN *with a book in his hand.*

LOPAKHIN. The train's arrived, thank God. What time is it?

DUNYASHA. Nearly two o'clock. [*Blows out the candle.*] It's already light.

LOPAKHIN. How late was the train then? A couple of hours at least. [*Yawns and stretches himself.*] And a prize idiot I am, making an ass of myself like this. I come out here specially so I can go and meet them at the station, then suddenly fall asleep and wake up too late. Dropped off in the chair. What a nuisance. You might have woken me.

DUNYASHA. I thought you'd gone. [*Listens.*] It sounds as if they're coming.

LOPAKHIN [*listening*]. No, they're not. There's the luggage to be got out and all that. [*Pause.*] Your mistress has been living abroad for five years and I've no idea what she's like now. She was always such a nice woman, unaffected and easy to get on with. I remember when I was a lad of fifteen and my father—he's not alive now, but he kept the village shop in those days—punched me in the face and made my nose bleed. We'd come round here for something or other and he had a bit of drink inside him. Lyuba Ranevsky—I can see her now—was still quite a slip of a girl. She brought me over to the wash-stand here in this very room, the nursery as it was. "Don't cry, little peasant," she said. "You'll soon be right as rain." [*Pause.*] Little peasant. It's true my father was a peasant, but here am I in my white waistcoat and brown boots, barging in like a bull in a china shop. The only thing is, I am rich. I have plenty of money, but when you really get down to it I'm just another country bumpkin. [*Turns the pages of his book.*] I was reading this book and couldn't make sense of it. Fell asleep over it. [*Pause.*]

DUNYASHA. The dogs have been awake all night, they can tell the family are coming.

LOPAKHIN. What's up with you, Dunyasha?

DUNYASHA. My hands are shaking. I think I'm going to faint.

LOPAKHIN. You're too sensitive altogether, my girl. You dress like a lady and do your hair like one too. We can't have that. Remember your place.

[YEPIKHODOV *comes in carrying a bunch of flowers. He wears a jacket and brightly polished high boots which make a loud squeak. Once inside the room he drops the flowers.*]

YEPIKHODOV [*picking up the flowers*]. The gardener sent these, says they're to go in the dining-room. [*Hands the flowers to* DUNYASHA.]

LOPAKHIN. And you might bring me some kvass.

DUNYASHA. Yes sir. [*Goes out.*]

YEPIKHODOV. There are three degrees of frost this morning and the cherry trees are in full bloom. I can't say I think much of our climate. [*Sighs.*] That I can't. It isn't exactly co-operative, our climate isn't. Then if you'll permit a further observation, Mr. Lopakhin, I bought these boots the day before yesterday and, as I make so bold to assure you, they squeak like something out of this world. What could I put on them?

LOPAKHIN. Leave me alone. I'm tired of you.

YEPIKHODOV. Every day something awful happens to me. Not that I complain, I'm used to it. Even raise a smile.

[DUNYASHA *comes in and hands* LOPAKHIN *the kvass.*]

YEPIKHODOV. I'll be off. [*Bumps into a chair and knocks it over.*] You see. [*With an air of triumph.*] There you are, if you'll pardon my language, that's just the kind of thing I mean, actually. Quite remarkable really. [*Goes out.*]

DUNYASHA. The fact is Yepikhodov has proposed to me, Mr. Lopakhin.

LOPAKHIN. Oh yes.

DUNYASHA. I really don't know what to do. He's the quiet type, only sometimes he gets talking and you can't make head or tail of what he says. It sounds ever so nice and romantic, but it just doesn't make sense. I do sort of like him, and he's mad about me. He's a most unfortunate man, every day something goes wrong. That's why he gets teased here. They call him "Simple Simon."

LOPAKHIN [*pricking up his ears*]. I think I hear them coming.

DUNYASHA. They're coming! Oh, whatever's the matter with me? I've gone all shivery.

LOPAKHIN. Yes, they really are coming. Let's go and meet them. I wonder if she'll know me, we haven't seen each other for five years.

DUNYASHA [*agitated*]. I'm going to faint. Oh dear, I'm going to faint.

[*Two carriages are heard driving up to the house. LOPAKHIN and DUNYASHA hurry out. The stage is empty. Noises begin to be heard from the adjoining rooms. FIRS, who has been to meet MRS. RANEVSKY at the station, hurries across the stage leaning on a stick. He wears an old-fashioned servant's livery and a top hat. He mutters something to himself, but not a word can be understood. The noises off stage become louder. A voice is heard: "Let's go through here." Enter, on their way through the room, MRS. RANEVSKY, ANYA and CHARLOTTE, with a small dog on a lead, all dressed in travelling clothes, VARYA, wearing an overcoat and a scarf over her head, GAYEV, SIMEONOV-PISHCHIK, LOPAKHIN, DUNYASHA carrying a bundle and an umbrella, and other servants with luggage.*]

ANYA. Let's go through here. You remember this room, don't you, Mother?

MRS. RANEVSKY [*happily, through tears*]. The nursery!

VARYA. How cold it is, my hands are quite numb. [*To* MRS. RANEVSKY.] Your rooms are just as they were, Mother, the white one and the mauve one.

MRS. RANEVSKY. The nursery! My lovely, heavenly room! I slept in here when I was a little girl. [*Weeps.*] And now I feel like a little girl again. [*Kisses her brother and* VARYA, *and then her brother again.*] Varya hasn't changed a bit, she still looks like a nun. And I recognized Dunyasha. [*Kisses* DUNYASHA.]

GAYEV. The train was two hours late. Pretty good, eh? What price that for efficiency?

CHARLOTTE [*to* PISHCHIK]. My dog eats nuts too.

PISHCHIK [*with surprise*]. Extraordinary thing.

[*All go out except* ANYA *and* DUNYASHA.]

DUNYASHA. We've been longing for you to get here. [*Helps* ANYA *off with her overcoat and hat.*]

ANYA. I've travelled four nights without sleep, and now I'm frozen.

DUNYASHA. You left before Easter in the snow and frost. What a difference now. Darling Anya! [*Laughs and kisses her.*] I've been longing to see you again, my precious angel. I must tell you at once, I can't keep it to myself a minute longer——

ANYA [*listlessly*]. Whatever is it this time?

DUNYASHA. Yepikhodov—you know, the clerk—proposed to me just after Easter.

ANYA. Can't you talk about something else? [*Tidying her hair.*] I've lost all my hair-pins. [*She is very tired and is actually swaying on her feet.*]

DUNYASHA. I really don't know what to think. He loves me so much, he really does.

ANYA [*fondly, looking through the door into her room*]. My own room, my own windows, just as if I'd never been away. I'm home again! I'll get up tomorrow and run straight out into the orchard. Oh, if I could only go to sleep. I didn't sleep at all on the way back, I was so worried.

DUNYASHA. Peter Trofimov arrived the day before yesterday.

ANYA [*joyfully*]. Peter!

DUNYASHA. He's sleeping in the bath-house, in fact he's living there. Afraid of being in the way, he says. [*With a glance at her pocket-watch.*] Someone ought to wake him up, but your sister said not to. "Don't you wake him," she said.

[VARYA *comes in. She has a bunch of keys on her belt.*]

VARYA. Dunyasha, go and get some coffee quickly. Mother wants some.

DUNYASHA. I'll see to it at once. [*Goes out.*]

VARYA. Well, thank heavens you're back. You're home again. [*Affectionately.*] My lovely, darling Anya's home again.

ANYA. I've had a terrible time.

VARYA. So I can imagine.

ANYA. I left just before Easter and it was cold then. On the way there Charlotte kept talking and doing those awful tricks of hers. Why you ever landed me with Charlotte——

VARYA. But you couldn't have gone on your own, darling. A girl of seventeen!

ANYA. It was cold and snowing when we got to Paris. My French is atrocious. I find Mother living on the fourth floor somewhere and when I get there she has visitors, French people—some ladies and an old priest with a little book. The place is full of smoke and awfully uncomfortable. Suddenly I felt sorry for Mother, so sorry, I took her head in my arms and held her and just couldn't let go. Afterwards Mother was terribly sweet to me and kept crying.

VARYA [*through tears*]. Don't, Anya, I can't bear it.

ANYA. She'd already sold her villa near Menton and had nothing left, nothing at all. I hadn't any money either, there was hardly enough for the journey. And Mother simply won't understand. If we have a meal in a station restaurant she asks for all the most expensive things and tips the waiters a rouble each. And Charlotte's no better. Then Yasha has to have his share as well, it was simply

awful. Mother has this servant Yasha, you know, we've
brought him with us——

VARYA. Yes, I've seen him. Isn't he foul?

ANYA. Well, how is everything? Have you paid the interest?

VARYA. What a hope.

ANYA. My God, how dreadful.

VARYA. This estate is up for sale in August.

ANYA. Oh my God!

LOPAKHIN [*peeping round the door and mooing like a cow*].
Moo-oo-oo. [*Disappears.*]

VARYA [*through tears*]. Oh, I could give him such a—. [*Shakes
her fist.*]

ANYA [*quietly embracing* VARYA]. Has he proposed, Varya?
[VARYA *shakes her head.*] But he does love you. Why can't
you get it all settled? What are you both waiting for?

VARYA. I don't think anything will come of it. He's so busy he
can't be bothered with me, he doesn't even notice me.
Wretched man, I'm fed up with the sight of him. Everyone's talking about our wedding and congratulating us,
when there's nothing in it at all actually and the whole
thing's so vague. [*In a different tone of voice.*] You've got a
brooch that looks like a bee or something.

ANYA [*sadly*]. Yes, Mother bought it. [*Goes to her room, now
talking away happily like a child.*] Do you know, in Paris I
went up in a balloon.

VARYA. My lovely, darling Anya's home again.

[DUNYASHA *has returned with the coffee-pot and is making
coffee.*]

VARYA [*standing near the door*]. You know, darling, while I'm
doing my jobs round the house I spend the whole day
dreaming. I imagine marrying you off to a rich man. That
would set my mind at rest and I'd go off to a convent, then
on to Kiev and Moscow, wandering from one holy place to
another. I'd just wander on and on. What bliss!

ANYA. The birds are singing in the orchard. What time is it?

VARYA. It must be nearly three. Time you were asleep, dear. [*Going into* ANYA's *room*.] What bliss!

[*Enter* YASHA *with a rug and a travelling bag*.]

YASHA [*crossing the stage and speaking in a refined manner*]. Is one permitted to pass this way?

DUNYASHA. I wouldn't have known you, Yasha. You've changed so much since you've been abroad.

YASHA. H'm! And who might you be?

DUNYASHA. When you left here I was no bigger than this. [*Shows her height from the floor*.] I'm Dunyasha, Theodore Kozoyedov's daughter. You won't remember me.

YASHA. H'm! Tasty little morsel. [*Looks round, then embraces her. She gives a squeak and drops a saucer.* YASHA *hurries out*.]

VARYA [*in the doorway, speaking angrily*]. What is it now?

DUNYASHA [*through tears*]. I've broken a saucer.

VARYA. That's supposed to be lucky.

ANYA [*coming out of her room*]. Someone ought to let Mother know that Peter's here.

VARYA. I told them not to wake him up.

ANYA [*thoughtfully*]. It's six years since Father died. And a month after that our brother Grisha was drowned in the river. He was a lovely little boy, only seven years old. It was too much for Mother, she went away, just dropped everything and went. [*Shudders*.] How well I understand her, if only she knew. [*Pause*.] Peter Trofimov was Grisha's tutor, he might bring back memories.

[FIRS *comes in wearing a jacket and a white waistcoat*.]

FIRS [*goes to the coffee-pot, anxiously*]. The mistress is going to have her coffee here. [*Puts on white gloves*.] Is it made? [*To* DUNYASHA, *sternly*.] You there! What about the cream?

DUNYASHA. Oh, goodness me. [*Goes out quickly*.]

FIRS [*fussing around the coffee-pot*]. The girl's a nincompoop. [*Muttering to himself*.] They've come from Paris. There was a time when the old master used to go to Paris, went by carriage. [*Laughs*.]

VARYA. What is it, Firs?

FIRS. Beg pardon, Miss Varya? [*Happily*.] The mistress is home. Home at last. Now I can die happy. [*Weeps with joy*.]

[*Enter* MRS. RANEVSKY, GAYEV *and* SIMEONOV-PISHCHIK, *the last wearing a sleeveless coat of fine cloth and wide trousers tucked inside his boots. As he comes in,* GAYEV *moves his arms and body as if making billiard shots*.]

MRS. RANEVSKY. How does it go now? Let me remember. "Pot the red in the corner. Double into the middle."

GAYEV. Screw shot into the corner. At one time, dear sister, we both used to sleep in this room. And now I'm fifty-one, unlikely as it may sound.

LOPAKHIN. Yes, time marches on.

GAYEV. What's that?

LOPAKHIN. Time. It marches on, I was saying.

GAYEV. This place smells of cheap scent.

ANYA. I'm going to bed. Good night, Mother. [*Kisses her mother*.]

MRS. RANEVSKY. My own beautiful little baby. [*Kisses* ANYA's *hands*.] Are you glad to be home? I still can't get used to it.

ANYA. Good night, Uncle.

GAYEV [*kissing her face and hands*]. God bless you. You look so like your mother. [*To his sister*.] You were just like her at that age, Lyuba.

[ANYA *shakes hands with* LOPAKHIN *and* PISHCHIK, *goes out and shuts the door behind her*.]

MRS. RANEVSKY. She's completely worn out.

PISHCHIK. Yes, it must have been a long journey.

VARYA [*to* LOPAKHIN *and* PISHCHIK]. Well, gentlemen? It's nearly three o'clock. Time you were on your way.

MRS. RANEVSKY [*laughing*]. Varya, you haven't changed a bit. [*Draws* VARYA *towards her and kisses her.*] I'll just drink this coffee, then we'll all go. [FIRS *puts a hassock under her feet.*] Thank you, my dear. I've got used to coffee, I drink it day and night. Thank you, dear old friend. [*Kisses* FIRS.]

VARYA. I'll go and see if they've brought all the luggage. [*Goes out.*]

MRS. RANEVSKY. Is it really me sitting here? [*Laughs.*] I feel like dancing and waving my arms about. [*Covers her face with her hands.*] But perhaps I'm only dreaming. God knows, I love my country, I love it dearly. I couldn't see anything from the train, I was crying so much. [*Through tears.*] But I must drink my coffee. Thank you, Firs. Thank you, dear old friend. I'm so glad you're still alive.

FIRS. The day before yesterday.

GAYEV. He's a bit deaf.

LOPAKHIN. I have to leave for Kharkov soon, about half past four. What a nuisance. I'd like to have seen a bit more of you and had a talk. You're just as wonderful as ever.

PISHCHIK [*breathes heavily*]. Even prettier. In that Parisian outfit. Well and truly bowled me over, and no mistake.

LOPAKHIN. This brother of yours calls me a lout of a peasant out for what I can get, but that doesn't bother me a bit. Let him talk. You just believe in me as you used to, that's all I ask, and look at me in the old way, with those wonderful, irresistible eyes. Merciful heavens! My father was a serf, belonged to your father and your grandfather before him. But you—you've done so much for me in the past that I've forgotten all that and love you as a brother. Or even more.

MRS. RANEVSKY. I can't sit still, I really can't. [*Jumps up and walks about in great excitement.*] I'll die of happiness. Laugh at me if you want, I'm silly. My own dear little book-case. [*Kisses the book-case.*] My own little table——

GAYEV. Nanny died while you were abroad.

MRS. RANEVSKY [*sitting down and drinking her coffee.*] Yes, God rest her soul. Someone wrote to me about it.

GAYEV. Anastasy has died too. Petrushka—remember the chap with the squint?—left me for another job, he's with the chief of police in town now. [*Takes a packet of sweets from his pocket and sucks one.*]

PISHCHIK. My daughter Dashenka sends her regards.

LOPAKHIN. I feel I want to tell you something nice and cheer-ful. [*With a glance at his watch.*] I'm just leaving and there isn't time to say much. Anyway, I'll be brief. As you know, the cherry orchard's being sold to pay your debts and the auction's on the twenty-second of August. But you needn't worry, dear friend, you can sleep in peace because there's a way out. Here's my plan. Please listen carefully. Your estate's only twelve miles or so from town and the new railway isn't far away. If you divide the cherry orchard and the land along the river into building plots and lease them out for summer cottages you'll have a yearly income of at least twenty-five thousand roubles.

GAYEV. Oh really, what rubbish.

MRS. RANEVSKY. I don't quite follow you, Yermolay.

LOPAKHIN. You'll get at least ten roubles an acre from your tenants every year. And if you advertise right away I bet you anything you won't have a scrap of land left by autumn, it'll all be snapped up. In fact I congratulate you. You're saved. The situation's magnificent and there's a good depth of river. But of course you will have to do a spot of tidying and clearing up. For instance, you'll have to pull down all the old buildings, let's say, and this house—it's no more use anyway, is it?—and cut down the old cherry orchard—

MRS. RANEVSKY. Cut it down? My dear man, forgive me, you don't know what you're talking about. If there's one inter-esting, in fact quite remarkable, thing in the whole county it's our cherry orchard.

LOPAKHIN. The only remarkable thing about that orchard is its size. It only gives a crop every other year and then no one knows what to do with the cherries. Nobody wants to buy them.

GAYEV. This orchard is even mentioned in the Encyclopaedia.

LOPAKHIN [*with a glance at his watch*]. If we don't make a plan and get something decided, that orchard—and the whole estate with it—is going to be auctioned on the twenty-second of August, you can make up your minds to that. There's no other way out, you can take it from me. And that's flat.

FIRS. In the old days, forty or fifty years ago, the cherries used to be dried, preserved and bottled. They used to make jam out of them, and time was——

GAYEV. Be quiet please, Firs.

FIRS. Time was when dried cherries used to be sent to Moscow and Kharkov by the wagon-load. They fetched a lot of money. Soft and juicy those dried cherries were, sweet and tasty. People had the knack of it in those days.

MRS. RANEVSKY. But where's the recipe now?

FIRS. Forgotten. No one remembers it.

PISHCHIK [*to* MRS. RANEVSKY]. How are things in Paris, eh? Eat any frogs?

MRS. RANEVSKY. I ate crocodiles.

PISHCHIK. Extraordinary thing.

LOPAKHIN. Until lately everyone in the countryside was a gentleman or a peasant, but now there are these holiday visitors as well. All our towns, even the smallest, are surrounded by summer cottages nowadays. And it looks as though in twenty years or so there are going to be fantastic numbers of these holiday-makers. So far your holiday-maker only has his tea on the balcony, but he may very well start growing things on his bit of land and then this cherry orchard will become a happy, rich, prosperous place.

GAYEV [*indignantly*]. That's all rubbish.

[*Enter* VARYA *and* YASHA.]

VARYA. Two telegrams came for you, Mother. [*Picks out a key and unlocks the old-fashioned book-case with a jingling noise.*] Here you are.

MRS. RANEVSKY. They're from Paris. [*Tears them up without reading them.*] I've finished with Paris.

GAYEV. Lyuba, do you know how old this book-case is? Last week I pulled out the bottom drawer and saw some figures burnt on it. This book-case was made exactly a hundred years ago. Not bad, eh? We might celebrate its centenary. It's an inanimate object, but all the same it is a book-case, you can't get away from that.

PISHCHIK [*in amazement*]. A hundred years. Extraordinary thing.

GAYEV. Yes, this really is quite something. [*Feeling round the book-case.*] Dear and most honoured book-case. In you I salute an existence devoted for over a hunded years to the glorious ideals of virtue and justice. In the course of the century your silent summons to creative work has never faltered, upholding [*through tears*] in several generations of our line confidence and faith in a better future and fostering in us the ideals of virtue and social consciousness. [*Pause.*]

LOPAKHIN. Yes.

MRS. RANEVSKY. Dear Leonid, you haven't changed a bit.

GAYEV [*somewhat embarrassed*]. In off on the right into the corner. Screw shot into the middle.

LOPAKHIN [*after a glance at his watch*]. Well, time for me to go.

YASHA [*handing some medicine to* MRS. RANEVSKY]. Would you care to take your pills now?

PISHCHIK. Don't ever take medicine, dear lady, it doesn't do any good. Or harm, if it comes to that. Here, give it to me, dearest lady. [*Takes the pills, pours them out on the palm of his hand, blows on them, puts them in his mouth and washes them down with kvass.*] There you are.

MRS. RANEVSKY [*terrified*]. You must be crazy!

PISHCHIK. I've taken the lot.

LOPAKHIN. You greedy pig. [*Everyone laughs.*]

FIRS. The gentleman was here at Easter. Ate over a gallon of pickled gherkins. [*Mutters.*]

MRS. RANEVSKY. What's he saying?

VARYA. He's been muttering like this for three years now. We've got used to it.

YASHA. It's a case of *anno domini*.

[CHARLOTTE *crosses the stage wearing a white dress. She is very thin and tightly laced and has a lorgnette attached to her belt.*]

LOPAKHIN. I'm sorry, Miss Charlotte, I haven't had a chance to say hallo. [*Tries to kiss her hand.*]

CHARLOTTE [*withdrawing her hand*]. If I let you kiss my hand it'll be my elbow next, then my shoulder——

LOPAKHIN. This is my unlucky day. [*Everyone laughs.*] Do us a trick, Charlotte.

MRS. RANEVSKY. Yes, do us a trick, Charlotte.

CHARLOTTE. Not now. I want to go to bed. [*Goes out.*]

LOPAKHIN. We'll meet again in three weeks. [*Kisses* MRS. RANEVSKY's *hand.*] Good-bye for now. I must go. [*To* GAYEV.] Fare you well [*kisses* PISHCHIK] for I must leave you. [*Shakes hands with* VARYA, *then with* FIRS *and* YASHA.] I don't really feel like going. [*To* MRS. RANEVSKY.] Think it over about those cottages, let me know if you decide to go ahead and I'll get you a loan of fifty thousand or so. Give it some serious thought.

VARYA [*angrily*]. Oh, do for heaven's sake *go*.

LOPAKHIN. All right, I'm going. [*Goes.*]

GAYEV. Ill-bred lout. Oh, I beg your pardon, Varya's going to marry him. He's Varya's "young man."

VARYA. Don't overdo it, Uncle.

MRS. RANEVSKY. But I should be only too pleased, Varya. He's such a nice man.

PISHCHIK. A most worthy fellow. Got to hand it to him. My daughter Dashenka says so too. She says all sorts of things actually. [*Gives a snore, but wakes up again straight away*.] By the way, dear lady, can you lend me two hundred and forty roubles? I've interest to pay on a mortgage tomorrow.

VARYA [*terrified*]. We haven't got it. Really.

MRS. RANEVSKY. Honestly, I've no money at all.

PISHCHIK. It'll turn up. [*Laughs*.] Never say die. The times I've thought, "This is the end of me, I'm finished." And then, lo and behold, they run a railway line over my land or something and I get some money. And sooner or later something will turn up this time, you'll see. Dashenka will win two hundred thousand. She has a ticket in the lottery.

MRS. RANEVSKY. I've finished my coffee. Now for some rest.

FIRS [*reprovingly, brushing* GAYEV's *clothes*]. You've got the wrong trousers on again. What am I to do with you?

VARYA [*in a low voice*]. Anya's asleep. [*Quietly opens a window*.] The sun's up now and it's not cold. Look, Mother, what marvellous trees! And the air is glorious. The starlings are singing.

GAYEV [*opening another window*]. The orchard is white all over. Lyuba, you haven't forgotten that long avenue, have you? It runs on and on, straight as an arrow. And it gleams on moonlit nights, remember? You can't have forgotten?

MRS. RANEVSKY [*looking through the window at the orchard*]. Oh, my childhood, my innocent childhood! This is the nursery where I slept and I used to look out at the orchard from here. When I woke up every morning happiness awoke with me, and the orchard was just the same in those days. Nothing's changed. [*Laughs happily*.] White! All white! Oh, my orchard! After the damp, dismal autumn and the cold winter here you are, young again and full of happiness. The angels in heaven have not forsaken you. If I could only shake off the heavy burden that weighs me down, if only I could forget my past.

GAYEV. Yes, and now the orchard's to be sold to pay our debts, unlikely as it may sound.

MRS. RANEVSKY. Look! Mother's walking in the orchard. In a white dress. [*Laughs happily*.] It's Mother.

GAYEV. Where?

VARYA. Really, Mother, what things you say!

MRS. RANEVSKY. There's no one there, I just imagined it. On the right at the turning to the summer-house there's a little white tree which has leant over, it looks like a woman.

[*Enter* TROFIMOV. *He is dressed in a shabby student's uniform and wears spectacles.*]

MRS. RANEVSKY. What a superb orchard! The great banks of white blossom, the blue sky——

TROFIMOV. Lyuba Ranevsky! [*She looks round at him.*] I'll just pay my respects and go away at once. [*Kisses her hand with great feeling.*] I was told to wait till later in the morning, but I was too impatient.

[MRS. RANEVSKY *looks at him in bewilderment.*]

VARYA [*through tears*]. This is Peter Trofimov.

TROFIMOV. I'm Peter Trofimov. I was Grisha's tutor. Can I have changed so much?

[MRS. RANEVSKY *embraces him and weeps quietly.*]

GAYEV [*embarrassed*]. There, Lyuba, don't cry.

VARYA [*weeping*]. I did tell you to wait till later, Peter.

MRS. RANEVSKY. Grisha, my—my little boy. Grisha, my son——

VARYA. It can't be helped, Mother, it was God's will.

TROFIMOV [*gently, through tears*]. Don't cry. Please don't.

MRS. RANEVSKY [*weeping quietly*]. I lost my little boy—drowned. Why? Why did it happen, my dear? [*In a quieter voice.*] Anya's asleep in there and here I am raising my voice and making all this noise. Well, Peter? Why have you grown so ugly? And why do you look so old?

TROFIMOV. A woman in the train called me "that seedy-looking gent."

MRS. RANEVSKY. You were only a boy in those days, just a nice little undergraduate. But now you're losing your hair and wear these spectacles. You can't still be a student, surely? [*Moves towards the door.*]

TROFIMOV. I'll obviously be a student for the rest of time.

MRS. RANEVSKY [*kisses her brother and then* VARYA]. Well, go to bed then. You look older too, Leonid.

PISHCHIK [*follows her*]. So we're off to bed now. Oh dear, my gout. I'd better stay the night here. And tomorrow morning, Lyuba my sweetheart, that little matter of two hundred and forty roubles.

GAYEV. Can't he think about anything else?

PISHCHIK. Two hundred and forty roubles to pay the interest on my mortgage.

MRS. RANEVSKY. But I've no money, my dear man.

PISHCHIK. I'll pay you back, dearest lady. A trifling sum.

MRS. RANEVSKY. All right then, Leonid will let you have it. Leonid, give him the money.

GAYEV. What, me give it him? Not likely!

MRS. RANEVSKY. Let him have it, what else can we do? He needs it, he'll pay us back.

[MRS. RANEVSKY, TROFIMOV, PISHCHIK *and* FIRS *go out*. GAYEV, VARYA *and* YASHA *remain behind*.]

GAYEV. My sister hasn't lost her habit of throwing money about. [*To* YASHA.] Out of the way, my man, you smell like a farmyard.

YASHA [*with an ironical grin*]. You haven't changed a bit, Mr. Gayev sir.

GAYEV. What's that? [*To* VARYA.] What did he say?

VARYA [*to* YASHA]. Your mother's come from the village. She's been waiting in the servants' quarters since yesterday and wants to see you.

YASHA. Why can't she leave me alone?

VARYA. You—you ought to be ashamed of yourself!

YASHA. What's the big idea? Couldn't she have come tomorrow? [*Goes out*.]

VARYA. Mother's just the same as ever, hasn't changed a bit. She'd give everything away if we let her.

GAYEV. Yes. [*Pause.*] When a lot of different remedies are suggested for a disease, that means it can't be cured. I've been thinking and racking my brains. I have plenty of remedies, any amount of them, and that means I haven't really got one. It would be a good thing if somebody left us some money. It would be a good thing to marry Anya to a very rich man. And it would be a good thing to go to Yaroslavl and try our luck with our aunt the Countess. Aunty is rich, you know, very much so.

VARYA [*crying*]. May God help us.

GAYEV. Stop that crying. Aunty's rich enough, but she doesn't like us. To start with, my sister married a lawyer, a social inferior——.

[ANYA *appears in the doorway.*]

GAYEV. She married beneath her, and the way she's behaved—well, she hasn't exactly been a model of propriety, has she? She's a good, kind, splendid person and I love her very much, but make what allowances you like, she's still a loose woman and you can't get away from it. It shows in every movement she makes.

VARYA [*in a whisper*]. Anya's in the doorway.

GAYEV. What's that? [*Pause.*] Curious thing, there's something in my right eye. Can't see properly. And on Thursday when I was at the County Court——

[ANYA *comes in.*]

VARYA. Why aren't you asleep, Anya?

ANYA. I can't. I just can't get to sleep.

GAYEV. My dear child. [*Kisses* ANYA's *face and hands.*] My little child. [*Through tears.*] You're not my niece, you're an angel, you're everything in the world to me. Do, do believe me.

ANYA. I do believe you, Uncle. Everyone loves and respects you. But, Uncle dear, you should keep quiet, just keep quiet. What were you saying just now about my mother, about your own sister? What made you say it?

GAYEV. Yes, yes. [*Takes her hand and covers his face with it.*] You're quite right, it was dreadful of me. Oh God! God, help me! And that speech I made to the book-case just now. How silly of me. And it was only when I'd finished that I saw how silly it was.

VARYA. It's true, Uncle dear, you oughtn't to talk. Just don't talk, that's all.

ANYA. If you stop talking you'll feel easier in your own mind.

GAYEV. I am silent. [*Kisses* ANYA's *and* VARYA's *hands.*] I am silent. There is something rather important, though. I was at the County Court last Thursday and—well, a lot of us got talking about this and that and about several other things as well. It seems we might manage to borrow some money and pay the interest to the bank.

VARYA. May God help us.

GAYEV. I'm going back there on Tuesday and I'll talk to them again. [*To* VARYA.] Stop that crying. [*To* ANYA.] Your mother's going to speak to Lopakhin and I'm sure he won't let her down. And when you've had a rest you can go and see your great-aunt the Countess at Yaroslavl. This way we'll be tackling the thing from three different directions at once and we simply can't fail. We shall pay that interest, I'm sure of it. [*Puts a sweet in his mouth.*] I give you my word of honour, I swear by anything you like, this estate isn't going to be sold. [*Elatedly.*] As I hope to be happy, I swear it. Here's my hand and you can call me a good-for-nothing scoundrel if I let it come to an auction. I won't, on that I'll stake my life.

ANYA [*has reverted to a calmer mood and is happy*]. What a good person you are, Uncle, you're so sensible. [*Embraces him.*] I feel calm now. Calm and happy.

[*Enter* FIRS.]

FIRS [*reproachfully*]. Mr. Leonid sir, you're past praying for. When are you going to bed?

GAYEV. At once, at once. You can go, Firs. It's all right, I'll undress myself. Well, children, bed-time. The details will keep till morning and you get to bed now. [*Kisses* ANYA *and* VARYA.] I'm a man of the eighties. No one has a good word to say for those days, but still I've suffered quite a bit for my convictions, I can tell you. Do you wonder the peasants like me so much? You have to know your peasant of course. You have to know how to——

ANYA. Uncle, you're off again.

VARYA. Uncle dear, do be quiet.

FIRS [*angrily*]. Mr. Leonid, sir!

GAYEV. I'm coming, I'm coming. Go to bed. Off two cushions into the middle. Pot the white. [*Goes off with* FIRS *tottering after him.*]

ANYA. I'm not worried now. I don't feel like going to Yaroslavl and I don't like my great-aunt, but I do feel less worried. Thanks to Uncle. [*Sits down.*]

VARYA. We must get to bed. I'm just going. Oh, something unpleasant happened here while you were away. As you know, there's no one living in the old servants' quarters except some of our old folk—Yefim, Polya, Yevstigney, oh yes, and Karp. They began letting odd tramps and people spend the night there. I kept quiet about it. But then I heard of a story they'd spread that I'd said they must be fed on nothing but dried peas. Out of meanness if you please. It was all Yevstigney's doing. All right, I thought. If that's the way things are, then you just wait. I sent for the man. [*Yawns.*] He came. "What's all this?" I said. "You stupid so-and-so." [*Looks at* ANYA.] Anya, dear! [*Pause.*] She's asleep. [*Takes* ANYA *by the arm.*] Come to bed, dear. Come on. [*Leads her by the arm.*] My little darling's gone to sleep. Come on. [*They move off.*]

[*A shepherd's pipe is heard playing from far away on the other side of the orchard.* TROFIMOV *crosses the stage, catches sight of* VARYA *and* ANYA *and stops.*]

VARYA. Sh! She's asleep—asleep. Come on, my dear.

ANYA [*quietly, half asleep*]. I'm so tired. I keep hearing bells. Uncle—dear—Mother and Uncle——

VARYA. Come on, dear, come on. [*They go into* ANYA's *room.*]

TROFIMOV [*deeply moved*]. Light of my being! My springtime!

CURTAIN

ACT TWO

In the open country. A small, tumble-down old chapel long ago abandoned. Near it a well, some large stones which look like old tombstones and an old bench. A road can be seen leading to GAYEV's *estate. Dark poplar trees loom on one side and beyond them the cherry orchard begins. There is a row of telegraph poles in the distance and far, far away on the horizon are the dim outlines of a big town, visible only in very fine, clear weather. It will soon be sunset.* CHARLOTTE, YASHA *and* DUNYASHA *are sitting on the bench.* YEPIKHODOV *stands near them playing a guitar, while the others sit lost in thought.* CHARLOTTE *wears a man's old peaked cap. She has taken a shot-gun from her shoulder and is adjusting the buckle on the strap.*

CHARLOTTE [*meditatively*]. I haven't any proper identity papers. I don't know how old I am and I always think of myself as a young girl. When I was little, Father and Mother used to go on tour round all the fairs giving performances, and very good ones too. I used to do the dive of death and lots of other tricks. When Father and Mother died a German lady adopted me and began educating me. Well, I grew up and became a governess. But where I come from and who I am I've no idea. Who my parents were I don't know either, very likely they weren't even married. [*Takes a cucumber out of her pocket and starts eating it.*] I don't know anything. [*Pause.*] I'm longing for someone to talk to, but there isn't anyone. I'm alone in the world.

YEPIKHODOV [*playing the guitar and singing*].
　　　"I'm tired of the world and its bustle,
　　　I'm tired of my friends and my foes."
How nice it is to play a mandolin.

DUNYASHA. That isn't a mandolin, it's a guitar. [*Looks at herself in a hand-mirror, and powders her face.*]

YEPIKHODOV. To a man crazed with love it's a mandolin. [*Sings softly.*]

> "If only my heart were delighted
> By the warmth of an ardour requited."

[YASHA *joins in.*]

CHARLOTTE. The awful way these people sing—ugh! Like a lot of hyenas.

DUNYASHA [*to* YASHA]. You're ever so lucky to have been abroad, though.

YASHA. Yes, of course. My sentiments precisely. [*Yawns, then lights a cigar.*]

YEPIKHODOV. It stands to reason. Abroad everything's pretty comprehensive like. Has been for ages.

YASHA. Oh, definitely.

YEPIKHODOV. I'm a cultured sort of person and read all kinds of remarkable books, but I just can't get a line on what it is I'm really after. Shall I go on living or shall I shoot myself, I mean? But anyway, I always carry a revolver. Here it is. [*Shows them his revolver.*]

CHARLOTTE. Well, that's that. I'm off. [*Slings the gun over her shoulder.*] Yepikhodov, you're a very clever man and a most alarming one. Women must be quite crazy about you. Brrr! [*Moves off.*] These clever men are all so stupid, I've no one to talk to. I'm lonely, oh so lonely. I'm on my own in the world, and—and who I am and what I'm for is a mystery. [*Goes out slowly.*]

YEPIKHODOV. Actually, other considerations apart, there's something I really must explain about myself at this juncture, which is that fate treats me most unkindly, like a storm buffeting a small boat. If I'm mistaken—which I allow is possible—why is it, to take a case in point, that I wake up this morning and there, sitting on my chest, is a spider of gigantic proportions? This size. [*Uses both hands to show the size.*] Or I pick up a glass of kvass to have a drink and lo and behold there's something highly improper inside it like a black-beetle. [*Pause.*] Have you ever read Buckle's

History of Civilization? [*Pause*.] Might I trouble you for the favour of a few words, Miss Dunyasha?

DUNYASHA. All right, carry on.

YEPIKHODOV. I should prefer it to be in private. [*Sighs*.]

DUNYASHA [*embarrassed*]. Very well then, only first go and get me my cape. You'll find it in the cupboard or somewhere. It's rather damp out here.

YEPIKHODOV. Oh certainly, I'm sure. At your service. Now I know what to do with my revolver. [*Takes the guitar and goes out strumming it*.]

YASHA. Simple Simon! The man's a fool, between you and me. [*Yawns*.]

DUNYASHA. Heavens, I hope he doesn't go and shoot himself. [*Pause*.] I've grown so so nervous and I feel worried all the time. The master and mistress took me in when I was a little girl and now I've lost touch with the way ordinary people live. Look at my hands, as white as white could be, just like a lady's. Yes, I've become all soft and refined and ladylike and easily frightened. I'm scared of everything. If you deceive me, Yasha, I can't think what it'll do to my nerves.

YASHA [*kissing her*]. Tasty little morsel. A girl should know her place, mind. There's nothing I dislike so much as loose behaviour in a girl.

DUNYASHA. I'm so much in love with you. You're so educated, you can talk about anything. [*Pause*.]

YASHA [*yawning*]. That's true enough. To my way of thinking, if a girl's in love with anybody that proves she's immoral. [*Pause*.] How nice to smoke a cigar out of doors. [*Pricks up his ears*.] There's somebody coming. It's the missis and the others.

[DUNYASHA *embraces him impulsively*.]

YASHA. Go back to the house as if you'd been down to the river for a bathe. Take that path, or else you'll meet them and they'll think we've been walking out together. I can't have that.

DUNYASHA [*coughing quietly*]. Your cigar's given me an awful headache. [*Goes off.*]

[YASHA *remains behind, sitting near the chapel. Enter* MRS. RANEVSKY, GAYEV *and* LOPAKHIN.]

LOPAKHIN. You must make up your minds once and for all, time's running out. And anyway it's a perfectly simple matter. Are you prepared to lease your land for summer cottages or aren't you? You can answer it in one word—yes or no. Just one single word.

MRS. RANEVSKY. Who's smoking disgusting cigars round here? [*Sits down.*]

GAYEV. How handy it is now they've built the railway. [*Sits down.*] We've been into town for lunch. Pot the red in the middle. I must go indoors now and have a game.

MRS. RANEVSKY. There's no hurry.

LOPAKHIN. One single word. [*Imploringly.*] Do give me an answer.

GAYEV [*yawning*]. What's that?

MRS. RANEVSKY [*looking in her purse*]. Yesterday I had lots of money, but I've hardly any left today. My poor Varya tries to save by feeding us all on milk soup and the old servants in the kitchen get nothing but peas to eat, while I go round simply squandering money, I can't think why. [*Drops her purse, scattering some gold coins.*] There, now I've dropped it all. [*Is annoyed.*]

YASHA. Allow me to pick it up, madam. [*Picks up the coins.*]

MRS. RANEVSKY. Please do, Yasha. Oh, whatever made me go out to lunch? That beastly restaurant of yours with its music and tablecloths smelling of soap. Does one have to drink so much, Leonid? Or eat so much? Or talk so much? You talked much too much again in the restaurant today, all most unsuitable stuff about the seventies and the decadent movement. And just think who you were speaking to. Fancy talking about the decadents to the waiters.

LOPAKHIN. Quite so.

GAYEV [*making a gesture of dismissal with his hand*]. I'm a hopeless case, obviously. [*To* YASHA, *irritably*.] Why is it I always see you hanging about everywhere?

YASHA [*laughing*]. I just can't help laughing when I hear your voice.

GAYEV [*to his sister*]. Either he goes or I do.

MRS. RANEVSKY. You may leave, Yasha. Off with you.

YASHA [*returning the purse to* MRS. RANEVSKY]. I'll go at once. [*Hardly able to contain his laughter*.] This very instant. [*Goes out*.]

LOPAKHIN. Do you know who's thinking of buying your property? A rich man called Deriganov. They say he's coming to the auction himself.

MRS. RANEVSKY. Oh? Where did you hear that?

LOPAKHIN. It's what they're saying in town.

GAYEV. Our aunt in Yaroslavl has promised to send money, but when she'll send it and how much it'll be, nobody knows.

LOPAKHIN. How much is she sending? A hundred thousand roubles? Two hundred thousand?

MRS. RANEVSKY. Oh, about ten or fifteen thousand, and we're lucky to get that much.

LOPAKHIN. With due respect, I've never met anyone as scatterbrained as you two, or as odd and unbusinesslike either. I tell you in plain language that your place is up for sale and you can't even seem to take it in.

MRS. RANEVSKY. But what are we to do about it? You tell us that.

LOPAKHIN. I *do* tell you. I tell you every day. Every day I say the same thing over and over again. The cherry orchard and the rest of the land must be leased out for summer cottages. You must act at once, without delay, the auction's almost on top of us. Do get that into your heads. Once you definitely decide on those cottages you can raise any amount of money and you'll be all right.

MRS. RANEVSKY. Cottages, summer visitors. Forgive me, but all that's so frightfully vulgar.

GAYEV. I entirely agree.

LOPAKHIN. I'm going to burst into tears or scream or faint. This is too much. I've had about all I can stand! [*To* GAYEV.] You're an old woman.

GAYEV. What's that?

LOPAKHIN. I say you're an old woman. [*Makes to leave*.]

MRS. RANEVSKY [*terrified*]. No, don't go away, my dear man. Stay with us, I implore you. Perhaps we'll think of something.

LOPAKHIN. "Think"? This isn't a question of thinking.

MRS. RANEVSKY. Don't go away, I beg you. Besides, it's more amusing with you around. [*Pause*.] I keep expecting something awful to happen, as if the house was going to collapse around our ears.

GAYEV [*deep in thought*]. Off the cushion into the corner. Across into the middle——

MRS. RANEVSKY. I suppose we've committed so many sins——

LOPAKHIN. Oh? What sins have you committed?

GAYEV [*putting a sweet in his mouth*]. People say I've wasted my substance on boiled sweets. [*Laughs*.]

MRS. RANEVSKY. Oh, my sins. Look at the mad way I've always wasted money, spent it like water, and I married a man who could do nothing but run up debts. My husband died of champagne, he drank like a fish, and then I had the bad luck to fall in love with someone else and have an affair with him. And just then came my first punishment, and what a cruel blow that was! In the river here——. My little boy was drowned and I went abroad, went right away, never meaning to return or see the river again. I shut my eyes and ran away, not knowing what I was doing, and *he* followed me. It was a cruel, brutal thing to do. I bought a villa near Menton because he fell ill there and for three years I had no rest, nursing him day and night. He utterly wore me out. All my feelings seemed to have dried up inside me. Then last year, when the villa had to be sold to pay my debts, I left for Paris where he robbed me, deserted me and took up with another woman. I tried to poison myself. It was all so stupid and humiliating. Then I suddenly longed to be back in Russia, back in my own country with my little girl. [*Dries her eyes.*] Lord, Lord, be merciful, forgive me my sins. Don't punish me any more. [*Takes a telegram from her pocket.*] This came from Paris today. He asks my forgiveness and begs me to go back. [*Tears up the telegram.*] Isn't that music I hear? [*Listens.*]

GAYEV. That's our famous Jewish band. You remember, the four fiddles, flute and double-bass?

MRS. RANEVSKY. Are they still about then? We must get them round here some time and have a party.

LOPAKHIN [*listening*]. I don't hear anything. [*Sings quietly.*]
        "For a spot of cash your Prussian
        Will frenchify a Russian."

[*Laughs.*] I saw a rather good play at the theatre last night, something really funny.

MRS. RANEVSKY. I don't suppose it was a bit funny. You people shouldn't go and see plays, you should try watching your own performance instead. What drab lives you all lead and what a lot of rubbish you talk!

LOPAKHIN. Quite right. To be honest, the life we lead is preposterous. [*Pause.*] My father was a peasant, an idiot who understood nothing, taught me nothing and just beat me when he was drunk, with a stick too. As a matter of fact I'm just as big a numskull and idiot myself. I never learned anything and my handwriting's awful. A pig could write about as well as I do, I'm ashamed to let anyone see it.

MRS. RANEVSKY. You ought to get married, my friend.

LOPAKHIN. Yes, that's true enough.

MRS. RANEVSKY. Why not marry Varya? She's a very nice girl.

LOPAKHIN. True.

MRS. RANEVSKY. She's a nice simple creature. She works all day long, and the great thing is she loves you. And you've been fond of her for some time too.

LOPAKHIN. All right, I've nothing against it. She is a very nice girl. [*Pause*.]

GAYEV. I've been offered a job in a bank. At six thousand roubles a year. Had you heard?

MRS. RANEVSKY. What, you in a bank! You stay where you are.

[FIRS *comes in with an overcoat*.]

FIRS [*to* GAYEV]. Please put this on, Mr. Leonid sir. It's damp out here.

GAYEV [*putting on the overcoat*]. You are a bore, my dear fellow.

FIRS. We can't have this. Goes off in the morning without so much as a word. [*Inspects him*.]

MRS. RANEVSKY. How you have aged, Firs!

FIRS. Beg pardon, madam?

LOPAKHIN. Your mistress says you look a lot older.

FIRS. Well, I've been alive a long time. They were arranging my wedding before your Dad was so much as thought of. [*Laughs*.] And when the serfs were freed I was already head valet. But I wouldn't have any of their freedom, I stayed on with the master and mistress. [*Pause*.] As I recall, everyone was very pleased, but what they were so pleased about they'd no idea themselves.

LOPAKHIN. Oh, it was a good life all right. At least there were plenty of floggings.

FIRS [*not hearing him*]. Yes, those were the days. The serfs had their masters and the masters had their serfs, but now everything's at sixes and sevens and you can't make head or tail of it.

GAYEV. Keep quiet a minute, Firs. I have to go to town tomorrow. I've been promised an introduction to a general who might let us have a loan.

LOPAKHIN. It won't come off and you won't pay the interest either, of that you may be sure.

MRS. RANEVSKY. He's only talking nonsense. There is no such general.

[*Enter* TROFIMOV, ANYA *and* VARYA.]

GAYEV. Ah, here come the children.

ANYA. Look, there's Mother.

MRS. RANEVSKY [*affectionately*]. Come, come to me. My darling girls. [*Embracing* ANYA *and* VARYA.] If you only knew how much I love you both. Sit beside me, that's right. [*All sit down.*]

LOPAKHIN. Our eternal student never strays far from the young ladies.

TROFIMOV. Mind your own business.

LOPAKHIN. He's nearly fifty and he's still a student.

TROFIMOV. Oh, stop making these idiotic jokes.

LOPAKHIN. But why so angry, my dear fellow?

TROFIMOV. Can't you leave me alone?

LOPAKHIN [*laughing*]. Just let me ask you one question. What's your opinion of me?

TROFIMOV. My opinion of you is simply this, Lopakhin. You're a rich man. You'll soon be a millionaire. Now, as part of the process whereby one form of matter is converted into another, nature needs beasts of prey which devour everything in their path. You fulfil that need. [*Everyone laughs.*]

VARYA. Oh Peter, couldn't you tell us something about the planets instead?

MRS. RANEVSKY. No, let's go on with what we were talking about yesterday.

TROFIMOV. What was that?

GAYEV. Pride.

TROFIMOV. We talked a lot yesterday, but we didn't get anywhere. A proud man in your sense of the word has something mystical about him. You may be right in a way. But if we look at the thing quite simply and don't try to be too clever, then what room is there for pride and what's the sense of it anyway, if in fact man is a pretty poor physiological specimen and if the great majority of the human race is crude, stupid and profoundly miserable? It's time we stopped admiring ourselves. The only thing to do is to work.

GAYEV. We shall all die anyway.

TROFIMOV. Why be so sure of that? And what does it mean anyway, "to die"? Perhaps man has a hundred senses and perhaps when he dies he loses only the five we know, while the other ninety-five live on.

MRS. RANEVSKY. How clever you are, Peter.

LOPAKHIN [*ironically*]. Oh, brilliant!

TROFIMOV. Mankind marches on, going from strength to strength. All that now eludes us will one day be well within our grasp, but, as I say, we must work and we must do all we can for those who are trying to find the truth. Here in Russia very few people do work at present. The kind of Russian intellectuals I know, far and away the greater part of them anyway, aren't looking for anything. They don't do anything. They still don't know the meaning of hard work. They call themselves an intelligentsia, but they speak to their servants as inferiors and treat the peasants like animals. They don't study properly, they never read anything serious, in fact they don't do anything at all. Science is something they just talk about and they know precious little about art. Oh, they're all very earnest. They all go round looking extremely solemn. They talk of nothing but weighty issues and they discuss abstract problems, while all the time everyone knows the workers are abominably fed and sleep without proper bedding, thirty or forty to a room—with bed-bugs everywhere, to say nothing of the stench, the damp, the moral degradation. And clearly all our fine talk is just meant to pull wool over our own eyes and other people's too. Tell me, where are those children's crèches that there's all this talk about? Where are the libraries? They're just things people write novels about, we haven't actually got any of them. What we have got is dirt, vulgarity and squalor. I loathe all these earnest faces. They scare me, and so do earnest conversations. Why can't we keep quiet for a change?

LOPAKHIN. I'm always up by five o'clock, you know. I work from morning till night, and then—well, I'm always handling money, my own and other people's, and I can see what sort of men and women I have around me. You only have to start a job of work to realize how few decent, honest folk there are about. When I can't sleep I sometimes think—the Lord gave us these huge forests, these boundless plains, these vast horizons, and we who live among them ought to be real giants.

MRS. RANEVSKY. You're calling for giants. They're all very well in fairy-tales, but elsewhere they might be rather alarming.

[YEPIKHODOV *crosses the back of the stage playing his guitar*.]

MRS. RANEVSKY [*pensively*]. There goes Yepikhodov.

ANYA [*pensively*]. There goes Yepikhodov.

GAYEV. The sun has set, my friends.

TROFIMOV. Yes.

GAYEV [*in a quiet voice, as if giving a recitation*]. Nature, glorious Nature, glowing with everlasting radiance, so beautiful, so cold—you, whom men call mother, in whom the living and the dead are joined together, you who give life and take it away——

VARYA [*imploring him*]. Uncle dear!

ANYA. Uncle, you're off again.

TROFIMOV. You'd far better pot the red in the middle.

GAYEV. I am silent. Silent.

[*Everyone sits deep in thought. It is very quiet. All that can be heard is* FIRS's *low muttering. Suddenly a distant sound is heard. It seems to come from the sky and is the sound of a breaking string. It dies away sadly*.]

MRS. RANEVSKY. What was that?

LOPAKHIN. I don't know. A cable must have broken somewhere away in the mines. But it must be a long, long way off.

GAYEV. Or perhaps it was a bird, a heron or something.

TROFIMOV. Or an owl.

MRS. RANEVSKY [*shudders*]. There was something disagreeable about it. [*Pause.*]

FIRS. The same thing happened before the troubles, the owl hooting and the samovar humming all the time.

GAYEV. What "troubles" were those?

FIRS. When the serfs were given their freedom. [*Pause.*]

MRS. RANEVSKY. Come, let's go in, everyone. It's getting late. [*To* ANYA.] You've tears in your eyes. What is it, child? [*Embraces her.*]

ANYA. It's nothing, Mother. I'm all right.

TROFIMOV. There's somebody coming.

[*The* PASSER-BY *appears. He wears a shabby, white peaked cap and an overcoat. He is slightly drunk.*]

PASSER-BY. Excuse me asking, but am I right for the station this way?

GAYEV. Yes. Follow that road.

PASSER-BY. I'm uncommonly obliged to you. [*With a cough.*] Splendid weather, this. [*Declaiming.*] "Brother, my suffering brother!" "Come out to the Volga, you whose groans—." [*To* VARYA.] Miss, could you spare a few copecks for a starving Russian?

[VARYA *takes fright and shrieks.*]

LOPAKHIN [*angrily*]. Even where you come from there's such a thing as being polite.

MRS. RANEVSKY [*flustered*]. Here, have this. [*Looks in her purse.*] I've no silver. Never mind, here's some gold.

PASSER-BY. I'm uncommonly obliged to you. [*Goes off.*]

[*Everyone laughs.*]

VARYA [*frightened*]. I'm going. I'm going away from here. Oh Mother, we've no food in the house for the servants and you gave him all that money.

MRS. RANEVSKY. What's to be done with me? I'm so silly. I'll give you all I have when we get home. Yermolay, lend me some more money.

LOPAKHIN. At your service.

MRS. RANEVSKY. Come on, everybody, it's time to go in. Varya, we've just fixed you up with a husband. Congratulations.

VARYA [*through tears*]. Don't make jokes about it, Mother.

LOPAKHIN. Amelia, get thee to a nunnery.

GAYEV. My hands are shaking. It's a long time since I had a game of billiards.

LOPAKHIN. Amelia, nymph, in thy orisons, be all my sins remembered.

MRS. RANEVSKY. Come on, all of you. It's nearly supper time.

VARYA. That man scared me. I still feel quite shaken.

LOPAKHIN. May I remind you all that the cherry orchard's going to be sold on the twenty-second of August? You must think about it. Give it some thought.

[*All go off except* TROFIMOV *and* ANYA.]

ANYA [*laughing*]. We should be grateful to that man for frightening Varya. Now we're alone.

TROFIMOV. Varya's afraid we might fall in love, so she follows us about for days on end. With her narrow outlook she can't understand that we're above love. To rid ourselves of the pettiness and the illusions which stop us being free and happy, that's the whole meaning and purpose of our lives. Forward then! We are marching triumphantly on towards that bright star shining there far away. On, on! No falling back, my friends.

ANYA [*clapping her hands*]. What splendid things you say! [*Pause.*] Isn't it heavenly here today?

TROFIMOV. Yes, it's wonderful weather.

ANYA. What have you done to me, Peter? Why is it I'm not so fond of the cherry orchard as I used to be? I loved it so dearly. I used to think there was no better place on earth than our orchard.

TROFIMOV. All Russia is our orchard. The earth is so wide, so beautiful, so full of wonderful places. [*Pause.*] Just think,

Anya. Your grandfather, your great-grandfather and all your ancestors owned serfs, they owned human souls. Don't you see that from every cherry-tree in the orchard, from every leaf and every trunk, men and women are gazing at you? Don't you hear their voices? Owning living souls, that's what has changed you all so completely, those who went before and those alive today, so that your mother, you yourself, your uncle—you don't realize that you're actually living on credit. You're living on other people, the very people you won't even let inside your own front door. We're at least a couple of hundred years behind the times. So far we haven't got anywhere at all and we've no real sense of the past. We just talk in airy generalizations, complain of boredom or drink vodka. But if we're to start living in the present isn't it abundantly clear that we've first got to redeem our past and make a clean break with it? And we can only redeem it by suffering and getting down to some real work for a change. You must understand that, Anya.

ANYA. The house we live in hasn't really been ours for a long time and I mean to leave it, I promise you.

TROFIMOV. If you have the keys of the place throw them in the well and go away. Be free, free as the wind.

ANYA [*carried away*]. How beautifully you put it.

TROFIMOV. Believe me, Anya. Trust me. I'm not yet thirty. I'm young and I'm still a student, but I've had my share of hardship. In winter time I'm always half-starved, ill, worried, desperately poor. And I've been landed in some pretty queer places. I've seen a thing or two in my time, I can tell you. Yet always, every moment of the day and night, I've been haunted by mysterious visions of the future. Happiness is coming, Anya, I feel it. I already see it——

ANYA [*pensively*]. The moon is rising.

[YEPIKHODOV *is heard playing his guitar, the same sad tune as before. The moon rises. Somewhere near the poplars* VARYA *is looking for* ANYA *and calling,* "Anya, where are you?"]

TROFIMOV. Yes, the moon is rising. [*Pause.*] Here it is! Happiness is here. Here it comes, nearer, ever nearer. Already I hear its footsteps. And if *we* never see it, if *we* never know it, what does that matter? Others will see it.

VARYA [*off stage*]. Anya! Where are you?

TROFIMOV. Varya's at it again. [*Angrily*.] She really is infuriating.

ANYA. Oh well, let's go down to the river. It's lovely there.

TROFIMOV. Come on then. [*They move off*.]

VARYA [*off stage*]. Anya! Anya!

CURTAIN

ACT THREE

The drawing-room. Beyond it, through an archway, the ballroom. The chandelier is lit. The Jewish band mentioned in Act Two is heard playing in the entrance-hall. It is evening. In the ballroom they are dancing a grand rond. SIMEONOV-PISHCHIK'*s voice is heard:* "Promenade à une paire!" *They come into the drawing-room, the first two dancers being* PISHCHIK *and* CHARLOTTE. TROFIMOV *and* MRS. RANEVSKY *form the second pair,* ANYA *and the* POST OFFICE CLERK *the third,* VARYA *and the* STATIONMASTER *the fourth and so on.* VARYA *is quietly weeping and dries her eyes as she dances. The last couple consists of* DUNYASHA *and a partner. They cross the drawing-room.* PISHCHIK *shouts,* "Grand rond, balancez!" *and* "Les cavaliers à genoux et remerciez vos dames!"

FIRS, *wearing a tail-coat, brings in soda-water on a tray.* PISHCHIK *and* TROFIMOV *come into the drawing-room.*

PISHCHIK. I've got high blood pressure, I've twice had a stroke and it's hard work dancing. Still, as the saying goes, those who run with the pack must wag their tails, even if they can't raise a bark. I'm as strong as a horse, though. My old father—he liked his little joke, God bless him—sometimes spoke about the family pedigree and he reckoned that the ancient line of the Simeonov-Pishchiks comes from a horse, the one Caligula made a senator. [*Sits down.*] Trouble is though, I've no money. A hungry dog thinks only of his supper. [*Snores, but wakes up again at once.*] I'm just the same, can't think of anything but money.

TROFIMOV. You know, you really are built rather like a horse.

PISHCHIK. Well, and why not? The horse is a fine animal. You can sell a horse.

[*From an adjoining room comes the sound of people playing billiards.* VARYA *appears in the ballroom beneath the archway.*]

TROFIMOV [*teasing her*]. Mrs. Lopakhin! Mrs. Lopakhin!

VARYA [*angrily*]. Seedy-looking gent!

TROFIMOV. Yes, I am a seedy-looking gent and I'm proud of it.

VARYA [*brooding unhappily*]. We've gone and hired this band,
but how are we to pay them?

[*Goes out.*]

TROFIMOV [*to* PISHCHIK]. Think of all the energy you've wasted
in your time looking for money to pay interest on your
loans. If you'd used it on something else you might have
turned the world upside down by now.

PISHCHIK. Nietzsche, the philosopher—tremendous fellow, very
famous, colossally clever chap—says in his works that there's
nothing wrong with forging bank-notes.

TROFIMOV. Have you read Nietzsche then?

PISHCHIK. Well, Dashenka told me about it actually. And the
way I'm fixed now, forging a few bank-notes is about my
only way out. I have to pay three hundred and ten roubles
the day after tomorrow. So far I've got a hundred and
thirty. [*Feels his pockets in alarm.*] My money's gone! I've
lost my money! [*Through tears.*] Where is it? [*Happily.*]
Oh, here it is in the lining. That gave me quite a turn.

[MRS. RANEVSKY *and* CHARLOTTE *come in.*]

MRS. RANEVSKY [*hums a Caucasian dance tune, the* Lezginka.]
Why is Leonid so long? What can he be doing in town? [*To*
DUNYASHA.] Dunyasha, ask the band if they'd care for some
tea.

TROFIMOV. Most likely the auction didn't even take place.

MRS. RANEVSKY. What a time to have the band here and what a
time to give a party! Oh well, never mind. [*Sits down and
hums quietly.*]

CHARLOTTE [*handing* PISHCHIK *a pack of cards*]. Here's a pack
of cards. Think of a card.

PISHCHIK. All right.

CHARLOTTE. Now shuffle the pack. That's fine. Now give them

to me, my dearest Mr. Pishchik. *Ein, zwei, drei!* And now look in your coat pocket. Is it there?

PISHCHIK [*taking a card out of his coat pocket*]. The eight of spades, you're quite right. [*In amazement*.] Extraordinary thing.

CHARLOTTE [*holding the pack of cards on the palm of her hand, to* TROFIMOV]. Tell me quick, what's the top card?

TROFIMOV. Well, say the queen of spades.

CHARLOTTE. And here she is! [*To* PISHCHIK.] Right. What's the top card now?

PISHCHIK. The ace of hearts.

CHARLOTTE. Correct. [*Claps her hand on the pack of cards, which disappears*.] What fine weather we've had today. [*She is answered by a mysterious female voice which seems to come from under the floor*: "Oh yes, magnificent weather, madam."] Oh you're so nice, quite charming in fact. [*The voice*: "I likes you very much too, madam."]

STATIONMASTER [*clapping his hands*]. Hurrah for our lady ventriloquist!

PISHCHIK [*astonished*]. Extraordinary thing. Miss Charlotte, you're utterly bewitching, I've quite fallen in love with you.

CHARLOTTE. In love? [*Shrugging her shoulders*.] As if you were capable of love. *Guter Mensch, aber schlechter Musikant.*

TROFIMOV [*claps* PISHCHIK *on the shoulder*]. Good for the old horse.

CHARLOTTE. Your attention, please. Another trick. [*Takes a rug from a chair*.] Here's a very fine rug, I'd like to sell it. [*Shakes it*.] Doesn't anyone want to buy?

PISHCHIK [*astonished*]. Extraordinary thing.

CHARLOTTE. *Ein, zwei, drei!* [*Quickly snatches up the rug, which she had allowed to fall down, to reveal* ANYA *standing behind it*. ANYA *curtsies, runs to her mother and embraces her, then runs back into the ballroom amid general enthusiasm*.]

MRS. RANEVSKY [*claps*]. Well done, well done!

CHARLOTTE. Now for another. *Ein, zwei, drei!* [*Raises the rug. Behind it stands* VARYA, *who bows*.]

PISHCHIK [*astonished*]. Extraordinary thing.

CHARLOTTE. The performance is over. [*Throws the rug at* PISHCHIK, *curtsies and runs off into the ballroom*.]

PISHCHIK [*hurries after her*]. What a naughty girl! Not bad, eh? Not bad at all. [*Goes out*.]

MRS. RANEVSKY. And still no sign of Leonid. I can't think what he's been up to in town all this time. The thing must be over by now. Either the estate's sold or the auction didn't take place, so why keep us in suspense all this time?

VARYA [*trying to console her*]. Uncle's bought it, he must have.

TROFIMOV [*with a sneer*]. Oh, of course.

VARYA. Our great-aunt sent him the authority to buy it in her name and transfer the mortgage to her. She's doing it for Anya's sake. Uncle will buy it, God willing, I'm sure of that.

MRS. RANEVSKY. Your great-aunt in Yaroslavl sent fifteen thousand to buy the estate in her name—she doesn't trust us—but that much wouldn't even pay the interest. [*Covers her face with her hands*.] My fate, my whole future is being decided today.

TROFIMOV [*teasing* VARYA]. Mrs. Lopakhin!

VARYA [*angrily*]. Hark at the eternal student. He's already been sent down from the university twice.

MRS. RANEVSKY. Why are you so cross, Varya? If he teases you about Lopakhin, what of it? If you want to marry Lopakhin, do—he's a nice, attractive man. And if you don't want to, don't. Nobody's forcing you, darling.

VARYA. I'm perfectly serious about this, Mother, I must tell you quite plainly. He is a nice man and I do like him.

MRS. RANEVSKY. Well, marry him then. What are you waiting for? That's what I can't see.

VARYA. I can't very well propose to him myself, can I? Everyone's been talking to me about him for the last two years. Everyone goes on and on about it, but he either says nothing or just makes jokes. And I see his point. He's making money, he has his business to look after and he hasn't time for me. If I had just a bit of money myself—even a hundred roubles would do—I'd drop everything and go right away. I'd go to a convent.

TROFIMOV. What bliss!

VARYA [*to* TROFIMOV]. Our student must show how witty he is, mustn't he? [*In a gentle voice, tearfully.*] Oh, you have grown ugly, Peter, and you do look old. [*She has stopped crying and speaks to* MRS. RANEVSKY.] But I can't stand having nothing to do, Mother, I must be doing something every minute of the day.

[*Enter* YASHA.]

YASHA [*hardly able to restrain his laughter*]. Yepikhodov's broken a billiard cue. [*Goes out.*]

VARYA. What is Yepikhodov doing here? And who said he could play billiards? I can't make these people out. [*Goes out.*]

MRS. RANEVSKY. Don't tease her, Peter. Don't you see she's unhappy enough already?

TROFIMOV. She's a great deal too officious. Why can't she mind her own business? She's been pestering me and Anya all summer, afraid we might have a love affair. What's it got to do with her? Not that I ever gave her cause to think such a thing, anyway, I'm beyond such trivialities. We are above love.

MRS. RANEVSKY. While I'm supposed to be beneath it, I imagine. [*Greatly agitated.*] Why isn't Leonid back? If only I knew whether the estate's been sold or not. I feel that such an awful thing just couldn't happen, so I don't know what to think, I'm at my wits' end. I'm liable to scream or do something silly. Help me, Peter. Oh, say something, do, for heaven's sake speak.

TROFIMOV. What does it matter whether the estate's been sold today or not? All that's over and done with. There's no turning back, that avenue is closed. Don't worry, my dear. But don't try and fool yourself either. For once in your life you must face the truth.

MRS. RANEVSKY. What truth? *You* can see what's true or untrue, but I seem to have lost my sight, I see nothing. You solve the most serious problems so confidently, but tell me, dear boy, isn't that because you're young—not old enough for any of your problems to have caused you real suffering? You face the future so bravely, but then you can't imagine anything terrible happening, can you? And isn't that because you're still too young to see what life's really like? You're bolder, more honest, more profound than we are, but try and put yourself in our place, do show a little generosity and spare my feelings. You see, I was born here, my father and mother lived here, and my grandfather too. I love this house. Without the cherry orchard life has no meaning for me and if it really must be sold then you'd better sell me with it. [*Embraces* TROFIMOV *and kisses him on the forehead*.] My little boy was drowned here, you know. [*Weeps*.] Don't be too hard on me, my good kind friend.

TROFIMOV. As you know, I feel for you with all my heart.

MRS. RANEVSKY. Well, that isn't the way to say it, it really isn't. [*Takes out her handkerchief. A telegram falls to the floor*.] I'm so depressed today, you just can't imagine. I hate all this noise. Every sound sends a shiver right through me. I'm trembling all over, but I can't go to my room, the silence frightens me when I'm on my own. Don't think too badly of me, Peter. I love you as my own son. I'd gladly let Anya marry you, I honestly would, only you really must study, dear boy, you must take your degree. You never do anything, you just drift about from place to place, that's what's so peculiar. Well, it is, isn't it? And you should do something about that beard, make it grow somehow. [*Laughs*.] You do look funny.

TROFIMOV [*picks up the telegram*]. I don't pretend to be particularly good-looking.

MRS. RANEVSKY. That telegram's from Paris. I get one every day. One came yesterday and there's another today. That

crazy creature is ill and in trouble again. He asks my
forgiveness, begs me to come to him, and I really ought to
go over to Paris and be near him for a bit. You look very
disapproving, Peter, but what else can I do, my dear boy,
what else can I do? He's ill, he's lonely and unhappy, and
who'll look after him there? Who'll stop him making a fool
of himself and give him his medicine at the right time?
And then, why make a secret of it, why not say so? I love
him, that's obvious. I love him, I love him. He's a millstone round my neck and he's dragging me down with him,
but I love my millstone and I can't live without it. [*Presses*
TROFIMOV's *hand.*] Don't think badly of me, Peter, and
don't say anything, don't talk.

TROFIMOV [*through tears*]. Excuse me being so blunt, for
heaven's sake, but he did rob you.

MRS. RANEVSKY. No, no, no, you mustn't say that. [*Puts her
hands over her ears.*]

TROFIMOV. Why, the man's a swine and you're the only one
who doesn't know it. He's a little swine, a nobody——

MRS. RANEVSKY [*angry, but restraining herself*]. You're twenty-
six or twenty-seven, but you're still a schoolboy.

TROFIMOV. What if I am?

MRS. RANEVSKY. You should be more of a man. At your age you
should understand people in love. And you should be in
love yourself, you should fall in love. [*Angrily.*] Yes, I
mean it. And you're not all that pure and innocent either,
you're just a prig, a ridiculous freak, a kind of monster——

TROFIMOV [*horrified*]. She can't know what she's saying!

MRS. RANEVSKY. "I am above love!" You're not above love,
you're just what our friend Firs calls a nincompoop. Fancy
being your age and not having a mistress!

TROFIMOV [*horrified*]. This is outrageous. She can't know
what she's saying! [*Goes quickly into the ballroom clutching his head.*] It's outrageous. I can't stand it, I'm going.
[*Goes out, but immediately comes back.*] All is over between
us. [*Goes out into the hall.*]

MRS. RANEVSKY [*shouting after him*]. Peter, wait a minute. Don't be silly, I was only joking. Peter!

[*There is a sound of rapid footsteps on the staircase in the hall and then of someone suddenly falling downstairs with a crash.* ANYA *and* VARYA *scream, but this is at once followed by laughter.*]

MRS. RANEVSKY. What's going on out there?

[ANYA *runs in.*]

ANYA [*laughing*]. Peter fell downstairs. [*Runs out.*]

MRS. RANEVSKY. What a funny boy Peter is.

[*The* STATIONMASTER *stands in the middle of the ballroom and begins to declaim* The Sinful Woman *by Aleksey Tolstoy. The others listen, but he has only recited a few lines when the sound of a waltz comes from the hall and the recitation is broken off. Everyone dances.* TROFIMOV, ANYA, VARYA *and* MRS. RANEVSKY *pass through from the hall.*]

MRS. RANEVSKY. Now, Peter. There now, my dear good boy. Please forgive me. Let's dance. [*Dances with* PETER.]

[ANYA *and* VARYA *dance together.* FIRS *comes in and stands his walking-stick near the side door.* YASHA *has also gone in from the drawing-room and is watching the dancing.*]

YASHA. How goes it, old boy?

FIRS. I don't feel so good. We used to have generals, barons and admirals at our dances in the old days, but now we send for the post office clerk and the stationmaster and even they aren't all that keen to come. I feel so frail somehow. The old master, Mr. Leonid's grandfather, used to dose us all with powdered sealing-wax no matter what was wrong with us. I've been taking sealing-wax every day for the last twenty years or more. Maybe that's what's kept me alive.

YASHA. Granddad, you make me tired. [*Yawns.*] It's time you were dead.

FIRS. Get away with you. Nincompoop! [*Mutters.*]

[TROFIMOV *and* MRS. RANEVSKY *dance in the ballroom, then in the drawing-room.*]

MRS. RANEVSKY. Thank you. I think I'll sit down a bit. [*Sits down.*] I'm tired.

[*Enter* ANYA.]

ANYA [*excitedly*]. There was someone in the kitchen just now saying the cherry orchard's been sold today.

MRS. RANEVSKY. Sold? Who to?

ANYA. He didn't say. He's gone away now. [*She and* TROFIMOV *dance off into the ballroom.*]

YASHA. It was only some old man's gossip. Nobody from here.

FIRS. And Mr. Leonid hasn't come yet, he's still not back. He's only got his light overcoat on and he'll catch cold, like as not. These young people never stop to think.

MRS. RANEVSKY. Oh, I shall die. Yasha, go and find out who bought it.

YASHA. But he's been gone some time, that old fellow. [*Laughs.*]

MRS. RANEVSKY [*somewhat annoyed*]. Well, what's so funny? What are you so pleased about?

YASHA. Yepikhodov really is a scream. The man's so futile. Simple Simon!

MRS. RANEVSKY. Firs, if the estate's sold where will you go?

FIRS. I'll go wherever you tell me.

MRS. RANEVSKY. Why do you look like that? Aren't you well? You ought to be in bed, you know.

FIRS. Oh yes. [*With amusement.*] I go off to bed and then who'll do the serving and look after everything? There's only me to run the whole house.

YASHA [*to* MRS. RANEVSKY]. Mrs. Ranevsky, may I ask you something, please? If you go back to Paris, do me a favour and take me with you. I can't stay here, that's out of the question. [*Looks round, in an undertone.*] It goes without saying, you can see for yourself, this is an uncivilized country and no one has any morals. Besides it's boring, the food they give you in the kitchen is something awful and on top of that there's old Firs wandering round mumbling and speaking out of turn. Do take me with you. Please.

[*Enter* PISHCHIK.]

PISHCHIK. May I have the pleasure of a little waltz, you ravishing creature? [MRS. RANEVSKY *goes with him*.] But I'll have a hundred and eighty roubles off you, my bewitching friend. That I will. [*Dances*.] Just a hundred and eighty roubles, that's all. [*They go into the ballroom*.]

YASHA [*singing softly*]. "Couldst thou but sense the trembling of my heart——"

[*In the ballroom a woman in a grey top hat and check trousers is seen jumping and waving her arms about. Shouts are heard*: "Well done, Charlotte!"]

DUNYASHA [*stops to powder her face*]. Miss Anya told me to join in the dancing. There are lots of gentlemen and only a few ladies. But I get giddy when I dance and it makes my heart beat so. I say, Mr. Firs, the man from the post office has just told me something that gave me quite a turn.

[*The music becomes quieter*.]

FIRS. What was that?

DUNYASHA. "You're like a flower," he said.

YASHA [*yawning*]. Shockin' ignorance. [*Goes out*.]

DUNYASHA. Like a flower. I'm such a sensitive girl and I like it ever so when people say such nice things.

FIRS. You'll end up in a real old mess.

[*Enter* YEPIKHODOV.]

YEPIKHODOV. You don't seem to want to see me, Miss Dunyasha, I might be an insect or something. [*Sighs*.] Oh, what a life!

DUNYASHA. What do you want?

YEPIKHODOV. Undoubtedly you may be right. [*Sighs*.] But of course, if one looks at things from a certain angle, as I venture to assert if you'll excuse my frankness, you've finally reduced me to a state of mind. I know what I'm up against. Every day something goes wrong, but I got used to that long ago, so I just smile at my fate. You gave me your promise, and though I——

DUNYASHA. Please! Can't we talk about it some other time? And you leave me alone now. I'm in a sort of dream. [*Plays with her fan.*]

YEPIKHODOV. Every day something goes wrong, but, as I make so bold to assert, I just smile. Even raise a laugh.

[VARYA *comes in from the ballroom.*]

VARYA. Are you still here, Simon? Really, you don't listen to anything you're told. [*To* DUNYASHA.] Be off with you, Dunyasha. [*To* YEPIKHODOV.] First you play billiards and break a cue, and now you wander round the drawing-room as if you were a guest.

YEPIKHODOV. You've no right to tell me off, permit me to inform you.

VARYA. I'm not telling you off, I'm just telling you. All you do is drift about from one place to another, you never do a stroke of work. Goodness knows why we keep a clerk at all.

YEPIKHODOV [*offended*]. Whether I work or drift about and whether I eat or play billiards, these are questions for older and wiser heads than yours.

VARYA. How dare you talk to me like that! [*Flaring up.*] How dare you! So I don't know what I'm talking about, don't I? Then get out of here! This instant!

YEPIKHODOV [*cowed*]. I must ask you to express yourself in a more refined manner.

VARYA [*losing her temper*]. Get out of here this instant! Out you go! [*He moves towards the door, and she follows him.*] Simple Simon! You clear out of here! Out of my sight! [YEPIKHODOV *goes out. His voice is heard from behind the door:* "I shall lodge a complaint."] Oh, so you're coming back, are you? [*Picks up the stick which* FIRS *left near the door.*] Come on then. All right——. Come on, I'll teach you. Ah, so you are coming, are you? Then take that. [*Lashes out just as* LOPAKHIN *comes in.*]

LOPAKHIN. Thank you very much.

VARYA [*angrily and derisively*]. I'm extremely sorry.

LOPAKHIN. Not at all. Thank you for such a warm welcome.

VARYA. Oh, don't mention it. [*Moves away, then looks round and asks gently.*] I didn't hurt you, did I?

LOPAKHIN. No, it's all right. I'm going to have a whacking great bruise, though.

[*Voices in the ballroom:* "Lopakhin's arrived! Yermolay! Mr. Lopakhin!"]

PISHCHIK. As large as life and twice as natural. [*Embraces LOPAKHIN.*] There's a slight whiff of brandy about you, dear old boy. We're having a pretty good time here too.

[MRS. RANEVSKY *comes in.*]

MRS. RANEVSKY. Is it you, Yermolay? Why have you been so long? Where's Leonid?

LOPAKHIN. We came together. He'll be along in a moment.

MRS. RANEVSKY [*agitated*]. Well? Did the auction take place? For heaven's sake speak!

LOPAKHIN [*embarrassed and fearing to betray his delight*]. The auction was over by four o'clock. We missed our train and had to wait till half past nine. [*Gives a heavy sigh.*] Oh dear, I feel a bit dizzy. [*Enter* GAYEV. *He carries some packages in his right hand and wipes away his tears with his left.*]

MRS. RANEVSKY. What happened, Leonid? Leonid, please! [*Impatiently, in tears.*] Hurry up! Tell me, for God's sake!

GAYEV [*not answering her and making a gesture of resignation with his hand. To* FIRS, *weeping*]. Here, take this, some anchovies and Black Sea herrings. I haven't eaten all day. I've had a frightful time. [*The door into the billiard room is open. The click of billiard balls is heard and* YASHA's *voice:* "Seven and eighteen!" GAYEV's *expression changes and he stops crying.*] I'm terribly tired. Come and help me change, Firs. [*Goes off through the ballroom to his own room followed by* FIRS.]

PISHCHIK. What happened at the sale? For heaven's sake tell us!

MRS. RANEVSKY. Was the cherry orchard sold?

LOPAKHIN. It was.

MRS. RANEVSKY. Who bought it?

LOPAKHIN. I did. [*Pause.*]

> [MRS. RANEVSKY *is overwhelmed and would have fallen if she had not been standing near an armchair and a table.* VARYA *takes the keys from her belt, throws them on the floor in the middle of the drawing-room and goes out.*]

LOPAKHIN. I bought it. Just a moment, everybody, if you don't mind. I feel a bit muddled, I can't talk. [*Laughs.*] When we got to the auction Deriganov was already there. Gayev only had fifteen thousand, and straight off Deriganov bid thirty on top of the arrears on the mortgage. I saw how things were going, so I weighed in myself and bid forty. He bid forty-five. I went up to fifty-five. He kept raising his bid five thousand, you see, and I was going up in tens. Anyway, it finished in the end. I bid ninety thousand roubles plus the arrears. And I got it. And now the cherry orchard is mine. Mine! [*Gives a loud laugh.*] Great God in heaven, the cherry orchard's mine! Tell me I'm drunk or crazy, say it's all a dream. [*Stamps his feet.*] Don't laugh at me. If my father and grandfather could only rise from their graves and see what happened, see how their Yermolay—Yermolay who was always being beaten, who could hardly write his name and ran round barefoot in winter—how this same Yermolay bought this estate, the most beautiful place in the world. I've bought the estate where my father and grandfather were slaves, where they weren't even allowed inside the kitchen. I must be dreaming, I must be imagining it all. It can't be true. This is all a figment of your imagination wrapped in the mists of obscurity. [*Picks up the keys, smiling fondly.*] She threw away the keys to show she's not in charge here now. [*Jingles the keys.*] Oh well, never mind. [*The band is heard tuning up.*] Hey, you in the band, give us a tune, I want to hear you. Come here, all of you, and you just watch Yermolay Lopakhin get his axe into that cherry orchard, watch the trees come crashing down. We'll fill the place with cottages. Our grandchildren and our great-grandchildren will see a few changes round here. Music, boys!

[*The band plays.* MRS. RANEVSKY *has sunk into a chair and is weeping bitterly.*]

LOPAKHIN [*reproachfully*]. But why, oh why, didn't you listen to me before? My poor dear friend, you can't put the clock back now. [*With tears.*] Oh, if all this could be over quickly, if our miserable, mixed-up lives could somehow hurry up and change.

PISHCHIK [*taking him by the arm, in an undertone*]. She's crying. Come into the other room and leave her alone. Come on. [*Takes him by the arm and leads him into the ballroom.*]

LOPAKHIN. Hey, what's up? You in the band, let's have you playing properly. Let's have everything the way *I* want it. [*Ironically.*] Here comes the new squire, the owner of the cherry orchard! [*Accidentally jogs a small table, nearly knocking over the candelabra.*] I can pay for everything. [*Goes out with* PISHCHIK.]

[*There is no one left in the ballroom or drawing-room except* MRS. RANEVSKY, *who sits hunched up, weeping bitterly. The band plays quietly.* ANYA *and* TROFIMOV *come in quickly.* ANYA *goes up to her mother and kneels down in front of her.* TROFIMOV *stays by the entrance to the ballroom.*]

ANYA. Mother! Mother, are you crying? My lovely, kind, good mother. My precious, I love you. God bless you. The cherry orchard's sold, it's gone. That's true, quite true, but don't cry, Mother, you still have your life to live. You're still here with your kind and innocent heart. Come with me, dear, come away. We shall plant a new orchard, more glorious than this one. And when you see it everything will make sense to you. Your heart will be filled with happiness—deep happiness and peace, descending from above like the sun at evening time. And then you'll smile again, Mother. Come, my dear, come with me.

CURTAIN

ACT FOUR

The scene is the same as in Act One. There are no window-curtains or pictures. Only a few pieces of furniture are left and have been stacked in one corner as if for sale. There is a feeling of emptiness. Suitcases, travelling bags and so on have been piled up near the outside door and at the back of the stage. The voices of VARYA *and* ANYA *can be heard through the door, left, which is open.* LOPAKHIN *stands waiting.* YASHA *is holding a tray with glasses of champagne on it.* YEPIKHODOV *is roping up a box in the hall. There is a murmur off stage at the rear, the voices of peasants who have come to say good-bye.* GAYEV's *voice is heard:* "Thank you, my good fellows, thank you very much."

YASHA. Some village people have come to say good-bye. If you ask my opinion, sir, the lower orders mean well, but they haven't got much sense.

[*The murmur of voices dies away.* MRS. RANEVSKY *and* GAYEV *come in through the hall. She is not crying, but she is pale, her face is working and she cannot speak.*]

GAYEV. You gave them your purse, Lyuba. You shouldn't do such things, you really shouldn't.

MRS. RANEVSKY. I couldn't help it, just couldn't help it.

[*Both go out.*]

LOPAKHIN [*calling through the door after them*]. Come along, please, come on. Let's have a little glass together before we go. I didn't think of bringing any from town and I could only get one bottle at the station. Come on. [*Pause.*] What's the matter? None of you want any? [*Comes back from the door.*] I wouldn't have bought it if I'd known. All right then, I won't have any either. [YASHA *carefully places the tray on a chair.*] You have some, Yasha, anyway.

YASHA. Here's to those that are leaving. And good luck to

them that aren't. [*Drinks.*] This champagne isn't the genuine article, you can take it from me.

LOPAKHIN. And at eight roubles a bottle. [*Pause.*] It's damn
cold in here.

YASHA. The stoves haven't been lit today. Never mind, we're
going away. [*Laughs.*]

LOPAKHIN. What's the joke?

YASHA. I feel so pleased.

LOPAKHIN. It's October now, but it might be summer, it's so
fine and sunny. Good building weather. [*Glances at his
watch and calls through the door.*] I say, don't forget the
train leaves in forty-seven minutes. So we must start for
the station twenty minutes from now. Better get a move
on.

[TROFIMOV *comes in from outside. He wears an overcoat.*]

TROFIMOV. I think it's time we were off. The carriages are at
the door. Damn it, where are my galoshes? They've disappeared. [*Through the door.*] Anya, I've lost my galoshes. I
can't find them anywhere.

LOPAKHIN. I've got to go to Kharkov. We're all taking the same
train. I'm spending the winter in Kharkov—I've been kicking my heels round here quite long enough and I'm fed up
with doing nothing. I can't stand not working—look, I
don't know what to do with my arms. See the absurd way
they flop about as if they belonged to someone else.

TROFIMOV. We'll soon be gone and then you can get back to
your useful labours again.

LOPAKHIN. Come on, have a drink.

TROFIMOV. Not for me, thank you.

LOPAKHIN. So you're off to Moscow, are you?

TROFIMOV. Yes, I'm seeing them as far as town and going on
to Moscow tomorrow.

LOPAKHIN. I see. Ah well, I daresay the professors haven't
started lecturing yet, they'll be waiting for you to turn up.

TROFIMOV. Oh, mind your own business.

LOPAKHIN. How many years is it you've been at the university?

TROFIMOV. Can't you say something new for a change? That joke's played out. [*Looks for his galoshes.*] Look here, you and I may never meet again, so let me give you a word of advice before we say good-bye. Stop waving your arms about. Cure yourself of that stupid habit. What's more, all this stuff about building cottages and working out that the owners will end up as smallholders—that's just as stupid as waving your arms about. Anyway, never mind, I still like you. You have sensitive fingers like an artist's and you're a fine, sensitive person too, deep down inside you.

LOPAKHIN [*embracing him*]. Good-bye, Peter. Thanks for everything. Let me give you some money for the journey, you may need it.

TROFIMOV. I don't. Why should I?

LOPAKHIN. Because you haven't any.

TROFIMOV. Yes I have, thank you very much. I got some for a translation, it's here in my pocket. [*Anxiously.*] But I still can't find my galoshes.

VARYA [*from another room*]. Oh, take the beastly things. [*Throws a pair of galoshes on to the stage.*]

TROFIMOV. Why are you so angry, Varya? I say, these aren't my galoshes.

LOPAKHIN. I put nearly three thousand acres down to poppy in the spring and made a clear forty thousand roubles. And when my poppies were in flower, that was a sight to see. What I'm trying to say is, I've made forty thousand and I'd like to lend it you because I can afford to. So why turn it down? I'm a peasant, I put it to you straight.

TROFIMOV. Your father was a peasant and mine worked in a chemist's shop, all of which proves precisely nothing. [LOPAKHIN *takes out his wallet.*] Oh, put it away, for heaven's sake. If you offered me two hundred thousand I still wouldn't take it. I'm a free man. And all the things that mean such a lot to you all, whether you're rich or poor—why, they have no more power over me than a bit of thistledown floating on the breeze. I can get on without you, I can pass you by. I'm strong and proud. Mankind is marching towards a higher truth, towards the greatest possible happiness on earth, and I'm in the vanguard.

LOPAKHIN. Will you get there?

TROFIMOV. I shall. [*Pause.*] I'll either get there or show others the way.

[*There is the sound of an axe striking a tree in the distance.*]

LOPAKHIN. Well, good-bye, my dear fellow. It's time to go. You and I look down our noses at each other, but life goes on without bothering about us. When I work for a long time at a stretch I feel a bit calmer, and I too seem to know why I exist. But there are lots of people in Russia, old boy, and why some of them exist is anyone's guess. Oh well, never mind, that's not what makes the world go round. I hear Gayev's taken a job at the bank at six thousand a year. He'll never stick it out, though, he's too lazy.

ANYA [*in the doorway*]. Mother says would you mind waiting till she's gone before cutting down the orchard.

TROFIMOV. Yes, you really might have shown more tact, I must say. [*Goes out through the hall.*]

LOPAKHIN. Right, I'll see to it. Those people are the limit. [*Goes out after him.*]

ANYA. Has Firs been taken to hospital yet?

YASHA. I told them to this morning. They must have taken him, I reckon.

ANYA [*to YEPIKHODOV, who is passing through the ballroom*]. Simon, please find out if Firs has been taken to hospital.

YASHA [*offended*]. I told Yegor this morning. Why keep on and on about it?

YEPIKHODOV. The aged Firs, or so I have finally concluded, is beyond repair. It's time he was gathered to his fathers. As for me, I can only envy him. [*Has placed a suitcase on a hat box and squashed it.*] Oh look, that had to happen. I knew it. [*Goes out.*]

YASHA [*with a sneer*]. Simple Simon.

VARYA [*from behind the door*]. Has Firs been taken to hospital?

ANYA. Yes.

VARYA. Then why didn't they take the letter to the doctor?

ANYA. Well, we'll have to send it on after him. [*Goes out.*]

VARYA [*from the next room*]. Where's Yasha? Tell him his mother's come to say good-bye.

YASHA [*with an impatient gesture*]. Oh, this is too much.

[*All this time* DUNYASHA *has been busy with the luggage. Now that* YASHA *is alone she goes up to him.*]

DUNYASHA. You might at least look at me, Yasha. You're going away, deserting me. [*Weeps and throws her arms round his neck.*]

YASHA. Why all the tears? [*Drinks champagne.*] I'll be back in Paris in a week. Tomorrow we catch the express and then you won't see us for smoke. I can hardly believe it somehow. *Veev la France!* It doesn't suit me here, this isn't the life for me and that's that. I've seen enough ignorance to last me a lifetime. [*Drinks champagne.*] So why the tears? You be a good girl and then you won't have anything to cry about.

DUNYASHA [*powders her face, looking in a hand-mirror*]. Write to me from Paris. You know, I did love you Yasha, I loved you so much. Oh Yasha, I'm such a soft-hearted girl.

YASHA. Somebody's coming. [*Attends to the suitcases, humming quietly.*]

[MRS. RANEVSKY, GAYEV, ANYA *and* CHARLOTTE *come in.*]

GAYEV. We ought to be going, there's not much time left. [*Looks at* YASHA.] Someone round here smells of herring.

MRS. RANEVSKY. We'd better be getting into the carriages in about ten minutes. [*Looks round the room.*] Good-bye, house. Good-bye, dear old place. Winter will pass, spring will come again and then you won't be here any more, you'll be pulled down. These walls have seen a few sights in their time. [*Kisses her daughter with great feeling.*] My treasure, you look radiant, your eyes are sparkling like diamonds. Are you very pleased? You are, aren't you?

ANYA. Oh yes, I am. This is the start of a new life, Mother.

GAYEV [*happily*]. It's quite true, everything's all right now. Before the cherry orchard was sold we were all worried and upset, but when things were settled once and for all and we'd burnt our boats, we all calmed down and actually cheered up a bit. I'm working at a bank now, I'm a financier. Pot the red in the middle. And you can say what you like, Lyuba, you're looking a lot better, no doubt about it.

MRS. RANEVSKY. Yes. I'm not so much on edge, that's true. [*Someone helps her on with her hat and coat.*] And I'm sleeping better. Take my things out, Yasha, it's time. [*To* ANYA.] We'll soon be seeing each other again, child. I'm going to Paris and I'll live on the money your great-aunt sent from Yaroslavl to buy the estate—good old Aunty! Not that it'll last very long.

ANYA. You'll come back soon, Mother. You will, won't you? I'm going to study and pass my school exams and then I'll work and help you. We'll read together, won't we, Mother— all sorts of books? [*Kisses her mother's hands.*] We'll read during the autumn evenings. We'll read lots of books and a wonderful new world will open up before us. [*Dreamily.*] Do come back, Mother.

MRS. RANEVSKY. I will, my precious [*Embraces her daughter.*]

[LOPAKHIN *comes in.* CHARLOTTE *quietly hums a tune.*]

GAYEV. Charlotte's happy, she's singing.

CHARLOTTE [*picking up a bundle which looks like a swaddled baby*]. Rock-a-bye, baby. [*A baby's cry is heard.*] Hush, my darling, my dear little boy. [*The cry is heard again.*] You poor little thing! [*Throws the bundle down.*] And please will you find me another job? I can't go on like this.

LOPAKHIN. We'll find you something, Charlotte, don't worry.

GAYEV. Everyone's deserting us. Varya's going, suddenly no one wants us any more.

CHARLOTTE. I haven't anywhere to live in town. I shall have to go away. [*Sings quietly*]. Anyway, I don't care.

[PISHCHIK *comes in*.]

LOPAKHIN. Oh, look who's come! Wonders will never cease.

PISHCHIK [*out of breath*]. Phew, I say, let me get my breath back. I'm all in. My good friends—. Give me some water.

GAYEV. Wants to borrow money, I'll be bound. I'll keep out of harm's way, thank you very much. [*Goes out*.]

PISHCHIK. Haven't been here for ages, dearest lady. [*To* LOPAKHIN.] You here too? Glad to see you. Tremendously clever fellow you are. Here. Take this. [*Gives* LOPAKHIN *money*.] Four hundred roubles. That leaves eight hundred and forty I owe you.

LOPAKHIN [*amazed, shrugging his shoulders*]. I must be seeing things. Where can you have got it?

PISHCHIK. Just a moment, I'm so hot. Most extraordinary occurrence. Some Englishmen came along and found a kind of white clay on my land. [*To* MRS. RANEVSKY.] And there's four hundred for you, you ravishing creature. [*Hands over the money*.] You'll get the rest later. [*Drinks some water*.] A young fellow on the train was just saying that some great philosopher advises everyone to go and jump off a roof. "Just you jump," he tells them, "and you'll find that solves your problem." [*With astonishment*.] Extraordinary thing. More water, please.

LOPAKHIN. But what Englishmen?

PISHCHIK. I've leased them this land with the clay on it for twenty-four years. But now you must excuse me, I can't stay. Must be running along. Going to see Znoykov. And Kardamonov. Owe them all money. [*Drinks*.] And the very best of luck to you. I'll look in on Thursday.

MRS. RANEVSKY. We're just leaving for town and I'm going abroad tomorrow.

PISHCHIK. What! [*Deeply concerned*.] Why go to town? Oh, I see, the furniture and luggage. Well, never mind. [*Through tears*.] It doesn't matter. Colossally clever fellows, these

English. Never mind. All the best to you. God bless you. It doesn't matter. Everything in this world comes to an end. [*Kisses* MRS. RANEVSKY's *hand*.] If you should ever hear that my end has come, just remember—remember the old horse, and say, "There once lived such-and-such a person, a certain Simeonov-Pishchik, may his bones rest in peace." Remarkable weather we're having. Yes. [*Goes out in great distress, but at once returns and speaks from the doorway*.] Dashenka sends her regards. [*Goes out*.]

MRS. RANEVSKY. Well, now we can go. I'm leaving with two worries. One is old Firs, who's ill. [*With a glance at her watch*.] We still have about five minutes.

ANYA. Firs has been taken to hospital, Mother. Yasha sent him off this morning.

MRS. RANEVSKY. My other worry's Varya. She's used to getting up early and working, and now she has nothing to do she's like a fish out of water. She's grown thin and pale and she's always crying, poor thing. [*Pause*.] As you know very well, Yermolay, I had hoped—to see her married to you, and it did look as if that was how things were shaping. [*Whispers to* ANYA, *who nods to* CHARLOTTE. *They both go out*.] She loves you, you're fond of her, and I haven't the faintest idea why you seem to avoid each other. It makes no sense to me.

LOPAKHIN. It makes no sense to me either, to be quite honest. It's a curious business, isn't it? If it's not too late I don't mind going ahead even now. Let's get it over and done with. I don't feel I'll ever propose to her without you here.

MRS. RANEVSKY. That's a very good idea. Why, it won't take more than a minute. I'll call her at once.

LOPAKHIN. There's even champagne laid on. [*Looks at the glasses*.] They're empty, someone must have drunk it. [YASHA *coughs*.] That's what I call really knocking it back.

MRS. RANEVSKY [*excitedly*]. I'm so glad. We'll go out. Yasha, *allez!* I'll call her. [*Through the door*.] Varya, leave what you're doing and come here a moment. Come on! [*Goes out with* YASHA.]

LOPAKHIN [*with a glance at his watch*]. Yes. [*Pause*.]

[*Suppressed laughter and whispering are heard from behind the door. After some time* VARYA *comes in.*]

VARYA [*spends a long time examining the luggage*]. That's funny, I can't find it anywhere.

LOPAKHIN. What are you looking for?

VARYA. I packed it myself and I still can't remember. [*Pause.*]

LOPAKHIN. Where are you going now, Varya?

VARYA. Me? To the Ragulins'. I've arranged to look after their place, a sort of housekeeper's job.

LOPAKHIN. That's in Yashnevo, isn't it? It must be fifty odd miles from here. [*Pause.*] So life has ended in this house.

VARYA [*examining the luggage*]. Oh, where can it be? Or could I have put it in the trunk? Yes, life has gone out of this house. And it will never come back.

LOPAKHIN. Well, I'm just off to Kharkov. By the next train. I have plenty to do there. And I'm leaving Yepikhodov in charge here, I've taken him on.

VARYA. Oh, have you?

LOPAKHIN. This time last year we already had snow, remember? But now it's calm and sunny. It's a bit cold though. Three degrees of frost, I should say.

VARYA. I haven't looked. [*Pause.*] Besides, our thermometer's broken. [*Pause.*]

[*A voice at the outer door*: "Mr. Lopakhin!"]

LOPAKHIN [*as if he had long been expecting this summons*]. I'm just coming. [*Goes out quickly.*]

[VARYA *sits on the floor with her head on a bundle of clothes, quietly sobbing. The door opens and* MRS. RANEVSKY *comes in cautiously.*]

MRS. RANEVSKY. Well? [*Pause.*] We'd better go.

VARYA [*has stopped crying and wiped her eyes*]. Yes, Mother, it's time. I can get to the Ragulins' today so long as I don't miss my train.

MRS. RANEVSKY [*calling through the door*]. Put your things on, Anya.

[ANYA *comes in followed by* GAYEV *and* CHARLOTTE. GAYEV *wears a warm overcoat with a hood. Servants and coachmen come in.* YEPIKHODOV *attends to the luggage.*]

MRS. RANEVSKY. Now we really can be on our way.

ANYA [*joyfully*]. On our way!

GAYEV. My friends, my dear good friends! As I leave this house for the last time, how can I be silent? How can I refrain from expressing as I leave the feelings that overwhelm my entire being?

ANYA [*beseechingly*]. Uncle.

VARYA. Uncle dear, please don't.

GAYEV [*despondently*]. Double the red into the middle. I am silent.

[TROFIMOV *comes in followed by* LOPAKHIN.]

TROFIMOV. Well everybody, it's time to go.

LOPAKHIN. My coat please, Yepikhodov.

MRS. RANEVSKY. I'll just stay another minute. I feel as though I'd never really looked at the walls or ceilings of this house before and now I can hardly take my eyes off them, I love them so dearly.

GAYEV. I remember when I was six years old sitting in this window on Trinity Sunday and watching Father go off to church.

MRS. RANEVSKY. Have they taken all the luggage out?

LOPAKHIN. It looks like it. [*Putting on his coat, to* YEPIKHODOV.] Make sure everything's all right, Yepikhodov, will you?

YEPIKHODOV [*speaking in a hoarse voice*]. Don't worry, Mr. Lopakhin!

LOPAKHIN. What's wrong with your voice?

YEPIKHODOV. I've just had some water, I must have swallowed something.

YASHA [*contemptuously*]. Shockin' ignorance.

MRS. RANEVSKY. When we've gone there will be no one left here. No one at all.

LOPAKHIN. Not till spring.

VARYA [*pulls an umbrella out of a bundle in such a way that it looks as if she meant to hit someone with it.* LOPAKHIN *pretends to be frightened*]. Oh, don't be silly, I didn't do it on purpose.

TROFIMOV. Come on, everyone, let's get into the carriages. It's time. The train will be in soon.

VARYA. There your galoshes are, Peter, just by that suitcase. [*Tearfully.*] And what dirty old things they are.

TROFIMOV [*putting on his galoshes*]. Come on, everyone.

GAYEV [*greatly distressed, afraid of bursting into tears*]. The train. The station. In off into the middle, double the white into the corner.

MRS. RANEVSKY. Come on then.

LOPAKHIN. Is everyone here? Nobody left behind? [*Locks the side door on the left.*] There are some things stored in there, so I'd better keep it locked. Come on.

ANYA. Good-bye, house. Good-bye, old life.

TROFIMOV. And welcome, new life. [*Goes out with* ANYA.]

[VARYA *looks round the room and goes out slowly.* YASHA *and* CHARLOTTE, *with her dog, follow.*]

LOPAKHIN. Till the spring then. Come along, everyone. Till we meet again. [*Goes out.*]

[MRS. RANEVSKY *and* GAYEV *are left alone. They seem to have been waiting for this moment and fling their arms round each other, sobbing quietly, restraining themselves, afraid of being heard.*]

GAYEV [*in despair*]. My sister, my dear sister——

MRS. RANEVSKY. Oh, my dear, sweet, beautiful orchard. My life, my youth, my happiness, good-bye. Good-bye.

ANYA [*off stage, happily and appealingly*]. Mother!

TROFIMOV [*off stage, happily and excitedly*]. Hallo there!

MRS. RANEVSKY. One last look at the walls and the windows. Our dear mother loved to walk about this room.

GAYEV. Oh Lyuba, my dear sister——

ANYA [*off stage*]. Mother!

TROFIMOV [*off stage*]. Hallo there!

MRS. RANEVSKY. We're coming. [*They go out.*]

> [*The stage is empty. The sound of all the doors being locked, then of carriages leaving. It grows quiet. In the silence a dull thud is heard, the noise of an axe striking a tree. It sounds lonely and sad. Footsteps are heard.* FIRS *appears from the door, right. He is dressed as always in jacket and white waistcoat, and wears slippers. He is ill.*]

FIRS [*goes up to the door and touches the handle*]. Locked. They've gone. [*Sits on the sofa.*] They forgot me. Never mind, I'll sit here a bit. And Mr. Leonid hasn't put his fur coat on, I'll be bound, he'll have gone off in his light one. [*Gives a worried sigh.*] I should have seen to it, these young folk have no sense. [*Mutters something which cannot be understood.*] Life's slipped by just as if I'd never lived at all. [*Lies down.*] I'll lie down a bit. You've got no strength left, got nothing left, nothing at all. You're just a—nincompoop. [*Lies motionless.*]

> [*A distant sound is heard. It seems to come from the sky and is the sound of a breaking string. It dies away sadly. Silence follows, broken only by the thud of an axe striking a tree far away in the orchard.*]

CURTAIN

Bantam Classics bring you the world's greatest literature—books that have stood the test of time. These beautifully designed books will be proud additions to your bookshelf. You'll want all these time-tested classics for your own reading pleasure.

Titles by the Brontës:

☐ 21140	JANE ERYE Charlotte Brontë	$2.25
☐ 21258	WUTHERING HEIGHTS Emily Brontë	$2.50

Titles by Charles Dickens:

☐ 21123	THE PICKWICK PAPERS	$4.95
☐ 21223	BLEAK HOUSE	$4.95
☐ 21265	NICHOLAS NICKLEBY	$4.95
☐ 21342	GREAT EXPECTATIONS	$2.95
☐ 21176	A TALE OF TWO CITIES	$2.50
☐ 21016	HARD TIMES	$2.95
☐ 21102	OLIVER TWIST	$2.50
☐ 21244	A CHRISTMAS CAROL & OTHER VICTORIAN TALES	$2.50

Titles by Henry James:

☐ 21127	PORTRAIT OF A LADY	$3.95
☐ 21059	THE TURN OF THE SCREW	$2.25

Look for them at your bookstore or use this page to order:

Bantam Books, Dept. CL3, 414 East Golf Road, Des Plaines, IL 60016

Please send me the items I have checked above. I am enclosing $_____ (please add $2.50 to cover postage and handling). Send check or money order, no cash or C.O.D.s please.

Mr/Ms _____

Address _____

City/State_____ Zip_____

CL3–2/91

Please allow four to six weeks for delivery.
Prices and availability subject to change without notice.

Bantam Classics bring you the world's greatest literature—books that have stood the test of time—at specially low prices. These beautifully designed books will be proud additions to your bookshelf. You'll want all these time-tested classics for your own reading pleasure.

Titles by Mark Twain:

☐	21079	**ADVENTURES OF HUCKLEBERRY FINN**	$1.95
☐	21128	**ADVENTURES OF TOM SAWYER**	$1.95
☐	21195	**COMPLETE SHORT STORIES**	$5.95
☐	21143	**A CONNECTICUT YANKEE IN KING ARTHUR'S COURT**	$2.95
☐	21349	**LIFE ON THE MISSISSIPPI**	$2.50
☐	21256	**THE PRINCE AND THE PAUPER**	$2.25
☐	21158	**PUDD'NHEAD WILSON**	$2.25

Other Great Classics:

☐	21274	**BILLY BUDD** Herman Melville	$2.95
☐	21311	**MOBY DICK** Herman Melville	$2.95
☐	21233	**THE CALL OF THE WILD & WHITE FANG** Jack London	$2.50
☐	21011	**THE RED BADGE OF COURAGE** Stephen Crane	$1.75
☐	21350	**THE COUNT OF MONTE CRISTO** Alexander Dumas	$4.95

- - - - - - - - - - - - - - - - - - - -

Bantam Books, Dept. CL2, 414 East Golf Road, Des Plaines, IL 60016

Please send me the items I have checked above. I am enclosing $_____
(please add $2.50 to cover postage and handling). Send check or money order, no cash or C.O.D.s please.

Mr/Ms _____

Address _____

City/State _____ Zip _____

CL2–2/91

Please allow four to six weeks for delivery.
Prices and availability subject to change without notice.

Bantam Classics bring you the world's greatest literature—
books that have stood the test of time—at specially low
prices. These beautifully designed books will be proud
additions to your bookshelf. You'll want all these time-tested
classics for your own reading pleasure.

Titles by Thomas Hardy:

☐ 21191	JUDE THE OBSCURE	$2.95
☐ 21024	THE MAYOR OF CASTERBRIDGE	$1.95
☐ 21269	THE RETURN OF THE NATIVE	$2.25
☐ 21168	TESS OF THE D'URBERVILLES	$2.95
☐ 21331	FAR FROM THE MADDING CROWD	$3.50

Titles by the Brontës:

☐ 21140	JANE EYRE Charlotte Brontë	$1.95
☐ 21258	WUTHERING HEIGHTS Emily Brontë	$2.25

Titles by Jane Austen:

☐ 21273	EMMA	$2.25
☐ 21276	MANSFIELD PARK	$3.95
☐ 21137	PERSUASION	$2.95
☐ 21310	PRIDE AND PREJUDICE	$2.25
☐ 21334	SENSE AND SENSIBILITY	$2.95
☐ 21197	NORTHANGER ABBEY	$2.50

Buy them at your local bookstore or use this page for ordering:

- -

Bantam Books, Dept. CL6, 414 East Golf Road, Des Plaines, IL 60016

Please send me the books I have checked above. I am enclosing
$_____ (please add $2.00 to cover postage and handling). Send
check or money order—no cash or C.O.D.s please.

Mr/Ms _____

Address _____

City/State _____ Zip _____

CL6—7/89

Please allow four to six weeks for delivery. This offer expires 1/90.
Prices and availability subject to change without notice.